RENAISSANCE
REVIVALS

A Victorian engraving expressing English theatrical continuity. Clockwise from the lower left: the Globe in 1613; the Princess; Haymarket; Victoria watching Windsor theatricals; Drury Lane; Sadler's Wells; Shakespeare's birthplace; Elizabeth watching a play at Court. In the center figures of Comedy, Tragedy (Sarah Siddons), Farce, and Pantomime hold the titles of popular plays from the seventeenth, eighteenth, and nineteenth centuries. (Harvard Theatre Collection)

RENAISSANCE REVIVALS

CITY COMEDY AND REVENGE TRAGEDY IN THE LONDON THEATRE 1576–1980

*

*   *

*

WENDY GRISWOLD

THE UNIVERSITY OF CHICAGO PRESS
Chicago and London

WENDY GRISWOLD is assistant professor of sociology at the University of Chicago.

THE UNIVERSITY OF CHICAGO PRESS, CHICAGO 60637
THE UNIVERSITY OF CHICAGO PRESS, LTD., LONDON
© 1986 by The University of Chicago
All rights reserved. Published 1986
Printed in the United States of America
95 94 93 92 91 90 89 88 87 86   12345

LIBRARY OF CONGRESS CATALOGING-IN-PUBLICATION DATA

Griswold, Wendy.
    Renaissance revivals.

    Bibliography: p.
    Includes index.
    1. Theater—England—London—History.   2. Literature
and society—England—London.   3. English drama—Early
modern and Elizabethan, 1500–1600—Social aspects.
4. English drama—17th century—Social aspects.
5. English drama—Early modern and Elizabethan,
1500–1600—Adaptations.   6. English drama—17th century
—Adaptations.   7. Cities and towns in literature.
8. Revenge in literature.   9. London (England)—Social
life and customs.   I. Title.
PN2596.L6G78   1986   306′.484   86-7059

ISBN 0-226-30923-1

This book is dedicated to my parents
Gladys Jauch Griswold
and
Raymond Lloyd Griswold

CONTENTS

FIGURES

TABLES

PLATES

Frontispiece: English theatre from Elizabeth I to Victoria

The plates follow page 128

ACKNOWLEDGMENTS

I am deeply grateful to Ann Swidler and Harrison C. White, who have generously given their advice and criticism as this study has made its way from dissertation to book. Other people who have helped me with their comments and responses to the manuscript include Howard S. Becker, the late Joseph Ben-David, Paul DiMaggio, Gary A. Fine, Richard A. Peterson, David Silverstein, and Gerald Suttles. A special thanks must go to my husband, John Frederick Padgett, who read, edited, supported, and lived with this project, offering continuing encouragement and sound suggestions for improvements. The manuscript was prepared by Angela Perez and Dee Marquez. Financial assistance came from the Frank Knox Fellowship for Research in the United Kingdom, the American Council of Learned Societies under a grant from the National Endowment for the Humanities, and the Stanford Humanities Center.

TIMBERS

In 1576 James Burbage, an actor and businessman who seems to have been something of a sharp operator, built the Theatre in Shoreditch, a disreputable suburb just north of London. The Theatre was the first permanent public playhouse in England. Burbage wanted to provide a secure home for Leicester's Men, the itinerant acting company to which he belonged, and to do so he went into partnership with his brother-in-law, John Brayne. In-laws being in-laws, Burbage and Brayne had different views on theatre management, and from the beginning the two were locked in conflict and litigation. After Brayne's death in 1586, his widow carried on the feud, at one point battling with Burbage and his sons over gate receipts at the Theatre's entrance; Richard Burbage, later to become the leading actor of Shakespeare's company, wielded a broomstick in the brawl. The Theatre had no shortage of problems even without the quarreling partners. Built in Shoreditch to put it beyond the reach of London authorities, it was not beyond the Puritans, who attacked it as a den of vice and idleness. This opposition prevented Burbage's other son, Cuthbert, from getting the lease to the land renewed in 1597. Cuthbert, who apparently inherited some of his father's entrepreneurial spirit, proceeded to dismantle the Theatre and cart off the timbers to the south bank of the Thames. where they were used to construct a new public theatre called the Globe.

The Theatre's stormy history emblemizes that of the English Renaissance theatre as a whole. From 1576 until the Long Parliament closed the playhouses in 1642, the theatres were beset with hostile civic officials on the one hand and Puritans on the other. Royal protection could never be taken for granted; the relationship between theatre and throne was intimate and tense, with the master of the revels scrutinizing plays for offenses against "Divinitie and State," and actors and playwrights were hauled off to prison with dismaying regularity.[1] With comparable regularity, outbreaks of plague closed the London theatres, sometimes for months.

From such adverse conditions emerged what is generally regarded as the apotheosis of literary culture in the English language: Renaissance drama. So venerated has this drama been during the four centuries since its inception that subsequent generations of writers have borne "the burden of the past," the sense that they could never match the achievements of their Elizabethan and Jacobean predecessors.[2] The enduring esteem in which English men and women have held these plays, and the theatrical and literary practices with which they have expressed and perpetuated this esteem, imply that the canonical drama of the Renaissance has been constantly and consistently meaningful to the English people.

But is this the case? There is a contemporary point of view, shared by many critics and sociologists, from which literary works appear less as enduring monuments fixed in a universally affirmed aesthetic hierarchy and more as products of human actors operating in concrete social, institutional, and cultural settings. Regarded in this way, even a monument must be actively maintained, situated anew, reconstructed, or it will retire into the darker recesses of the cultural museum.

A revival of an old play is a moment where such cultural reconstruction is particularly visible, and its success or lack of success particularly evident. Focusing on the revival patterns of certain clusters of Renaissance plays over the centuries forces the recognition that these plays, far from holding an unwavering position in the theatrical pantheon, have had periods of high visibility and periods of being essentially moribund. By investigating the circumstances under which old plays attain new life, the history of revivals helps us understand the ongoing, mutually influential relationship between a society and its cultural products.

In the following study of Renaissance revivals, therefore, I will be investigating the ongoing reconstruction of the meaning of Renaissance drama. Metaphors involving building seem particularly suited to cultural constructions.[3] Just as the Theatre's timbers had to be set in a particular place by men with particular objectives before they constituted a playhouse, so cultural timbers are not simply floating in the collective consciousness but are situated by human beings pursuing specific ends. Just as the Burbage timbers had a history, now holding up one playhouse and now another, so do cultural timbers have pasts that influence, but do not determine, their future meanings. These future meanings are a function of both the cultural building materials and the social contexts in which the constructions take place. The purpose of this book is to elucidate this ongoing process.

My subject is the revival of two distinctive dramatic genres, city comedy and revenge tragedy. After reviewing what is understood to be the cultural, theatrical, and social backgrounds of city comedy and revenge tragedy in order to interpret some of the meanings these genres had in their original

contexts, I shall investigate how their meanings changed over time by chart-
ing their revival histories in the London theatre from the Restoration to the
present day. Revival patterns, waves of interest and neglect, will be shown to
depend upon how the institutional and social conditions in which drama is
produced interact with the form and thematic content of plays themselves. I
shall set these empirical findings within a theory of the metaphoric relationship between society and culture, the ongoing interaction between societal tenor and cultural vehicle wherein each is interpreted according to the
other.

CULTURE AS SOCIAL ACTION

A particular conception of culture underlies the following study, a conception that encourages a combined humanistic and sociological exploration of
cultural phenomena. Research organized around the question of meaning, I
suggest, allows for a socioeconomic account of the cultural entity in question
while leaving analytically accessible the peculiar symbolic capacities of what
we call culture. Max Weber's familiar definition of an interpretive sociology
sets the starting point:

> Sociology . . . is a science concerning itself with the in-
> terpretive understanding of social action and thereby with a
> causal explanation of its course and consequences. We shall
> speak of "action" insofar as the acting individual attaches a
> subjective meaning to his behavior—be it overt or covert,
> omission or acquiescence. Action is "social" insofar as it
> takes account of the behavior of others and is thereby ori-
> ented in its course.[4]

It follows that if a playwright fashions the role of a grasping usurer named
Pecunius Lucre because he expects the character to amuse an audience of
highborn spendthrifts by allowing them to vent their disdain for the usurers
upon whom they must depend, this creation is a sociologically accessible act
in Weber's terms.[5] If a number of dramatists incorporate usurers into their
plots, thereby developing a convention of "the usurer," this convention and
the shared meanings it implies will reward sociological analysis. Similarly,
when several theatre managers decide independently to revive plays featuring
usurers, when members of the audience laugh at or sympathize with the usurer, when critics discuss the usurer in their reviews—these are all sociologically significant actions.

   Regarded from this Weberian viewpoint, "meaning" lies as much in the
minds of human beings as in the dramatic object. Pecunius Lucre may mean
one thing to the Jacobean dramatist Thomas Middleton, something else to a

member of the audience at Saint Paul's in the early seventeenth century, and something quite different again to the Londoner who sees the comedy seven years after the end of the Second World War. Each meaning, insofar as it is shared with others, is open to sociological analysis, but none is privileged; as Weber went on to say, there is no "objectively 'correct' meaning or one which is 'true' in any metaphysical sense." While a cultural object like a play or a pot may appear static, its meaning never is.[6]

Applying this conception of cultural meaning to Renaissance genres raises the questions, What did these plays mean to their creators? Their audiences? What gave them their forms and conventions? What meanings have men and women found in the plays since? The object of the present investigation of dramatic "meaning" is to understand how the meaning of a cultural object such as a genre is created, shared, and changed over time by the community of dramatic producers and consumers. A dramatist writes a play, a director revives a play, an audience member reacts to a play. In all of these social actions, the study at hand asks, how does the subject, a human being, interact with the predicate, a cultural object, to produce meaning? As the human beings who experience the play change over time, and as the social context in which they interact with the play changes, what happens to the meaning? What changes and what stays constant?

Research addressing these questions requires two phases. The first is to delineate the meanings a type of play may have had for its authors and audiences in its original context. The specification of such meanings will not explain why any particular play came out the way it did, but it will suggest why a certain type of play succeeded, thereby becoming an established dramatic genre having distinctive characteristics. The second phase is to try to understand the changes in the genres' cultural meanings over time, to determine when the plays have been meaningful and to whom, to see what makes them available for the reconstruction of meaning at certain times and not others. In Weberian terminology, the research must both interpret these cultural objects of social action in their initial settings and explain their histories.

The methods of both the humanist and the social scientist are needed for the job, for the combination of these two traditions yields a more powerful means of understanding any cultural object than does either perspective by itself. The ultimate confirmation of this claim must be sought in the substance of the chapters that follow. Before beginning the analysis itself, however, I first want to clarify the meaning of "cultural object"; second, I shall propose the "cultural diamond" as a helpful tool for the analysis of cultural objects; and third, I shall indicate why dramatic revivals constitute particularly good materials for the exploration of the aesthetic and social roots of meaning.

THE CULTURAL OBJECT

A cultural object, such as a single play or a dramatic genre, is shared significance embodied in form. Significance refers to the object's incorporation of one or more symbols, which suggest a set of denotations and connotations, emotions and memories. The symbol-containing object is more than a signal pointing to one idea, as when a red light means stop. It is more than a sign, natural or artificial, which has some logical or causal relationship to a primary social meaning, as when the trucks parked in front of a diner are a sign of good food within. A significant object refers to, symbolizes, an extended set of meanings. It is economical, the way poetry is an economical use of language. It must be shared as well. Everyone has a multitude of personally significant objects, products of individual biography and psychology, but in spite of their capacity for signification, these are not cultural objects. This essential property of being shared implies that something is a cultural object only with respect to a particular group of people. The Black Hills were a cultural object for the Sioux, who saw them as infused with spiritual power, but not for the prospectors who regarded them only as a potential economic resource. One may speak of the culture of a nation, of a children's playgroup, of the regulars at the neighborhood bar, or of a coterie of young Elizabethan gallants.[7]

By embodied, I mean that the cultural object is humanly crafted, worked on. This may be a case of hands fashioning a material object, as when someone crochets a shawl or carves a piece of marble. Human beings also work on cultural objects through words, spoken or written. In a cultural object, be it a folktale, an opera, or a quilt, meaning is made manifest by human activity. This manifestation takes a formal pattern, an arrangement of elements potentially understood by more people than just the object's creator, which allows the object's meaning to endure with and within the group, to be communicated repeatedly. Once the form is understood by a group, the meaning is conveyed even when the form is imperfectly reproduced.[8] A cultural convention, understood as simply a persistent and widely recognized form, may be modified, extended, broken, inverted, or otherwise manipulated; the original form and its attendant meaning are evoked by the modified version, and the latter is comprehended with respect to the former.

Given this working definition of a cultural object, it remains to set forth a basic axiom: "society," represented by social institutions and human actors, and "culture," represented by cultural objects, may be considered separately from each other. This is only an analytic distinction, for neither culture nor society exists outside of the minds of human beings who believe and act as though they exist. Furthermore one no sooner makes such a separation than one is struck by the fact, or what I take to be the fact, that the cultural and the social are engaged in ongoing mutual construction. Nevertheless, in order to undertake the empirical investigation of culture that is intended here, it is practical as an initial technique to proceed with the fiction of separateness. For example, chapters 2 and 3 will first examine dramatic genres as cultural objects and the theatre as a social institution before considering the relationship between the two. The reality lies in the relationship, but the analytic distinction yields a vocabulary with which to discuss the elements of the relationship.[9]

The Cultural Diamond

There are two common ways of thinking about a cultural object. One is to regard it as *archive,* a repository of symbolic forms and works accumulated by a people over time. It can be drawn upon, is occasionally replenished, is never exhausted. As Matthew Arnold put it, culture is what a society acknowledges as "the best that has been thought and known" by its past and present members.[10]

The second recurrent conception sees culture as *activity,* the practices and beliefs operating here and now. Culture is the sum of a society's current vehicles of expression, constituting a web of clues, a text, a set of data; through the interpretation of culture, one may understand much about the social arrangements prevailing. This view often takes account of the circumstances of production and distribution, the filters and channels that allow some forms of expression to come into existence and not others. Just as the archive view tends to be associated with much traditional scholarship in the humanities, the activity conception has been commonly assumed in the social sciences.[11]

A fundamental premise of the following study is that archive and activity, or what is saved and what is done, are two aspects of the same cultural system, and comprehensive cultural analysis should look at both. While disciplinary habits of emphasizing either one conception or the other have discouraged this two-pronged research strategy, such artificial constraints may be giving way. The "new literary history" school in criticism converges with the "art-worlds" school in sociology in their common interest in the collective constructions of the means by which human beings perceive and represent their experience, constructions that are both historically situated and historically persistent.

Critics associated with the new literary history, far from accepting the authority of any canon or canonical work as given, seek the ideological and institutional foundation upon which a canon is erected and maintained over time. They interpret the political, economic, and social texts—subversive or legitimating—that lie embedded in never-innocent works of literature. Instead of reducing all writing to a simple signification of social meaning, thereby leveling distinctions of literary value, these critics seek to untangle the complex ideological messages wherever they are most intricately and compellingly encoded, in literary works veined with ambiguity, multivocality, and significance beyond the author's conscious intention. Thus the new literary history critics preserve an operating conception of literary "value" even as, with a wink, they study its "contingencies."[12]

Sociological investigators of art worlds, most notably Howard S. Becker, likewise deny the autonomy of works of art, regarding them instead as "joint products of all the people who cooperate via an art world's characteristic conventions to bring works like that into existence."[13] The emphasis here is on *all* the people, for an art world is the entire network of people whose activities produce art, from the man who makes the paintbrushes to the woman who operates the Soho gallery; art is indeed, as Becker has repeatedly stressed, a collective activity. Such an expansive conception of art worlds demands that those seeking to understand any particular artistic or literary object need to take account of the structure of professional opportunities for its creators, the organizational and market systems through which cultural creators reach their audiences, and the skills, expectations, and situations of those who experience the object. Production and consumption are central processes that must be understood, and guiding metaphors are drawn from collective action and from plumbing.[14] The existence, persistence, and prestige of "works like that" are understood by both the art-worlds approach and the new literary historicism to be functions of the interplay of institutions and ideologies, conventions and common sense, inert artifacts and interested actors.

Such an interplay takes place over time, and to investigate its temporal dimension requires a research strategy that is both cross-sectional and longitudinal. One way of formulating research of this sort is to think of it as examining the activity of going into the archive. Revivals of cultural objects offer the archetypal case with which to explore the question: When and why does a society reach into its cultural archive and pull something out?

My methodological approach to understanding cultural objects as both archive and activity begins with a simple device: I conceive of the linkages between a cultural object and the social world as forming a diamond, as illustrated in figure 1. At the apex there is a social context, such as Elizabethan England; at the base there is a cultural object, such as the genre city comedy. The left point of the diamond represents creators or artists, here a set of dramatists and theatrical personnel, while the right point stands for the recipients, the audience.

The cultural diamond is not a theory. It has nothing to say about how its

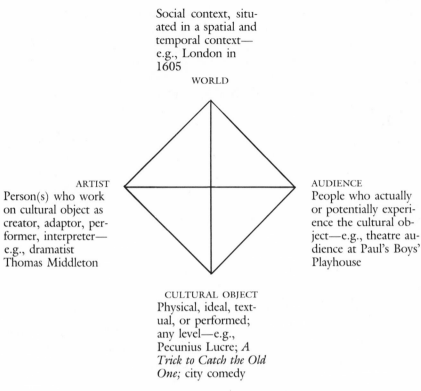

Social context, situated in a spatial and temporal context—e.g., London in 1605
WORLD

ARTIST
Person(s) who work on cultural object as creator, adaptor, performer, interpreter—e.g., dramatist Thomas Middleton

AUDIENCE
People who actually or potentially experience the cultural object—e.g., theatre audience at Paul's Boys' Playhouse

CULTURAL OBJECT
Physical, ideal, textual, or performed; any level—e.g., *Pecunius Lucre; A Trick to Catch the Old One;* city comedy

FIG. 1 The Cultural Diamond

points might be related, only that they must be related. Nor is it in itself a model, for it implies no causal direction. Any point or linkage may be specified as the dependent variable. Furthermore, each link is an arrow understood to have two heads; cultural objects influence audiences and audiences influence cultural objects, to take just one obvious example of mutual structuring. What the cultural diamond is, instead, is an accounting heuristic. Regardless of what is the primary research object, the dependent variable to be explained, the diamond compels the investigator to address all of the primary elements of the social-cultural interaction. I am contending that cultural analysis demands the investigation of the four points and six connecting lines of this diamond; studies that neglect some points or connections are incomplete.

While the analyst may designate any point or link on the cultural diamond as the phenomenon to be explained. the present study seeks to account for the cultural object itself. Moreover, the concern here is with the meaning of the cultural object as it has been revived, not only as it was written. Any cultural object such as a dramatic genre has a history that is subject to, but not predicated entirely upon, socioeconomic changes. Audience, artists, and the institutions that link them to have semi-independent histories as well. Thus the method of this study entails moving the cultural diamond over time by examining the artists, audiences, and social contexts of the cultural object's history. I am examining not just a diamond, but a parallelepiped.

REVIVALS

Revivals of preexisting cultural objects provide extraordinarily rich data for the historical study of sociocultural interaction because they encompass the power of both reflection and reception theories of culture without permitting the researcher to succumb to the empirical naïveté that both approaches sometimes entail.

Reflection, the assumed capacity of cultural objects to mirror some aspect of the social system, has been the dominant metaphor behind most sociological (and many humanist) analyses of the culture-society relationship.[15] Culture is said to reflect social values, social conflicts, class interests, social pathology, the spirit of the age. To take an example from the Frankfurt School branch of this tradition, Leo Lowenthal once analyzed the changes in biographical sketches appearing in popular magazines from the early to the mid-twentieth century.[16] He found that the "mass idols" of the earlier period were achievers (politicians, entrepreneurs, inventors, scientists, artists) while the later idols were leisure-time heroes (mass entertainers such as film stars and sports figures) whose lives were presented in the most quotidian detail regarding what foods they liked and what cigarettes they smoked. Lowenthal concluded that this change reflected a shift from production to consumption values that had taken place during the first half of the century, a period during which the average man had come to be increasingly impressed with the limitations on his ability to achieve. Cultural analysis based on the mirror metaphor can be more complex than such an economic-change-gives-rise-to-cultural-change type of model. Persuasive research has shown that various cultural works reflect, for example, "a polyvalent mental structure," technologically based national myths, the social isolation of their audience, the professional anxieties of a group of artists, and the cognitive style or "period eye" of a particular time and place.[17]

The most deterministic types of reflectionism, those that concentrate on the vertical axis of the cultural diamond with the arrow pointing resolutely downward, are easy to dismiss, but even the more sophisticated versions raise a fundamental problem: the more completely, the more complexly, a cultural object is shown to reflect the context of its origin, the less would seem to be its ability to transcend its origins and be enjoyable or comprehensible to people removed in time or space. This paradox of the tight embrace, which plagues interpretive anthropology as well, is not intrinsic to the mirror metaphor itself. Mirrors, after all, reflect whatever is put in front of them, so it may be argued that each age has its own Shakespeare, for example, reflecting its own interests. Too strong a version of this position, on the other hand, denigrates the reflectionist insights regarding why a cultural object possesses certain characteristics and not others, and such intense historical relativism cannot elucidate why and when certain cultural objects, and not others, are preserved (put in the archive) or selected (revived).

The historical study of the careers of cultural objects as they are experienced over generations of recipients suggests a solution to the tight-embrace paradox without denying the initial social context-cultural object linkages. Both theoretical and empirical support for such an investigation can be found. According to Hans Robert Jauss and the German school of reception aesthetics, readers position a work of literature against their "horizon of expectations," that background of literary knowledge and know-how formed by what they have read and what they have experienced, and interpret the text according to this horizon.[18] Similarly, Robert Escarpit has drawn attention to the way in which literary works "betray" the intentions of their authors by appealing to publics other than the one for which they were written; a different "community of assumptions" produces a different reading of the same book through an act of "creative treason."[19] Such approaches have tended to concentrate on the expectations generated by cultural rather than social experience, but they can and should be extended to the latter, which is what the present study attempts to do.

The theoretical elaboration of reception theories has not yet produced a commensurate empirical payoff, but over the past thirty years a few reception studies have appeared, often prompted more by curiosity about shifts in popularity and repertory than by any explicit theoretical agenda. One study, *Dickens and His Readers,* which looked at both the critical esteem and the general popularity of Dickens from 1836 to the early 1950s, found that the waning and waxing of his reputation among literary critics was inversely related to the ascent and descent of the criterion of realism in fiction; the common reader, unimpressed with shifts in critical tenets, never lost enthusiasm.[20] Sociological studies of theatrical and operatic repertories have emphasized not so much changes in aesthetic standards as the economic pressures that incline larger performing organizations toward artistic conservativism.[21] More theoretically oriented is the emerging field of interpretive history, which seeks to account for the changing nature of the dialogue between a text and its critics.[22] George Steiner has set forth the philosophical, theatrical, and philological careers of the various *Antigones*.[23]

The study bearing the closest resemblance to the present one is John Mueller's 1951 examination of the repertories of major American symphony orchestras over their century-long existence.[24] Amassing program data for eleven leading orchestras from 1842, when the New York Philharmonic Society gave its first concert, until 1950, Mueller compared the life spans of composers in the orchestras' performance histories. He found six distinct patterns: composers who have maintained their preeminence (e.g., Beethoven, Brahms); composers with lower but stable popularity (e.g., Haydn, Handel); composers in the ascending stage of their life cycles (e.g., Strauss, Mahler); composers in the descending phase (e.g., Schumann, Schubert); composers who display the full life cycle (e.g., Dvořák, Saint-Saëns); and composers once prominent but now forgotten (e.g., Spohr, Kalliwoda). Mueller associates the careers of the composers both with the nature of their music (Liszt has come to be seen as midway between Berlioz and Strauss in the evolution of the tone poem, and thus has been rendered somewhat obsolete by the latter) and with their institutional contexts (Leopold Stokowski, who conducted the Philadelphia Orchestra for twenty-four years, personally championed Bach and transformed him from a musician's musician to a dominant figure in the twentieth-century repertory).[25]

Mueller's painstaking collection of data and his sensitivity to cultural and institutional variables produce an exemplary study of the cultural-societal interaction over time, but his reliance on the life-cycle metaphor strikes me as misconceived, and the misconception points out the importance of looking at revivals. It is not the case that an artist must either enjoy eternal life in a repertory or live and then die forever. This and similar conceptions of art as "lasting" or not imply too smooth and parabolic a cultural trajectory and draw attention away from the phenomenon of rediscoveries or revivals.[26] The same institutional, social, and aesthetic variables that may explain the health of an artist's or a work's reputation at one time may also contribute to the renewal of interest in cultural objects or figures long buried; or, on the other hand, a different set of variables may prompt a resurgence of esteem. This is where the study of cultural revivals can make a crucial contribution to the understanding of the cultural-social interplay.[27]

Revivals, which need be neither resurrections into life eternal nor exhumations prompted by a morbid curiosity, offer dramatic witness to the capacity of cultural and social interactions to create meanings for particular people at particular times. They are not necessarily incremental, as the life-cycle analysis of trends implies, but may burst on the cultural scene for the most idiosyncratic of reasons. When they catch on, when they last, when they influence similar cultural activities, revivals offer demonstrations of the reconstruction of meanings, from the most occasional to the most universal.

Drama, especially Renaissance drama, has a number of advantages over other cultural objects for the study of the interaction between culture and society over time. The relation of a performed play to the society in which it is produced is immediate and public. A play is thrown onto a market, and its degree of initial success is critically proclaimed in print or word-of-mouth and commercially confirmed or denied. It is subject to revivals and dormant periods, and competes for attention with other old plays as well as with new ones. To be sure, the decisions involved in determining which plays are to be produced have much in common with other cultural choices such as a publisher's decisions about which novels to bring out, for publishers also must choose among established classics, relatively forgotten works out of print, and new novels clamoring for attention.[28] Plays offer better data for the study of cultural revival, however, insofar as their production and reception are more centralized, they receive more concentrated critical attention per unit, their commercial success or failure is immediate, and their influence on subsequent revival attempts is often quite direct. It therefore makes sense to approach questions of the interaction between literature and society by looking at that form of literature where the interaction is most apparent. Plays, especially plays written sufficiently long ago to have had long-term patterns of revivals and neglect, and even more especially plays regarded since their first performances as being significant works of drama, constitute ideal data for the exploration of revivals. Drama from the English Renaissance fulfills these criteria.

The present study of Renaissance revivals focuses on two genres, city comedy and revenge tragedy. I chose to examine the revival histories of these particular genres for several reasons. First, there has been a sufficient amount of scholarly agreement about the characteristics and the core membership of each of them so that I do not have to put forward extraordinary claims for their thematic coherence. Second, neither city comedy nor revenge tragedy is dominated by one playwright, nor is either dependent on the phenomenon of Shakespearean productions. It seemed important to identify sets of plays where neither the stylistic particularities of a single dramatist nor the operations of the Shakespeare industry would obscure the role thematic content played in the revival histories. Third, research on dramatic revivals requires something like a critical mass of plays that have actually been revived in the London theatre. A sufficient number of city comedies and revenge tragedies have both survived and have been performed in London at some time from the Restoration to the present so that one may seek patterns of revivals; this is in contrast with domestic tragedy, for example, a Renaissance genre that would have met the first two criteria. Excluding the Shakespeare canon, no other standard Renaissance genre has had so rich a revival history as city comedy and revenge tragedy.

A brief outline of what is to come: first the archive of Renaissance drama, specifically city comedies and revenge tragedies, is explored. Any cultural object, such as a genre employing distinctive conventions, is a re-creation as well as a creation. It is shaped by preexisting cultural objects and conventions, by the institutional context for which it is fashioned, and by the shared understandings, the common sense, in which its creators participate and to which they are trying to appeal. In chapters 2 and 3 I investigate this creation and re-creation of city comedy and revenge tragedy. After considering the characteristics of each genre as a coherent dramatic category, I examine its cultural antecedents, the dramatists who created it, its audience, its theatrical context, and the interests and concerns that it addressed. These chapters look synchronically at the cultural diamond for both genres.

I then turn to an examination of the activity of going into the cultural archive. In chapters 4, 5, and 6, I look at the revivals of city comedies and revenge tragedies in the London theatres from 1660 to 1979. The chronological pattern of revivals tells the story of the ongoing relationship among these particular cultural objects, the theatre as institution, and English society. By moving the cultural diamond over time, looking at periods of greater and lesser revival activity, one can see periods of greater and lesser fit between these genres and their societal and institutional contexts. The theoretical task then is to account for this variation in fit. This is the subject of chapter 7, which suggests that the operation of metaphor along three analytically distinct levels—the topical, the archetypal, and the social—may be the key to understanding the constructions and reconstructions of cultural meanings.

CITY COMEDIES

City comedy presents wily, ambitious characters pursuing fortune, status, and love.[1] The genre celebrates the adventures of urban and urbane rascals operating in the wide-open economic milieu of Renaissance London. Its characters demonstrate skills appropriate to an age of expanding opportunities, as they unblushingly lie, scheme, take risks, ignore propriety, flout conventional morality, fleece the gullible, and enjoy themselves hugely all the while.

This study examines the revival careers of thirteen city comedies, selected according to the following criteria: (1) each play has been considered to be a city comedy in one or more of the major discussions of the genre (listed in note 1); (2) each play is set in or oriented toward London; (3) each play has been revived in the London theatre at some time between the Restoration and 1979. The plays included are: Lording Barry's *Ram Alley;* George Chapman, Ben Jonson, and John Marston's *Eastward Ho!;* John Fletcher's *Wit without Money;* Ben Jonson's *The Alchemist, Bartholomew Fair, The Devil Is an Ass, Epicoene,* and *Every Man in His Humour*[2]; John Marston's *The Dutch Courtesan;* Philip Massinger's *A New Way to Pay Old Debts;* and Thomas Middleton's *A Chaste Maid in Cheapside, A Mad World, My Masters,* and *A Trick to Catch the Old One.*[3] Table 1 gives the date and company for each play's first performance.[4]

To understand why a cultural object like city comedy arises and becomes popular at some particular time, one must investigate the aesthetic background that made it pleasing and comprehensible, the institutions that produced it, and social context that found it meaningful and supported it. Any dramatic genre or convention is the product of three histories: literary, theatrical, and social. The present chapter accounts for the emergence and success of city comedy by first delineating the characteristics of the genre; next it considers the nature of the theatre in which city comedy flourished; and finally it explores how the topical, archetypal, and social appeal of the genre, suggesting that city comedy playwrights modified the trickster archetype to fashion a cultural resolution to a social dilemma.

TABLE 1   City Comedies

Author	Title	Year	Company
Jonson	*Every Man in His Humour*	1598	Chamberlain's (Curtain?)
Marston	*The Dutch Courtesan*	1604 (1603–4)	Queen's Revels (Blackfriars)
Middleton	*A Trick to Catch the Old One*	1605 (1604–7)	Paul's Boys (Paul's)
Chapman, Jonson, Marston	*Eastward Ho!*	1605	Queen's Revels (Blackfriars)
Middleton	*A Mad World, My Masters*	1606 (1604–7)	Paul's Boys (Paul's)
Barry	*Ram Alley, or Merry Tricks*	1608 (1607–8)	King's Revels (Whitefriars)
Jonson	*Epicoene, or The Silent Woman*	1609	Queen's Revels (Whitefriars)
Jonson	*The Alchemist*	1610	King's Men (Blackfriars, Globe)
Middleton	*A Chaste Maid in Cheapside*	1611 (1611–13)	Lady Elizabeth's Men (Swan)
Jonson	*Bartholomew Fair*	1614	Lady Elizabeth's Men (Hope)
Fletcher	*Wit without Money*	1614 (1614–20)	Lady Elizabeth's Men(?) (unknown)
Jonson	*The Devil Is An Ass*	1616	King's Men (Blackfriars, Globe)
Massinger	*A New Way to Pay Old Debts*	1621 (1621–25)	Red Bull(?) (Red Bull)

CHARACTERISTICS OF CITY COMEDY

A number of specific characteristics define city comedy and distinguish it from other contemporary comic genres such as romantic comedy. Most discussions of the genre mention the following as being typical features.[5] Each

of the thirteen city comedies of the present study has most or all of these
characteristics.

London Setting

> Our scene is London, 'cause we would make known
> No country's mirth is better than our own.
> No clime breeds better matter for your whore,
> Bawd, squire, imposter, many persons more,
> Whose manners, now called humors, feed the stage,
> And which have still been subject for the rage
> Or spleen of comic writers.
> *(The Alchemist,* Prologue, 5–11)

City comedy took the dramatic tradition of entertaining an audience with
vice, tricks, and temptation, a tradition well established in the late mystery
and morality plays, and gave it local color by setting it squarely within the
streets, taverns, and houses of Renaissance London. The playwrights seemed
of two minds regarding the city. Some avowed an innocent, nationalistic
pride, as when Lording Barry assured his audience in *Ram Alley* that "Home-
bred mirth our Muse does sing," with no satire intended. At the same time,
pride in the breeding ground of such mirth often took the form of a perverse
satisfaction in the enormities spawned in London. In *The Devil Is an Ass,* a
minor devil named Pug tries to bring vice to London, but the city's inhabitants turn out to be far more vicious than he. "Why, Hell is a grammar school
to this!" he cries (4.4.170–71). An exasperated Satan admonishes Pug for
jeopardizing the reputation of devils by exposing himself to London's overwhelming competition.

City comedy's preoccupation with London is manifest in detailed references to the city's streets, neighborhoods, taverns, conduits, and landmarks.
The Devil Is an Ass has one character virtually draw a map of the city:

> Child of hell, this is nothing! I will fetch thee a leap
> From the top of Paul's steeple to the Standard in Cheap
> And lead the dance through the streets without fail,
> Like a needle of Spain, with a thread at my tail.
> We will survey the suburbs, and make forth our sallies
> Down Petticoat Lane, and up the Smock-Alleys,
> To Shoreditch, Whitechapel, and so to Saint Kathern's
> To drink with the Dutch there, and take forth their patterns.
> From thence we will put in at Custom-house quay there,
> And see how the factors and prentices play there
> False with their masters; and geld many a full pack,
> To spend it in pies, at the Dagger, and the Woolsack.
> (1.1.55–66)

The London orientation of the plays is as much a matter of social semiotics as of geographical setting. Urban sites represented urban manners and morals, offering the playwright a code through which he could efficiently communicate his characters' reputations and plans. The audience knew all about the clientele of the Dagger and the Woolsack, the popularity of Barn Elms as a rendevous for lovers (*A Chaste Maid in Cheapside*), the proximity of Cuckhold's Haven to Billingsgate (*Eastward Ho!*), and the likelihood of finding a chaste maid in Cheapside, a virgin in Ram-Alley, or a bear "to be yet seen in Paris Garden, living upon nothing but toasted cheese and green onions" (*The Dutch Courtesan* 2.3.54–55).[6]

Socially Heterogeneous Characters

LOVELL: I can advance you.
MARGARET: To a hill of sorrow,
Where every hour I may expect to fall,
But never hope firm footing. You are noble,
I of low descent, however rich;
And tissues match'd with scarlet suit but ill.
(*A New Way to Pay Old Debts* 3.2.195–99)

Fabrics had social significance for Renaissance Londoners, as they have for us today. Tissue, lavishly ornamental and often interwoven with gold or silver thread, represented the aristocracy; scarlet was a much heavier material, connoting riches but not nobility. Margaret's response is a typical example of how city comedy characters carefully mark social distinctions. Plots often involve a conflict between those who strive to maintain distance between social groups versus those who attempt to bridge the gap.

There are plenty of gaps, for city comedy characters come from a wide variety of social backgrounds. The most active characters are usually gentlemen, middle-class citizens, or out-and-out criminals. Though usually of gentle birth, protagonists are typically disinherited or otherwise penniless. Welborne in *A New Way to Pay Old Debts* and Witgood in *A Trick to Catch the Old One* have lost their property through dissolute living; in *Epicoene* Sir Dauphine is about to be disinherited by his uncle; in *Ram Alley* William has lost his property and lusts after the widow Taffeta's wealth as well as her body; Winwife and Quarlous (*Bartholomew Fair*) also need wealthy wives; in *A Mad World, My Masters* Follywit wants to obtain his legacy from his uncle without having to wait for the old man to die. Other leading characters (in the welter of characters found in most city comedies, the term protagonist is somewhat misleading) include confidence men such as Subtle and Face (the alchemist and the entrepreneurial butler of *The Alchemist*) or Meercraft (the projector of *The Devil Is an Ass*). Such rogues, and their prostitute and low-life companions, abound and frequently prosper. Titled aristocrats appear in most plays, often as victims of various forms of trickery and arbiters of the final disposition of rewards and punishment. Minor characters represent a variety of conventional urban types. Puritans are invariably hypocrites, servants may be loyal or treacherous, knights are generally ineffectual, merchants are grasping and their wives available.

The Dutch Courtesan presents a typical London panoply. It contains two old knights, genial but slow to catch on, their nubile daughters, the city gallants who court the girls, an assortment of tradesmen (Master Mulligrub, the vintner, and his social-climbing wife) and craftsmen (Master Burnish, the goldsmith), servants and apprentices, and—most vital of the characters—the rogues: Francesca the whore, the old woman who panders for her, and the unparalleled thief, Cocledemoy. Thus the comedy includes members of every social stratum from the lesser aristocracy to the underworld.

Trickery

> Every part of the world shoots up daily into more
> subtlety; the very spider weaves her cauls with
> more art and cunning to entrap the fly.
> The shallow ploughman can distinguish now
> 'Twixt simple truth and a dissembling brow;
> Your base mechanic fellow can spy out
> A weakness in a lord, and learns to flout.
> How does't behoove us then that live by sleight,
> To have our wits wound up to their stretched height.
> (*A Mad World, My Masters* 1.1.153–61)

Thus does a mother instruct her prostitute daughter as to the ways of the world. The daughter presumably requires little instruction ("Mother, I am too deep a scholar grown / To learn my first rules now"), for the pair have already sold the girl's maidenhead some fifteen times. Characters possessing such ingenious capacity to "live by sleight" are a distinguishing feature of city comedy. Trickery or "cozenage" and gullibility structure the plots and subplots. "Wit without money" is the common plight, and all of the main characters must say with Fletcher's gallant, "My wit's my plough" (1.1).

Two tricksters recur: the rogue—a criminal, whore, or confidence man, clearly operating on the far side of the law—and the young gallant, whose schemes, while no less elaborate than those of the rogue, violate moral though not always legal sanctions.[7] The principal difference between the rogue and the gallant is that the gallant is born a gentleman, while the rogue is from a lower social stratum. Cocledemoy is a classic rogue. He tricks a citizen's wife into handing over a gilded goblet by offering to have her husband's coat of arms engraved on it before a feast, supporting his fabrication about the feast by giving the wife "a jowl of fresh salmon" to prepare for the meal; having thus stolen the goblet, he later returns to steal the salmon. Like all such rogues he takes pride in his cunning and calls the audience's attention to his cleverness in frequent asides like, "I must have the salmon too, worshipful Cocledemoy, now for thy masterpiece!"[8]

Gallants are younger, disinherited, or bankrupt sons of the elite who seek money commensurate with their ascribed social position.[9] Follywit, the gallant in *A Mad World, My Masters* is representative of the type. Preparing to rob his own uncle, he explains his predicament to his companions:[10]

> You all know the possibilities of my hereafter fortunes, and
> the humour of my frolic grandsire Sir Bounteous Progress,
> whose death makes all possible to me: I shall have all, when
> he has nothing, but now he has all, I shall have nothing. I
> think one mind runs through a million of 'em; they love to
> keep us sober all the while they're alive, that when they're
> dead we may drink to their healths; they cannot abide to see
> us merry all the while they're above ground; and that makes
> so many laugh at their fathers' funerals. . . . Then since he
> has no will to do me good as long as he lives, by mine own
> will, I'll do myself good before he dies. (1.1.38–47, 54–55)

Thus justifying his nepotistic predation, he sets out to take an advance on his inheritance by abusing the old man's fawning hospitality to a "nobleman," Lord Owemuch, who of course is Follywit in disguise. Gallants like Follywit are students of human greed, vainglory, and folly. Both gallants and rogues attune their schemes to the specific weakness or "humour" of a selected victim; for example, Follywit and Cocledemoy both cater to their gulls' desires to enhance their social status by making a good showing before important guests.

Some city comedy tricksters defy neat categorization. Sir Giles Overreach (*A New Way to Pay Old Debts*) operates within the law, amassing wealth by foreclosing on mortgages to improvident landowners, but his extreme violation of the moral law, along with the violence he uses to back up his legal extortion, make him a quasi-rogue. Similarly, while most gallants are motivated by love and profit, with the emphasis on profit, there are a few who act entirely for love.[11] Finally, some tricksters act more from delight in trickery than from any personal desire for love or profit. Brainworm (*Every Man in His Humour*) simply likes to demonstrate his wit (although as a servant, he may profit from aiding his master); Truewit (*Epicoene*) similarly enjoys exercising his cleverness at unmasking hypocrites; Freevill's cruel tricks on his friend Malhereaux (*The Dutch Courtesan*) are designed to cure the latter's love for a whore. Such disinterestedness, which harkens back to early comic tricksters like Diccon (*Gammer Gurton's Needle*) and Merrygreek (*Roister Doister*), is exceptional.

The rascals of city comedy often go unpunished, and even become objects of their victims' admiration. In *The Alchemist* Lovewit forgives Face, his butler, who during his master's absence has converted the household into a den of confidence games. Lovewit concludes that it behooves a master to "be a little indulgent to that servant's wit," especially since that wit has brought him a wealthy bride. Similarly, Sir Bounteous Progress forgives his nephew for fleecing him (*A Mad World, My Masters*), his indignation giving way to amusement when he realizes that Follywit has unsuspectingly married his uncle's cast-off whore.

Money

Pooh, the plot's ripe! Come, to your business, lad;
Though guilt condemns, 'tis gilt must make us glad.
(*A Mad World, My Masters* 2.2.30–31)

Money, its acquisition or its recovery, motivates the action in city comedy. Impatient rogues and gallants refuse to see duller folk or miserly relatives enjoying all the money while they go without. They calculate their chances and take their risks to win financial security, knowing that "he that ne'er strives, says wit, shall ne'er excel" (*A Trick to Catch the Old One* 3.3.142).

The rascals excel because they recognize the greed of everyone else. Pursuit of gilt is universal in city comedy London, and as always the most avaricious are the easiest to con. For example, *A Trick to Catch the Old One* begins with Witgood facing the typical problem of the gallant, the contradiction between his gentle birth and his empty pockets: "All's gone! Still thou'rt a gentleman—that's all; but a poor one—that's nothing" (1.1.1–3). After meditating on the miserliness of his uncle, who holds the mortgage on his property, Witgood reaches the inevitable conclusion of the city comedy trickster:

Well, how should a man live now that has no living—hum?
Why, are there not a million of men in the world that only
sojourn upon their brain, and make their wits their mercers;
and am I but one amongst that million, and cannot thrive
upon't? Any trick, out of the compass of law, now would
come happily to me. (1.1.22–28)

He then concocts a scheme to fool his uncle, Pecunious Lucre, and a rival of the uncle named Walkadine Hoard, by convincing both old men that he is about to marry a wealthy widow. Lucre decides to help his nephew financially in hopes of regaining his affection and eventually getting hold of the widow's fortune, while Hoard sets out to capture the widow for himself. By playing off the greed and rivalry of the two old men, Witgood manages to get his mortgage back from his uncle, his debts paid, and "the widow," his former mistress toward whom he feels some responsibility, well provided for in a marriage with Hoard.

Witgood also wins his sweetheart, Hoard's niece. Pecuniary and amatory motives are frequently intertwined in city comedies, but the lust for money tends to be the primary concern and the sine qua non for success in love; in Witgood's case the clearing of his debts and regularizing of his affairs are necessary before he can consider marriage. The prodigal of *Wit without Money* plays upon the convention by inverting it; he swears he wants neither the return of his mortgaged lands nor the love of the wealthy widow, though of course he ends up with both. Less sympathetic characters often regard their erotic interests as equivalent to and interchangeable with their monetary ones. Sir Walter Whorehound, about to wed a girl whose citizen parents are virtually selling her for the enhanced status a titled marriage would bring their family, looks forward to his wedding day as an excellent bargain:

> . . . ere tomorrow noon,
> I shall receive two thousand pound in gold,
> And a sweet maidenhead worth forty.
> (*A Chaste Maid in Cheapside* 4.3.75–78)

Sir Walter's equation of love and money is repugnant, and is punished. In contrast, the gallants who must give money priority over love are sympathetically presented, and they are rewarded with both.

Social Mobility

> Nay, when my ears are pierc'd with widow's cries
> And undone orphans wash with tears my threshold,
> I only think what 'tis to have my daughter
> Right honourable; and 'tis a powerful charm
> Makes me insensible of remorse or pity
> Or the least sting of conscience.
> (*A New Way to Pay Old Debts* 4.1.126–31)

In his naked desire to convert his wealth into lasting social position for his family, Sir Giles Overreach lacks subtlety as well as compassion, but his aspiration for upward social mobility is widely shared by the rogues, citizens, and fools of city comedy. Social climbers change their dress as well as their behavior in emulation of their betters. In *The Alchemist,* Face puts off the "honest, plain, livery-three-pound-thrum" of a butler for the silks of a city gallant, while Kastril comes to town to learn how to quarrel like a gentleman, and Doll Common, in "a kind of modern happiness," parades as a noble dame. Contradictions between economic and social position motivate characters who, as in the case of Sir Giles, have money but no title, or in the reverse situation typical for the gallant, have gentle blood but no money.

City merchants and small businessmen, and especially their wives, often make fools of themselves attempting to imitate the styles and manners of their social superiors, but they also take practical steps toward securing the social position of the next generation. Strategies vary. A typical example from *A Chaste Maid in Cheapside* occurs when Tim, the son of a wealthy goldsmith, is sent to the university in order to mix with and take on the characteristics of the young gentlemen there. In *The Devil Is an Ass*, another goldsmith takes a different approach:

> All this is to make you a gentleman
> I'll have you learn, son. Wherefore have I plac'd you
> With Sir Paul Eitherside, but to have so much law
> To keep your own? Besides, he is a justice
> Here i' the town; and dwelling, son, with him,
> You shall learn that in a year, shall be worth twenty
> Of having stay'd you at Oxford or at Cambridge,
> Or sending you to the Inns of Court, or France.
>   (*The Devil Is an Ass* 3.1.1–8)

The ambitious father waxes eloquent over how preying on other men's folly enables a citizen to secure social position for his offspring:

> We live by finding fools out to be trusted.
> Our shop-books are our pastures, our corn-grounds
> We lay 'em op'n, for them to come into;
> And when we have 'em there, we drive 'em up
> Int' one of our two pounds, the compters straight,
> And this is to make you a gentleman!
> We citizens never trust, but we do cozen:
> For if our debtors pay, we cozen them,
> And if they do not, then we cozen ourselves.
> But that's a hazard every one must run
> That hopes to make his son a gentleman!
>   (17–26)

Emblematic of all of the social climbers are the prostitutes who plot to be "made honest" through marriage. Frank Gullman, the courtesan kept by the old knight in *A Mad World, My Masters*, succeeds in marrying her lover's young nephew. Her mother's comment, "So, girl, here was a bird well caught," reflects the pair's cool manipulation to achieve social status. The success of such prostitutes, in contrast with the failure of other social climbers, may be due to their limited aspirations; they seek to be made "honest," but not "honourable."

Cynicism

> Think of it. Come away! Virtue, let sleep thy passions;
> "What old times held as crimes are now but fashions."
>   (*The Dutch Courtesan* 3.1.270–71)

City comedy offers a relentlessly cynical view of human motivations. Greed, vanity, and lust drive the characters to action. The dramatists satirize this behavior, but except for Jonson in his earlier plays, they don't seem to expect anything better. Such an attitude distinguishes city comedy from the comedies of dramatists like Dekker and Heywood, which, though set in London and representing many social classes, take a more benign view. Dekker's *The Shoemaker's Holiday,* for example, lacks the bitterness of city comedies; its characters are insufficiently rapacious, its tone sentimental.[12]

City comedy rascals, sharing their creators' cynicism, are able to spot and exploit the individual desires gnawing at their gulls. They con them with offers of phony titles, opportunities for quick wealth, or the chance to sleep with the queen of the fairies (*The Alchemist*). Greed motivates rascals and victims alike; they are distinguished only by the rascals' cunning versus the gulls' credulousness.

Moral Ambiguity

> And here forever I disclaim
> The cause of youth's undoing, game,
> Chiefly dice, those true outlanders,
> That shake out beggars, thieves, and panders,
> Soul-wasting surfeits, sinful riots,
> Queans' evils, doctors' diets,
> 'Pothecaries' drugs, surgeons' glisters,
> Stabbing of arms for a common mistress,
> Riband favors, ribald speeches,
> Dear perfumed jackets, penniless breeches,
> Dutch flapdragons, healths in urine,
> Drabs that keep a man too sure in—
> I do defy you all.
> Lend me each honest hand, for here I rise,
> A reclaimed man, loathing the general vice.
> (*A Trick to Catch the Old One* 5.2.191–205)

Thus does Witgood, on his knees before those he has tricked, pledge himself to future probity. He apparently does not want to be outdone by the Courtesan, his partner in crime, who has just assured her new husband that he need not fear being cuckolded ("She that knows sin, knows best how to hate sin") and has offered the company an elaborate catalogue of the wanton ways she is now abandoning:

> Henceforth forever I defy
> The glances of a sinful eye,
> Waving of fans (which some suppose
> Tricks of fancy), treading of toes,

Wringing of fingers, biting the lip,
The wanton gait, th' alluring trip,
All secret friends and private meetings,
Close-borne letters and bawds' greetings, . . .
Removing chambers, shifting beds,
To welcome friends in husbands' steads,
Them to enjoy, and you to marry,
They first served, while you must tarry,
They to spend, and you to gather,
They to get, and you to father—
These and thousand thousand more
New reclaimed, I now abhore.
                          (5.2.169–76, 181–88)

Both passages are remarkable for the sensuous imagery employed, the penitents clearly delighting in their lush descriptions of forsaken ways. Beyond the contradiction between the miscreants' expressed loathing of their past vices and their zest for talking about them lies a more fundamental contradiction. Both Witgood and the Courtesan have greatly profited from their duplicity and immorality. She, as Hoard's wife, is now wealthy, honest, and free to play the amatory games she knows so well; Witgood has his debts paid, his mortgage returned, and a virgin bride. If the two schemers have forsaken sin, it may be because they have already achieved everything they sought through sinning. This pattern appears repeatedly. Rascals like Face, Quicksilver, and Follywit issue public recantations only after they have attained their goals or to avoid imminent punishment. Even Sir Walter Whorehound's quasi-deathbed conversion to virtue is prompted by his conclusion that he has made a bad bargain in exchanging his soul for a life of profligacy.

All such changes of heart are supremely unconvincing. Hence, the moral message of a city comedy tends to be ambiguous or ironic. Traditional moral sentiments, uttered sententiously by the rascals in the final acts, are at sharp variance with the comedies' richly elaborated portrayal of trickery, sensuality, and the amoral but successful pursuit of profit. It is not so much that city comedy has no moral signposts,[13] but the signposts point in opposite directions.

A comparison between *Roister Doister,* generally regarded as the earliest English secular comedy, and city comedy indicates the novelty of the latter's relatively unabashed depiction of material and social acquisitiveness, a depiction that often verged on celebration. *Roister Doister,* a secular comedy modeled after Plautus and Terence, was written by Nicholas Udall sometime between 1538 and 1553. The play deals with love and money, it is set in the streets of town, and its characters include a parasitic prankster, a braggart soldier, and a flock of silly servants. Notwithstanding its resemblances to city comedy, however, *Roister Doister's* tone is entirely different. The town setting is unspecified and featureless; there is no street life, nor are characters shown pursuing their trades. Social mobility plays no part in motivating the characters, and even money is relatively insignificant; true, Ralph Roister Doister is attracted to the widow Custance in part because of her wealth, but he tends to fall in love often, in fact with every woman who smiles at him. His parasite, Merrygreek, has fun with his gullible patron, but this protorascal plays his tricks for amusement, not for profit; indeed, were Roister Doister ever to catch on, Merrygreek's intriguing would conflict with his self-interest. The morality of the play is completely conventional with respect to honest women, faithful servants, and the perils of vanity. Sex is reserved for the marriage bed; Merrygreek won't help Roister Doister before asking, "But is your love, tell me first, in any wise / In the way of marriage, or of merchandise?," and Ralph hastens to reassure him. Udall takes a sunny view of human nature, far removed from the cynicism of city comedy; his play is about love and pranks. The characters in *Roister Doister* may be foolish or tricky, but they are not corrupt, and, slaves to their own humors, they have little eye for the main chance. Face would have found them contemptibly naïve.

CITY COMEDY IN INSTITUTIONAL CONTEXT

Upon reviewing these standard city comedy characteristics, it is tempting to draw conclusions based on the reflection metaphor. City comedy reflected the mores of the late Elizabethan and Jacobean period, an era of increasing materialism, cynicism, and sharp dealing; or, city comedy reflected an abhorrence for these developments based on the popular tradition of precapitalist community shared by its authors and its audience.[14] As always, however, sheer reflection is too simple a model. While few would deny some connection between social experience and cultural objects, these connections are always mediated by the institutions through which the cultural objects are produced.

Setting the genre of city comedy as the cultural object at the bottom point of the cultural diamond reminds the analyst that, while there may be some direct linkage between top and bottom as the simple reflection model suggests, the side points of the diamond mediate and modify how city comedy represents the social world from which it emerged. A particular type of social world encourages certain groups of people, and not others, to become playwrights; it encourages certain groups, and not others, to constitute an audience. The tastes of this audience and the professional concerns of these playwrights shape the plays that get produced. Thus the resulting drama will be selective in its social representations, emphasizing certain aspects of social experience and ignoring or obscuring others. It may present an indirect, transformed, or even inverted image of social reality. Moreover, it will be influenced by aesthetic considerations, including cultural conventions, as perceived by artists and audiences.

A schematic device like the cultural diamond is an oversimplification, of course, for each link between two points on the diamond is itself complex and mediated. For example, if we take the cultural object to be a play as written, its link with an audience in a theatre is affected by the conditions of its staging and the interpretative decisions of its performers. Nevertheless, the diamond does direct attention to some institutional considerations that must be taken into account before any claims can be made about the relationship between city comedy and the Elizabethan and Jacobean social world. It is to such institutional considerations for city comedy that we now turn.

The Theatres

From 1576 to 1613 at least twelve permanent theatres operated in or near London. Eight were public: the Theatre, the Curtain, the Rose, the Swan, the first Globe, the first Fortune, the Red Bull, and, less conveniently located, Newington Butts. Four were private: Paul's Boys, first Blackfriars, second Blackfriars, and Whitefriars.[15] The Globe burned down in 1613 and was rebuilt the following year. Also in 1613 the Bear Garden was converted into the Hope, a public theatre that could also accommodate the bears. Four years later the Cockpit was converted into a private theatre, later to be renamed the Phoenix. In 1621 the Fortune burned; it too was rebuilt in a year.

City comedy took shape in the so-called private theatres, in which most of the genre's early productions were concentrated. These theatres, although open to anyone who could afford the admission price, catered to a more fashionable audience than did public theatres like the Globe.[16] They were more expensive; admission to the public theatres ranged from one to three pence and up, while the cheapest entrance price for a private theatre was six pence.[17] Private theatres were indoor, rectangular, and relatively small, whereas public theatres as a rule were open to the sky (the galleries and stage were roofed), circular, and large. The capacities of these theatres, like almost everything else about them, is largely conjectural, but second Blackfriars is believed to have held about 700 people, while the Swan and the second Globe may have held close to 3,000.[18] Extra patrons could be squeezed into the public theatres if necessary because of the large standing room for the "groundlings," who paid the lowest admission price; all patrons at the private theatres appear to have been seated. Most of the audience at either type of theatre sat in galleries, typically stacked in three tiers. At least in the private playhouses, a privileged and ostentatious few actually sat on the stage.

The stage itself was a platform stage, as shown in plate 1. Since the stage

was raised and jutted out amid the audience, actors were surrounded by viewers on three sides, a spatial configuration very different from the proscenium
arch theatre of later centuries (see figure 2 for this comparison). This arrangement allowed little in the way of scenic elaboration. Several doors at the rear
of the stage and a balcony above constituted the basic set.[19]

In contrast with their eighteenth- and nineteenth-century counterparts,
Elizabethan audiences seem to have been relatively well behaved and attentive. Puritans and City officials often charged the playhouses with being well-
springs of civil disturbances, but most trouble that did occur happened
outside the theatres. (The real danger from such large gatherings was the
spread of plague, and the theatres were frequently closed during epidem-
ics.)[20] Even if the audience members confined their noise to the cracking of
nuts, however, the fact that everyone seems to have been able to hear is
initially surprising. Renaissance drama, which required its audience to follow
an intricate flow of language, flourished in a theatre filled with several thousand people, many standing. with neither amplification nor, in most cases,
even the minimal accoustical aid afforded by a roof.

At least two factors enabled the playgoers to both hear and follow the
lines. First, Elizabethans knew how to listen and listen closely. In an era when
illiteracy was still the rule (although most of the male merchants and gentlemen of a London audience would have been literate themselves), people
depended on, and cultivated, their listening skills.[21] Elizabethans were accustomed, for example, to sitting through hours of sermons with complex
expository structures; they had plenty of practice following intricate oral pre-
sentations. Second, the openness of the platform stage, with the actors posi-
tioned out in the middle of the audience, combined with the declamatory
style of acting then prevalent, contributed to making Marlowe's mighty line
accessible to most auditors most of the time.

The Audience

The number of extant city comedies plus the development of formulas and
conventions within the genre indicate that the city comedy formula was popular with Elizabethan and Jacobean playgoers, but the social makeup of this
audience has been a matter of some debate. The most familiar view emphasizes the heterogeniety of "Shakespeare's audience." From the groundlings
cracking nuts to the gallants loitering on the stages. and not excluding the
sober citizens in the galleries, the playgoers represented "just about every
class, with the possible exception of the highest nobility."[22] Thus the Globe
was truly a theatre of the world.

This image requires qualification, particularly when considering non-
Shakespearean Renaissance drama or productions after 1609. Shakespeare's
audience may indeed have been mixed, but that was because the Globe was

ELIZABETHAN VERSUS PROSCENIUM ARCH THEATRE

ELIZABETHAN PUBLIC THEATRE

NINETEENTH-CENTURY PROSCENIUM ARCH THEATRE

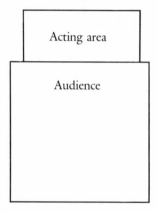

FIG. 2 Elizabethan vs. Proscenium-arch Theatre

one of the large public theatres. Alfred Harbage, stressing the public/private split, proposed a three-tier audience stratification:

> There was the genteel audience of the private theatres; there was the plebeian audience of such theatres as the Red Bull and perhaps the Fortune after the private houses had filched the gentry away; and then there was that audience both genteel and plebeian, or neither, of the nineties and because of its peculiar prestige, of the Globe in the early decades of the seventeenth century. It was the audience for which nearly all the great Elizabethan plays were written.[23]

Harbage contends that the private theatres were the haunts of a coterie of young gallants who could afford the admission price; the public theatres, on the other hand, offer little evidence for selection on the basis of "class, occupation, sex, or respectability," although the audience may have been disproportionately youthful.

Recently Ann Jennalie Cook has challenged this standard view of the Elizabethan-Jacobean audience, arguing that persons of social and economic privilege, with both money and leisure time in the afternoon, dominated the theatre-going public and exerted a major influence on playwrights.[24] In the public theatres as well as the private ones, the well-born, educated, moneyed, and landed made up the bulk of those in attendance. Although Cook's definition of this privileged group is somewhat protean,[25] her general point that theatre-goers were far from being perfectly representative of the London social composition is persuasive. While the seventy to eighty-five percent of the London populace who were not privileged by any definition were not excluded from either the public or private theatres by admission price alone, it does seem likely that they would have been underrepresented because of considerations of free time, the choice of how to spend limited entertainment money, and taste.[26]

The dispute over audience composition involves only the public theatres. Harbage, Cook, and all other accounts concur on the prominence of young gentlemen, the real-life gallants, in the private theatre audiences. This group of students from the Inns of Court, gentlemen apprentices, idle aristocrats, hopeful hangers-on at court waiting for an office, and country gentlemen visiting town for business or pleasure were acknowledged by the playwrights and observers to be the dominant taste-setters in the private theatres.

The influence of an audience of gallants is particularly significant in the case of city comedy, because the conventions of this genre were established in the private theatres. Six of the seven city comedies first performed before or during 1609, the year the King's Men took over Blackfriars, were performed in private theatres by the children's companies. The tastes of the audience of Blackfriars, Whitefriars, and Paul's, an audience dominated by elite young men, set the initial limits of possibility for city comedy. Furthermore, since established dramatic conventions and formulas are conservative by definition, the influence of this audience continued even when later city comedies had moved to public theatres like the Swan and the Red Bull.

The importance of the gallants in the private theatre audience should not obscure the fact that they were not the only patrons, for through the first decades of the seventeenth century, private as well as public theatre audiences seem to have been mixed to a considerable degree. The dramatists thought so, in any event. In his prologue to *Epicoene,* written for the Children of the Queen's Revels to be performed at Whitefriars, Ben Jonson expressed his anxiety about pleasing all the social groups to be found in his audience:

> Our wishes, like to those make public feasts,
> Are not to please the cook's taste but the guests. . . .
> The poet prays you then, with better thought
> To sit; and when his cates are all in brought,
> Though there be none far-fet, there will dear-bought,
> Be fit for ladies: some for lords, knights, squires;
> Some for your waiting-wench, and city-wires;
> Some for your men, and daughters of Whitefriars.
>   (*Epicoene*, Prologue, 8–9, 19–24)

Such an attempt at a broad appeal was especially prudent in light of the fact that successful plays often migrated between the public and the private theatres.[27] So while the city comedy playwrights sought to cater to the tastes of the young gallants in particular, they had to please other palates as well.

During the later Jacobean and especially the Caroline period, the stratification between the public and private theatre audiences intensified. This was reflected in the declining prestige of the Globe after the King's Men began playing in both it and Blackfriars in 1609. It became increasingly possible for dramatists to appeal only to a genteel audience during this later period, or only to a popular one. Nevertheless, even the city comedies performed at the public theatres during the late Jacobean period largely adhered to the conventions that had been formulated for the elite young audience of Paul's and Blackfriars some twenty years earlier.

The Playwrights

Ben Jonson's concern with catering to a variety of tastes reminds us once again that performing arts do not automatically mirror the interests of their viewers. In order for drama to correspond to audience tastes, there must exist both a means whereby the playwrights and producers become aware of audience preferences and the incentives for them to take such preferences into account. The professional dramatists of the Elizabethan and Jacobean period had both feedback and motivation.

Not all contemporary playwrights were professionals, and the system of amateur production was quite different from that in which the city comedy dramatists operated.[28] Amateur poets, often aristocrats wishing to display the learning and sensibility appropriate to a courtier, wrote plays for private production and limited manuscript circulation. These self-proclaimed writers of trifles, who scorned profiting from their pens, seldom wrote more than one or two plays. Although they did not compete with professional dramatists for the attention of the commercial acting companies, their attitudes reinforced the low status of those who wrote for a living.

Most playwrights did just that. Over three-quarters of the plays whose authors are known to us were written by professionals, that is, by men who supported themselves during most of their literary careers by the regular composition of drama for the commercial theatre.[29] Except for Barry, every dramatist included in this study was a professional, although only Massinger, Fletcher, and Shakespeare had long attachments to one of the companies. Indeed, the professionalization of dramatists and actors, as well as the construction of buildings designated primarily for theatrical productions, were the institutional changes most responsible for the flourishing of dramatic writing during the Renaissance period.

In contrast to the aristocratic amateurs, professionals often came from middle-class or craft backgrounds. (Table 2 presents a summary of what is known about the social position of city comedy and revenge tragedy authors.) Unable to secure patronage as a steady source of income, much as they tried, such dramatists experienced general financial insecurity during most of their careers.[30] For these men, catering to the tastes of their audiences was a practical necessity. Amateurs could afford to scorn the crowd; professionals needed it.

The acting companies were the intermediaries between authors and audiences. The professional dramatist, whether independent or attached by contract to a particular company, sold his script and all subsequent rights to the companies, and to do so he needed to persuade these potential buyers of the stageworthiness of his work, not simply its dramatic merit. Playwrights read their finished manuscripts, or gave preliminary readings of unfinished ones, to the assembled actors prior to purchase. Even after a company had bought a play, the script went through considerable revision, both in its presentation on the stage and in its later revivals; contracts between dramatist and company sometimes specified that the dramatist must undertake to revise his play if necessary in the future.[31] Thus the dramatists' professional concerns, the intimacy of the author-actor relationship, the ongoing revision of the scripts, and the competition among the London theatres all support the conclusion that any play or cluster of plays achieving popularity satisfied the tastes of contemporary playgoers.

While it is difficult to assess the popularity of individual plays, indirect evidence comes from mere survival: popular plays were the most likely to be published, and published plays were the most likely to be preserved. Typically the publication of a play followed its performance by several years. Those professionals under contractual obligations to acting companies, such as Massinger, were prohibited from publishing without the company's consent. The companies believed it was in their interest to forestall publication while the play was enjoying a popular career on the stage. They were not always successful; players and sometimes the playwrights themselves got pirated copies of plays published. Nevertheless, the fact that half of the plays of an extremely

TABLE 2   Social Status of Dramatists

Dramatist	Family background	Education and career
Barry 1580–1628	father a fishmonger	education unknown; Whitefriars shareholder; pirate
Beaumont ca. 1584–1616	father justice of Common Pleas	Oxford, no degree; Inner Temple; collaborated with Fletcher
Chapman ca. 1560–1634	yeoman family	Oxford (?); soldier; served earl of Somerset
Chettle ca. 1560–ca. 1607	father a dyer	apprenticed as printer; worked as printer; wrote for Admiral's and Worcester's Men
Fletcher 1579–1625	father a bishop, queen's chaplain, left only debts	Cambridge, probably no degree; collaborated with Beaumont
Ford 1586–ca. 1639	landed gentry	Oxford, no degree; Middle Temple; never admitted to bar; disinherited
Jonson ca. 1572–1637	father clergyman, died before birth; stepfather a bricklayer	no university; worked as bricklayer, soldier; actor and poet
Kyd 1558–94	father a scrivner	Merchant Tailor's School; no university
Marlowe 1564–93	father a cobbler	graduated Cambridge; actor(?)
Marston 1576–1634	father lawyer, chamberlain to Herberts	graduated Oxford, Middle Temple; wrote for Pauls; shareholder in Queen's Revels; became clergyman in 1609
Massinger 1583–1640	father agent of earl of Pembroke	Oxford, no degree; disinherited(?)
Middleton 1580–1627	father citizen, bricklayer	Oxford, no degree; wrote for several companies and city

(*continued*)

TABLE 2 (*Continued*)

Dramatist	Family background	Education and career
		pageants; London Chronologer 1620
Rowley ca. 1585–ca. 1624	unknown	education unknown; actor and dramatist, collaborator
Shakespeare 1564–1616	father a glover, received arms 1596	no university; actor and shareholder of Admiral's–King's Men
Tourneur 1570s–1526	unknown	education unknown; served Vere and Cecils; in diplomatic service
Webster ca. 1580–ca. 1638	father member of Merchant Taylors(?)	education unknown; Merchant Taylor(?)

popular writer like Shakespeare were not published until ten years after his retirement indicates how well the companies controlled dramatic publishing.

Shakespeare was attached to a company, but the unattached dramatists seldom waited that long, for they had reputations to build through the publication of their plays. Prestige was their only incentive, however. The stationer to whom the play was sold made all the profits from its retail sale; author royalties did not exist. Under such a system, while the unattached dramatists often took a keen interest in the publication of their works, the stationers sought to publish those least risky plays that had enjoyed or were enjoying a popular reception on stage.[32] Thus there is reason to believe that the title pages of plays that typically introduced the play "As it hath bin lately in Action by the children of Paules" or "As in diuers places it hath often beene acted" contained as much truth as puffery.[33]

Some further evidence supporting the contention that the plays that survived were among the most popular comes from the records kept by Philip Henslowe, who had a financial interest in the Admiral's Men and whose account books have provided the fullest documentation we have of daily theatrical operations. Some seventy percent of the plays mentioned in Henslowe's papers, which cover the 1590s, would have been completely unknown were it not for his records.[34] In the years from 1592 to 1597, where Henslowe provides unusually good data, we know the titles of 114 different plays that were performed, of which twenty-two (19%) survive.[35] These surviving plays were performed an average of eleven times apiece during the six-year period, while the lost plays averaged seven performances each. (See appendix A for a year-by-year breakdown.)

Therefore, while it is discouraging to remember that the majority of Elizabethan and Jacobean plays have been lost, most without leaving a trace, one may nevertheless be confident in assuming that those plays that actually got printed and preserved were among the most popular with the Renaissance audience. Furthermore, plays that spawned imitations, such as *Eastward Ho!* and *Every Man in His Humour*, must have been audience pleasers, and genres like city comedy, whose basic formulas were repeated over and over, must have been well attended. All of this evidence justifies the conclusion that city comedies were enthusiastically received on the Elizabethan and Jacobean stage, and that those that have been preserved were among the favourites.

THREE DIMENSIONS OF CITY COMEDY APPEAL

If city comedies were popular, their content should offer clues as to the source of their appeal. The following discussion focuses on what I take to be the essence of city comedy: cunning individuals—gallants and rogues—pursuing their economic, social, and amatory interests in the urban London milieu. The appeal of these characters' adventures, I shall suggest, depended in part on their topicality, which prompted their audience's amused recognition of familiar places, schemes, and character types. The attraction of city comedy gallants and rogues also derived from their participation in the archetypal appeal of the trickster, a dramatically compelling figure long established on the English stage. A third source of the genre's appeal lay in its representation of recurrent concerns about social mobility and social order.

The analytical purpose served by sorting out dramatic content into these three levels—the topical, the archetypal, and the social—is to help distinguish among the characteristics of plays that made them immediately popular, the characteristics that enhanced their chances for being preserved in the cultural archive, and the characteristics that encouraged their revival at some times more than others. Popularity, preservation, and revival, all social actions upon cultural objects, are sequential enabling factors. The more popular a Renaissance play or genre was, the more likely was its preservation. Mere preservation is essential for revival, and prominence in a cultural archive—for example if a play exists in published editions rather than only in manuscript form—enhances the likelihood of its rediscovery. While elements representing what I have called the social basis of appeal powerfully influence the chances of any particular play being selected for revival at a certain time, its topical and archetypical characteristics, by enhancing its chances of achieving popularity and preservation, allow it to be a candidate for revival in the first place. The analytic strategy of breaking down genres of plays such as city comedy into three types of appeal allows the separate consideration of the processes whereby a cultural object may win approval, enter the cultural archive, and later be revived.

City Comedy and Iron Age Londoners

Topicality was one of city comedy's most prominent attractions. These plays amused their audiences by giving stylized expression to the urban sophistication, shared knowledge, and common sense of Londoners at a particular historical moment. To put it colloquially, everyone likes to have the inside dope, and city comedy dramatists flattered their audiences by implicitly assuming that they had it.[36]

Success in the commercial theatre could not depend solely on representing the consciousness of a single audience segment, even that of the highly visible gallants. Though tilting toward the privileged, the audience was too heterogeneous for the dramatists to pursue such a strategy exclusively. What almost all playgoers from lords to waiting wenches did share was the urbanite's familiarity with local culture and city gossip, along with the self-satisfaction of the cosmopolitan. City comedies utilized collective understanding of local geography and its connotations, giving the audience the pleasure of being in the know about the pie shops of Ram Alley, the pleasant walks through Moorfields, or the ample meals served at the Mitre tavern.[37]

City comedies sometimes expressed the Londoner's pride in his sophistication through the spectacle of city slickers mocking country rubes. In *The Devil Is an Ass* for example, Fitzdotteral, a Norfolk squire, hopes to cut an impressive figure at Blackfriars, but he has to rent the clothing he needs to do so. Wittipol, the urbane gallant, remarks that

> He dares not miss a new play, or a feast,
> What rate soever clothes be at, and thinks
> Himself still new in other men's old.
> (1.4.23–25)

So much for country bumpkins attempting to pass.

Londoners enjoyed being knowledgeable about persons as well as places, but here the dramatists needed to exercise discretion. Direct or obvious allusions to influential people provoked censorship.[38] Explicit references to political figures were especially dangerous, for Elizabethan-Jacobean censorship was particularly concerned with perceived offences to "Divinitie and State." Thus the not very innocent satire on the Scots in *Eastward Ho!*, offensive to a

Scottish king and court, landed Chapman and Jonson in jail and for a while threatened them with the loss of their ears. Such direct, personal satire on political figures was avoided by the discreet for understandable reasons.

Instead, dramatists presented "characters." To Renaissance Londoners, a "character" was a short sketch of some general psychological, moral, or social type, the vogue for characters having been set off by the publication of the Latin translation of Theophrastus' *Characters* in 1592. Theophrastus, a collaborator with and successor to Aristotle, had depicted deviants from the moral norm like "the flatterer" and "the grumbler"; his popular work may have influenced Ben Jonson's comedy of humours. A multitude of English character books were written in the early seventeenth century, including those by Bishop Joseph Hall (1608), Sir Thomas Overbury (1614), and John Earle (1628).[39] In the hands of these writers, as was true to some degree in Jonson, the characters were more likely to be social than moral types; classifications included occupations (the lawyer, the common bawd), social rank (the younger son, the gentleman, the citizen), social relationships (the parasite, the good wife), and religion (the Papist, the Puritan) as well as the humours. All late Elizabethan, Jacobean, and Caroline dramatists were unquestionably familiar with the popular character books. Webster had Bosola and Flamineo toss off a number of polished characters in *The Duchess of Malfi* and *The White Devil,* while Jonson included sketches of "the severall Character of every Person" in published version of *Every Man out of His Humour* (1600).[40]

By presenting a range of conventional characters in their plays as a form of literary shorthand, city comedy dramatists accomplished a number of things. They could be topical, appealing to their audience's knowledgeability, without risking the censorship that more individually directed satire would draw. They could sequentially address the social groups within their audience; "topical portraits seemed drawn sometimes to set one part of the house laughing at the other."[41] They could dispense with the time-consuming business of establishing motivations, since everyone knew what motivated "the university scholar," "the citizen's wife," or "the younger brother." In offering a character, the playwright was setting forth a convenient marker for a conventional social type; since he could take recognition of the type for granted, he could therefore concentrate on the language and plot.

In addition to catering to its audience's familiarity with places and social types, city comedy appealed to the Elizabethan Londoner's fascination with money and how to acquire it. Money was a topic of compelling interest for all social groups; as Ben Jonson put it: "How hath all true reputation fallen since money began to have any. Yet the great herd, the multitude, that in all other things are divided, in this alone conspire and agree: to love money."[42] More particularly, insofar as city comedy was crafted for the private theatre audience dominated by younger sons, law students, aspiring young gentlemen from the country, and entrepreneurial urbanites, the genre engagingly treated a subject of immediate and admitted concern to such an audience. City comedy equated London with money, just as the gallants in the audience did. In *Wit without Money,* to cite one instance, the widow determines to flee the city to escape the suitors who pursue her and her sister for their fortunes, while her servants regard leaving London as a sentence of death from rural boredom. In such plays, and to the audience of such plays, London represented money, opportunity, and excitement, while the country represented social prestige, security, and traditional torpor.

City comedies have an internal logic that depends on their audience's familiarity with the money convention. When the pursuit of money is recognized to be the principal goal of the tricksters, the anomalies of a play like *Epicoene* begin to clear up. In Jonson's comedy Dauphine and Truewit con Morose, a man with a pathological hatred of noise, into marrying "the silent woman." No sooner has the wedding taken place than Morose discovers his bride has a tongue and mind of her own, both of which she uses to torment him. The tricksters meanwhile introduce noise and disorder into the household, finally driving Morose to sleep perched on the rafters. In the ensuing confusion, some vainglorious dullards including Sir Jack Daw and Sir Amorous La-Foole are exposed and mocked. At the climax, Dauphine, who is Morose's nephew, offers to free his uncle from the terrible marriage in return for an annuity and guaranteed inheritance. Morose agrees, and Dauphine reveals that the marriage is null because Epicoene is really a young boy. This final trick, for which neither the audience nor even Truewit have been prepared, has struck many as gratuitous, a joke played on the audience rather than one shared with them.[43]

Under the assumption that the Elizabethan audience understood that money is always the object of city comedy action, however, then the ending is not gratuitous after all. In the first scene, Dauphine mentions that he believes his uncle is going to disinherit him. Little is made of this, and it might appear that the uncle's plans serve only to justify his torture by the tricksters, but to an audience that expected money and the restoration of social position that money could buy to be the nephew's prime concern, and that recognized that his delight in harassing fools and his lust for women would be subsidiary to and in service of the profit motive, the ultimate revelation of Epicoene's male sex would come as less of a surprise. The nephew wanted to achieve his monetary ends and thus could hardly countenance a real marriage, which might produce an heir, for his uncle. The apparently random trickery of the plot is structured by this convention of the gallant doing anything to get money. Later audiences and readers, less familiar with the conventions of city comedy, found the play to be formless and the final trick meaningless.

Similarly, the bizarre climax of *Ram Alley,* where Smallshanks holds a knife to the wealthy widow's throat and delivers a courting speech that encompasses an extraordinary mixture of lust, sadism, and greed, makes sense in light of the money convention. True, Smallshanks has longed for the lovely widow, but as he threatens her with immediate extinction, he is unabashed about revealing the root of his despair:

> Come you shall kiss, why so, I'll stab by heaven
> If you but stir. Now hear, first kiss again,
> Why so, stir not. Now come I to the point:
> My hopes are past, nor can my present state
> Afford a single half-penny; my father
> Hates me deadly; to beg, my birth forbids,
> To steal, the law, the hangman, and the rope
> With one consent deny; to go a trust,
> The City common-council has forbad it.
> Therefore my state is desperate, stir not,
> And I by much will rather choose to hang,
> Then in a ditch or prison-hole to starve.
> Resolve, wed me, and take me to your bed,
> Or by my soul I'll straight cut off your head,
> Then kill my self, for I had rather die,
> Then in a street live poor and lousily.
>   (5.1.2195–2210)

When Taffeta, won over by this remarkable confession, agrees to marry Smallshanks, he responds, "Then straight let's both to bed," the more important financial considerations having been settled. To the audience of White-friars, Smallshank's methods might be extreme but his priorities would be unexceptionable.

City Comedy and Tricksters

While the ne'er-do-well gallants and shifty rogues whose enterprises structure the plots of city comedies were recognizable character types of Elizabethan London, they were also representatives of a timeless figure of folktale, prose narrative, and drama: the trickster. An examination of the trickster in folklore, in drama, and in the popular literature of the English Renaissance will reveal how the gallants and rogues were adaptations of a longstanding cultural archtype.[44] Table 3 summarizes the various literary tricksters under consideration.

The trickster appears in folklore throughout the world.[45] He is a bundle of diverse qualities: weak yet able to overcome the strong through his cunning, sly yet sometimes stupid, sneaking and untrustworthy yet often a culture hero who has made human life possible. Animal tricksters include carrion eaters

TABLE 3   Tricksters in Drama and Popular Literature

Character	Status	Opposition	Methods	Outcome
Trickster (folklore)	weak animal or person	stronger animal or person	cunning, flattery, turning opponent's strength against him	sometimes succeeds, sometimes is himself tricked
Witty slave (Roman comedy)	slave of household; has considerable freedom; assists young son	father, head of household	duplicity, brazen lies; quick responses to changing situations	succeeds in gaining son's objectives and escaping punishment
Parasite (Roman comedy)	freeborn, unattached to household; looking for free meals	head of household	flattery; clever and open pursuit of self-interest	suceeds
Devil (mystery plays)	strong theological figure, defined as God's adversary	Eve, Christ	temptation	ultimate failure, but temporary success; lord of "this world"
Vice (morality plays)	allegorical figure, ethical personification	tries to capture human soul; resisted by Virtues	temptation, seductiveness, play on human weaknesses; uses humor, friendliness	foiled; may capture some sinners but not primary soul under contention
Cony-catcher (pamphlets)	criminal, vagabond	respectable owners of property	con games, preying on foolishness, greed of victims; thief	succeeds repeatedly; may be punished at end or not
Rogue (city comedy)	criminal, social outcast, or lower-class	respectable owners of property, es-	temptation, preying on weaknesses,	often succeeds, and usually avoids

(*continued*)

TABLE 3   (*Continued*)

Character	Status	Opposition	Methods	Outcome
	person	pecially "citizens"	elaborate con games	punishment
Gallant (city comedy)	elite birth; usually penniless, disinherited	wealthy older relatives and other people with property	preying on greed and weaknesses; elaborate schemes	always succeeds in getting money and usually woman; forgiven by victims, restored to elite status

(coyote and raven in North American Indian tales) and spiders (Anansi of West Africa and the Caribbean), relatively weak animals who achieve the perquisites of the strong—consumption of meat—through cunning. Brer Rabbit is a familiar trickster from Afro-American folklore.

The trickster capitalizes on the vanity of others. An Indian tale describes a monarch who promises a jewel to whomever can travel around his kingdom first.[46] Many start the long race, but the trickster simply walks around the monarch, asserting that the king and his kingdom are one. Flattered, the ruler awards him the prize. Tricksters are themselves often tricked, on the other hand, for their greed and pride may tempt them to outreach themselves.

In spite of his hubris, irresponsibility, and other undesirable traits, the trickster is immensely entertaining because he represents antistructure and possibility. He is "the spirit of disorder, the enemy of boundaries."[47] In the structured world of everyday life, the strong dominate the weak; the trickster tries to beat the odds and often succeeds. Thus the appeal of the trickster in narrative lies in his defiance of the hierarchy of power. Ignoring natural limits and boundaries, he possesses the wisdom and freedom of the outlaw, the jester, the one who "gets away with it."

This powerful narrative figure has been employed in a wide variety of literary forms. His contribution is unpredictability. A tale about a fox catching a rabbit has little appeal, even though, indeed because, it accurately depicts the power relationship between the two species. A tale of a rabbit outsmarting a fox, on the other hand, is immensely attractive. It allows the teller to exercise his imagination (the tar baby; " 'Hang me des ez high as you please, Brer Fox,' sez Brer Rabbit, sezee, 'but do fer de Lord's sake don't fling in dat brier patch,' sezee") and leaves the audience with a sense of optimism (the strong don't always win).[48] Tricksters in written literature, in addition to the reworked folktales of Joel Chandler Harris, include the clever slave and the parasite of Roman comedy, the picaresque hero, the confidence man, the private detective, and the antihero of modernism.

To say that the trickster archetype has functioned in a variety of literary settings, however, does not explain why he took the forms of the gallant and the rogue in city comedy. An understanding of these characters must take into account the cultural history of the trickster in English drama, because previous versions of the archetype influenced both the dramatists' imaginations and their audience's expectations. Elizabethans were not familiar with Anansi or Brer Rabbit, but they knew all about the dramatic power of Titivillus and Merrygreek. Exploring the community of assumptions of Renaissance playwrights and playgoers requires an examination of some of these cultural ancestors on the family tree who lie between the universal trickster and Richard Follywit.

City comedy tricksters bear traces of two distinct dramatic traditions: Roman comedy and late medieval English drama. The influence of Roman comedy was both direct and mediated through Italian Renaissance comedies and stories. Tudor playwrights admired and imitated the plays of Plautus and Terence, incorporating into their comedies the Roman witty slave who helps his love-struck but not terribly bright young master fool the older generation and get the girl. *Roister Doister* sets the Roman pattern in an English village, with Ralph Roister as braggart (*miles gloriousus*) and Merrygreek as the clever parasite and assistant. Jonson's comedies, from the servant Brainworm of *Every Man in His Humour* to the nest of rascals and cheaters in *Bartholomew Fair,* draw on and manipulate the Roman model quite explicitly.

Important differences exist between the intriguers of Roman comedy and the rogues and gallants of city comedy, however. Social status is the main one. The Roman intriguer was a slave or parasite; the city comedy gallant combines the intriguer with the youth from a good family (*adolescentulus*), while the city comedy rogue is usually a criminal, not a servant.[49] Second, in sharp contrast to city comedy rascals, the Roman intriguer responds to events rather than initiates them. For example, in Plautus' *Mostellaria,* a young man has filled his father's house with drinking companions and girls in an endless party; when his father returns unexpectedly, the slave Tranio must exercise his ingenuity to keep the old man from entering the house and seeing what his son has been up to. This is the same situation Face must deal with in *The Alchemist,* but in Jonson's play it is Face himself who has organized the various con games going on within the house. City comedy tricksters do not use their wits just to get out of tight spots, as did the Roman tricksters; they use their wits to get into tight spots in order to make profits. A third and related difference is that the city comedy characters typically express far more confidence in their schemes and their wits than do their Roman counterparts. Tranio, for example, is always bemoaning his incapacities.

> Oh, what a rogue
> And peasant slave am I! And scared to death.
> There's no worse ill the flesh is heir to than conscience,
> Especially a guilty conscience. And I've got a beaut!
> But however it all turns out, I plan to proceed
> To continue to confuse things as chaotically as I can:
> That looks like what they demand.
>   (*Mostellaria* 3.1)[50]

Of course Tranio immediately does proceed to handle the difficulties most adroitly. The point is that the city comedy tricksters seldom experience such a failure of confidence and never, never feel any guilt.

A more immediate ancestor of the gallant and rogue was the Vice of the morality play tradition, who may have derived some of his dramatic characteristics from the devil as depicted in mystery plays. The mystery plays, themselves descendants of liturgical drama that had appeared as part of the mass in about the tenth century, were enactments of biblical scenes. Cycles of plays, presented by the guilds over several days at Corpus Christi, depicted the history of the human race from the Creation to the Last Judgment. In this cosmic drama the role of the devil was severely constrained by biblical precedent and, even when liberties were taken, by his theological position. Dramatists could never give their inventiveness full rein with the devil, for Satan had to maintain a certain dignity, or at least seriousness, benefitting his position as God's adversary. He could roar, be quarrelsome, even smell bad, all characteristics of the popular image of Satan, but he was by no means comical and could not stray far from his scriptural basis.[51]

If not comical, the devil was nevertheless compelling. He was elaborately costumed in feathers, long fur, and masks; he often brandished a club.[52] Because of his extraordinary appearance or perhaps because it was deemed unseemly for human biblical characters to engage in advertising, it was the devil who ran about the town promoting the play. The devil exerted the fascination of the trickster, the spirit of disorder, the defier of the heavenly hierarchy.

With the development of the allegorical morality plays, the trickster's dramatic function expanded through the character of the irrepressible Vice. While the devil, if present at all, was reduced to a minor figure in the morality plays, the Vice was the active agent, tempting human beings into earthly pleasures and the forfeit of their souls. Representing a single deadly sin or a composite, the Vice studied human psychology in his pursuit of souls. When a direct assault on Mankind in *The Castle of Perseverance* failed, for example, Covetousness lured the aged Mankind out of the castle by appealing to his desire for security in his old age. Vices bragged, amused their audiences with extravagant language, scatological humor, and satire, and were exceedingly worldly.

This is not to suggest that the Vices simply "descended from" the devil, but that they performed an analogous dramatic function: they supplied a trickster—sly, outrageous, and entertaining—for Christian drama.[53] The devil suggested possibilities that the Vice realized. The morality dramatists, having so much more freedom to shape the role of the Vice than mystery playwrights had with the devil, created an energetic, enterprising, and witty character who threatened to overshadow the allegorical point of the play altogether. The troupes of players were well aware of the dramatic power of the Vice; he was played by the leading actor and was seldom doubled.[54] The Vice interacted directly with the audience, cajoling money from them, running among them, letting them in on his plans, seducing them into laughter—and then bringing them up short in the recognition of their momentary complicity in the evil he represented.[55] Like the devil, the Vice was a trickster who ultimately had to lose (although he made off with a few sinners on the way), but he captivated his audience if not Everyman.

Such a vital character of such proven dramaturgical utility was not forgotten when secular drama eclipsed the morality plays. Playwrights made passing reference to the conventional figure of the Vice. Jonson explicitly parodied the morality tradition in *The Devil Is an Ass;* Shakespeare referred to the Vice's habitual playing on words in *Two Gentlemen of Verona* (3.1), and to his "dagger of lath" in *Twelfth Night* (4.2). More important, the characteristics of the Vice—his seductiveness, his duplicity, his wit, his enterprise, his amorality—gave a model that late Elizabethan and Jacobean dramatists used for their villains (Iago, Bosola, Richard III) and their clowns (Diccon, Falstaff). The same model influenced the rogue and gallant of city comedy.

To sum up the case so far: English dramatists were aware of the dramatic potential of the trickster archetype, a potential based on his unpredictability and his defiance of structure, and they cast him in a variety of roles. As the devil, the possibilities of the trickster were severely limited, but nevertheless he was established as a flamboyant figure having a special degree of interaction with the audience. Playwrights could go much further with the Vice, who openly attempted to entertain his audience with every dramatic device from acrobatics and jokes to letting his viewers in on his plots, but even the Vice was constrained by the Christian premises of the allegory; he had to lose. When drama became secularized, the characteristics of the Vice, which had already been proved to be dramatically potent, were applied to a wide variety of characters, and, for the first time, the fate of these trickster characters was not theologically predetermined.

The gallants and rogues of city comedy were dramatic offspring of the Vice and traced their ancestry back to the primordial trickster, but there was one characteristic they shared that was not inherited from their cultural antecedents: their single-minded pursuit of money. Profit motivated neither the devil nor the Vice, and although Roman tricksters and Tudor clowns sometimes sought money, it was less important than their pursuit of food, sex, good times, and escape from punishment. So the question is, even if the trickster was dramatically effective and had immediate theatrical precedents, why was he presented in city comedy as primarily, if not entirely, motivated by profit seeking?

One potential explanation of the prominence of the economic theme is that the Elizabethan-Jacobean age saw a tremendous burgeoning of commercial and protocapitalist economic activities, which made the pursuit of profit more visible and more acceptable than before. According to L. C. Knights, the most prominent exponent of this argument, city comedy represented the dramatists' various attitudes toward the new economic ethos of acquisition, attitudes ranging from disgust (Jonson and Massinger) to ambivalence tinged with admiration (Middleton).[56] This conception of cultural objects responding to economic changes strikes me as both plausible and incomplete. To the extent that the period was preoccupied with economic acquisition (though this charge had been leveled at every era since the thirteenth century), such a shared preoccupation would help explain why most city comedy tricksters pursued money first and foremost. On the other hand, the economic change argument does not account for the characters' other attributes: their craftiness, their humor, their bragging about their wit, and their blatant disregard for customary morality. If the essential theme is greed, greed can be portrayed in many ways. The most obvious exemplars of a new economic ethos would have been the wealthy merchant, the ambitious citizen, the worldly clergyman or Puritan, and the usurer; all of these figures occasionally appeared in city comedy, but they are not portrayed as successful tricksters. So the question is, Why did the acquisitory urge get grafted onto the trickster archetype instead of being assigned to other, more obvious social types?

A well-established cultural model already existed that brought together economic aggression and the wiles of the trickster, and this model existed in the pages of the tremendously popular cony-catcher pamphlets. Since the city comedy dramatists could not help but be impressed by the success of this minor genre, the cony-catcher suggested to them how economic observations and commentary might be fashioned into the characterizations of city comedy tricksters. Just as the Vice had suggested the utility of trickster figures in the commercial theatre, the cony-catcher provided an image of how tricksters might operate in contemporary London, and ensured that the tricksters' chief objectives would be monetary.

Cony-catchers (a cony is a rabbit) were thieves and swindlers who emerged from the mass of vagabonds of the late Tudor period.[57] Vagabonds, much feared by the Elizabethans, were the homeless, wandering poor—ex-soldiers, peasants thrown off the land because of enclosure, and former servants released from the dissolved monasteries or let go by the belt-tightening landed classes. Though most of these unfortunates remained harmless vagrants and beggars, the more aggressive among them contrived various illegal ways of gaining a living. These included "hookers," who stole hanging clothing with long sticks; "crossbiters," who had their wives lure a cony into bed and then burst in on the pair demanding reparation for the outrage; "rufflers," who begged for pity for their nonexistent or self-inflicted war injuries; card and dice cheats; and the familiar cutpurses. Pamphlet writers cataloged the varieties and practices of the cony-catchers. The proliferation of cony-catching pamphlets during the late sixteenth century indicates a significant popular fascination with these new forms of theft. Most prominent among the pamphleteers was Robert Greene (1558–92), whose readers were offered sensational material under the guise of sober advice as to how to avoid being victimized.

The operations of the cony-catcher were those of the trickster, involving the usual combination of opportunism, temptation, flattery, and cleverness. A 1552 pamphlet on dice-play cheaters illustrates the pattern.[58] First the cheaters find a promising victim in "a raw courtier, as one that come from school not many months afore." Spotting such an innocent in Saint Paul's, a popular meeting place for fashionable young men, the cony-catchers befriend him and invite him home for a capon supper. After the feast, the dice and cards appear. The cony-catchers expertly manipulate their victim, only letting him play a little the first night but urging him to return. He comes back daily, gradually losing more and more money while still convinced that his gambling companions are gentlemen. After weeks of being systematically fleeced, the gull tells his troubles to a more sophisticated friend, who sets him straight. The times are such, says the friend, that "wit, first planted in a few, hath in time taken so many roots, that in every corner ye may find new branches budding and issuing from the same." Thus with cony-catchers.

> Now, such is the misery of our time, or such is the licentious outrage of idle misgoverned persons, that of only dicers a man might have half an army, the greatest number so gaily beseen and so full of money, that they bash not to insinuate themselves into the company of the highest . . . always shining like blazing stars in their apparel, by night taverning with [s]trumpets, by day spoiling gentlemen of their inheritance. And to speak all at once, like as all good and liberal sciences had a rude beginning, and by the industry of good men, being augmented by little and by little, at last grew to a just perfection, so this detestable privy robbery, from a few and deceitful rules is in a few years grown to the body of an art. . . .[59]

The friend enumerates the various shifts and devices of the cheaters and ends by urging the gull to "withdraw yourself from yonder costly company," to which the erstwhile victim readily complies.

The elaborate stratagems of the dice cheaters, representative of the schemes of other cony-catchers described in period pamphlets, are analogous to the operations of the city comedy rogues and gallants.[60] All need money; all look for likely victims; all invest without certainty of return; all follow complicated plans involving considerable risk; all seek profit; all enjoy outwitting their fellows. Eyeing a gullible citizen or a wealthy uncle, the rogue or gallant is one with the housebreaker who says, "we must of necessity use some policy, when strength will not serve."[61] All such tricksters come up with policies that do indeed serve.

Respectable Elizabethans seemed to feel a certain ambivalence toward the cony-catchers. Though fearing their depredations, they also admired their cunning and shared their contempt for gulls. As one woman warned a recent victim, "By my troth, never speak more of it. When they shall understand of it in the parish, they will but laugh you to scorn."[62] Greene's "merry jests" and "pleasant tales" about cony-catchers reveal an affectionate admiration for their subjects that sharply contradicted his overlay of traditional morality.

Putting the case for cony-catching far more aggressively than Greene's equivocation, the remarkable pamphlet entitled "A Defence of Cony-Catching," written by 1592 by "Cuthbert Cony-Catcher" in reply to Greene, maintained that cony-catchers were no different from respectable people, only the latter were more hypocritical. "Cuthbert" contended that writers like Greene concentrate on minor thieves, while the major depredators go unchallenged:

> I am resolved to make an apology, and to answer his li-
> bellous invectives, and to prove that we cony-catchers are
> like little flies in the grass, which live: or little leaves and do
> no more harm: whereas there be in England other profes-
> sions that be great cony-catchers and caterpillars, that make
> barren the fields wherein they bait.[63]

Parodying the pamphleteers, he cataloged these greater thieves: the usurer, the "miller with the gilden thumb," the lawyers, the drapers who show their fabric in dim light to hide its imperfections, the chandlers with two sets of weights, the pawnbrokers, the tailors. Cuthbert even accused Greene of being a bit of a cony-catcher himself, for he once sold the same play to two different acting companies! Everyone has his tricks for, in Renaissance England,

> there is no mystery nor science almost, wherein a man may
> thrive, without it be linked to this famous art of cony-catch-
> ing. . . . What trade can maintain his traffic, what science
> uphold itself, what man live, unless he grow into the nature
> of a cony-catcher?[64]

The merry jests Cuthbert uses to illustrate his thesis generally portray the trickster tricked, but the trickery itself he regarded as endemic. In this respect he was at one with the city comedy dramatists.

The link between cony-catchers and city comedy characters is not only one of analogy, but one wherein a small circle of professional writers borrowed ideas from each other. Sometimes the pamphleteers were themselves playwrights. The prolific Greene, who was one of the first professionals to support himself entirely by writing, also wrote at least half a dozen plays. One of these, *Friar Bacon and Friar Bungay,* is filled with tricksters and their plots, although the object is love and the setting medieval. Thomas Dekker, who wrote "citizen comedy" if not city comedy, produced a number of cony-catcher collections. The cony-catching pamphlets frequently compared the status of the writer with the cony-catcher, in that both had insecure incomes that forced them to live by their wits.

The main connection between the playwrights and the pamphleteers was simply one of imitation, for in the small world of London authors, everyone knew what was selling. The literate buyers of the cony-catcher pamphlets, the gallants who hung around the booksellers at Saint Paul's, were the very audience that dramatists, especially those writing for the private theatres, wanted to attract. So it is not surprising that cony-catchers show up in city comedies. Face, Cocledemoy, Francesca and their ilk could all have stepped straight out of one of the pamphlets, for their creators knew the formula, knew it was popular, and knew it could incorporate both the archetypal appeal of trickery and the particular appeal of topicality. The gallants and rogues of city comedy were cony-catchers in their calculation, their predation, and their shamelessness; the gallants were just cony-catchers from good families. These characters delighted their audiences, as tricksters always do, by portraying the triumph of the (economically) weak over the strong. They were tricksters operating as cony-catchers in the specific milieu of Iron Age London. For as Cuthbert, sounding like the panderer-mother of *A Mad World, My Masters,* summed up the mores of the day:

> Truth it is, that this is the Iron Age, wherein iniquity hath the upper hand, and all conditions and estates of men seek to live by their wits, and he is counted wisest that hath the deepest insight into the getting of gains: every thing now that is found profitable is counted honest and lawful; and men are valued by their wealth, not by their virtues. He that cannot dissemble cannot live.[65]

City Comedy and Social Mobility

A puzzle remains. City comedy writers incorporated the trickster, an archetype familiar to English audiences and readers through his manifestations as the devil, Vice, and cony-catcher, into their plays, but they did more than dress him up in Elizabethan clothing. They transformed his ultimate social position. In previous literary forms the trickster had been an outsider, a disreputable character, a liminal figure—the carrion eater, the vagabond, the parasite, the enemy of God. City comedy rogues fit this pattern, but the gallants were strikingly different. Born within the social elite, gallants became outsiders only through their temporary poverty, and upon achieving financial rehabilitation they are welcomed back into the society of gentlemen. The question is, What accounts for this new social status of the old trickster archetype?

It is possible to identify moments in cultural history when an extraordinary number of recombinations and innovations occur, and one such moment was the late Elizabethan-Jacobean era.[66] A variety of contingencies— institutional (the establishment of permanent playhouses), demographic (London's accelerated growth), socioeconomic (the effect of commercial capitalism on the experiences and attitudes of Londoners), political (the arts' role in the celebration of the cult of Elizabeth)—gave rise to a drama in which old conventions and categories, not entirely suited to new circumstances, were mixed together with abandon. Renaissance drama, a "hodge-podge" according to John Lyly, mixed the classical forms and models advocated by the humanists with indigenous elements from the native popular tradition, and the social meanings of such mixtures derived from their contemporary contexts. The gallant was a recombination from the classical and popular trickster traditions embodied in a "character," that of the younger son of the elite, and as such he was a cultural innovation that addressed very real social concerns. His career in city comedy plots, in which his cleverness wins him reentry into elite society, resulted from dramatists taking a powerful and proven narrative figure, making him a contemporary urban type with which much of the private theatre audience could identify, and giving him a career that corresponded to this audience's aspirations and fantasies.

Understanding the social transformation of the trickster in the character of the gallant begins with the recognition that city comedy gallants and rogues were not simply London character types, or only tricksters, although they were surely both. They had significant social meaning as well. They offered previously taboo techniques and attitudes to a people whose circumstances required the mastery of new coping strategies. Furthermore, they offered the promise that enterprise would be rewarded economically while the basic social structure would remain intact.

City comedy gave cultural representation to a vexing problem of the late sixteenth and early seventeenth centuries, that of widespread social mobility. During the century before the Civil War, "English society experienced a seismic upheaval of unprecedented magnitude."[67] There was both a horizontal and a vertical component of this upheaval. Geographic movement involved migration between villages of as much as thirty to forty percent of the population in a decade, settlement of previously undeveloped fens and forests, and massive urbanization. The chief recipient of the rural to urban flow was London; the population of London grew from 70,000 in 1550 to 200,000 by the turn of the century and to 400,000 by 1650.[68]

Vertical mobility was equally spectacular. One contemporary described the English social structure of the 1580s as follows: "We in England divide our people commonly into four sorts, as gentlemen, citizens or burgesses, yeomen, and artificers or laborers."[69] All four of these groups were undergoing changes brought about by the expansion of commerce and a century of inflation. Of the lower two orders, who constituted ninety to ninety-five percent of the population, some of the landowning yeomen were able to prosper because of rising agricultural prices, and some country lads did come to London and find their fortunes as in the Dick Whittington model. For most of the poorer formers and laborers, on the other hand, the standard of living fell as a result of inflation, the expansion of population within these groups, and lower wages in relative terms.

The crisis of the landowning classes, the consequence of fixed rents in a time of high inflation, resulted in massive sales of lands. City comedies often refer directly to these transfers:

> We see those changes daily: the fair lands
> That were the clients', are the lawyers' now;
> And those rich manors there, of goodman tailor's,
> Had once more wood upon 'em than the yard
> By which th' were measur'd out of the last purchase.
> Nature hath these vicissitudes. She makes
> No man a state of perpetuity, sir.
> *(The Devil Is an Ass 2.4.33–39)*

The economic squeeze on the landed aristocracy created a particular problem for their younger sons. Primogeniture had been practiced with increasing strictness since the early sixteenth century. The English version differed from the Continental in two respects: it penetrated down the social scale to the least of the gentry, and it did not customarily include any significant provision for the younger sons.[70] Keeping their estates intact was especially a problem for the lesser gentry, whose numbers had increased sharply during the late Tudor period; for such families primogeniture was more necessity than custom.[71] The eldest brother inherited the lands, and often all the others got was, as one such younger brother put it, "that which the catt left on the malt heape."[72]

Increasingly strict primogeniture coincided with an increase in fertility beginning around 1570, a baby boom particularly strong among the elite.[73] By the 1580s this combination, along with the absence of monasteries as repositories for surplus sons, was producing a wave of young cadets of gentle birth but little money. Some went to the universities. Most poured into London to "go into traffic," that is, commerce or a trade, after serving an apprenticeship, to study law in the Inns of court, or to seek a patron or court preferment. These were the real-life gallants, so conspicuous at Saint Paul's, the ordinaries and taverns, and the private theatres.

Though the situation of the younger sons of the landed elite was often desperate, some groups profited from the troubles of the country aristocracy. In *A New Way to Pay Old Debts,* Wellborn has lost his lands to Sir Giles Overreach, one of the "new men" attempting to convert wealth into social prestige by acquiring country property. Contemporary observers believed this to be a common pattern.[74] In another shaking of the social ladder, the titled aristocracy was gaining new members at an accelerating rate. Elizabeth knighted wealthy merchants and daring seamen who had performed heroic services for the nation, setting a precedent despite her restraint in terms of actual numbers. Following her example to the point of absurdity, James I simply met his perpetual need for cash by selling titles. The increase in peerages and inflation of honors during the Jacobean period further undermined the self-confidence of the aristocracy and exacerbated concerns about the ultimate consequences of excessive social mobility.[75]

At the same time the merchant groups were increasing in both size and wealth. Younger sons of the gentry forced into commerce mixed with the ambitious country youth from humbler backgrounds pouring into London as apprentices, and both helped swell the ranks of the middle class. William Harrison commented on the considerable movement between the gentry and the growing middle class: "In this place also are our merchants to be installed, as amongst the citizens (although they often change estate with gentlemen, as gentlemen do with them, by a mutual conversion of the one into the other), whose number is so increased in these days."[76] Many of these "citizens and burgesses" were frustrated because of monopolies that restricted their activities and because their political power and social status were lagging behind their incomes. The London middle class was self-conscious of its rising position and prerogatives, and its prosperous members eagerly sought the luxuries that had formerly been the preserve of the well-to-do (a class characteristic mocked in city comedies).[77] They had a strong interest in learning, and avidly read handbooks on self-improvement. Their pride in their accomplishments was encouraged by Elizabeth as an expression of English nationalism, but this very pride made them sensitive to any obstacles to their economic and social advancement.[78]

Such widespread and visible mobility generated intense interest and concern. The rapid growth of London, for example, troubled Elizabeth and James I. With the support of the city, they repeatedly enacted and enforced legislation to prevent the construction of new housing and further buildup of the London metropolitan area, but their efforts failed to slow the flood of newcomers.[79]

Just as the throne was caught unprepared for the surge of urban immigration, so in many respects popular attitudes had not caught up with social realities. Younger sons of the landed elite were forced into apprenticeships and trades by sheer financial necessity, yet conventional attitudes among members of their class scorned entering into "traffic."[80] Making profits was fine, so long as it was through land or capital investments in grand enterprises like mining and overseas ventures, but for a gentleman to engage directly in commerce was still considered inappropriate. In his 1628 character book John Earle succinctly expressed the paradoxical dilemma of the younger brother: "His birth and bringing up will not suffer him to descend to the means to get wealth: but he stands at the mercy of the world, and, which is worse, of his brother."[81]

The younger sons were not alone in their contradictory positions. Titled gentry had lost the lands and income necessary to maintain the open houses and sumptuous style of life expected of them, yet often increased their debts trying to do so. Commercial men resented the fact that their greater wealth could not always buy them social prestige. Lawyers and merchants were unable to break into the administrative circles; officials and courtiers were, with rare exceptions, unable to enter the special sphere of being royal favorites. Intellectuals trained at the universities found an insufficient number of positions in church or state.[82] Courtiers elaborated theories of individual merit whereby they might penetrate the inner circles of social power, while titled aristocrats elaborated theories of exclusivity whereby the same courtiers could be kept out.[83] Meanwhile the numbers of the poor were getting larger, with vagabondage increasing in spite of restrictive legislation.

Thus Elizabethan and Jacobean England was a society with massive mobility, much discontent among the most mobile classes, much hostility to the upwardly mobile among the groups who felt invaded by the new men, and much general worrying about the changing social structure. Practical concerns about mobility and stability animated conflict at the level of ideas between, on the one hand, the medieval world picture of degree and inherent social position and, on the other hand, a more modern conception of social rank based on achievement rather than birth. No general consensus dominated regarding questions about mobility; what was dominant was the question itself. Renaissance hymns to the organic conception of society, the so-called chain of being that ordered both the heavenly and human realms, testified to what people worried about, not what they believed with any confidence. One of the best known of these, Ulysses' speech on degree in Shakespeare's *Troilus and Cressida*, expresses the conservative anxiety:

> Take but degree away, untune that string,
> And hark what discord follows. Each thing meets
> In mere oppugnancy. The bounded waters
> Should lift their bosoms higher than the shores
> And make a sop of all this solid globe;
> Strength should be lord of imbecility,

And the rude son should strike his father dead;
Force should be right, or rather right and wrong,
Between whose endless jar justice resides,
Should lose their names, and so should justice too;
Then everything include itself in power,
Power into will, will into appetite.
And appetite, an universal wolf,
So doubly seconded with will and power
Must make perforce an universal prey
And last eat up himself.

                                                                 (1.2.85–124)

City comedies, especially late ones like *Wit without Money* and *A New Way to Pay Old Debts,* contain comparable nervous hymns to social degree. The social mobility of the late Tudor and Stuart era upset traditionalists not only because it threatened their own circumstances but because it violated the law of God and nature. While the existential terror once believed to be part of the "Elizabethan world picture" was not felt by most people, and while sectarians, radicals, and entrepreneurs welcomed a cleansing or profitable disorder, the literary evidence does suggest that many among the educated elite feared the disruption of the correspondence between heavenly and earthly order, a correspondence that happened to legitimate their own preeminence.[84]

City comedies depicted these concerns about social mobility and offered a quasi-resolution to make everyone happy. In city comedy the smart and aggressive, be they younger sons, servants, or con men, achieved wealth, forgiveness, and sometimes even respectability. At the same time, those who profited from the loss of lands or the downfall of others, the Sir Giles Overreach types, were punished.[85] Most important, the gallants reclaimed their inherited social standing by relying on their wits to accumulate the necessary capital. This portrait of the reconciliation of economic activism with elite social status was obviously appealing to the young gentlemen in the private theatre audience, for it made a cultural virtue of their economic necessity.

The fundamental message of city comedy, borne by the gallant as transformed trickster, is that despite all of the social striving and economic activism represented, the basic structure of society was not changed. As table 3 indicates, the gallant is remarkable in that he comes from an elite social background, unlike any of the other tricksters, and at the end of each play he was reinstated to his rightful social position. Fallen aristocrats or gentlemen were returned to their former statuses, but newcomers did not break in. Marriages adhered to class lines. Butlers like Face became wealthy, but they remained butlers. City comedies generally closed with some titled character commenting on the restoration or order, the clearing up of confusion, and the general happiness of all parties. Everyone except the most flagrantly unworthy came out a winner, yet at the same time the social hierarchy was essentially undisturbed.

The Devil Is an Ass illustrates how city comedy reconciled economic gains with the preservation of the social order. Fitzdottrel, a country squire with more money than brains, is looking for new investments, and thus is a target of Meercraft, the projector (a type of entrepreneur who acquired monopolies over commodities or processes). Having monopolized adulterated aqua vitae, Meercraft tempts Fitzdottrel with his plans for controlling bottled ale, dogs' skins to be sold for leather, and making wine from raisins.

> ENGINE: Is not that strange, sir, to make wine of raisins?
> MEERCRAFT: Yes, and as true a wine as th' wines of France
>   Or Spain or Italy. Look of what grape
>   My raisin is, that wine I'll render perfect,
>   As of the muscatel grape I'll render muscatel,
>   Of the Canary, his; the claret, his;
>   So of all kinds, and bate you of the prices,
>   Of wine, throughout the kingdom, half in half.
> ENGINE: But, how sir, if you raise the other commodity,
>   Raisins?
> MEERCRAFT: Why, then I'll make it out of blackberries,
>   And it shall do the same. 'Tis but more art,
>   And the charge less.
>   (2.1.98–109)

But Fitzdottrel wants more than money; he wants a title. Meercraft finally seduces him with a fens-drainage scheme that will make him Duke of Drown'd Lands.[86] Through no fault of his own, Fitzdottrel is saved from losing his lands to Meercraft, and the Epilogue proclaims that "the Projector here is overthrown." Another ironic ending: Meercraft is by no means overthrown, just stymied in one of his many enterprises; Drown'd Lands may not work out, but he has meanwhile entered into a monopoly for face powder with the wealthy Lady Tailbush, and he is about to seize control of toothpicks. Meercraft's plans for the promotion of this newest monopoly gave Jonson the occasion to write the play's most unforgettable lines, as he describes his patent

> For serving the whole state with tooth-picks;
> Somewhat an intricate business to discourse, but
> I show how much the subject is abus'd,
> First, in that one commodity; then what diseases
> And putrefactions in the gums are bred,
> By those are made of adult'rate and false wood.
> My plot for reformation of these follows:
> To have all toothpicks, brought unto an office,
> There seal'd; and such as counterfeit 'em, mulcted.

And last, for venting 'em to have a book
Printed, to teach their use, which every child
Shall have throughout the kingdom, that can read
And learn to pick his teeth by. Which beginning
Early to practice, with some other rules,
Of never sleeping with the mouth open, chewing
Some grains of mastic, will preserve the breath
Pure, and so free from taint. . . .

(4.2.39–55)

With such energy and craft, such a thoroughly modern grasp of marketing techniques, the projector is sure to prosper. At the same time, the social position of the characters in the play are unchanged. Meercraft is uninterested in titles or prestige; his mobility is strictly economic. Lady Tailbush is a fool, but she remains a lady. Fitzdottrel neither loses his lands nor gains a title. Thus, smart men make money, titled or landed fools retain position, and degree does not dissolve into mere oppugnancy.

City comedy simultaneously displayed economic mobility while soothing social anxieties. Economically up-to-date yet socially conservative, the genre tried to demonstrate that both economic advancement and the existing social structure could coexist.[87] City comedy's particular hodge-podge included both the medieval and the modern world pictures, both images of organic community and of acquisitive individualism—contradictory elements coexisting in the medium of dramatic invention. In this medium, there could be winners without losers, social changes without social disorder, new men without the universal wolf.

Culture is artifice, and the city comedy social resolution was an artificial one. It involved a formal balancing of rewards that was easier to accomplish in drama than in the actual socioeconomic world of Renaissance England. For in this real world of London, and in its theatres, there were losers, losers of money and of social position. In a city where these losers in the contest for income and prestige were all too evident, the city comedy presentation of enterprise rewarded within a stable social order was a very attractive image. It appealed to the insecure young gentlemen attending the private theatres and to everyone else who feared, with Shakespeare, that degree, priority, and place might be giving way to power, will, and appetite.

REVENGE TRAGEDIES

Murder, delayed revenge, a ghost, madness, sexual viciousness, a bloody de-
nouement: *Hamlet* has impressed revenge tragedy conventions on English-
speaking readers and playgoers for four centuries. By 1599 the genre's formula was so familiar that it could be scorned; the Induction to *A Warning for
Fair Women* parodies the typical revenge tragedy plot, which tells

> How some damnd tyrant, to obtaine a crowne,
> Stabs, hangs, impoysons, smothers, cutteth throats,
> And then a Chorus too comes howling in,
> And tels us of the worrying of a cat,
> Then of a filthie whining ghost,
> Lapt in some fowle sheet, of a leather pelch,
> Comes skreaming like a pigge halfe stickt,
> And cries *Vindicta,* revenge, revenge.[1]

Despite mockery of such clichés, the revenge tragedy formula in its various
versions was extraordinarily robust, surviving on the London stage until Parliament closed the theatres in 1642.

Critical discussions of the genre usually begin with Thomas Kyd's *The
Spanish Tragedy* and include, at a minimum, *Hamlet* and *Titus Andronicus,*
John Marston's *Antonio's Revenge,* Henry Chettle's *Hoffman, or A Revenge for
a Father,* Cyril Tourneur's *The Atheist's Tragedy, or The Honest Man's Revenge,*
George Chapman's *The Revenge of Bussy D'Ambois,* and *The Revenger's Tragedy,* which may have been written by Tourneur, Middleton, or some unknown playwright.[2] The titles attest to the thematic self-consciousness of the
genre in its early period. Beyond this core of relatively pure examples lie the
later tragedies of dramatists like Webster and Ford, plays on the boundary of
the genre in which the formula has undergone considerable modification.
Some critics, stressing the difference between the earlier "Kydian" plays and
the later ones prefer to designate the latter as tragedy of blood, following J.

A. Symonds, or simply as Jacobean tragedy. The present study follows the predominant practice, established with perhaps excessive zeal by Fredson Bowers, of construing the revenge tragedy genre broadly and applying it to plays from the late Elizabethan through the early Caroline periods.[3]

I have selected sixteen plays as representing revenge tragedy in its most popular form: the seven plays already mentioned except for *Hamlet,* Francis Beaumont and John Fletcher's *The Maid's Tragedy,* Fletcher's *Valentinian,* John Ford's *'Tis Pity She's a Whore,* Christopher Marlowe's *The Jew of Malta,* Philip Massinger's *The Duke of Milan,* Thomas Middleton and William Rowley's *The Changeling,* Middleton's *Women Beware Women,* and John Webster's *The Duchess of Malfi* and *The White Devil, or Vittoria Corombona.* Table 4 indicates the first performance of each play. My criteria for inclusion were initially the same as those for city comedy: first, the play must be considered a member of the genre by most critical discussions, and second, it must have been revived in London between 1660 and 1979. However, I have included four plays that do not meet the second criterion, because they are central to all standard considerations of the genre. Two, *The Spanish Tragedy* and *Antonio's Revenge,* have had major repertory revivals in Glasgow and Nottingham respectively in the 1970s (and in 1982 *The Spanish Tragedy* was revived at the National Theatre in London), while the other two (*Hoffman* and *The Atheist's Tragedy*) have never been revived. The revival patterns described in later chapters are not affected by the inclusion of these four plays. The only major revenge tragedy not included is *Hamlet,* which is left out because its revival pattern has less to do with its characteristics as a revenge tragedy than with its membership in the elite circle of Shakespeare's best-known plays. On the other hand, *Titus Andronicus,* although it has been produced more than its intrinsic merits would warrant because of its author, does show variation in its revival career comparable to that of other revenge tragedies, so it is included in my sample.

The present chapter will draw attention to several aspects of revenge tragedy that powerfully influenced the popularity, canonization, and revival history of the genre. As in the previous chapter, I shall first delineate the characteristics of revenge tragedy, and I shall show how these derived in part from the institutional context in which it originated, the Elizabethan public theatres. Then I shall suggest how, within this context, a set of sociopolitical concerns combined with certain literary antecedents to produce a drama that engaged its audience in three distinct ways. Revenge tragedy's topical appeal derived from its representation of a popular ideological configuration of Protestantism and nationalism. Its archetypal interest came from its highly elaborated depiction of horror. And its social significance lay in its display and formal resolution of the tension between centralized authority and individual justice.

TABLE 4 Revenge Tragedies

Author	Title	Year	Company
Kyd	*The Spanish Tragedy*	1587 (1582–92)	Lord Strange's Men (Rose)
Marlowe	*The Jew of Malta*	1589 (ca. 1589–90)	Lord Strange's Men (Rose)
Shakespeare	*Titus Andronicus*	1594 (earlier?)	Derby's, Pembroke's, or Sussex's Men (Rose)
Marston	*Antonio's Revenge*	1600 (1599–1601)	Paul's Boys (Paul's)
Chettle	*Hoffman*	1602	Admiral's Men (Fortune)
Tourneur (?)	*The Revenger's Tragedy*	1606 (1606–7)	King's Men (Globe)
Tourneur	*The Atheist's Tragedy*	1609 (1607–11)	King's Men(?) (theatre unknown)
Chapman	*The Revenge of Bussy D'Ambois*	1610 (1601–12)	Queen's Revels (Whitefriars)
Beaumont and Fletcher	*The Maid's Tragedy*	1610 (1608–11)	King's Men (Blackfriars)
Webster	*The White Devil*	1612 (1609–12)	Queen Anne's Men (Red Bull)
Webster	*The Duchess of Malfi*	1614 (1612–14)	King's Men (Blackfriars & Globe)
Fletcher	*Valentinian*	1614 (1610–14)	King's Men (Blackfriars?)
Middleton	*Women Beware Women*	1621 (1620–27)	King's Men(?) (theatre unknown)
Massinger	*The Duke of Milan*	1621 (1621–23)	King's Men (Blackfriars)
Middleton and Rowley	*The Changeling*	1622	Lady Elizabeth's Men (Phoenix)
Ford	*'Tis Pity She's a Whore*	1632 (1629–33)	Queen Henrietta's Men (Phoenix)

CHARACTERISTICS OF REVENGE TRAGEDY

Following are what most critical discussions take to be the typical features of revenge tragedy. Some of the plays, especially the later ones, lack one or more of these characteristics, but all emphasize revenge as a motivation for action. While clustering plays in thematic genres obscures important differences, the practice and rhetoric of vengeance combined with a lavish display of horrors distinguish revenge tragedy from other contemporary genres.

Court Setting

Oh, happy they that never saw the Court,
Nor ever know great men but by report.
(*The White Devil* 5.6.261–62)

Revenge tragedies are typically set in courts or palaces, and the principal characters are noble. The court might be classical, Spanish, French, or German (or Danish), but is most often Italian. The English Renaissance popular imagination, fed by the novellas then being translated, saw Italian courts as riddled with corruption and diabolic intrigue, festering with fascinating sins, and thus appropriate for plays involving passion, hatred, and blood. The courts are presented in dark, claustraphobic imagery; people flee or are banished, travelers and rumors arrive, yet the focus of attention is internal. Most wicked deeds are planned and executed within the court, although there is sometimes a shift to another dark place: the graveyard in *Antonio's Revenge,* the cave in *Hoffman,* the forest clearing in *Titus Andronicus,* all places cut off from the flow of everyday life. *The Revenger's Tragedy* and *Valentinian* contrast the country, seat of light and virtue, with the evil twilight of the court.

When the protagonist is the main revenger, he is often an aristocrat who is not fully integrated into courtly circles. Titus and Maximus (*Valentinian*) are generals who have spent most of their lives off on campaigns; Vindici (*The Revenger's Tragedy*) has avoided the court because of his poverty; Hieronimo (*The Spanish Tragedy*) has held high office, but is stigmatized by not being from one of the noblest families; Francisco had been "a thing obscure, almost without a name" until favored by the Duke of Milan; Charlemont (*The Atheist's Tragedy*) and Hoffman have been driven out of the court. One typical pattern is that the protagonist, an insider by birth and rights, becomes an outsider by circumstances which may have to do with his victimization, and then returns to become an insider again but one who bears watching; this socially ambiguous position, sometimes facilitated by disguise or feigned madness, gives him access to court secrets while temporarily maintaining his moral distance from court evils.[4] Even in the case of *The Jew of Malta,* where Barabas is an outsider from the beginning by definition, he comes to enter the circles of the ruling elite in the course of enacting his revenge against this very elite. In the later revenge tragedies, where the protagonist is the object of revenge or equivalent to the other characters in wickedness, there is less stress on the insider-outsider-insider movement. The latest revenge tragedy included in this study, *'Tis Pity She's a Whore,* is exceptional in that it involves private citizens and takes place in a city rather than a court; on the other hand, it is an Italian city, the characters are wealthy, and one central figure, Soranzo, is a nobleman.

Revenge Motivates Action

> Behooves thee then, Hieronimo, to be reveng'd.
> The plot is laid of dire revenge:
> On then, Hieronimo, pursue revenge,
> For nothing wants but acting of revenge.
> (*The Spanish Tragedy* 4.3.27–30)

The essential feature of revenge tragedy, emphasized to the point of tedium by revengers like Hieronimo, is a series of actions motivated by the desire for revenge. Usually the initiating action is the murder of a kinsman or lover, although sometimes rape, incest, or adultery sets a revenger in motion. The incident inciting revenge may have occurred before the play begins. In *Hoffman,* the execution of the revenger's father has taken place years ago, but Hoffman keeps his father's skeleton hanging on the wall to remind himself of his filial responsibility of blood vengeance. In *The Revenger's Tragedy,* Vindici's mistress was poisoned nine years earlier; like Hoffman, Vindici has her skull on hand as a *momento vindicti.* Other plays have the revenge-inciting act occur during the play itself, as when Titus Andronicus' daughter is raped and mutilated in the second act.

Regardless of when the crime has occurred, there is some delay in achieving the desired revenge. This delay may be due to indecision, lack of opportunity, an unsuccessful first appeal to institutions of justice (*The Spanish Tragedy*), temporarily incapacitating madness (*Titus Andronicus*), intervention of a friend (*Valentinian*) or even a ghost (*The Atheist's Tragedy*), or the delay may be unexplained, as the case of Vindici's delay of nine years or Ferdinand's delay for enough time for his sister, the Duchess of Malfi, to produce three babies. The delay is dramaturgically necessary, for it allows an intricate vengeance plot to be developed, displaying the revenger's cunning as he plans his moves. Revenge is intrinsically more dramatic than immediate retaliation both because it takes longer and because it allows the revenger to give rhetorical display of his emotions and intentions.

In the early, Kydian revenge tragedies that established the conventions of the genre, the protagonist is the revenger. He ranges from a decent individual driven mad by suffering (e.g., Hieronimo) to a character whose single-minded pursuit of revenge makes him monstrous right from the beginning (e.g., Hoffman). Most revenger-protagonists begin with the sympathy of the audience, for they have been grievously wronged, but they forfeit much of the sympathy during the course of the play by becoming sadistic killers who enjoy their revenge far too much, slaughtering totally innocent people along the way. Barabas, who poisons an entire convent of nuns just to kill one person (his own daughter), or Antonio, who butchers a trusting child just to get indirect revenge on the boy's father, exemplify the revenger's tendency to alienate through excess. In the later revenge tragedies of Webster and Ford, the protagonist is not the revenger but the object of revenge. This reversal may have been due to the dramatists' problem with sustaining interest in a character who had degenerated into a bloodthirsty cliché. By performing a pathetic inversion, for example, making the foolish but blameless Duchess of Malfi the target of her brothers' cruel revenge, the Jacobean and Caroline dramatists managed to breathe new life into the genre.

To talk of whether the protagonist is the subject or object of revenge is itself a bit misleading, for revenge plots proliferate in a single play. In *Titus Andronicus,* Tamora seeks revenge upon Titus for the sacrifice of her son; he seeks revenge on her and her sons for the violation of his daughter. There are at least a dozen revenge plots in *The Revenger's Tragedy,* to such an extent that some have suspected that the author intended the apostrophe of the title to follow the *s,* not precede it. As the schemes of the multiple revengers in *Women Beware Women* intersect and the bodies begin to fall, one doomed character realizes that

> vengeance met vengeance
> Like a set match, as if the plague[s] of sin
> Had been agreed to meet here altogether. . . .
> (5.1.198–200)

Revenge is not only enacted; it is talked about constantly, it is sworn solemnly, it is howled for by unappeased ghosts. In *The Spanish Tragedy,* revenge is personified. He sits on the stage like a chorus, explaining his slow but sure procedures to Andrea's impatient ghost. *The Spanish Tragedy's* excesses prompted parody shortly after they were first seen, but the immense popularity of the play and the return of later tragedians to Kydian conventions testify to the power the revenge theme had to fascinate Renaissance audiences.

Blood and Sex

> I'll damn you at your pleasure: precious deed!
> After your lust, O, 'twill be fine to bleed.
> (*The Revenger's Tragedy* 2.2.126–27)

Bloodletting abounds in revenge tragedies, often in bizarre forms. Murderers and revengers lure their victims into kissing poisoned corpses, poisoned skeletons, and poisoned Bibles. Death comes from being boiled in oil, crowned with a burning crown, hung up in a tree, slaughtered and baked into a pie. Body parts are carried about or waved for dramatic effect—heads, hands, fingers, a leg, a heart. Revengers often resort to torture to prolong the satisfactions of their vengeance, as when Antonio binds Piero, tears out his tongue, offers him a stew made from his slaughtered little boy, taunts him, and finally stabs him, an act of mercy for the audience as well as for Piero.[5]

Sexual sensationalism is similarly omnipresent. Incest occurs or threatens in *'Tis Pity She's a Whore*, *The Atheist's Tragedy*, *The Revenger's Tragedy*, *Hoffman*, *Women Beware Women*, and, arguably, *The Duchess of Malfi*. Necrophilia is almost as common, and rape and adultery are staples.[6] Somewhat more exotic are Middleton and Rowley's treatment of erotic attraction between the beautiful and the ugly in *The Changeling* and Shakespeare's portrait of interracial adultery in *Titus Andronicus*.

Sex and death are linked explicitly and repeatedly. Kisses are poisonous. Isabella (*The White Devil*) dies from kissing the poisoned portrait of her husband, while the Duke of Milan dies from kissing the poisoned lips of his dead wife, whom he himself has slain. In *The Revenger's Tragedy* another Duke dies from an attempted liaison with a country wench, a mannequin topped with the poisoned skull of Vindici's dead mistress, whom the Duke himself had killed for refusing his advances nine years earlier. The seduction scene is splendidly ironic, as Vindici himself introduces the Duke to the country girl ("a little bashful at first as most of them are, but after the first kiss, my lord, the worst is past with them. . . . Sh'as somewhat a grave look . . ."), meanwhile frantically signaling an accomplice to spray more perfume in the air to mask the odor of putrefaction. Beyond its black comedy, the scene is multiply emblematic, at once representing final justice, the embrace of physical and moral corruption, and the vanity of earthly passion.

Sex leads to death even for relatively innocent characters such as the wife of the Duke of Milan, stabbed in a fit of uxorious jealousy, and Annebella of *'Tis Pity She's a Whore*, who managed to maintain her purity of heart through her incestuous affair. In *The Atheist's Tragedy*, two young sweethearts sleep chastely side by side, the picture of innocent love, but they sleep in a graveyard, their heads pillowed on skulls. Earlier in that same graveyard, there had occurred an attempted murder, a slaying, an attempted incestuous rape, and a seduction that miscarries into necrophilia. Even the sincerity of the two sweethearts is overwhelmed by the medieval vanity imagery, as when the lover offers his sweetheart a skull, "the pillows whereon men sleep best."

Such sex-death linkage is far more prominent in revenge tragedies than in other tragedies of the period. *Othello*, *King Lear*, *Doctor Faustus*, domestic tragedies like *A Woman Killed with Kindness*—all contained murder and sexual passion aplenty, for such is the nature of tragedy. Nevertheless, the lurid scenes of revenge tragedy far surpass the tepid stabbings and seductions of these other plays in their sheer multiple horrors. The grotesque marriage of blood and sex that the common usage of the term "Jacobean" denotes is a distinctive feature of these plays.

Trickery

> Why, is not this
> A kingly kind of trade to purchase towns
> By treachery, and sell 'em by deceit?
> Now tell me, worldlings, underneath the sun,
> If greater falsehood ever has been done.
> (*The Jew of Malta* 5.5.46–50)

Protagonists in revenge tragedy are unable to achieve their desired ends through orthodox or officially sanctioned means, and so, like their city comedy counterparts, they resort to trickery. Disguises are frequently employed, with the same character sometimes assuming multiple roles. In *The Revenger's Tragedy* Vindici disguises himself as a pimp, deceiving the Duke's son and his own mother and sister as well; he then reappears as a country malcontent and again fools the Duke's son. Both disguises, as well as his brother's disguise as Carlo and the aforementioned disguising of a corpse as a shy-but-willing country wench, are part of an elaborate plot to exact revenge on the Duke, destroy his sons, and test the virtue of Vindici's own sister and mother.

In addition to disguises, the revenge tragedy includes contrivances such as planted letters and rumors, feigned madness, and the deadly play-within-a-play, which is frequently allegorical on more than one level. *Women Beware Women* ends in a wedding masque, with characters representing Hymen, Juno, shepherds, cupids, and nymphs, all staged to celebrate the marriage of the Duke and his paramour, but it is a masque of revengers, who proceed to attack the audience and each other. One nymph poisons Juno with burning incense, Juno retaliates by pouring flaming gold on her, the cupids shoot real arrows dipped in poison, and the wedding toast presented by the masquers kills two members of the audience. Since the marriage being celebrated is that of a murderer and a whore, this perversion of ritual hymeneal allegory is itself perfectly appropriate and constitutes yet another reworking of the sex/death equation.

Ghosts

> Thy pangs of anguish rip my cerecloth up;
> And lo, the ghost of old Andrugio
> Forsakes his coffin! Antonio, revenge!

> I was empoisoned by Piero's hand;
> Revenge my blood!—take spirit, gentle boy—
> Revenge my blood!
>
> *(Antonio's Revenge* 3.1)

Ghosts or supernatural portents often urge the revenger on. Ghosts are particularly prominent in the early, more Kydian revenge tragedies, although in *The Spanish Tragedy* itself the ghost serves as a chorus and has no direct contact with the living. One use of the ghost convention made familiar through *Hamlet* is for the ghost to demand revenge for his slaying, encourage the revenger, and provide him with crucial information about the murder. When Antonio goes to the church at midnight to pray over the laid-out body of his father, Andrugio's ghost appears. He names Piero as his murderer, confirms that Antonio's beloved is wrongfully accused of adultery, and urges the young man to "rouse up thy blood, invent some strategem of vengeance." Thus inspired ("take spirit, gentle boy"), Antonio begins to rant and rave in classic revenge tragedy style:

> By the astonishing terror of swart night,
> By the infectious damps of clammy graves,
> And by the mould that presseth down
> My dear father's skull, I'll be revenged!
>
> (3.2)

Meanwhile his understandably distressed mother urges him to go to bed. After she leaves, Andrugio and a companion ghost continue to remind him of his duty, and he continues to vow to "suck red vengeance [o]ut of Piero's wounds." The chance to do so comes at once, for Piero enters. Antonio lets his opportunity to kill Piero pass, not because of any Hamletesque indecision but because a quick stabbing is too good for Piero; he deserves torture, as Antonio vows: "I'll force him feed on life till he shall loath it." Piero leaves, not knowing how close he has come to being murdered, but the opportunity for Antonio to torture him immediately presents itself in the person of his young son Julio, a blameless child who adores Antonio. Antonio does hesitate momentarily in face of the child's guileless trust, but Andrugio's ghost shrieks "Revenge!" and Antonio obediently stabs the little boy, pours his blood over Andrugio's hearse, and vows further vengeance.

This pattern of the ghost urging revenge is found in *The Revenge of Bussy D'Ambois* and *The White Devil;* in *The Changeling,* Alonzo's ghost appears to discourage the villains, a pattern more like that of *Richard III* than *Hamlet*. *The Atheist's Tragedy* turns convention upside down, as the ghost of Montferrers repeatedly urges his son to forgo revenge: "Attend with patience the success of things, / But leave revenge unto the King of kings" (2.6.21–22).

Revenge tragedies, even those lacking an actual ghost, are replete with natural and supernatural portents. A comet foretells the approach of vengeance in *The Revenger's Tragedy,* as the guilty young Duke realizes: "I am not pleased at that ill-knotted fire . . . they say, whom art and learning weds, / When stars wear locks they threaten great men's heads" (5.3.18, 22–23). A storm representing the wrath of heaven spurs Hoffman to revenge and provides him with the opportunity for its execution by shipwrecking the son of his enemy. In *The Duchess of Malfi* an echo gives Antonio the premonition that his wife and children are dead, while a stumbling horse in *Valentinian,* a sleepless night in *Titus Andronicus,* even the morning star in *The Changeling* prefigure approaching horrors. Ill omens and terrifying dreams are strewn throughout the plays with a peculiarly Jacobean lavishness; Piero sums up their general atmosphere as he walks at night, smeared with the blood of a recent victim:

> 'Tis yet dead night, yet all the earth is clutched
> In the dull leaden hand of snoring sleep;
> No breath disturbs the quiet of the air,
> No spirit moves upon the breast of earth,
> Save howling dogs, nightcrows, and screeching owls,
> Save meager ghosts, Piero, and black thoughts.
> (*Antonio's Revenge* 1.1)

Revenge tragedy characters are quite at home among the ghosts and ominous birds of such a night.

Success, Death, Restoration

> May not we set as well as the duke's son?
> Thou hast no conscience. Are we not revenged?
> Is there one enemy left alive amongst those?
> 'Tis time to die when we are ourselves our foes.
> (*The Revenger's Tragedy* 5.3.106–9)

Revenge tragedy revengers succeed, but then are killed. In the typical case, the principal revenger's cause is just; he has been victimized and is unable to gain redress from the authorities, who are usually implicated in the crime he has suffered. This is the pattern set by *The Spanish Tragedy* and perpetuated in *Titus Andronicus, Hoffman, The Revenger's Tragedy, Antonio's Revenge, Valentinian,* and even *The Jew of Malta,* in all of which the revenger is the protagonist. It is also the pattern from the point of view of Tomaso, a lesser character in *The Changeling.* Later revenge tragedies tend to have revengers like Giovanni (*'Tis Pity She's a Whore*) or Livia (*Women Beware Women*), whose motives for revenge are far more questionable, yet even in such a late play as *The Duke of Milan,* the villainous Francisco turns out to be a seriously wronged character (his sister was seduced and abandoned by the Duke) whose desire for revenge is understandable even if his wanton cruelty is not. Perhaps most complex is *The Duchess of Malfi*. The brothers' stated reason for seeking revenge on the Duchess, her marrying without their consent, seems disproportionate to their rage. Yet even in this play Bosola eventually vows revenge on the brothers for their murders of the Duchess and her children as well as the destruction of his own soul; Bosola is perverse, but his final cause is just, as he belatedly assumes the role of revenger. Other villain revengers like Aaron (*Titus Andronicus*) seem to act primarily from pure deviltry, with revenge simply a convenient label for their evil deeds. Even in cases where the act of revenge is not justifiable, the revenger succeeds, and his object, relatively innocent as the Duchess of Malfi or wicked as Vittoria Corombona (*The White Devil*), is slain.

The revenger, though he may begin with a just cause, is altered and corrupted by his pursuit of revenge. As he becomes ever more obsessed with his grievances, he turns into a sadistic monster: Antonio butchers a loving child; Valentinian betrays his faithful old friend. These characters, along with Vindici, Francisco, Hoffman, Titus, and Hieronimo, forfeit their audience's original sympathy as their campaigns of slaughter render them as evil as their original malefactors. Such revengers' displays of overt madness are emblematic of their moral state and, like mad dogs, they must be destroyed. They usually die, but they die unrepentant, satisfied with their achievements like Vindici, or, like Hoffman, spurning forgiveness with a curse.

Many variations on this basic Kydian pattern appear. Antonio does not die, but retreats to a monastary, an act that constitutes a social if not a physical death. Potential revengers who forswear revenge (Charlemont in *The Atheist's Tragedy*) or who are ineffectual (Tomaso in *The Changeling*) live on. So does Francisco de Medici (*The White Devil*), although other revengers in that play (Lodovico, Flamineo) fit the pattern of success followed by destruction. Clermont (*The Revenge of Bussy D'Ambois*) succeeds and dies by his own hand, but never forfeits his audience's admiration. Such variations appeared after the basic formula had become familiar.

The deaths of the revenger and his last victims often occur at banquets. Dinner parties are dramatically efficient, for they bring together the principal characters, contain masques that both conceal the revengers and allow for multiple allegory of revenge, and permit various poisonings and cannibalism. More than dramatic convenience is involved, however, for it is at these bloody banquets or some functionally equivalent final gathering that a restoration of order is achieved. Typically, a ritual feast is intended to celebrate a wedding or coronation, but that ritual is undone in blood. In its place, what is celebrated is the return of order following the period of disorder represented by all those dead bodies lying about. A relatively blameless, and often minor, character steps forward over the bodies and restores order. The assembled nobility proclaim a new ruler or, as in *Valentinian,* retire to select one. A young heir is hopefully set on the throne. A wise old counsellor takes over. Often this representative of corruption's purge and virtue's triumph closes the play with some sententious lines, as does Giovanni, new Duke of Brachiano, who intones, "Let guilty men remember, their black deeds / Do lean on crutches made of slender reeds" (*The White Devil* 5.6.302–3).

The Duke of Milan offers a good illustration of this restoration pattern. Throughout the play the Marquis Pescara has given sound advice, generally ignored, to the impetuous Duke. At the end of the play, the Duke, mortally wounded, orders that Francisco be taken off for torture. Pescara merely echoes the Duke's order—"Away with him!"—but the lord Tiberio immediately replies to Pescara, "In all things we will serve you," this before the old Duke has expired. When he finally does so, Pescara picks up the fallen reigns of authority before they hit the ground, restoring both government control and conventional morality in the closing lines:

> It is in vain to labour
> To call him back. We'll give him funeral,
> And then determine of the state affairs.
> And learn from this example, there's no trust
> In a foundation that is built on lust.
> (5.2.265–69)

Such restoration scenes suggest the emergence of more solid foundations for state authority.

Revenge Tragedy in Institutional Context

Before asking what type of society would have created and supported these gory tales of vengeance in high places, one must first consider the nature of the theatrical institution that produced them. In many respects the institutional context of revenge tragedy was identical to that of city comedy. As table 2 indicates, revenge tragedy dramatists were middle-class professionals; indeed, they were some of the same men—Middleton, Chapman, Massinger—who wrote city comedy. They were concerned with attracting a large popular audience to the commercial theatres. They were not subsidized to any significant extent by patronage, nor did they have private means. They had to ascertain and cater to their audience's theatrical tastes.

Despite these similarities, the context of revenge tragedy did differ from that of city comedy in two important respects: duration and location. The first difference involves the length of time revenge tragedies occupied the English stage. Although they flourished during the first fifteen years of the seventeenth century, as did city comedy and theatrical life in general, revenge tragedies were written and performed long before and long after. *The Spanish Tragedy* may have appeared as early as 1582, although a recent review of the evidence contends that a date around 1590 seems more probable.[7] By the early nineties the lost Ur-*Hamlet* and Marlowe's *The Jew of Malta* had been produced, with *Titus Andronicus* coming some time before 1594. Thus the genre was well established before the turn of the century, enough so that by 1596 knowing jokes could be made about stage ghosts crying for revenge "like an oister wife."[8] At the other end of the age of revenge tragedy, *'Tis Pity She's a Whore* was first performed no earlier than 1629. The harshly Kydian *Hoffman* was popular with the Phoenix audience perhaps as late as 1631.[9] Indeed, the play often regarded as the last revenge tragedy, James Shirley's *The Cardinal,* was produced in 1641 a few months before the theatres were closed, but this was more of a throwback than the end of a continuous line. In contrast, the earliest city comedy, *Every Man in His Humour,* appeared in 1599, the latest in 1621.[10] Thus while the age of city comedy lasted only slightly over twenty years, revenge tragedy held the stage steadily for twice that long. This enduring vitality suggests that the appeal of revenge tragedy was more broadly based than that of city comedy, surviving such institutional changes as the increasing polarization of the theatre audience and the passing of the first generation of great tragic dramatists.

A second and related difference between the contexts of the two genres is that revenge tragedy was originally crafted for the public theatres. As we have seen, the early city comedy dramatists wrote for a private theatre audience at a time when public and private theatres were competing vigorously, as Hamlet and Rosencrantz's rather nervous discussion of the "little eyases" illustrates.[11] If we take 1609, the year the King's Men took over Blackfriars, as a dividing point, we see that seven of the present study's sixteen revenge tragedies were staged by that year, and of these only one, *Antonio's Revenge,* first appeared in a private theatre. In contrast, only one of the seven city comedies performed by 1609 was *not* performed in private theatre.

After 1609 the public/private theatre relationship changed. The King's Men, the most prestigious company, now played at the public Globe in summer and the private Blackfriars in winter; to see some play owned and acted by the King's Men, a playgoer could select either a public or a private house. At about the same time the boys' companies, up until that time the principal performers of city comedy, went into a permanent decline, thereby no longer offering serious competition to the adult companies. Thus by the second decade of the seventeenth century, the decision to attend a public versus a private theatre no longer depended on a preference for adult players versus children, nor were playgoers forced to attend a public theatre if they wanted to see the best actors or the plays of their repertory. The decision had become more purely economic. The social gap between the public and private theatre audiences grew wider and perpetuated itself. The Red Bull and the Fortune became infamous for catering to the vulgar, while the elite frequented the private theatres such as Blackfriars or the Phoenix. Late revenge tragedy seems to have found an audience at both types of playhouses. Of the nine revenge tragedies first performed after 1609, five were produced by the King's Men, appearing probably at both public and private theatres, one (*The White Devil*) was first performed at a public theatre, and three at private theatres.

Therefore while it behooved early city comedy writers to pay close attention to the tastes of the elite private theatre audience, especially the young gallants, there was no comparable core of supporters for revenge tragedy. These plays were originally written for a public theatre audience that, privileged or not, was far more socially heterogeneous than that of the private theatre. They were written at a time when they faced major competition from the boys' companies and at times, earlier and later, when there were no boys' companies. They were written when the commercial theatre was only a decade old, they were written twenty years later when it was flourishing, they were written twenty years later still when it had become decadent.

All this meant that there was no thematic equivalent to "the problem of the younger sons" that revenge tragedy writers could seize on for its certain appeal to an influential segment of the audience. These playwrights needed to paint with broader strokes, dealing with matters of either widespread human interest—blood and sex—or widespread popular concern.

A similar breadth appears in the tragedies' use of subplots. Comedy seems more conducive to multiple plots than tragedy; a lively degree of confusion enhances the comic atmosphere but detracts from the tragic.[12] Nevertheless, the multiple, cumulative revenge plots of *The Spanish Tragedy, Titus Andronicus, Women Beware Women,* or *The Revenger's Tragedy* provide variations and implicit commentaries on the primary revenge action. More structurally problematic is the revenge tragedy propensity to include comic subplots or characters that set an emotional tone at odds with the rest of the play. It is the notorious comic plot of *The Changeling,* as well as the clowns and fools of *Hoffman, Antonio's Revenge, The Atheist's Tragedy,* or *'Tis Pity She's a Whore,* that demand explanation. How can one take Antonio's report of his dream of bleeding ghosts howling for revenge seriously when it is followed by Balurdo's account of his own dream about "the abominable ghost of a misshapen Simile"?

The dominant analytic treatment of comic episodes in Renaissance tragedy has been to see them as constituting thematic analogues and foils to the main tragic action, and no doubt they do. On the other hand, to view the madhouse scenes and disguises of *The Changeling,* for example, as only a comic counterpoint to the gradual moral revelation of Beatrice in the main plot is too restrictive, an error of regarding the plays as drama and not theatre. Particularly in the formative years of the genre, revenge tragedies had to appeal to the wide range of tastes represented at the Globe and the Fortune. The comic seduction of Langbeau Snuffe (*The Atheist's Tragedy*), the absurd posturings of the feckless Jerome (*Hoffman*), the madhouse episodes, and the like may well have been devices whereby dramatists hedged their bets; if the naturalism of the atheist didn't provoke a shudder in every member of the audience, perhaps the hypocrisy and coitus interruptus of Snuffe would move these unresponsive playgoers to laughter. Clowns and farcical subplots worked the same way the chopped off hands and poisoned skulls worked: both allowed for spectacular effects in a theatre where visual spectacle was severely limited, and both appealed to the tastes of those who favored the vividly concrete over the abstract. Beyond their thematic connections with the main plot, connections that may be more apparent upon reflection or reading than in actual performance, the subplots were theatrical stunts designed to get an audience reaction from that segment of the audience least impressed with the moral complexity of Vittoria Corombona's legal defense or the issues raised by D'Amville's rationalism.

The necessity of attracting and entertaining an audience must have impressed itself on the tragedians with a particular urgency, for they were writing in a genre that was significantly less popular than comedy. From the 1570s until the close of the theatres, twice as many comedies as tragedies were written (see appendix A for data). This ratio remained quite steady over the entire period, as figure 3 indicates. Performances seem to have followed a comparable pattern. We know of 884 dramatic performances that took place between 1592 and 1597. Of these, 200 (23%) were of comedies, and 134 (15%) were of tragedies. Individual tragedies such as *The Jew of Malta* and *The Spanish Tragedy* were exceedingly popular, but the tragic genre as a whole never won a dominant place on the Elizabethan stage. Since the theatre was unequivocally commercial, the subordination of tragedy must have reflected consumer tastes. So given that the demand for tragedy was never too keen to begin with, it behooved tragic writers to be cautious, stick with tested conventions such as those set by the popular *Spanish Tragedy,* and practice a multivocal dramaturgy speaking to as diverse an audience as possible.

THREE DIMENSIONS OF REVENGE TRAGEDY APPEAL

Institutional factors suggest that Renaissance dramatists sought professional success by writing tragedies that contained multiple plots and appealed to a rather wide variety of audience tastes, but such factors do not go very far toward accounting for the substantive content of revenge tragedy. It is to that content, to that particular combination of characteristics described at the be-

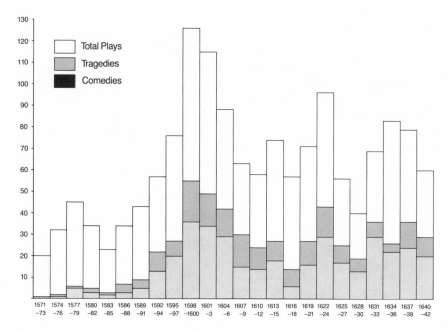

FIG. 3 Comedy and Tragedy in Renaissance Drama

ginning of this chapter, that we now must turn. As in the case of city comedy, I suggest that it is profitable to analyze the conventions of the revenge tragedy formula along three dimensions: their topicality, which contributed to their initial stage success; their archetypal representations, which contributed to their preservation in the literary canon; and their depiction of recurrent social concerns, which influenced the patterns of their subsequent revivals. The remainder of this chapter will address these three dimensions in order.

Revenge Tragedy and Political Protestantism

The first question to ask about any popular genre is: What made it become so popular in the first place? Once a formula has been locked into its audience's consciousness, it may be elaborated and manipulated in any number of ways while still remaining recognizable, but the initial success of the formula, its early engagement with a large enough portion of the relevant audience to establish it as conventional, needs to be explained and not simply taken as given. What made revenge tragedies such extraordinary crowd-pleasers right from the start?

Part of the appeal a type of drama has for a particular audience in a particular time and place lies in its representation of subjects that are of particular concern to that audience, in other words in its topicality, so one must ask what made bloody intrigues in foreign courts seem timely to Londoners of the late Renaissance. I suggest that the early and enduring popularity of revenge tragedy derived in large part from its representation of some of the most disturbing political and religious issues of the late Tudor period. In its sensational depictions of dynastic struggles and court corruption in continental, usually Catholic, counties, revenge tragedy presented a nightmare inversion of three things its audience valued: (1) effective central government with orderly succession, (2) English strength and prestige, and (3) the lasting establishment of English Protestantism. Revenge tragedy catered to a popular ideology wherein these three concerns coincided, in which stable government, English superiority, and Protestantism were mutually reinforcing.

The background of this ideological configuration lay in the centralization of authority that had been achieved during the sixteenth century. Henry VII's consolidation of power under the crown brought welcome relief from such feudal death throes as the War of the Roses. The crown's claim that law and order required a strong monarch was taken further when Henry VIII renounced papal ecclesiastical supremacy as well. The story is familiar: Henry needed to free himself from the aging Catherine of Aragon in order to produce a legitimate male heir to perpetuate the Tudor dynasty. He spent three years trying to get his divorce approved without actually severing the ties with Rome, but Ann Boleyn's pregnancy in 1533 forced the ultimate break to ensure the legitimacy of the heir-to-be. Thus the Act in Restraint of Appeals declared England to be an empire, with courts competent to handle all internal matters including the king's marital status; appeals to Rome were prohibited. The next year the Act of Supremacy confirmed Henry as head of the English Church.

During the 1530s, religious struggle inflamed the nation, though Henry tried to maintain control through parliamentary acts and a rather even-handed policy of executing troublesome Protestants and Catholics alike. The Catholic "Pilgrimage of Grace" revolt was suppressed, but the threat to the king represented by supporters of Mary Tudor, Catherine's daughter and a staunch Catholic, persisted. Henry himself vacillated between a nonpapal Catholicism and a more straightforward Protestant orientation, but the events of the decade outstripped his own rather half-hearted Reformation. The publication of the Bible in English, the advantages gained by newly landed groups following the dissolution of the monasteries and subsequent sale of crown lands, and the widespread disgust with the corruption of the old religion's clergy had moved much of the English population toward an irremediable Protestantism.

This movement did not seem irreversible at the time, however, and the years from the Act of Supremacy until the beginning of Elizabeth's reign were a quarter century of religious instability during which England lurched first toward, then away from, Protestantism. The Reformation was fostered under Edward VI's reign (1547–53), but then severely repressed under Mary Tudor (1553–58). Mary's Spanish blood and marriage, the loss of Calais because of English involvement in the Habsburg-Valois war on behalf of her consort, and her public burnings of over three hundred Protestant clergy, artisans, and peasants united the populace in revulsion against their queen. Her death was greeted with jubilation.

In light of this history of royal sponsorship setting the possibilities of sectarian advances, Prostestant leaders immediately recognized that it was advantageous to glorify the newly crowned Queen Elizabeth and promote the congruence of the monarchy, English nationalism, and Protestant theology. The linkage itself was not new.[13] The title page of the 1535 Coverdale Bible, the first complete Bible printed in English, had featured Holbein's print of Henry VIII handing the Bible to kneeling bishops and lords. Holbein had expanded on this imagery on the cover of the next English Bible, the Great Bible of 1539; here Henry received the Word of God directly from Christ, then passed it down to prelates and lords who in turn passed it to aristocrats and commoners (these latter two groups distinguished themselves from one another by shouting either "Vivat Rex" or "God Save the King," according to their status). Iconography and literature associating royal supremacy with the Protestant cause had especially flourished under the Edward VI protectorate.

With years of experience in back of the recent five-year setback, Protestant propogandists responded to Elizabeth's accession by emphasizing anew a cultural association between royal authority and Reformation. By far their most influential expression of the Elizabeth-nationalism-Protestantism linkage was John Foxe's *Acts and Monuments,* popularly known as the Book of Martyrs.[14] Published in English in 1562, vastly enlarged in 1570, and running through five editions during Elizabeth's reign alone, outsold only by the Bible, the Book of Martyrs was a Protestant version of world history that appealed to both the faithful and the sensation-seeking with its lurid accounts of the Marian martyrs. It presented the English Church as the true and original Church, founded by Joseph of Arimathea, with Papism being a relatively recent and distinctly un-English deviation. England was an elect nation, comparable to the Old Testament Israelites, in which God took a special interest. Martyrdoms from as far back as Wyclif to the recent burnings of Cranmer and Latimer under Bloody Mary had tested the English faith, but now the ordeal was over; Elizabeth would usher in a new dawn of godliness and prosperity. This was a most attractive message to Protestants and patriots, and also to a queen determined to secure the royal prerogative established by her father and grandfather. Elizabeth was shrewd enough to take advantage of the ideological opportunity the Book of Martyrs offered, and to cultivate the linkage among herself, nationalism, Protestantism, and royal authority.[15]

This Protestant-based system of symbolic interactions also tended to reinforce the increasingly problematic concept of divine right, a point that was not lost on Elizabeth. The divine right controversy in England had its roots in the old struggle between the pope and the Holy Roman Emperor.[16] The theory had been that Christ was the head of the Empire, with the pope and emperor being equal subordinates with coterminous powers; in practice, such an arrangement was largely unworkable, and papal claims of being first among equals had been regularly countered by the reverse claims of the emperors. Popes and emperors had argued from the same premises—the acknowledged necessity of a single earthly authority, the accepted theological basis of politics, and the priority of obedience over liberty—but had drawn opposite conclusions. The claims of the English monarchs, who had resisted papal interference in domestic affairs as far back as Edward I, had long echoed the traditional rhetoric of this struggle. In the fourteenth century the proto-Protestant Wyclif had elaborated an argument for the supremacy of royal over papal authority. Thus Henry VIII's ultimate break with Rome had been prefigured for centuries.

The doctrine of monarchal supremacy contained internal contradictions, however. Legitimism, whereby the king reigns through indefeasible hereditary right, was incompatible with absolutism, whereby the king has the power to select his successor. Even absolutists like Henry VII claimed legitimacy; such claims were feeble, but they indicated respect for the popular belief in royal blood. An additional complication was the generally accepted theory of the king's two bodies, according to which a king had a body natural, subject to change and death, and a body politic, which was immortal and passed from one body natural to another.[17] The obvious question was, Could the king (body natural) decide on whose body natural the body politic was to land next?

The issues came to a head in the Elizabethan succession controversy over who would inherit the throne if the queen bore no children.[18] Henry VIII's will had stipulated that if his children produced no issue, the throne should not go to the Catholic Stuart line of his eldest sister, but to the Protestant Suffolk line of his younger sister. His position was absolutist, for legitimism would favor the elder sister, but this absolutism was backed up by an act of Parliament allowing him to alter the customary line of succession. Advocates of Mary Stuart's claims reasoned that Henry had no right to make such a will because the king (body politic) never dies and therefore cannot name an heir, and legitimism supported the Stuarts. Elizabeth simply forbade public discussion of the matter, maintaining the absolutist position that she had the right to determine her successor while avoiding mobilizing opposition by actually doing so.

From the Protestant standpoint, the best way to ensure a Protestant line was to celebrate the absolute powers of this Protestant queen, who could then either bear a successor or name one. The papal act of excommunication (1571) intensified the identification of Elizabeth's political ends with the Protestant clergy's religious ends, and their implicit partnership was reinforced by a series of Catholic rebellions and plots—the Revolt of the Northern Earls (1569), the Ridolfi Plot (1571–72), the Throgmorton Plot (1583), the Babington Plot (1586)—as well as by the Jesuit activities of the 1580s and the ominous presence of Mary Stuart until her execution in 1587. Elizabeth, who was nothing if not an expert at "self-fashioning," went along with the Protestant-inspired association in which political and religious autonomy were identified with her person.[19]

Thus only fifty years after Henry VIII's divorce problems, belief in the congruence of strong central government, internal order, English national-ism, and Protestantism, all emblematized by the queen, was widely shared. Each strand in this braid of ideas drew strength from the others. The braiding also made inescapable its opposite, the interweaving of Catholicism, treason, corruption, foreign intervention in English affairs, intrigue, and anarchy. This association remained viable throughout much of the seventeenth cen-tury, when the popular fear of Catholics far exceeded their actual political threat.[20]

Revenge tragedy captured these politico-religious concerns, representing the lurid background against which England and the English monarchy ap-peared in sharp relief. The genre's typically Catholic courts seethed with plots, hatred, and murder. Catholic clergy were variously portrayed as wicked (the cardinals in Webster's pair), opportunistic (the cardinal in *'Tis Pity She's a Whore*), ineffectual (the friar in the same play), or ambitious (the cardinal in *Women Beware Women*), but more significant was the message conveyed by their context: this is the sort of court chaos and bloody mayhem one finds in those pope-ridden countries across the Channel. Eight of the sixteen revenge tragedies covered by this study are set in Italy, two in Spain, two in France; of the remainder, three are in classical settings and one in Germany. While the conventional Catholic locales made the point most directly, all revenge tragedies suggested the contrast between the foreign horrors—dynastic struggles, intrigues, bloodshed at court—and the English self-conception, fostered by the Protestants and used by Elizabeth, of order, stable central government, and peaceful succession. In addition, the use of Continental settings allowed the dramatists to address problems such as court corruption or dynastic instability, problems of real concern to their audiences, without risking censorship or imprisonment.

Italian settings were especially effective for heightening the English/non-English contrast because the Elizabethan attitude toward Italy combined fascination with abhorrence. A vogue for Italian musicians, players, and teachers of dancing and fencing, with cultivated Londoners including the queen speaking some Italian, coexisted with strong anti-Catholic sentiments and fears of papal political activities.[21] Italy was a polyvalent icon, a metaphor for the luxurious, the elegant, the corrupt, the diabolical, the menacing. One aspect of this general view was the English conviction, reinforced by translations of novellas, that Italians were particularly prone to bloody revenge. Thomas Nash was merely echoing popular wisdom when his "unfortunate traveller" reported in 1594 that "these Italians are old dogs and will carry an injury a whole age in memory. I have heard of a box on the ear that hath been revenged thirty year after."[22]

While popular ideology associated religion, nationalism, and stable monarchy, one figure who represented a challenge to the linkage was Machiavelli, which may be why he was usually characterized on stage as the personification of wickedness. (*Antonio's Revenge* is an exception, for Antonio speaks of Machiavelli with admiration.) Tudor attitudes toward the Florentine's political theories combined horror with interest, as was typical for all things Italian; some theorists openly agreed with his secular ethics, and even more traditional thinkers were able to absorb Machiavelli's practical statecraft while overlooking his underlying assumption of the separation of religion from politics.[23] But that assumption was there, and Tudor Englishmen as different as Cardinal Pole, agent for the Counter-Reformation and Mary's favorite churchman, and Roger Ascham, Elizabeth's Protestant tutor who abhorred the papacy, both hated Machiavelli for the same reason: his relegation of politics to an ethical sphere uncontrolled by religion. Both Protestant and Catholic activists used the epithet "Machiavellian" as something of an all-purpose insult, for neither wanted to dispense with God as their ally or justifier.[24] Thus regardless of the fact that English political theorists, notably Francis Bacon, were beginning to think along the same lines as Machiavelli, popular cultural forms like revenge tragedy had little room for ambivalence, because to accept the separation of religion from politics would be to remove the divine auspices of the Elizabeth/nationalism/Protestantism configuration itself.[25]

I have suggested that this linkage of political stability, nationalism, and Protestantism reached its apotheosis under Elizabeth's reign, during which revenge tragedy developed its conventional depiction of the complementary linkage of dynastic instability, foreign corruption, and Catholicism. Had concerns over such issues diminished under James I's reign, now that this particular Stuart had converted to an acceptable Protestantism, it seems likely that revenge tragedy would have declined in popularity. Instead the opposite happened. Although there had already been a rise in corruption of the bureaucracy late in Elizabeth's reign, under James such offenses were increasingly flagrant.[26] A poor judge of character, the new king surrounded himself with venal courtiers and pursued an extravagant way of life financed by the sale of titles. Whereas Elizabeth had promoted the image of mutual love binding subjects and monarch as an ideological support to her absolute authority, James bolstered his authority by promoting their very separateness, the awe and mystery of the monarch; whereas Elizabeth used her body as metaphor of inviolability from foreign enemies and partnership with her subjects, James withdrew his person, in ideology and actuality, behind a veil of "the secrets of state."[27] Popular misgivings over corruption at court under a weak monarch combined with panic about Catholic treachery fueled by the 1605 Guy Fawkes plot to produce a general apprehension that the religious and governmental reforms of the Tudors might not hold. In such an atmosphere, the conventions of revenge tragedy continued to be salient.

The question of royal prerogatives grew increasingly urgent under the Stuarts, of course, and revenge tragedy playwrights were by no means of a single mind. Fletcher strongly supported legitimism and divine right, for example, while Webster pointedly questioned both. Ideological agreement is not the point; the shared preoccupations of a group are revealed through their common sense of what are the important problems of the day, not what are the solutions. Jacobean and Caroline playwrights saw the Stuarts perpetuating the Tudor theory of divinely ordained monarchy without possessing the underlying political or public relations skills that had made Elizabeth the object of public adoration. The Stuarts were trapped in the royalist ideology that the Tudors had promoted.[28] At the same time, James and then Charles appropriated the theatres and players for their patronage and service, thus pressing the conventions of Protestant nationalism into the service of the Stuart version of divine right. Some playwrights succumbed openly, some sidestepped into the psychological horrors of foreign courts or bourgeois life. Whatever a dramatist's particular resolution and representation of the formula, the basic revenge tragedy conventions continued to be compellingly topical, for the political-religious issues they represented were growing more pressing every year.

Revenge Tragedy and Horror

A question different from that of the meaning of revenge tragedy for Renaissance Londoners, a question of greater bearing on revivals, is: What has revenge tragedy meant to succeeding generations? For the genre has been a fixture of the English literary canon even when it has been seldom present on the stage. The first edition of Robert Dodsley's *A Select Collection of Old English Plays,* published in 1744, included four revenge tragedies; when the second edition (1780) added two more, revenge tragedies accounted for over ten percent of the plays in the collection.[29] When Charles Lamb brought out his "Specimens" (short extracts from plays contemporary with Shakespeare) in the early nineteenth century, ten of the ninety specimens were from revenge tragedies.[30] *The Spanish Tragedy,* not performed in London from the Restoration until 1982, enjoyed three editions in the eighteenth century, four in the nineteenth century, and six in the twentieth century before 1959, when the modern revival boom for revenge tragedy was just getting under way.[31] *The Atheist's Tragedy,* a much less important play historically, has received at least five twentieth-century editions.[32] Such enduring interest in revenge tragedy as literature, if not always as theatre, could not have been due solely to the genre's once-topical depictions of Protestant or nationalist ideology, but must have depended to a large extent on its treatment of more general, even universal, themes.[33] I suggest that part of the explanation for the continuing interest in revenge tragedy, for the genre's secure position in the English literary canon, lies in its striking, elaborate, and manifold representations of the archetype of horror.

Revenge tragedy horror is based on more than just buckets of blood, plentiful though they be. While there is no gainsaying the popular appeal of carnage, it appears in too many types of entertainment to explain the genre's specific fascination.[34] An account of revenge tragedy's lasting appeal must be able to distinguish it from other types of tragedy, bear baitings, ballads about murderers, and public executions, all of which featured bloody events and competed with revenge tragedy for Renaissance audiences. Furthermore, given the plethora of literary and cultural depictions of slaughter and gore in the years since the Renaissance, the mere presence of sensational bloodletting does not go very far to account for the genre's continuing literary prominence.

Does Aristotle's conception of tragedy, the arousing of terror and pity through the fate of a famous or prosperous character capable of moral choice, offer much help in understanding the attraction of revenge tragedy? Though such a definition does eliminate bear baitings and hangings from the field, I believe the answer is no for at least two reasons. First, while one may expand the Aristotelian definition to say that the Elizabethan tragic protagonist must be seen as being capable of making virtuous decisions even if he doesn't actually make any (thus Macbeth and Lear are tragic because of their unfulfilled capacity for virtue, while Richard III is not because he lacks moral capacity), many revenge tragedies do not conform even to this enlarged definition. Pity and terror attending an intrinsically virtuous character are found in some plays—Titus, Clermont, and Hieronimo seem to fit this pattern—but most revenge tragedy protagonists such as Antonio, Beatrice, Hoffman, Vindici, the Duke of Milan, Giovanni, and the Jew of Malta do not impress one as being morally competent in the first place. Purely virtuous characters, inevitably suffering and often doomed, are minor figures like Antonio (*The Revenger's Tragedy*) or Isabella (*The White Devil*); they evoke pity but little terror, for they are not fully enough developed for the audience or reader to identify with them. Most of the major figures, on the other hand, evoke neither terror nor pity, for they are, or become, too wicked for audience identification, and by the end of the play they deserve their downfall. The second problem with applying Aristotle's definition to revenge tragedy is that it encompasses too much. Even for those plays in which the "terror and pity for a noble but flawed character" definition seems appropriate, Webster's pair or *Titus Andronicus* for example, this definition cannot distinguish revenge tragedy from other tragedies. A preoccupation with revenge is an obvious additional discriminating rule, but even this seems insufficient. The insistence on revenge is louder in *Titus* than in *The Duchess of Malfi*, for example, yet the two plays strike most people as being cut from the same cloth. So the question remains as to why a cluster of largely un-Aristotelian tragedies, to which the convenient but not completely enlightening label of revenge tragedy has been attached, has occupied such a lasting and esteemed position in the canon.

What distinguishes revenge tragedy both from its contemporaries and from other literary treatments of the revenge theme, I suggest, is the genre's capacity to produce an overwhelming sense of horror in its viewers or readers. To understand how such dramatic horror operates, one must first bear in mind the difference between horror and terror. Terror is the extreme fear human beings feel in the face of something bad that is about to happen. It may be produced by experience (people being terrified by someone pointing a gun at them) or by identification (people empathizing with the misfortunes, actual or imminent, of a tragic character with whom they identify). Playwrights can move their audiences to terror, but they must first create a character with whom the audience can identify. Since most readers and playgoers regard themselves as morally responsible beings, they can identify more readily with a Hieronimo than with a Hoffman; thus while some revengers inspire tragic terror, others, indeed most others, do not.

Horror is very different, for it achieves its impact by violating what is regarded as natural by mixing cultural categories that are customarily separate.[35] For example, though most Americans enjoy eating veal, they would be horrified (though not terrified) if presented with a soup made from puppies, because their cultural distinctions between edible and nonedible animals would be violated. Horror is universal in form but not in content; a Muslim will be repulsed by a soup made with pork, a noncannibal by a soup with human flesh, and an American by a soup containing puppies. The revulsion originates not from what is in the soup, but from the insertion of what is categorized as nonfood into the category of food.

An artist, storyteller, or writer can easily construct the horrible. Probably the most common horror tales involve the "living dead"—ghost stories passed around campfires, movies about zombies and vampires, Poe's short stories, and Hamlet's visit from his slain father are familiar examples. All draw their horror from the violation of the Western understanding of the impermeable membrane separating life from death, a separation believed to be absolute in this world, though not in the next.[36]

Horror's fascination derives from its flagrant display of mixed categories. It intrigues us with possibilities: What if one could be both dead and living? Both man and wolf? Both brother and lover? Such ambiguities compel attention, but at the same time social institutions and individual cognitive bearings depend on separate and discrete categories; their intermingling is abhorrent because human beings cannot cope with such indetermination. Horror is a freak show, attracting with its forbidden mixtures—bearded ladies and other "cultural monsters."[37] We gape, but then return to the open air with a shudder, relieved by our socially shared convictions that such monsters cannot exist in our everyday world.

A homology exists between horrors and tricksters, as well as an essential difference. Both compel attention by crossing culturally defended boundaries, and at times the distinction between the two is blurred, as in the cases of the grotesque, the privileged fool or court dwarf, the androgyne or eunuch; on the other hand, their motivation and capacities for identification are quite distinct. Tricksters pursue recognizably human goals—money, food, and sex—and thus allow their audience to identify with their personified denial of limits: perhaps I too can outwit my stronger adversaries and win the prize. Horror is inhuman, and often is not even personified. If the horrible object is a bleeding portrait or a swarm of killer bees, issues of motivation or identification do not arise. If the horror is incarnate in a werewolf, a madman, or someone not altogether dead, motivation tends to be somewhat irrelevant to the malign actions (werewolves just act that way), nor do most people imagine themselves achieving any conceivable goals through similar behavior. In short, human beings are able to take a lesson from the trickster more readily than from the horrible.

Multiple horrors characterize revenge tragedy, horrors that are greater in quantity and more various and elaborate in quality than those found in comparable genres. Revenge tragedy ghosts and necrophilia horrify by mixing the categories of living and dead, while incest and rape violate the distinctions between those who are and are not available for sexual relations. Madness crosses the line between human (i.e., rational, predictable) and inhuman, and one variety, Ferdinand's lyncanthropy (*The Duchess of Malfi*), crosses the human/animal boundary as well. Severed hands and heads mix the categories of body/environment, while the cannibalism and poisoned banquets cross both the food/not-food line and that between life-giving and death-giving. The sheer number of such horrific devices distinguishes revenge tragedy from more restrained tragic genres that have perhaps one mad scene or a single ghost.[38]

The most striking revenge tragedy horror is the repeated equation of sex and death. Necrophilia, poisonous kisses, lovers in graveyards, lovers in arbors stalked by their killers, the inexorable death following the passion of the Duchess of Malfi or the Duke of Milan, wedding masques with Cupid's poisoned arrows and Danse's scalding shower of love, Giovanni carrying his paramour's heart impaled on his dagger—in virtually every revenge tragedy there appears this direct linkage of sex with death. Moreover, these are not Romeo and Juliet stories in which lovers die because of the social context of their love. In revenge tragedy, death is a part of love, is embodied in it from the beginning; sex is fertile, and death its offspring. A scene from *The Maid's Tragedy* vividly portrays the sex-death equation, as the courtesan Evadne ties the King to his bed while he assumes she is playing an erotic game:

> KING: What pretty new device is this, Evadne?
> What, do you tie me to you? By my love,
> This is a quaint one. Come my dear and kiss me,
> I'll be thy Mars; to bed my Queen of love,
> Let us be caught together, that the gods may see
> And envie our embraces.
> EVADNE: Stay, Sir, stay,
> You are too hot, and I have brought you physick
> To temper your high veins.
> KING: Prethee to bed then, let me take it warm,
> Here thou shalt know the state of my body better.
> EVADNE: I know you have a surfeited foul body,
> And you must bleed.
>
>   (5.1.47–58)

And so he does, but not until she has taken another fifty lines to tell him how his death is the price of her past sexual favors. The Renaissance convention of orgasm as a little death is taken very literally in revenge tragedy.

Horror, an archetype characterized by the formal structure of crossed cultural categories, and revenge, the motivation for a line of action, constitute a powerful narrative combination that has been used repeatedly in Western literature, but revenge tragedy depicts both horror and revenge in peculiar and distinctive ways. The special character of revenge tragedy's expression of this combination, on which rests both its archetypal and its social appeal, may be seen by comparing that genre with other literary forms embodying horror and revenge. Table 5 summarizes some of the similarities and differences between revenge tragedy and three comparable genres: Seneca's tragedies, seventeenth-century Spanish honor plays, and some continental novellas translated in William Painter's popular collection, *The Palace of Pleasure*. The argument to be pursued is not primarily one of influence—Seneca and the novellas undoubtedly had some influence on both the Spanish plays and revenge tragedy, but how much is debatable—but one of differentiation. Although all four genres contain horrors and vengeance, I propose to show that revenge tragedy was radically and significantly different from the others in its treatment of both horror and revenge. Revenge tragedy's unique depiction of horror contributed to the genre's enduring literary interest, while its unique presentation of revenge (to be discussed in the final section of this chapter) contributed to its sometimes latent social meaning.

The earliest works of literature usually said to have marked affinity with revenge tragedy are the plays attributed to Seneca.[39] During the Renaissance, Seneca's aphorisms were more familiar to more people than his drama, but some portion of educated Englishmen knew and admired his plays as well.[40] Eight of Seneca's plays were translated between 1559 and 1567, and in 1581 all ten tragedies were published together.[41] The Latin versions were performed at Cambridge during the 1550s and '60s, and the first known English tragedy, *Gorboduc,* which was acted at Inner Temple in 1561, was explicitly modeled after Seneca.

So by the 1580s when the earliest revenge tragedies were emerging, at least some playwrights and audiences were familiar with Senecan conventions, including hyperbolic rhetoric, blood and sensationalism, and characters overwhelmed by passions, including rage and the desire for revenge. Such conventions are not exclusive to Seneca, of course—medieval saints' legends featured comparable bloodbaths, for example—but their combination has been traditionally labeled "Senecan." Furthermore, Kyd and other early revenge tragedy writers indicated that they believed themselves to be borrowing from Seneca's models; Hieronimo, for example, carries a book of Seneca's plays on stage and quotes from it as he works himself up to his revenge. It seems appropriate, therefore, to ask just how the Renaissance "Senecan" drama differed from its predecessor.

Thyestes will serve as an example of Seneca's own treatment of both horror and revenge. The play opens as the ghost of Tantalus, whose infanticide condemned him to perpetual hunger and his progeny to generations of woe, is brought by the Fury to the house of his grandson Atreus, king of Argos. The Fury claims that Tantalus will instigate new horrors on the house through his vengeance.[42]

TABLE 5   Revenge and Horror in Drama and Popular Literature

Type of literature	Revenger and object	Horrors	Revenger's fate	Attitude of ruler and community	Other characteristics
Seneca's tragedies	Most frequent: ruler seeks revenge on nonruler; god or ghost seeks revenge on human. Less frequent: someone with magic power seeks revenge on ordinary person; nonruler seeks revenge on ruler; nonruler seeks revenge on other nonruler.	Murder (usually intentional) of relative most common. Assorted other horrors: incest, cannibalism, murder of nonkin, poisoned robes, and miscellaneous gruesome (Theseus piecing son's body together) or ironic (Polyxena preparing for wedding) events. Ghosts often appear.	Succeeds; usually is unharmed and boastingly triumphant. A few revengers, because of error or twist of fate, are left desolate by their success. Often indications that cycle of revenge to continue.	Ruler is either the revenger or the object of revenge; acts freely. Community not sympathetic to revenger, may be thrown into chaos by his success.	No institutional or supernatural power above the revenge action to ratify or condemn it; all levels (humans, ghosts, gods) caught up in same system of revenge motivating action, passion overwhelming reason. Universal injustice.
Spanish honor plays	Most frequent: husband seeks revenge on wife and her lover. Also peasants seeks revenge on local	Social horrors (actions inappropriate to one's status and obligations) most comon. Murder	Succeeds and is pardoned by ruler. If a peasant, revenger is ennobled, made commander (e.g., Peribanez) or	Ruler is told the truth; he pardons revenger and declares his actions in keeping with justice and demands	Honor, usually in terms of defending wife from sexual violation or punishing her and lover, is the moral

	tyrant; heavens, via king, revenge past injustice; person of higher or equal status seeks revenge on someone for insult or disrespect.	(often of wife and lover) typical, also rape and seduction. Little macabre horror; no cannibalism, few mutilations. Killing often done offstage. No ghosts.	otherwise elevated, whereby defense of his honor is fully appropriate.	of honor. Revenger's friends and community approve of his action.	imperative. Honor not just property of nobility; military leader who acts tyrannically violates code of honor, while peasant may act honorably.
Tales from *The Palace of Pleasure*	Revenge plots evenly divided among revenge between equals, revenge of weaker on stronger, revenge of husband on wife or her lover, and revenge of stronger on weaker. Less frequent is revenge of wife on husband. Several tales of the revenge of men on women who had scorned them.	Murder of kin most frequent (incl. wife, daughter, sister, husband) followed by other murders. Rapes, social horrors, mutilations also quite comon. Some tales have no horrors per se (e.g., tale of queen and gentleman who get revenge on king for having affair with latter's wife by cuck-olding him).	Usually, but not always, succeeds; sometimes is pardoned, sometimes punished for revenge. Often revenge is private, domestic; no authority involved (e.g., lover's revenge on cruel mistress).	Varies as to whether community and/or ruler is involved. If community opinion mentioned, may side with or against revenger; ruler may either punish the revenger or pardon.	Tales vary widely from light-hearted to horrific. No dominant line or set of attitudes toward revenge; revenge is used for its narrative power and inherent fascination, not because it is morally necessary or problematic.

(continued)

TABLE 5 (*Continued*)

Type of literature	Revenger and object	Horrors	Revenger's fate	Attitude of ruler and community	Other characteristics
Revenge tragedies	Most frequent: weaker character seeks revenge on stronger, e.g., subject on ruler. Revenge between equals or by stronger on weaker also found, though less frequent. Multiple revenge plots typical.	Murders of nonkin far more frequent than murders of kin, though both frequent; suicides fairly common. Social horrors involve betrayals (political or personal). Macabre physical and sexual horrors (mutilations, incest, poisoned corpses, etc.) very common; ghosts and supernatural signs also fairly frequent.	Multiple revengers. Principal revenger always succeeds, but then is usually killed. Minor revengers may or may not succeed, and are often, though not inevitably, killed.	Typically a new ruler or other authority steps in to restore order, is ratified by assembled elite. Final lines spoken by new ruler often express sententious optimism about future peace under state now purged of evil. Attitude of community outside court seldom mentioned.	Much more bloody and horrific than other revenge literature. Many more revenge actions and killings. Justice seen as possible at state level; injustice, wicked rulers represent aberration, must be cast out, but individual revenge seen to be highly problematic.

> Let havoc rule this house; call blood and strive
> And death; let every corner of this place
> Be filled with revenge of Tantalus!

Though Tantalus is reluctant, the Fury urges him on, and the house awaits the coming atrocities set in motion by his passing over. Atreus appears, berating himself for having delayed taking revenge against his brother, Thyestes, who raped his wife and stole his kingdom long ago; Atreus is back on the throne and Thyestes in exile, but Atreus is not satisfied because "You cannot say you have avenged a crime unless you better it." An adviser tries to dissuade him, but Atreus, spurred on by the malign influence of the ghost, decides to commit "no act that common anger knows . . . some deed more wonderful": to make Thyestes feast on his own sons' flesh. Atreus lures his brother and nephews back to Argos with the promise of sharing the throne, past enmity forgotten. Thyestes returns with some misgivings, expressed in his soliloquy on the simple country life, but is encouraged by his sons to accept his brother's effusive welcome. Later, in a hidden cypress grove within the palace, Atreus slaughters his three nephews, supervises the roasting of their flesh, and serves them to their unsuspecting father. After the banquet, Thyestes starts to worry about his missing children, at which point Atreus exhibits their heads and reveals the ingredients of the meal just finished. Thyestes is in agony, but Atreus still has not had enough vengeance: "There are bounds / To limit willful sin; but sin's requital / Acknowledges no limits." Thyestes prays that he will be avenged by the gods, and the play closes by indicating that the cycle of revenge will go on.

Like Seneca's other tragedies, *Thyestes* shares many characteristics with revenge tragedy—sensational and bloody horrors, noble characters in a court setting, a ghost, a revenge plot involving trickery, a final banquet, sexual transgression (in the past), and characters talking endlessly and exuberantly about revenge—and such resemblances alone may justify referring to the latter plays as "Senecan," regardless the degree of direct influence involved. Commentators promoting the influence argument have pointed out that *The Spanish Tragedy* and some of its successors incorporated Seneca's rhetorical devices and relentlessly quoted him, sometimes in undigested form, as when Hieronimo sprinkles his vengeance monologue with Senecan aphorisms. Those wishing to downplay Seneca's influence on Elizabethan writers point out that the playwrights were practical craftsmen who understood the archetypal appeal of horror, and while some may have borrowed liberally from Seneca, they had plenty of other sources for their horrific dramaturgy.

Setting aside the influence debate for now, I want to point out some differences between the horrors found in Seneca and those of revenge tragedy. First is the sheer extent of violence. In the nine complete plays traditionally attributed to Seneca there occur thirty violent deaths, or 3.33 per play; in the sixteen revenge tragedies under consideration, there are 112 violent deaths, seven per play.[43] Three of the Senecan deaths (10%) are suicides, as are a slightly larger proportion of the revenge tragedy deaths (16, or 14%); the rest are murders. Thus while it is certainly the case that Seneca's tragedies are bloody, revenge tragedies are far more so, having over twice as many violent deaths per play.

Second, Senecan murder is usually a family affair, whereas revenge tragedy murders go well beyond the circle of kinship. Almost two-thirds (17) of the twenty-seven murders in the Senecan canon are perpetrated by a relative of the victim, while only twenty-nine percent of the ninety-six revenge tragedy murders are between kin. Kinship murder is especially horrible, for while murder means killing someone from the category of people one is forbidden to kill (unlike killing enemy soldiers, for example), killing a relative is a double horror, for the victim belongs to two protected categories: those people whom the murderer is not socially permitted to kill, and those people who are in the murderer's family. Both Senecan plays and revenge tragedies average a little under two relative-murders per play, but revenge tragedies involve a proliferation of extrafamilial killings as well.

Third, there is a different distribution of horror in the Senecan plays, and hence a different texture to the overall effect, than in the Renaissance plays. In the typical Senecan play, the horror comes from one or two overwhelmingly horrible and luridly described events: Atreus' trick, Clytemnestra's treachery, Medea's two episodes of slaughter (that of Creusa and Creon and that of her two sons), Hercules' insane slaying of wife and children. The weight of such acts (which is largely due to the fact that they take place between kin) and the detailed description of them (in sharp contrast to the Greek versions)[44] gives them a stunning effect, but the fact remains that there are relatively few such horrors in each play, and everything in a play like *Medea* or *Thyestes* prefigures or reinforces the one or two major horrors of the climax. In contrast, horrible acts and images are casually, prodigiously strewn throughout most revenge tragedies, so their overall effect comes more from the sheer number of horrors, many of which are only lightly sketched, than from a focus on any one central incident. A good example of this is the number of severed hands, tongues, fingers, heads, and other body parts that are waved around in revenge tragedy. When Seneca gives an extensive description of the slaughtering, dismembering, roasting, boiling, serving, and eating of Thyestes' sons, the gruesome details make palpable the horrors of turning nonfood into food and making a father, who gives life and nourishment to his children, unwittingly take nourishment from them; the display of the preserved heads of the sons is a part of this action. When the Duchess of Malfi is given a severed hand to kiss, or when her brother is reported to have carried a man's leg from the graveyard because he thought he was a wolf, these episodes contribute by adding to the cumulation of similar episodes more than by their organic relationship to other horrors. As G. K. Hunter has pointed out, such accumulations are more Gothic than classical, and are not found in Seneca.[45]

Fourth, the horrors in Seneca have cosmic sanction. Human actors are victims and agents of the ghosts and gods, who are carrying out their own feuds and rivalries through the manipulation of men and women. As a result, some of the most horrific acts in Seneca are entirely unwitting, such as Hercules killing his family or Deianira giving her husband the poisoned robe. In revenge tragedy, murders are often unwitting, but only because the murderer intended to murder someone else and made a mistake. Revenge tragedy horrors are human, not divine, in inspiration. The ghosts that do appear are essentially onlookers or advisers; human passions are sufficient to account for the chain of horrors that ensue, and the cosmos is accorded little blame.

The distinctiveness of the revenge tragedy representation of horror becomes still clearer when the plays are compared with the very different treatment of horror found in the Spanish honor plays of Lope de Vega and Claderón, which were roughly contemporary with Jacobean and Caroline drama and which may have been influenced by some of the same sources, including Seneca and popular medieval theatre.[46] In the Spanish plays, horror is social. The emphasis is on punishment for sexual transgressions and for violations of social roles; there is relatively little sensationalism and virtually no supernatural intervention. The typical plot begins when the protagonist's honor has been insulted. Usually the man is noble and the insult takes the form of an adulterous wife and her lover, but sometimes the honor of a peasant is insulted by a military commander or other aristocrat who misuses his office through sexual and other predations on the peasantry, thereby acting in ways inappropriate to the responsibilities of his office and class. The protagonist seeks revenge, understood as a reestablishment of correct social relations, which will thereby restore his honor. He kills the offenders, throws himself on the mercy of the king, and is pardoned and often elevated for his scrupulous attention to the demands of honor, upon which the social order depends.

There is a certain economy to the violence of the Spanish plays, in sharp contrast to revenge tragedies. Typically only one or two offenders are killed; the virtue of economy is made explicit in Calderón's *Three Judgments at a Blow,* where Don Lope's garroting punishes Don Mendo for an old seduction, Donna Blanca for concealing the truth about Don Lope (whom she had claimed to be her son), and Don Lope himself, who had struck the man he knew as his father. Most slayings take place offstage, and there is little description of the Senecan sort. Nor are there ghosts, supernatural sanctions beyond a general sense that God is concerned with people meeting their social responsibilities, or the brandishing of severed body parts. The revenger may employ trickery, for instance by concealing his crime and the dishonor that provoked it (*Secret Vengeance for Secret Insult* and *The Surgeon of His Honor* are examples) or by avoiding doing the actual killing himself (in *Justice without Revenge,* the betrayed husband tricks his wife's lover into killing her, then brings in the authorities to execute the lover), but such trickery is less of the macabre, poisoned-lips-of-a-corpse variety common to revenge tragedy and more in service of apt social symbolism. Compared with revenge tragedy, Spanish honor plays, though similarly involving murder, rape, adultery, and revenge, seem almost ascetic.

The creators of the continental novellas also recognized the narrative attractions of horror and used it effectively, but once again we find a different type of horror from that of revenge tragedy. To construct a comparison, I have used William Painter's English translation of Italian novellas and classical stories, *The Palace of Pleasure,* which first appeared in 1566 and which provided a sourcebook for many Renaissance plays, including *The Duchess of Malfi.*[47] I selected every tale that involves revenge, a total of eighteen, and have examined the expression of the horrible in each.[48] This procedure first of all offers a reminder that revenge may be comic as well as tragic, something that a concentration on Spanish honor plays and Seneca obscures, for among the novellas one finds lighthearted stories of comic revenge that do not involve horror at all except of the mildest turn-about-is-fair-play variety; a typical tale tells how the queen and gentleman get revenge on the king, who is having an affair with the gentleman's wife, by cuckolding him. The majority of *Palace of Pleasure* revenge tales do involve more explicit horrors in some form or other, however, and these are the subject of our particular interest. Examples of social horrors are common, both in the crimes that instigate the revenge (the treacherous schoolmaster who delivers his pupils to the enemy general; the three unnaturally cruel ladies who reject their would-be lover), and in the revenge itself (the schoolmaster is stripped and whipped by his pupils; the cruel ladies are exposed naked to their husbands, their faces hidden, as if they were whores). In such cases violations of social responsibilities or amatory ethics are punished by a dramatic and public structural inversion that implicitly restores, by drawing attention to, more correct social relationships.

Some of the *Palace* tales do contain horrors that would have met Seneca's standards of gruesomeness: the betrayed husband who forces his wife to hang her lover, then seals her in a room with his rotting corpse until she dies; the father who sends his daughter the heart of her lover in a gold cup (she adds poison to the cup, drinks, and dies clasping the heart); the betrayed wife who kills her husband in bed, tears out his eyes, tongue, and heart, and then throws all the parts out the window, an action that would have delighted a revenge tragedy audience. This type of sensational horror occurs in only about a third of the revenge novellas, however. The rest involve either social horrors or relatively straightforward (and, by Senecan standards, under-described) murders. Murder, when it does occur, is likely to be a family affair; fifty-six percent of the murders are between kin, a proportion only slightly less than that of the Senecan plays.[49]

The primary impression given by the tales' treatment of horror is one of great variety. The storytellers are happy to use whatever material adds to the interest of their stories, and horror certainly does so, but the collection as a whole presents no single pattern or type of horrific representation. Murders (16), mutilations (5), rapes or seductions (4), social horrors (7) all occur, yet almost half of the revenge novellas contain no killings at all. Those tales that do involve bloody revenge resemble the Senecan model in their concentration on one horrific act; the multiple revenge pattern does not occur. One tale resembles the Spanish pattern in that the betrayed husband manages to keep his dishonor and his crime (he murders his wife with a poisoned salad) secret, while the tale preceding it has a very un-Spanish outcome in that the betrayed husband, having tortured his wife by making her drink from the skull of her dead lover, eventually forgives her. While women are sometimes subject to sadistic revenge actions, they also are the principal revengers in almost a third of the tales and often perpetrate physical or social horrors. In sum, the attractions of the horror archetype, and the narrative power of combining horror and revenge, were understood and employed by the novella writers, but beyond this, at least in the collection most familiar to Renaissance England, no dominating pattern appears.

The comparison of revenge tragedy with Spanish honor plays and with the revenge tales from *The Palace of Pleasure* reinforces the observations made following the Senecan comparison: while all four literary genres make effective use of the horror archetype, revenge tragedy is far more lavish in its expressions of horror. Revenge tragedy contains many more deaths and mutilations; its killings are matters of policy as well as of intrafamilial passion; its horrors are more dispersed through the work; it contains an immense variety of sexual, physical, supernatural, and social horrors; and its emphasis on the sex-death equation is unique. The sheer number of horrors and the vast variety of cultural categories that get crossed constitute an accumulation that makes the revenge tragedy treatment of the archetype qualitatively different from literary forms that use horror as either a plot embellishment or a characteristic of one central action. In revenge tragedy, horror must be savored for its own sake. Charles Lamb's description of Webster's ability "to move a horror skilfully, to touch a soul to the quick, to lay upon fear as much as it can bear" can stand for the entire genre.[50] This overwhelming repetition and elaboration of the horror archetype has fascinated readers for centuries, and has helped revenge tragedy retain a special place in the dramatic canon, that place reserved for the skillful expression of that which is simultaneously repulsive and irresistible.

Revenge Tragedy and the State

Revenge tragedies feature revenge, and this defining characteristic of the genre, essential neither to horror stories nor to elaborations of Protestant nationalist ideology, must now be addressed on its own terms. In the remainder of this chapter I shall demonstrate that the distinctive English Renaissance treatment of the revenge theme constituted a metaphor for the social tension between state authority and individual justice, a tension that was widely felt during the Elizabethan and Jacobean age. Like city comedy, revenge tragedy both portrayed a pressing dilemma and offered a satisfying formal resolution to the dilemma. This social meaning represented by the revenge theme itself contributed to the genre's immediate popularity and, more significant for the present study, influenced its subsequent revivals.

Revenge is the return in kind of an injury done to oneself or to one's group, a balancing the accounts of pain. From the late feudal period until the present, revenge's popular fascination has drawn on the contradiction between its public condemnation and its private satisfactions, a contradiction that was historically possible only once the state had taken upon itself the provision of punishment for injuries. More fundamentally, revenge motivates action, often violent or spectacular action, and thus has great utility for the storyteller or dramatist. As the literature represented in table 5 indicates, horror and revenge have a particular narrative affinity, for each may instigate and justify the other.

Just as all horror stories are not the same, however, so the structures of revenge plots vary in significant ways. Revenge tragedy resembles other literary genres featuring vengeance and horror, but it also developed peculiarly English characteristics as it moved away from the Senecan prototypes represented in Kyd's popular and influential *The Spanish Tragedy*. In this area of distinctiveness may be found the clues to the genre's social meaning.

In addition to the previously discussed differences in the structure of horror, revenge tragedy differs from Seneca's dramatic depictions of revenge in the following respects:

1. Revenge tragedies have multiple revengers, while Senecan tragedy concentrates on a single individual's revenge.
2. Revenge tragedy revengers are usually less powerful than the objects of their revenge, while Senecan revengers are typically more powerful.[51] Sixty-one percent of revenge tragedy revengers are weaker than their victims in terms of social power; examples include nonrulers seeking revenge on rulers (the most prominent type of revenge), sons on fathers, and wives

on husbands. In contrast, seventy-nine percent of the Senecan revengers are stronger than their victims; examples are rulers seeking revenge on subjects, gods on mortals, and magicians on nonmagicians.

3. Revenge tragedy revengers are often in a quandry over whether revenge is the right course of action, and they are frequently delayed or stymied before they can begin the revenge action. Sometimes they require prompting from a ghost or another revenger. Even revengers who act decisively from the beginning, such as Webster's villains, are tormented by second thoughts afterward. Seneca's revengers, in contrast, act directly and with assurance, never questioning the correctness of their course and paying little attention to the nurses or advisers who try to dissuade them. Senecan revengers may be temporarily immobilized by their passions, but they are not slowed down by opposition or infirmity of purpose.[52]

4. Revenge tragedy revengers employ far more trickery and dissembling. The English revengers' plots are more complicated than those of Senecan revengers like Medea or Atreus, who use only one or two tricks, though these are tremendous.

5. Revenge tragedies include comic elements unknown in Seneca.[53] Comic figures and subplots have dramaturgical utility in their appeal to a mixed audience, a problem Seneca did not have. In addition, the comic plots parody the main plots, acting as distancing devices that make the main actions more open to contemplation.

6. Although they are successful in obtaining their revenge, revenge tragedy protagonists, and most lesser revengers as well, are typically killed in the final act. Variations of this include their withdrawing from society (*Antonio's Revenge*) or vowing to commit suicide (*The Maid's Tragedy*). Senecan revengers never die, though a curse or prophesy may foretell that the full revenge cycle is not yet over.

All of these differences present revenge as being more problematic and complex for the Renaissance revenger, and for his audience, than for the Senecan prototype. Revenge tragedies depict revenge as neither unquestionably desirable nor easy to accomplish, and, once achieved, it brings destruction upon the revengers as well as their victims. With destruction comes closure; the English plays end with a conclusiveness—most of the principals are dead—that is absent in Seneca.

This closure is extremely important, for it represents revenge tragedy's fundamentally different vision of the relationship between order and chaos. In Seneca's neo-stoic view, life is inevitably an evil business, states are corrupt and tyrants unexceptional, human passions routinely overwhelm human reason, and only a studied indifference to worldly concerns allows one to retain dignity and even serenity. Thyestes, for example, adopts a submissive posture in the face of his losses:

> Then may eternal night endure, may darkness
> Cover these vast immeasurable sins
> For evermore. Sun, never move again,
> And I shall be content. . . . My revenge
> The gods will give. I have no other wish
> But to entrust to them your punishment.
>
> (5, pp. 92, 93)

Thyestes' stance is based on his belated recognition that chaos is normal in human affairs, ever threatening to break through, and justice is beyond the capacity of men. (Such Stoicism is rarely seen in revenge tragedy; two characters who do espouse a Stoic ethos, Pandulpho in *Antonio's Revenge* and Clermont in *The Revenge of Bussy D'Ambois,* later change their minds and become active revengers.) The ignorant chorus parodies Thyestes' discovery. For most of the play, the chorus voices popular opinion while remaining utterly in the dark about what is taking place. At the end of the second act, in which Atreus has spelled out his ploy for luring his brother back under a pretense of forgiveness, the chorus rejoices that "At last this royal seat, this ancient race of Inachus / Sees its old fratricidal feud composed, strife laid to rest," and goes on to sing platitudes praising the peaceful life. After Thyestes has walked into Atreus' trap in the next act, the chorus chirps on about the strength of family ties. When act 4 finally confronts them with a recitation of Atreus' atrocities, the chorus faces the source of all terror:

> This is the fear, the fear that knocks at the heart,
> That the whole world is now to fall in the ruin
> Which Fate foretells; that Chaos will come again
> To bury the world of gods and men; . . .
> And are we chosen out of all earth's children
> To perish in the last catastrophe
> Of a disjointed universe? . . .
>
> (4, pp. 81, 83)

The chorus disappears completely from act 5 because its structuring work is done; it has represented the naïve mind for, having once believed that order and harmony are possible, it has become disabused of this optimism.[54] The movement of the play is from calm to chaos.

The revenge tragedy movement is the reverse: from chaos to order. Revenge tragedy assumes that order and justice are possible, and possible especially at court.[55] Thus those final scenes of cleansing and restoration where the former ruler, often a tyrant, lies dead next to the revenger, and hope rests on a new, legitimate ruler who, crowned amid the pile of bodies, sententiously expresses the hope that peace and justice will now prevail. Such a restoration scene was not included in the earliest and most "Senecan" revenge tragedy, *The Spanish Tragedy,* but was quickly added to the genre's formula; the return of state authority was presented in ironic terms in *The Jew of Malta,* in lugubrious form in *Titus Andronicus,* and thereafter was conventional. Even in the bourgeois tragedy of *'Tis Pity She's a Whore,* the Cardinal restores order at the close, cleansing the city with one burial, one banishment, and the Church's confiscation of the sinners' property. Revenge tragedy paradoxically offers a vision of an unspeakably corrupt court coupled with a sturdy political optimism, expressed in the conclusion, that government can be better.

The individual revenger represents anarchy in revenge tragedy, and while his actions may clear away the corruption that has obstructed justice, his destruction gives renewed vitality to state authority. *Valentinian* exemplifies the formula. At its opening, the Roman Empire has become decadent, its soldiers mutinous from idleness, and its emperor Valentinian more concerned with seducing women than directing affairs of state. The revenge action is initiated when Valentinian rapes Lucina, then cooly informs her that there is no appeal for her victimization:

> LUCINA: As long as there is motion in my body
> And life to give me words, I'll cry for justice.
> EMPEROR: Justice shall never hear you; I am justice.
> (3.1.32–34)

She calls for the gods to bring vengeance on Valentinian, then kills herself. When her husband Maximus learns what has happened, he vows to kill the emperor, while his friend Aecius tries to dissuade him through a typically Fletcherian divine right argument:

> . . . were it any man's
> But his life, that is life of us, he lost it
> For doing this mischief; I would take it,
> And to your rest give you a brave revenge:
> But as the rule now stands, and as he rules,
> And as the nations hold, in disobedience
> One pillar failing, all must fall; I dare not.
> Nor is it just you should be suffered in it.
> Therefore again take heed: On foreign foes
> We are our own revengers, but at home
> On Princes that are eminent and ours,
> 'Tis fit the Gods should judge us.
> (3.3.147–58)

Knowing that Aecius will try to thwart his plans, Maximus plants a rumor that leads to his friend's death; he then poisons Valentinian, who dies in slow agony on stage. Chaos ensues, as Maximus gloats over the fruits of his vengeance:

> Gods, what a sluice of blood have I let open!
> My happy ends are come to birth, he's dead,
> And I revenged; the Empire all afire,
> And desolation everywhere inhabits.
>
> (5.3.1–4)

If the play were by Seneca, it would have ended right here, but revenge tragedy goes on to cleansing, restoration, and closure. Maximus has himself proclaimed the new emperor and attempts to cement his authority by marrying Eudoxa, Valentinian's widow. She gets her own revenge at the coronation banquet by poisoning him, and the senators retire to select yet another emperor and restore order; one of them closes the play with the conventional hope:

> Rome yet has many noble heirs. Let's in
> And pray before we choose, then plant a Caesar
> Above the reach of envy, blood, and murder.
>
> (5.8.117–19)

Conceiving of such a Caesar in the face of all the contrary evidence distinguishes the political optimism of revenge tragedy from the Senecan pessimism.

The Spanish honor plays bear a certain resemblance to the English plays in that they too end conclusively with a celebration of the state's capacity for providing order and justice, but their treatment of revenge, and the revenger's moral position vis-à-vis the ruler, are completely different. In the Spanish plays the revenger is usually stronger than his object, as when an outraged husband seeks revenge on his faithless wife, and thus in a good position to achieve his ends. Where the revenger is in a socially weaker position, as is true of the peasant revengers, he is reinforced by widespread community support. The Spanish revenger proceeds with no qualms about the appropriateness of his revenge, which he understands to be vital to the defense of his honor. He may be delayed by practical obstacles or his desire for an exquisite fit between the crime and the vengeance (as in *Secret Vengeance for Secret Insult*), but he is not held back by any questions about the morality of revenge itself. The revenger eventually succeeds, is pardoned and often elevated, and lives on. The king, far from being the source of the injury as in revenge tragedy, is the source of the honor; the revenge action takes place between private citizens, and the king, learning of the episode, expresses his approval and forgiveness, thereby ratifying the honor code itself. The Spanish plays exhibit a stability at the top levels of government and an acceptance of the obligation of revenge that are absent from the English plays.[56]

The problematic nature of revenge, the conflict between the individual revenger and the state, and the restoration of a purged central authority at the conclusion of the revenge action, which has been fatal to the revenger—these are distinctive to English revenge tragedy, and it is this distinctive treatment of revenge that lies at the root of the genre's social meaning. To understand this meaning, one must understand what revenge represented to Renaissance England. The official Elizabethan attitude toward private revenge, based on the hard-won establishment of a centralized, all-encompassing rule of law and promulgated by government and church, was one of absolute condemnation. Such condemnation was a recent phenomenon in England, where the legal status of revenge had changed dramatically since the feudal period.[57] Anglo-Saxon law held that an act of violence against an individual was of concern only to his kinsmen, with the state having no interest; for example, a murderer or his kinsmen had to pay his victim's family a reparation (wergeld) to avoid being in a state of war with them. During the pre-Norman expansion of central authority, the king had come to get a share of the wergeld, and by the mid-tenth century responsibility for payment was restricted to the slayer alone, thus ending the collective blood-feud in law though not always in practice. The Normans introduced a new legal procedure, the appeal, whereby the nearest kin of a victim could move to prosecute his murderer. While increasing the potential involvement of the state, the system's dependence on a widow or male heir to initiate the appeal perpetuated the idea that the injury done was a tort, a private wrong, rather than a crime. Furthermore the appeal continued to favor the powerful because, although trial by jury was possible, the accused could request judicial combat, a throwback to the direct revenge pattern that effectively prevented weaker individuals from securing justice.

As part of his consolidation of central authority following the War of the Roses, Henry VII established the indictment as the means whereby the kin of a murder victim could seek justice, and this was the crucial step that moved revenge from private duty to public responsibility. Under the indictment procedure, which was the legal means of prosecuting murders throughout the Tudor period and remains the system operating today, relatives of the victim presented their information to the governing officials, and from that point on the handling of the case, including the punishment of the accused, was entirely the state's prerogative.[58] As Sir Thomas Smith described it: "If I began first to pursue him by information or denunciation to enditement, I am now no partie but the Prince, who for his dutie to God and his common wealth and subietes, must see justice executed against all malefactors and offenders against the peace, which is called Gods and his."[59] The responsibility for providing justice was entirely in the hands of the state. Moreover, just as Protestant clergy supported state authority in general, so did they firmly condemn private revenge, which was held to be a violation of the scriptural injunction, "Vengeance is mine; I will repay, saith the Lord" (Rom. 12:19).[60]

The monarch, God's regent on earth, was to be the sole source of temporal punishment.

While there is no question about the official prohibition of revenge, there has been a great deal of debate over what the popular attitude was: Did the Renaissance English approve or disapprove of private revenge in cases where the state was unable or unwilling to provide redress for injuries? Those scholars advocating the approval theory contend that the folk memory of blood revenge persisted among all social strata, providing a popular countercode to the official position. Fredson Bowers, the leading proponent of this position, claims that in spite of the law of God and the state,

> there was a very real tradition existing in favor of revenge under certain circumstances, and especially of the heir's legal duty to revenge his father. . . . Many thoughtful men refused to condemn revenge entered upon in cases where recourse to the law was impossible. There would be few Elizabethans who would condemn the son's blood-revenge on a treacherous murderer whom the law could not apprehend for lack of proper legal evidence.[61]

Thus according to this argument, the revenge tragedy audience would be inclined to be sympathetic to the revenger, who would forfeit their approval only when he lost control and began to indulge in a bloodbath. Proponents of the popular disapproval thesis, on the contrary, cite pamphlet literature, ballads, poetry, and other nonofficial sources that express strong moral antipathy toward acts of revenge, despite some sympathy toward their causes. Eleanor Prosser, who has made a strong case against the countercode hypothesis, concludes that

> we must not make the error of equating sympathy with moral approval. . . . We identify even with Macbeth, yet we still condemn him on moral grounds: indeed, our knowledge that he is violating moral law increases our compassion. The same is even more true of the revenge play, for the revenger's dilemma is closer to us than that of Macbeth. . . . Is it at least possible that the Elizabethan audience could instinctively identify with the revenger and yet—either at the same time or later, when released from emotional involvement—judge him, too?[62]

Retrospective attitude construction is notoriously difficult, but it seems plausible, given the evidence both sides of the debate have mustered, that the Renaissance attitude toward revenge was the same as the modern attitude, one of profound ambivalence. To see murder go unpunished is mightily offensive, but to see people take justice into their own hands is frightening. The Renaissance version of this ambivalence would have been different from our present feelings in two contradictory respects—both the belief in ultimate providential justice and the folk tradition of revenge would have been stronger—but the ethical dilemma would be the same as ours: how to reconcile the longing for justice with the longing for order. When the two do not coincide, as epitomized by the private revenger, the Renaissance mind may have been as troubled as our own.[63]

Evidence for a Renaissance ambivalence may be found in the abrupt shifts of direction in Bacon's essay "Of Revenge," which has been cited on both sides of the popular-attitudes debate.[64] Bacon calls revenge a "wild justice," the adjective as unsettling as the noun is satisfying, and while admitting its attractions, argues that "the more man's nature runs to, the more ought law to weed it out. For as for the first wrong, it doth but offend the law, but the revenge of that wrong putteth the law out of office." After quoting Scripture attesting to "the glory of a man to pass by an offense" (Prov. 19:11), he contends that one should forgo revenge both because "it is a prince's part to pardon" (and punish) and because the wise man will hardly be surprised when an enemy wrongs him. This latter rise-above-it-all argument rings a bit hollow, and Bacon immediately turns back to the quesiion of law, now from a new angle: "The most tolerable sort of revenge is for those wrongs which there is no law to remedy." In such cases he offers practical advice to the revenger ("take heed the revenge be such as there is no law to punish") and instruction on how to enact revenge nobly (let your victim know who you are). Reversing himself again, he quotes Cosimo de' Medici on forgiving enemies but not friends, and then suggests that Job was "in better tune" regarding the necessity of accepting evil as well as good from God; he undercuts this scriptural reference with the rather utilitarian remark that the revenger "keeps his own wounds green, which otherwise would heal . . . [and they] live the life of witches, who as they are mischievous, so end they unfortunate." This essay, a caricature of ambivalence, might be paraphrased: revenge is understandable but dangerous to law and order, so try to rise above it, but if the law cannot provide justice, it may be tolerable if conducted openly and safely; on the other hand, it's probably wiser to be patient like Job and besides it will be better for you here on earth. Casting around for a reason for exercising Job's forbearance, Bacon's secularism will not permit his argument to proceed from the premise of providential justice; without such a premise, he finds it hard to state just why revenge should be eschewed in his extreme case—when the law cannot help and the injured party can achieve revenge honorably and safely. Best not do it anyway, he concludes vaguely, because it probably is bad for you. Though he wants to make a case for law and order, Bacon is unable to sound very convincing. I suggest that his mixed emotions regarding revenge were shared by the dramatists and playgoers of his era.

Which brings us back to revenge tragedy, where the representation of a problematic revenge action coupled with a final restoration of state authority expresses social ambivalence while concluding with political affirmation.[65] The genre presents the historically recurrent tension between order and disorder, wherein potential order is represented by the state and potential disorder by individual action, and this is the political innovation made by Renaissance dramatists when they reversed the Senecan movement from order to chaos. In revenge tragedy the dilemma is between state-guaranteed order without justice on the one hand, and individual-level justice without order on the other. To put it simply, what if the government cannot do all that it has promised to do, in this case punish crime, but the alternative to central control is anarchy? Unlike Seneca, Elizabethan dramatists did not believe that chaos was normal and only temporarily held back by tyranny. Unlike the Spanish dramatists, they recognized that justice and state authority were by no means always congruent, but believed they could be made so. The revenge tragedy playwrights maintained the ideal of strong government providing both order and justice, despite past examples to the contrary. This was the Tudor promise that Elizabeth as Astraea, the virgin angel of justice, embodied.[66] In the queen, order and justice were one.[67]

Revenge, the private administration of justice and punishment, which the Tudors had established as public functions, was a vehicle well suited for focusing dramatic attention onto the problems of state capacities. The revenger explicitly denies the state's ability to provide justice, hence displaying doubts about the strength and will of the government in an extreme form. To act on these doubts, however, to have private citizens carrying out their own systems of justice, meant anarchy. No matter how concerned they were about incompetence or corruption at court, no groups in the late sixteenth or early seventeenth century except the most extreme sectarians wanted the destruction of the apparatus of the state. As one man put it:

> Take Soveraignty from the face of the earth, and you turne it into a Cockpit. Men would become cut-throats and cannibals one unto another. Murder, adulteries, incests, rapes, robberies, perjuries, witchcrafts, blasphemies, all kinds of villanies, outrages, and savage cruelty, would overflow all Countries. We should have a very hell upon earth, and the face of it covered with blood, as it was once with water.[68]

This description sounds like the chorus of *Thyestes*, but what was inevitable for Seneca was, for the Renaissance Englishman, unthinkable.

Virtually all Renaissance tragedies end with the restoration of governmental authority.[69] The state is preserved, and although revenge tragedy sharply poses the question of whether or not it is worth preserving, the conclusion is affirmative. In its depiction of not simply a struggle for the throne or the evil deeds of ambitious men but the deeper problem of justice versus social order, revenge tragedy displayed and offered a quasi-resolution to what was in fact becoming an impossible dilemma. The genre portrays a corrupt court incapable of dispensing justice and evokes the traditionally satisfying picture of an aggrieved individual taking justice into his own hands. He cannot succeed and live, according to a straight eye-for-an-eye formula, however, for such unpunished success would suggest the desirability of institutional anarchy. So his success must be qualified; hence the convention of the revenger himself becoming corrupt in the course of his revenge, destroying the wicked duke or other source of evil, and then being himself destroyed while a previously minor figure reestablishes order. The formula satisfies everyone: justice is achieved, corruption is rooted out, anarchy is avoided, and the state ends up firmly in control.[70]

Two points deserve emphasis: first, this restoration of order is at the institutional and not the individual level, and second, the restoration is insisted upon even in the face of evidence that all government authority is subject to corruption. There can be no correction of a wrong and restoration of balance for people like Antonio or Vindici, for they have gone too far, becoming creatures of their passion beyond redemption in this world.[71] Their individual destruction, far from being antithetical to institutional restoration, is essential to it: radical individual action must give way to state necessity. As the new Duke of *The Revenger's Tragedy* puts it in the play's last line, "Pray heaven their [the revengers'] blood may wash away all treason." A particularly notorious example of a restoration scene where political optimism outweighs contrary evidence concludes *The White Devil*. Young Giovanni, the new duke of Brachiano, may turn out little better than his wicked predecessor, or so the cynic Flamineo suspects ("He hath his uncle's villainous look already. . . . So, the wolf and the raven are very pretty fools when they are young" [5.4]), but the play still ends with Giovanni in firm control. While optimism is a misleading term for Webster's political expectations, he nevertheless counters the logic of his own skepticism by his conventional conclusion. There is surely a heavy dose of irony in Webster's conclusion, but the restoration convention itself promises future institutional durability despite the individual morality of any particular Giovanni.[72]

Revenge tragedy's conventions embodied an ultimate political optimism by representing the coexistence of both justice and order. The structure of a corrupt government being replaced by a better one was homologous to the theory of the king's two bodies; a ruler must die so the Rule could live.

Change and continuity, justice and order, individual freedom and institutional virtue—all were balanced. In its representation of shared concerns about the capacity of the central government, revenge tragedy offered a formal resolution, one that was as aesthetically satisfying as it was politically unrealistic, and in this resolution of the revenge problem lay the genre's original and continuing social meaning.

* 4 *

RENAISSANCE REVIVALS FROM
THE RESTORATION THROUGH
THE AGE OF GARRICK

In the two preceding chapters I have tried to discern traces of meaning, in terms of both intention and significance, in the conventions of city comedy and revenge tragedy.[1] I have suggested that authors working in these genres crafted their plays from familiar cultural materials and popular social concerns within specific institutional boundaries of possibilities. I have analyzed the results of their craftsmanship, the genres themselves, by assigning their themes and conventions to three categories: the topical, the archetypal, and the social. These analytic categories are useful not because they represent a dramatist's way of conceptualizing his composition—for surely they do not—but because they draw attention to the distinctive properties a play (or any cultural object) might have that influence its popularity, its preservation, and its revival.

Now it is time to investigate revivals themselves. If the organizing question for the two previous chapters was what made city comedy and revenge tragedy so popular in the Renaissance theatre, the next three chapters address the questions of when and how post-Renaissance theatres and theatregoers reconstructed the meanings of these genres. As before, the focus will be on the interactions between cultural materials and social contexts within institutional settings, the points and links of the cultural diamond. Understanding the institutional circumstances that encouraged the rediscovery or neglect of city comedy, revenge tragedy, or Renaissance drama in general requires taking into account the social composition and physical arrangement of theatre audiences; the economic and organizational context in which managers and producers made their repertory decisions; the prevalent dramatic conventions; the competing modes of entertainment attracting audiences and worrying managers; and the socially based concerns and commonplaces, expectations and attitudes, of those individuals in each era that made up the London theatre's "art world."

Figure 4 indicates the overall revival patterns for city comedy and revenge

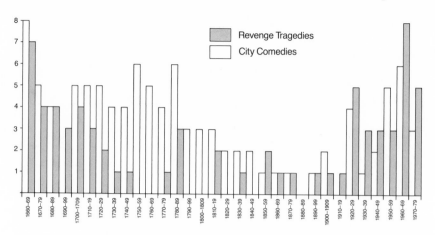

FIG. 4 Renaissance Revivals by Decade, 1660–1979

tragedy in the London theatre from the Restoration to the late twentieth century. (For a complete list of city comedy and revénge tragedy revivals, see appendix B.) My objective is to determine why city comedy or revenge tragedy fit the requirements of the London theatre better at some times than at others. The revival of a play is a rediscovery, a decision, and an investment. Above all, mounting a revival means taking a risk. Any production is risky in a theatre that depends on winning an audience for some major portion of its revenues, but revivals are especially so, for they display conventions, language, and topics that time has made unfamiliar to potential playgoers. To understand why theatre companies and their managers sometimes take a chance on a revival is to begin to understand the interaction between a society and its cultural creations over time.

In their capacity to influence whether a play will be revived, institutional and thematic factors are separate and not equal, for the former are the sine qua non. An old play in the cultural archive may eloquently address contemporary social issues, but if there is not some institutional capacity to support the production of this type of play, it is unlikely to be revived. There are occasional exceptions, the nature of which must be examined to see what makes them exceptional, but they seldom are repeated. As a rule, institutional factors are the gatekeepers of the cultural archive, and the broad fluctuations in revival patterns derive from institutional changes.[2] It is thus necessary to begin the examination of Restoration and eighteenth-century revivals by reviewing the institutional arrangements that facilitated or hindered the production of Renaissance drama.

RESTORATION AND EIGHTEENTH-CENTURY LONDON THEATRE

Rarely do established cultural institutions abruptly disappear for the better part of a generation, but such was the fate of the English theatre during the Commonwealth. The Puritans had been suspicious of art in all forms, and particularly of the blatantly secular, morally suspect and dismayingly popular stage.[3] There were many city merchants who shared the Puritans' attitude toward the theatre, if not always their religious convictions. Despite its popularity, the London theatres and players had always been on shaky ground politically, and with Parliament's seizure of control, there was a dearth of nobles ready to defend their "servants." The Long Parliament closed the theatres on 2 September 1642. They were not to reopen until 1660.

All dramatic activity did not cease, however. Plays were legally performed in the schools and possibly in the private theatres on occasion, for the 1642 ordinance had specified only the public theatres. Forty-two plays were first performed in England during the years from 1643 through 1659, usually staged at schools or in private homes.[4] Even a few public theatre productions were illegally offered, sometimes under the cover of being called drolls, short scenes from familiar plays. The government usually looked the other way, but raided and closed such performances just often enough to make them risky as commercial ventures.

The principal dramatic activity was play publication, which flourished during the Commonwealth.[5] Over 108 plays are known to have been written during that period; these were either intended as closet drama, were staged outside of England, or their possible performances are unknown.[6] Most of these were promptly published. Many more plays performed before 1643 were published or brought out in new editions during the Commonwealth period. Booksellers openly promoted these plays, which were popular with the literate minority.

Since the new plays almost invariably reflected royalist sentiments, and often specifically satirized the Puritans, one must wonder why the government exhibited such unusual tolerance. Louis Wright suggests two possible reasons. First, the censors were so busy running down political pamphlets that directly attacked the government that they had little time to worry about drama. Second, the government's real concern was less with the immorality or impiety of the drama than with the danger presented by large public gatherings, the old concern of the Elizabethans. Under the Commonwealth, the Venetian ambassador reported: "They have absolutely forbidden plays, suspecting that these gatherings of the people might occasion some disadvantage to the present state of affairs."[7] Without this potential for crowd formation, plays could be published and read w1th minimal government interference.

Such reading helped shape the Restoration audience. Prior to the Commonwealth, most strata in society attended the theatres, and dramatists catered to their various tastes. When drama became accessible only to the literate for nearly two decades, the upper classes of the latent theatre audience were cultivated while the lower-class audience atrophied.[8] In addition, royalists in exile on the continent were at leisure to pursue their theatrical interests. Thus the potential theatre audience on the eve of the Restoration was more homogeneous than that of earlier in the century, and bluer of blood.

Theatre of the Court

The stage was restored as soon as the king was. Indeed, Samuel Pepys reported a production on 6 June 1660, while he was still on board his ship at Dover waiting to land, where he heard that "the two Dukes [brothers of Charles] do haunt the Parke much, and they were at a play, *Madame Epicene*, the other day."[9] Charles II loved theatre, his taste having been developed on the continent during his exile, and his patronage made the theatre fashionable at the very moment of its rebirth. He issued patents to two royalists who had shared his exile, Thomas Killigrew for the King's Company and Sir William Davenant for the Duke's Company. No other companies were permitted to produce plays. The pattern was set for two centuries of theatrical monopoly in London.

Killigrew and Davenant shared and attended to the tastes of the Court. Experienced men of the theatre, they and the patentees who followed them were businessmen first of all. They had no literary or aesthetic axes to grind, and were more concerned with satisfying the tastes of their audiences than with refining them. Hence they produced the works of socially prominent playwrights who themselves knew how to flatter the court.[10]

Their efforts paid off. In the early days of the Restoration, Charles and his courtiers supported the theatre with their purses and their presence. During the 1660s, royalty attended the theatre over 130 times.[11] The protection offered by the royal patronage allowed the Restoration theatre a period of incubation, in particular sheltering it from the antitheatre sentiment that continued to smolder.

The Restoration audience was aristocratic in taste, if not entirely in composition. Pepys, an avid theatregoer, loved to enumerate the galaxy of notables in attendance on any particular night. A typical entry in his diary, from 21 December 1668, reads:

> Thence to the Duke's playhouse and saw Mackbeth, The King and Court there, and we sat just under them and my Lady Castlemayne, and close to the woman that comes into the pit, a kind of loose gossip, that pretends to like hers . . . it vexed me to see Moll Davis [one of Charles's mistresses, a

former actress] in the box over his [the king's] and my Lady
Castlemayne's head, look down upon the King and he up to
her; and so did my Lady Castlemayne once, to see who it
was; but when she saw her, she blushed like fire.[12]

At the same time, although not himself a member of the titled aristocracy,
Pepys expressed a strong distaste for any "citizens"—members of the merchant class—who happened to be present, making such remarks as, "The
house was full of citizens, and so the less pleasant."[13] More than simply a
display of snobbishness, for Pepys was a tailor's son and had many friends
and professional acquaintances among the merchant community, such a comment reveals Pepys's belief that "citizens" were alien to the theatre, therefore
unwelcome.

The roots of this attitude, which Pepys shared with members of the royalist elite, were political. It was commonly assumed that the business and merchant classes had supported the Puritans during the Revolution and
Interregnum. Many royalists had lost property to the Puritans, many had fled
into exile, and all had been humiliated. Now in power, they were not about
to miss a chance to express scorn for their old enemies. The Restoration
theatre, reflecting the sentiments of its patrons, treated the business classes
with savage contempt, a contempt that was easy to maintain inasmuch as the
"citizens" did not provide any significant portion of the financial support of
the theatre. Even in the 1660s, however, the Restoration audience was not
altogether homogeneous.[14] Charles and his court were undoubtedly interested and influential. Restoration audiences also included the nobility, following court-set fashion. and other persons of high distinction in public life:
members of the Privy Council, the archbishop of Canterbury, men of high
rank in the professions and in the military, including Pepys of the navy.
Members of Parliament attended the theatres, and so did a group to be reck-
oned with since Elizabethan times, young Templars reading law at the nearby
Inns of Court. Pepys also mentions friends and neighbors, particularly fellow
naval personnel of various ranks, who often attended in family groups. And
there were the "citizens." So while the Restoration audience appears to have
been overwhelmingly drawn from the higher ranks of the social order, it was
not composed entirely of aristocrats.

The drama that entertained this audience flattered them by emphasizing
their wit, their sophistication, and their removal from everyday concerns.
Comedy of manners, the most important Restoration dramatic legacy and
something quite unlike the comedy that prevailed during most of the Renaissance, presented aristocratic characters engaging in polished and clever conversation as they followed their sexual inclinations wherever those might lead
them. They exhibited their brilliant repartee in lovers' duels and their social
discrimination in satires on those who did not fit into their rarified circles.

Comedies by writers such as Etherege, Wycherly, and Congreve celebrated sophistication, emphasized fashion even by mocking it, and let their characters' sparkling verbal dexterity overshadow their lack of both morals and substance. The second distinctive Restoration genre, heroic tragedy, featured noble characters torn between honor and love as they pursued glorious conquests in exotic lands. The language was bombastic, the characters exaggerations of virtue or viciousness, and the genre was barely a decade old when Buckingham subjected it to the withering satire of *The Rehearsal*. But heroic tragedy, like its comic counterpart, was well suited to its institutional context. Both genres catered to their audience's desire for splendid, witty versions of themselves. This was not a drama that provoked its audience, but one that held up before it a rose-tinted mirror.

This is not to suggest that Restoration drama simply reflected the manners and mores of its audience. It is always a mistake to read social history naïvely through literature, and the Restoration period does not seem to have been especially immoral by any standard.[15] Even within the narrow stratum of the society that set theatrical fashion, opinions differed. Men from the city, Pepys included, were uncomfortable with the gross immorality on stage that the court countenanced.[16] Nevertheless, it was the court that provided the patents and protection, and hence called the tune. What the court wanted to see was the witty, the insouciant, the sexually playful—all of which, beyond self-flattery, were in pointed contrast to the Puritan manners and mores imposed during the preceding decades. Restoration drama reflected class ideology and class divisions, not necessarily class practice.

In the closing years of the seventeenth century, there were fewer courtiers and more bureaucrats, businessmen, and other "citizens" at the average performance. Prejudice against such an audience continued, however. In 1702, John Dennis, after praising both the quality and the taste of the audience of Charles II's reign, notes acerbically the numbers of newly wealthy or ambitious men in the audience. Such people would never have the time or the capacity to develop a refined appreciation of the drama; they are "attentive to the events of affairs, and too full of great and real events to receive due impressions from the imaginary ones of the theatre."[17] Dennis's perception of audience degradation notwithstanding, turn-of-the-century ticket prices were still too high to admit large numbers of the middle, let alone the lower, classes. Class representation had broadened somewhat, but the early eighteenth-century theatre was not a popular one.

Nor was it a free one. Dramatic censorship was a fact of life during the Restoration and long after, although at the time there was considerable ambiguity as to where the jurisdiction of lord chamberlain versus that of the master of the revels lay. Sexual material was tolerated during the Restoration, but political and religious subjects were severely censored.

The actual productions during the late seventeenth century differed from their Elizabethan predecessors in a number of ways beyond the social makeup of the audience. Women played women's parts for the first time; this innovation aroused surprisingly little opposition and was adopted uniformly. The new theatres, Dorset Garden and the two in Drury Lane, were moderate in size. Theatre Royal in Drury Lane (opened in 1674) is estimated to have seated about 1,000, while Dorset Garden (1671) was somewhat larger. There were now seats in the pit; indeed, in contrast with the Elizabethan theatres, the pit had now become the principal seating area. There were also boxes—front boxes facing the stage, side boxes, and boxes actually on the stage—and these held the most expensive seats. The least expensive were in the one or two galleries; here one was most likely to find "citizens."

The stage itself consisted of a large forestage or apron, recalling the Elizabethan platform stage, on which most of the acting took place. The proscenium arch appeared in public theatres during the Restoration (see plate 2), but that inner part of the stage behind the proscenium was mainly for background effects. Changeable backdrops were introduced, and there began to be some efforts toward scenic spectacle. Before the Commonwealth, visually lavish productions had been confined to the masques, for which the technology had been highly developed by Inigo Jones and his peers. With the Restoration and the courtly tastes of the theatre audience, spectacle moved into the public theatres; Dorset Garden was particularly well suited for staging elaborate productions.

There was elaboration of the program as well. There began to be spoken prologues and epilogues written by someone other than the author of the play himself. Entr'acte entertainment in the form of singing, dancing, acrobatics, and other specialty acts appeared. This trend toward a broad and varied program, which was to go much farther in the next two centuries, prevented the audience becoming too intellectually or emotionally involved in the play itself, for the play was just an interrupted part of the afternoon's entertainment.

Above all, the theatre centered on its actors. Restoration audiences were interested in seeing how this particular actor, or this actor this time, interpreted the well-known role. Although an actor's theatre, it did not yet have a star system; actors rotated roles, and no individual star could claim to "own" a part in the manner of their eighteenth-century successors. Restoration theatre was not a literary theatre, as the Elizabethan had been, and not a theatre of illusion, as nineteenth-century theatre would be. It was an arena in which talented individuals displayed their skills before a discriminating audience.

In spite of all this effort directed toward pleasing the court, royal patronage waned eventually, to the extent that the two theatre companies were no longer viable by the early 1680s. They merged, in 1682, into the United Company, and for the next thirteen years London had a single theatre. During James II's brief and troubled reign, he and his courtiers seem to have been too preoccupied with political difficulties to spend much time at the theatre, despite the monarch's enjoyment of it. William and Mary shared a rather tepid attitude toward the theatre; following the Glorious Revolution, the days of enthusiastic royal patronage were over, not to come again until the Hanovers.

Theatre of the Town

Drury Lane manager David Garrick so dominated the London theatre world that one may think of the eighteenth-century theatre as falling into three periods: before Garrick, the age of Garrick, and after Garrick. The first was a time of an increase in audience size and in the number of theatres. The tolerance of the lord chamberlain regarding theatre licensing and political censorship was continually tested until the Licensing Act of 1737 reimposed government control of the theatres. Following the Act, and roughly coincident with Garrick's long career as manager of Drury Lane, was a period of theatrical stability and prosperity. Yet by the final decades of the century, drama was giving way to spectacle, the middle-class members of the audience were giving way to the working classes, and the intellectuals were declaring the theatre moribund.

The century began inauspiciously, with organizational instability and an outburst of antistage propaganda. As noted above, a decline in the size of late seventeenth-century audiences had led to the formation of the United Company in 1682. The United Company's management was taken over by Christopher Rich and Thomas Skipwith, two businessmen whose interest in profits was unsullied by a concern for drama or fair employment practices. The Company rapidly deteriorated. The actors were in a continual state of rebellion against salary cuts and shoddy production until, in 1695, Thomas Betterton and most of the leading actors seceded and formed a second company. From then on, there were always at least two operating theatres in London.

Institutional flux coincided with a renewed burst of hostility toward the theatre.[18] Jeremy Collier's 1798 diatribe, *A Short View of the Immorality and Profaneness of the English Stage,* let loose a flood of pro- and antitheatrical tracts that debated whether the theatres were fulfilling the only purpose that justified their existence: "to recommend Virtue, and discountenance Vice."[19] Collier's target was Restoration comedy—he specifically exempted Renaissance playwrights from his charges—and he was less hyperbolic than some of his successors insofar as he called for reformation, not suppresion. Others, harkening back to Prynne's view of the stage as unsalvageable, regarded the theatre as "a *Sink of Sin*, a *Cage of Uncleanness*, and the Original Cause of all our Profaneness."[20] The result of Collier and his ilk was to mobilize anti-theatrical suspicions and put the stage in the position of defending itself according to the extent to which it did "recommend Virtue."

More theatres and companies appeared and disappeared in the early eighteenth century, testing the meaning of the royal patents and the tolerance of the lord chamberlain. By the 1730s, there were more than a half-dozen theatres operating in London, plus occasional theatres such as those at the fairs, a situation that was a far cry from the monopoly privileges granted the Restoration patentees. Competition drew audiences and stimulated politically daring plays, including Henry Fielding's satires. Theatre professionals, in light of their need to justify their activities in terms of moral instruction, regarded the situation to be dangerously chaotic. As one put it: "The noblest and most instructive Diversion may be lost, for Want of the State's taking it under its Direction, and commissioning Officers to see it kept up to the Dignity and Decorum of its first Design. . . ."[21]

The state took the theatre under its direction once and for all with the Licensing Act of 21 June 1737, which reimposed a strict monopoly that was to last over a century. The Act was pushed through by Walpole, who was angered by Fielding's well-aimed satirical attacks, currently on stage at one of the illegitimate theatres. The Act limited theatres to those two having the royal patents, authorized the lord chamberlain to prohibit performances at his discretion, and required all plays, old and new, and all prologues and epilogues to be submitted to the lord chamberlain for licensing prior to performance. Now only Covent Garden and Drury Lane were legitimate theatres. Fielding withdrew from theatrical activity altogether. Other operators of the minor theatres attempted to evade the law for a time. At Goodman's Fields, for example, plays were performed with music at the beginning and end; the proprietors called the entertainment a "concert," with the play thrown in for free. Plays also continued to be performed at the fairs. A 1747 law ended such evasions by explicitly limiting theatrical productions to the two patented houses. In 1766 the Little Theatre in Haymarket received a third patent, but its performances were limited to the summer months when Drury Lane and Covent Garden were closed.[22]

Under the stability imposed by the Licensing Act, London theatre flourished. Drury Lane, which had lapsed into chaos during the 1730s, became the leading playhouse in Europe under David Garrick's management, which lasted from 1747 to 1776. Himself a brilliant actor, Garrick instituted many reforms, including the requirement that actors attend rehearsals, the removal of spectators from the stage boxes, concealed lighting, and more naturalistic scenery and acting. John Rich and the managers who followed him at Covent Garden took a similarly professional approach. The two patented houses were no longer the experimental and competitive enterprises that theatres had been earlier in the century; they had become complex, profitable institutions, and the twin pillars of an oligopoly.

Their managers were careful to protect their flanks from the never dormant criticism of the stage's immorality by espousing the neoclassic view that art's primary duty was to inculcate virtue. Lessons in virtue that emanated from the stage, argued Drury Lane prompter Chetwood, made stronger impressions than those from the pulpit:

> For a Play well wrote, and well perform'd, where Virtue suffers, or meets its just Reward, must have strong Force upon the Mind, where the Eye is suppos'd to view the very Persons in the real Circumstances of History. . . . So reasonable an entertainment, as the Drama in its Purity, must be, in some sort, a Promoter to Virtue; therefore every Manager of a Theatre should make it his Study to exhibit no other Pieces but what aim to the End; and, by Degrees, throw off the looser Drama. . . .[23]

Such being the case, the managers conspicuously enlisted in the front ranks of virtue's army.

Much of what had previously been haphazard was rationalized during the Garrick era. Advertising developed, both in the direct form of playbills, newspaper announcements, and announcements in the theatres concerning future productions, and in the indirect form of "puffs," reviews planted in the newspapers by the theatre managers themselves. Theatrical criticism flourished in the popular press. Attempts were made to systematize acting, which to the neoclassical mind was subject to rules and analysis like other arts; actors, following Garrick's lead, gradually gave up formal, declamatory acting for a more natural style. Contracts for actors, specifying four levels of the professional thespian hierarchy, now offered some protection for both theatre and players. In typical oligopolistic fashion, Drury Lane and Covent Garden made tacit agreements not to steal each other's players and not to compete with simultaneous performances of the same plays.[24]

Prosperity seemed never-ending. Both theatres expanded their size, yet still the crowds appeared an hour or more before the doors opened, to jam into the theatres. A newspaper of 26 December 1757 reported: "Last Night two or three Persons were squeezed to Death in attempting to get into Drury Lane Playhouse, and several others very much hurt."[25]

The increasing heterogeneity of the audience, already in evidence at the beginning of the century, led to a mid-century theatre catering to a wide variety of middle- and upper-middle-class tastes. Businessmen, younger brothers, military men of lesser rank, foreigners—John Dennis had mentioned all these groups with disgust, and all were increasingly visible as the century advanced. Complaints were heard about the young fops who regularly attended the theatres to pursue their social activities but were quite indifferent to what might be taking place on the stage. Despite some nostalgia for the good old days of the courtly audience, the managers encouraged this more heterogeneous audience, recognizing that it meant a broader market for the theatre and one less subject to the whims of fashion.

Court and Town met in the theatres. Many in the audience were regulars, interested in drama and attending often. The theatre continued to be a haunt of the aristocracy. Visible royal support had waned under Queen Anne, who preferred to have the players come to court, but George I, who ascended the throne in 1714, frequently attended the public theatre. People of fashion attended the theatres during the winter "season," then transferred to Bath for the summer. Yet gradually the Town, those middle- and upper-middle-class merchants, small entrepreneurs, professionals, men engaged in finance and commerce, and their wives began to dominate theatre audiences. Certain groups attended en masse. Freemasons often came together, and are reported to have constituted a most peaceful and attentive part of the audience. Considerably more raucous were the Templars, who sat in the pit and prided themselves on being witty and critical, frequently engaging actors or other members of the audience in noisy debates. Lower still on the social hierarchy, apprentices, seamen, even servants were by no means uncommon.

The theatre of the Garrick era was emblematic of the social structure of the day.[26] The nobility and the more fashionable people occupied the boxes; the ladies generally sat in the front boxes (in the back of the theatre but facing the stage), the beaux and wits in the side or stage boxes. The city fops, the Templars, critics and intellectuals, and some male members of the nobility sat in the pit. The galleries were occupied by the sailors, apprentices, and members of the lower classes. These were the "gallery gods," the rowdiest and most responsive part of the house, corresponding to the groundlings of the Elizabethan theatre. Young men of fashion roamed from box to pit during the performances. Members of the upper middle class might be found everywhere.

The eighteenth-century audience, although including representatives from all levels of society, was tilted toward the prosperous. Less affluent men and women were not able to afford the theatre as easily as had their Elizabethan counterparts.[27] They attended now and then, but the gallery gods were a definite minority presence. The audience was largely from the upper-middle classes, and it was their tastes that predominated in the managers' selection of the repertory. Located between the commercial and financial establishments of the city to the east and the increasingly desirable residential neighborhoods of the West End and Westminster, Drury Lane and Covent Garden were geographically and socially situated as the meeting ground of Town and court, new money and old families.

The audience was tumultuous to a degree unknown in the modern theatre. There was constant coming and going. Fashionable people ate late, and seldom arrived at their boxes before the second or third act; less fashionable people also waited until the third act in order to get in cheaply, paying the afterprice. "Women of the town" circulated freely. Members of the audience often sat on the stage, and not just in the stage boxes provided for that purpose, until Garrick ended this practice. Applause was fervid, criticism was loud and immediate, ranging from heckling to impromptu speeches by members of the audience. Missiles were tossed at the actors, including in one case "a lighted serpent."[28] Outbreaks of violence with fists and swords were not uncommon, and full-scale riots broke out periodically throughout the century. Although the vast majority of performances were more peaceful, they entailed considerable audience participation. The actors themselves responded directly to this audience, greeting and bowing to particular friends, addressing the wits and hecklers with as much good humor as they could muster, and occasionally making impassioned pleas for order.

Though intimate, the relationship between theatrical professionals and their audience also tended to be antagonistic. The Town was replacing the court as arbiter of taste.[29] Like the coffeehouses, the theatres were public arenas for the expression of wit, and establishing a reputation for wit was a strategy for the upwardly mobile, especially for provincial young men down from the universities. These self-appointed critics arrived at the theatre early, stayed late, and voiced their opinions to the general audience. The activities of these critics were supplemented by the presence of other playwrights, who were admitted to the theatres for free during the eighteenth century, and who had their own motivations for lending loud support to hostile criticism; rival playwrights showed up in force on opening nights. During the early years of the century, playwrights and theatrical managers fought back.[30] One finds in the prologues and epilogues of this period an absence of the audience flattery that characterized those of the Elizabethan and Restoration periods. Instead, they were more inclined to denounce the audience for oversophistication and lack of real taste. Colley Cibber blamed the critics for preventing new playwrights from getting a fair hearing:

> They come now to a new Play, like Hounds to a Carcass, and are all in a full Cry, sometimes for an Hour together, before the Curtain rises, to throw it amongst them. . . . The Play then seems rather to fall by Assassins, than by a lawful Sentence. . . . While this is the Case, while the Theatre is so turbulent a Sea, and so infested with Pirates, what Poetical Merchants, of any Substance, will venture to trade in it?[31]

Pirates notwithstanding, the managers were determined to give the audience its money's worth, as plate 3 indicates. An evening at the theatre began at 6:00 and ran upwards of three and a half hours. The play or "mainpiece" was generally preceded by several musical pieces played by the house orchestra. Plays themselves were in five acts, and between each act was an entr'acte entertainment of dancing or singing. A play was sandwiched between a prologue and an epilogue, often written for the occasion. Following the epilogue came the afterpiece, generally a scaled-down comedy, a farce, or one of the popular harlequinades or pantomimes. The elaboration of the afterpiece derived from the managers' desire to attract those of the Town, whose business affairs kept them occupied until after 6:00 and who were always concerned with getting good value for their entertainment expenditures.

Garrick incessantly reminded his audiences that the repertory was in direct response to their expressions of preference, thus attempting to dampen audience combustibility. Garrick's good nature never seemed to fail him, no matter how violently that audience expressed its preferences. A newspaper clipping dated 20 November 1755 reports a riot that took place in Drury Lane after one of the critics in the pit took it upon himself to beat one of the actors with a stick. The next performing night,

> Mr. Garrick addressing himself to the House observed, that many gentlemen having on the Saturday night prohibited its being performed any more, he should be sorry to incur their displeasure by contradicting their commands . . . therefore beg'd they would determine how he should act. The House on this seem'd divided, but the dissidents appearing in the minority, it was performed on Tuesday.[32]

The repertory was extraordinarily varied. Fifty or more different plays were performed during a season, which ran from mid-September to mid-June, six nights a week except during Lent. Popular plays were revived year after year. When a play became a favorite vehicle of some star actor, it did not leave the stage until he or she did.

Audiences favored comedy, so the managers offered comedy far more often than tragedy and propped up tragedies with comic afterpieces.[33] During the years from 1700 through 1728, the London theatres produced 5,823 performances of 350 different comedies and 2,361 performances of 145 different tragedies; ten comedies and five tragedies received a hundred performances or more.[34] The prevalence of comedy increased during the Garrick years (1747–76), which saw 11,365 performances of comedy and 3,802 of tragedy; thirty-three comedies and twelve tragedies were performed one hundred times or more. Thus a comedy to tragedy performance ratio of 2.5/1 in the first quarter of the century rose to 3/1 by mid-century.

All of these institutional developments were conducive to improvements in acting, staging, playhouse construction, theatre administration, and drama criticism, all of which flourished. What they were not conducive to was the cultivation of new playwrights. With no real competition, with an assured audience increasingly dominated by Town tastes, and with hostile critics lying in wait, managers had few incentives to experiment with new plays. By the last quarter of the eighteenth century, Drury Lane was introducing only an average of four new plays per year, Covent Garden five.[35] The critical reaction to new works was almost always unfavorable, hardly surprising since they were being compared with polished stock pieces and given that the limited market did not encourage many able writers to attempt drama. New plays were usually weak and unsuccessful; more than half did not survive their first season.[36] Thus dramatic innovation was neither fostered nor rewarded. Throughout the century critics complained of the decline in the quality of dramatic writing, but the theatres remained filled.

What filled the theatres was what appealed to middle-class tastes, and that was, above all, sentiment. Sentiment was the justifying device by means of which the stage could claim to offer an instructive model of virtue. Sentimental comedies aimed for the heart rather than the brain or those organs that comedy of manners was accused of exciting. Their heroes and heroines were bourgeois, kind, honorable, polite, and apparently unmoved by any sexual impulses whatsoever. Sentimental tragedies featured the same species of characters, whose fates were more pathetic than terrifying. Most of the authors of such works have been forgotten, and the canon tends to emphasize Goldsmith and Sheridan, playwrights whose disgust with the prevailing sentiment prompted them to write brilliant reversions to the comedy of manners such as *The School for Scandal,* but their antisentimentalism was distinctly a minority position. It was the vacuous portrayals of virtue triumphant, represented at its best by playwrights such as Steele, Kelly, and Cumberland, that dominated the stage and established the sentimental norms that would be perpetuated by the melodramas of the next century.

Renaissance Revivals in the Seventeenth and Eighteenth Centuries

Institutional changes notwithstanding, theatre managers always face the same problem: deciding what plays to perform. One of the options available to London theatres since the Restoration has been the revival of a Renaissance play. The history of Renaissance revival activity from the days of Samuel Pepys spying on Lady Castlemayne through the theatrical heyday of the Garrick years is the story of how the general institutional pressures working against Renaissance drama were countered by some specific social concerns, represented in city comedy, that allowed it to survive on the eighteenth-century stage long after most of its contemporaries had disappeared. The remainder of this chapter will trace the gradual eclipse of non-Shakespearean Renaissance revivals, the establishment of Shakespeare as the premier English dramatist, and the reasons for city comedy's exceptional revival status.

The displacement of Renaissance by Restoration drama was remarkably swift. Following the Commonwealth hiatus, Killigrew and Davenant began their management having only the plays of a previous era to offer, but new playwrights quickly appeared. By the end of the decade, the Restoration dramatists dominated the stage. Of the fifty-eight known productions during the 1661–62 season, fifty-four were pre-Restoration.[37] By 1667–68, Renaissance and Restoration drama were equally represented; the season saw thirty-three old plays and thirty-two new works, of which twelve were new that season. Thereafter, the preponderance of plays staged were Restoration drama. In the forty years between the Restoration and the beginning of the eighteenth century, 440 new plays and 120 old plays (almost all Renaissance) were performed on the London stage.[38]

The comedies of Francis Beaumont and John Fletcher were by far the most popular Renaissance revivals. Written for the Jacobean elite, their polished wit and verbal playfulness appealed to the courtly audiences of Charles II's reign. In the 1660s, performances of the Beaumont and Fletcher canon outnumbered performances of Shakespeare and Jonson combined by more than two to one.[39] Fifteen or sixteen plays by the Beaumont and Fletcher team were produced during single seasons, while Shakespeare productions never exceeded six. The Beaumont and Fletcher canon had a firm hold on the stage until the early eighteenth century, then declined.

Shakespeare was not neglected on the Restoration stage, but he was less popular than either Beaumont and Fletcher or Ben Jonson. He had not yet achieved exceptional status as national bard. Rigid neoclassicists like Thomas Rymer voiced the orthodox dogma that Shakespeare's plots were improbable and his characters violated decorum. Even a far more sensitive and enthusiastic critic like John Dryden was dismayed by Shakespeare's sprawling plots, neglect of the unities of time, place, and action, and unrestrained play with words, although Dryden was happy to make concessions to genius. Performances of Shakespeare's plays met with no particular reverence, and an observer like Pepys did not hesitate to call *A Midsummer Night's Dream* "insipid."

A number of revenge tragedies and city comedies were revived during the Restoration. Ben Jonson's comedies appeared often. Jonson continued to be both more popular in performance and more highly esteemed as a dramatist than Shakespeare.[40] His comedies were especially favored; six were produced during the Restoration, while *Cataline* was the only tragedy that appeared. Pepys, who seems to have preferred comedies in general, enjoyed Jonson's in particular.

Restoration productions of revenge tragedies and city comedies exemplify the speed with which Renaissance drama fell from favor. Fifteen of our sample plays were performed in the 1660s, nine in the '70s, eight in the '80s, three in the '90s. All theatrical activity was in something of a slump following the early 1670s, and new dramatists had arisen to challenge the dominance of the old; even Beaumont and Fletcher were slipping by the 1680s. Nevertheless, the decline of interest in the older works, with only the partial exceptions of Jonson, Beaumont and Fletcher, and Shakespeare, is striking.

Since the managers of the late seventeenth century prided themselves on being good businessmen, one must conclude that the new audience was not generally receptive to Renaissance plays. Part of the problem may have been that their Elizabethan language not only seemed jarring to ears attuned to Restoration verbal polish but had rapidly become unfamiliar and old-fashioned. Dryden remarked in his *Preface to Troilus* that "many of [Shakespeare's] words, and more of his phrases, are scarce intelligible. And of those which we understand, some are ungrammatical, others coarse; and his whole style is so pestered with figurative expressions, that it is as affected as it is obscure."[41]

The return of theatrical prosperity in the eighteenth century brought renewed attention to some, but not all, of the Renaissance canon. Eighteenth-century Renaissance revivals exhibited three significant patterns: the emergence of Shakespeare as a national institution, the popularity of certain city comedies, and the absence of revenge tragedies. David Garrick organized the first Shakespeare festival at Stratford-upon-Avon and, quite literally, set the playwright on a pedestal (see plate 4). Garrick did not exactly rediscover Shakespeare, for interest had been slowly building since the turn of the century.[42] During the age of Colley Cibber, the period from 1710 to 1742, only ten of Shakespeare's works were stock pieces. The standard tragedies and histories were acted over and over, the comedies neglected. Within this rather monotonous repertory, there was a series of Shakespeare revivals, each somewhat more lasting than the one before, and prior to Garrick's management, Shakespearean comedies began to enter the repertory.

Garrick recognized and capitalized on Shakespeare's rise in popularity, retaining both the stock tragedies and histories and the newly revived comedies in the Drury Lane repertory. The 1769 Stratford Festival brought hundreds of visitors to celebrate the bard for three days in the pouring rain. The festivities included the recitation of speeches, odes, and eulogies written by Garrick, though not so much as a line written by Shakespeare himself was heard. Neither this odd omission nor the weather seem to have dampened the English enthusiasm for Shakespeare. After the Festival, Garrick organized "The Jubilee," a grand procession of Shakespearean characters, which ran for ninety nights at Drury Lane. During the Garrick era, Shakespeare accounted for almost one-fifth of the main-piece performances at Drury Lane and only slightly less at Covent Garden.[43] By the end of Garrick's tenure, Shakespeare's preeminence among English dramatists was firmly established.

Shakespeare aside, Renaissance plays were not often seen on the eighteenth-century stage. A few plays by Beaumont and Fletcher, especially Fletcher's *Rule a Wife and Have a Wife*, remained in the repertory, but many popular playwrights of the Renaissance, including Kyd, Marlowe, Webster, and Dekker, were all but forgotten. Unfamiliar Renaissance plays faced the same difficulties new plays encountered in trying to break into the repertory of established Restoration and eighteenth-century favorites. Theatre managers had no incentives to take risks when they could fill their two houses nightly with tried-and-true pieces like Colley Cibber's *The Provok'd Husband* or John Gay's *The Beggar's Opera*, both of which were performed season after season. Elizabethan conventions and language were increasingly unfamiliar to the theatrical audience, and therefore welcome.

Both critical neoclassicism and popular tastes discouraged Renaissance revivals. Samuel Johnson, the most perceptive of his age, was less bound by neoclassical tenets than most of his contemporaries, and he granted that Shakespeare's psychological truths far outweighed his plot weaknesses and unfortunate punning.[44] But even he shared the century's conviction that drama should instruct as well as delight, and he worried about what he regarded as Shakespeare's lack of moral purpose. Renaissance dramatists who had not been idolized were all the more vulnerable to charges that they violated decorum and the unities without contributing to moral improvement. As for the popular audience, Renaissance comedy was too coarse, and tragedy too bleak, for their increasingly sentimental tastes. Garrick himself deplored the trend toward unabashed sentimentality. In a letter to a would-be comic dramatist, he called for "a Comedy of Character . . . One calculated more to make an Audience Laugh than cry—the Comedie Larmoyante is getting too Much ground upon Us . . . [If our comic writers do not] make a Stand for ye Genuine Comedy . . . the Stage in a few Years will be (as Hamlet says) like Niobe all tears."[45] It was a losing battle. Old plays could be altered (Garrick himself worked Wycherly's comedy of manners, *The Country Wife*, into a less shocking adaptation called *The Country Girl*), but as a rule it was easier to ignore old drama than to try to sanitize or sentimentalize it.

City comedy, including but not limited to those of Jonson, was the one type of non-Shakespearean Renaissance play that was regularly revived throughout the century. This was not just a case of continuity from the previous century, for city comedies had disappeared from the London stage during the 1690s. There seems to have been a genuine reawakening of interest in this type of play, as figure 4 suggests. Even during the middle of the eighteenth century, city comedies were being rediscovered, were found to be popular with contemporary audiences, and were added to the permanent repertories of Drury Lane and Covent Garden. For example, in 1751 *Every Man in His Humor* was revived at Drury Lane for the first time since 1670; it stayed in the repertory for the next thirty-seven years. *A New Way to Pay Old Debts,* revived by Garrick in 1748, had not been performed for forty years. Though this first revival was not successful, and ran for only four performances, it paved the way for the subsequent, more lasting revivals. Three to six city comedies were performed on the London stage during every decade of the eighteenth century.

In contrast, the few attempts made to revive revenge tragedies failed, and the genre virtually disappeared from the stage. This was true even for *Titus Andronicus,* which did not rise with the Shakespeare star. Although spot revivals occurred (*Titus Andronicus* in the 1720s, *The Duke of Milan* in 1779, *The Changeling* in 1789), they did not succeed in attracting an audience, so they did not get added to the theatres' repertories. Omission of dramatists who wrote revenge tragedies are striking. Marlowe was never performed in the eighteenth century, and Webster never after 1707. This absence of interest in revenge tragedies is especially remarkable when compared with the great popularity of Shakespeare's tragedies. Eighteenth-century audiences were not entirely wedded to the sentimental comedies of the period, but non-Shakespearean tragedies of blood and revenge failed to move them.

Three Renaissance Dramatists

A closer look at the revivals of Jonson, Fletcher, and Massinger reveals that their city comedies received considerably greater attention during the eighteenth century than did their other plays. In the case of Jonson, R. G. Noyes had found his stage history from the Restoration to the late eighteenth century as amounting to the persistent popularity of a few comedies gradually undercut by changing critical and dramatic tastes.[46] The late seventeenth-century attitude was one of "uncompromising adulation" coupled with a fascination with the poet's quirky personality; this personality cult was perpetuated by the jest-book anecdotes of the eighteenth century. Jonson won praise for his classicism and his realism, although his satire was seldom mentioned. At the same time his critics, and even his supporters, found his comedies to be cold and loveless, and he suffered in comparison with Shakespeare's romantic comedies. As neoclassicism began to give way to Romanticism and sentiment in the mid-eighteenth century, Jonson's strengths became liabilities. Garrick's commitment and the skilled productions of his company kept Jonson alive, but with Garrick's retirement, and with the shift in popular taste toward sentimental comedy and pantomime, Jonson's works all but disappeared from the stage.

Noyes's attribution of Jonson's stage popularity and subsequent decline to his neoclassicism and personality leaves some questions unanswered that are of particular interest here: First, why were Jonson's tragedies virtually ignored during the eighteenth century? And second, why did *The Devil Is an Ass* go unperformed when his other city comedies were flourishing? While it is true that the eighteenth-century stage was not kind to tragedies in general, some were revived. Aside from Shakespeare, Fletcher's popularity, although resting mainly on his comedies, prompted several revivals of his tragic plays. *Bonduca* and *The Maid's Tragedy* were performed often; *The Bloody Brother* and *Valentinian* were revived during the early decades of the century, although apparently with less success. In contrast, Jonson's two major tragedies, *Cataline's Conspiracy* and *Sejanus,* were never revived during the eighteenth century. Jonson's tragedies are undoubtedly inferior to his comedies, but, as the comparison with Fletcher indicates, dramatic quality is hardly a prerequisite for revivals; *Sejanus* is not noticeably worse than *Valentinian.* The neglect of Jonson's tragedies makes one suspect that it was not simply Jonson's reputation or his classicism, but something in particular about his comedies, that drew the interest of eighteenth-century audiences and, therefore, of managers.

Some comedies were more compelling than others, however, for the bases of their appeal were not perfectly congruent. *The Alchemist, Volpone,* and *Epicoene* were the long-term favorites, with *Every Man in His Humour* also winning great popularity following its mid-century revival. *Bartholomew Fair's* popularity was limited to the first third of the century, and *The Devil Is an Ass* was ignored. It seems that Georgian audiences enjoyed Jonson's city comedies insofar as they portrayed trickery, the pursuit of money, and social ambition (in these respects, *Volpone* resembles the London comedies). Garrick himself remarked in a letter about the stage having "so many *Cheaters* & *Cheatees* upon the Stage, Such as are in the Alchymist, Albumazar, etc."[47] Topical satire, on the other hand, is a perishable good. Satire of common human foibles amuses, and amused eighteenth-century London audiences, but too-specific a satire on Renaissance London neighborhoods, manners and mores, such as that found in *The Devil Is an Ass* and *Bartholomew Fair,* may have been less appealing to an audience remote in time. Similarly, *Eastward Ho!* failed dismally during its 1751 revival, while *Every Man in His Humour,* revived the same season, was a great success; the former play skewers particular Jacobean character types, such as the new-made knight, while the latter aims at more general types like ne'er-do-well sons and blustering soldiers.[48] *The Devil Is an Ass* may have been additionally handicapped by its parody of the morality play tradition. A Jacobean audience recognized devils and Vices as old-fashioned dramatic conventions, good to poke fun at; a Georgian audience, unfamiliar with the conventions, would have missed the humor.

The impulse for the revival of a single play may come from various sources, as the stage history of *The Alchemist* illustrates, for this play's career on the Restoration and eighteenth-century stage was enhanced, sequentially, by its structure, its topicality, and its possession of what developed into a star role. Dryden regarded the play as Jonson's finest, its unity and balance of plot structure more than compensating for its lapse in poetic justice represented by Face's success.[49] More rigid and less sensitive neoclassicists agreed; Charles Gilden, for example, cited the first act as a model of efficient introduction, "where the Audience is let into the Design and Characters, by a quarrel between *Subtle* and *Face,* who are the chief Managers of the whole Design."[50] In the 1720s, *The Alchemist* was found to be remarkably topical, for its presentation of gullible men transformed into fools by their greed seemed an apt depiction of the recent craze of speculation and crash epitomized by the South Sea Bubble. An epilogue to a 1721 performance, later published as a broadside, made the analogy explicit, and suggested that Jonson's knaves, alchemists, and bands were small-time operators in comparison:

> Our Knaves Sin higher Now than those of Old,
> Kingdoms, not Private Men, are Bought and Sold,
> Witness the South-sea Project. . . .[51]

Still later, David Garrick's stunning success in the previously minor role of Abel Drugger (Garrick's interpretation combined Drugger's greedy simplicity with Kastril's inept pugnaciousness) charmed London audiences for over thirty years (see plate 5). Well after Garrick's retirement, adaptations of *The Alchemist,* including Francis Gentleman's farce *The Tobacconist,* continued to appear, with the engaging role of Drugger persisting until the early nineteenth century.

Fletcher, alone or with a coauthor, dominated Restoration and eighteenth-century Renaissance revivals. Of his fifty extant works that fit into conventional dramatic genres, twenty-five were comedies, sixteen were tragicomedies, and nine were tragedies; of these, only two tragedies and one comedy went unrevived.[52] Tragedy seems to have fallen behind the other two categories during the eighteenth century; while two-thirds of both the comedies and the tragicomedies were performed on the Georgian stage, only four of the tragedies were, and only *The Maid's Tragedy* and *Bonduca* showed any strength from season to season. Both comedy and tragicomedy declined in popularity during the century, and they declined at the same rate. If we count as a "revival" each play performed at any time during a given decade (as in figure 4), we find that sixty-two percent of the eighteenth-century revivals of Fletcher's comedies and sixty-three percent of his tragicomedies occurred before 1750. His tragedies declined even more sharply: only twenty-five percent of the century's revivals followed 1750. Not only do comedy and tragedy follow the same pattern, but no mid-to-late-century recovery of Fletcher's comedies occurred, in contrast with the city comedy increase shown in figure 4.

Apart from the audiences' gradual rejection of tragedy, Fletcher's popularity seems to have been independent of the actual content of individual plays. The accepted explanation of this popularity has been that, as a gentleman and "entertainer to the Jacobean gentry," Fletcher produced a drama of polished conversation and decorous incident that appealed to aristocratic and upper-middle-class tastes.[53] Restoration critics agreed with Dryden's comment that "in easy dialogue is Fletcher's praise." They admired his "courtly elegance and gentle familiarity of style," his "witty raillery"; they enjoyed "that witty obscenity in his Playes, which like poison infused in pleasant liquor, is alwayes the more dangerous the more delightful."[54] The sheer number of his plays produced something like a critical mass of performances during the Restoration, embedding Fletcher in the dramatic memories of theatre professionals and audiences alike. Furthermore, changing tastes toward sentimental comedy in the eighteenth century were less disadvantageous to Fletcher than to Jonson, for Fletcher's plays were full of love and sentiment.

Fletcher's *Wit without Money* perpetuated the city comedy formula, and while one may suspect that it was Fletcher's general popularity and not an interest in city comedy that sustained this play during the eighteenth century, there is some evidence that *Wit without Money* had more appeal for the Georgians than for their Restoration ancestors. Pepys did not care for the play, once walking out before its performance, and it is not known to have been revived at all between 1672 and 1707. After this thirty-five-year absence it seems to have had strong appeal, for it was regularly performed until the mid-1760s and at least once in 1782. One anonymous commentator in 1732, although exaggerating the decline in Fletcher's popularity, made the revealing comment that "few of the Plays of Beaumont and Fletcher are now either prized or acted; the *Scornful Lady* and *Wit without Money* are almost the only ones, which at this time of Day are capable of entertaining the Town. . . ."[55]

Philip Massinger, the third city comedy dramatist revived in the eighteenth century through the "amazing career" of *A New Way to Pay Old Debts*, differed from Fletcher and Jonson in that he was not popular during the Restoration, nor indeed during most of the eighteenth century.[56] A number of his plays, including *The Duke of Milan, The Bashful Lover, The Emperor of the East, The Unnatural Combat, The Renegado,* and *A Very Woman,* seem to have been fleetingly revived in the 1660s, but we know of only a single performance in each case, so apparently they did not capture the Restoration fancy. His late throwback to the city comedy genre, *The City Madam,* seems to have gone unperformed until late in the eighteenth century. Some of his collaborations with Fletcher, especially *The Beggar's Bush* and *The Prophetess,* did better, but it would seem that Massinger was being carried along by the popularity of his coauthor. *The Roman Actor* was revived occasionally. Not quite as neglected in the eighteenth century as tragedians like Marlowe and Webster, Massinger seems to have been always lurking in the recesses of the theatre without ever moving to center stage.

He was not forgotten, however, and there were occasional movements toward his rediscovery, most notably by the publisher and bookseller Robert Dodsley. Dodsley published five of Massinger's plays in his first *Select Collection of Old Plays* in 1744.[57] The same year he published a separate edition of *A New Way to Pay Old Debts.* This publication may have prompted David Garrick's revival of the play four years later; in any case, in 1748 Dodsley published a new edition of the play as acted that year at Drury Lane. In 1759 Thomas Coxeter put out a four-volume edition, *The Dramatic Works of Philip Massinger.*[58] In the second edition published in 1761, an anonymous essay, which George Colman admitted to have written, called for the stage revival of Massinger's plays.[59] The essay was addressed to Garrick, who, Colman suggested, had been so successful in establishing Shakespeare's preeminence that other pre-Commonwealth writers had been eclipsed by comparison:

> Has not the Contemplation of Shakespeare's Excellencies almost dazzled and extinguished your Judgment of his Contemporaries? Under your Dominion, have not Beaumont and Fletcher, nay even Jonson, suffered a kind of theatrical Disgrace? And has not poor Massinger, whose cause I have now undertaken, been permitted to languish in Obscurity, and remained almost entirely unknown?[60]

A New Way to Pay Old Debts was to be the vehicle that brought Massinger out of exile. The play was largely dormant for over a century; we know of only one performance in 1662, another in 1708. Ball suggests that the reasons for this neglect lie in the contrast between it and the Restoration comedy of manners, for *A New Way to Pay Old Debts* was grim and lacked the "amoral suavity" of Restoration comedy. "Its purpose is to tell a highly edifying story about an extortioner . . . there are definite characters and strong passions expressed in blunt language. Wit and grace are lacking; the intrigue does not exist for itself but for the plot. . . ."[61] Nor did it meet the criteria of decorum valued in the neoclassical period. The play languished until David Garrick attempted a revival in 1748. Garrick clearly saw contemporary possibilities in the play, for he produced it several times during the 1748–49 season, several times again ten years later, and again during the fall of 1769. None of these productions seems to have been particularly successful, however, and Garrick himself did not act in the play.

It was not until the comedy was defined as a star vehicle that it established a firm hold on the London stage. This occurred in the Covent Garden production of 1781, when John Henderson, who had a personal interest in Massinger and may have been responsible for the play's revival, triumphed in the role of the irrepressible villain Sir Giles Overreach. Henderson so impressed London audiences that he was ordered to give a command performance for Queen Charlotte only eight days after he opened the play. Thereafter Sir Giles was a role that all leading actors wanted to play. The play was performed frequently in the 1780s, although Henderson himself died in 1785. It appeared at least once in the 1790s, and it achieved its greatest prominence in the first decades of the nineteenth century. The rapidity with which Henderson had made the role of Sir Giles a major one in the English theatre is indicated by Cumberland's memorial to Henderson: "He was an actor of uncommon powers. . . . What he was on the stage, those who recollect his Falstaff, Shylock, Sir Giles Overreach, and many other parts of the strong cast, can fully testify. . . ."[62] Sir Giles was keeping good company. John Philip Kemble played the role from 1781 until 1816. His cool, classic style was not especially well suited to the role, and he was compared unfavorably with Henderson and with George Frederick Cook, who played Sir Giles in the early nineteenth century. Still to come was Edmund Kean's brilliant Romantic version. A single, sought-after role kept *A New Way to Pay Old Debts* on the London stage for years after most city comedies had disappeared.

City Comedy Exceptionalism

To sum up, the period from the era of Davenant and Killgrew through the age of Garrick was not hospitable to most Renaissance plays. When theatre managers began to have a choice, for at the outset of the Restoration they had none, they selected a repertory that tickled the elite sensibility with witty language. As the audience grew increasingly middle class, the risqué changed to the sentimental, the heroic became the pathetic. Theatre managers depended on, and sought to please, the members of their audiences. Their decisions were conservative and prudent, for they sought to satisfy their patrons, not challenge, educate, or shock them. Shakespeare gradually displaced his contemporaries in the repertory. A Renaissance revival, especially of a play by an unfamiliar writer, was usually not regarded as a risk worth taking.

During the eighteenth century, city comedy withstood this filtering of Renaissance drama from the repertory to a considerable extent, and this puzzling exceptionalism, especially surprising given the distinctly unsentimental tone of the genre, requires explanation. It was not simply a matter of the theatrical bias toward comedy. We have seen that during the Garrick era the performance ratio of comedy to tragedy was three to one. During the same period there were 299 performances of city comedy, and none of revenge tragedy.[63] Each city comedy revival seems to have its own unique causes, such as Garrick's dogged championing of Jonson or Henderson's capitalizing on the star vehicle Sir Giles offered, but these individual causes do not adequately account for what appears to be a continuing pressure on the managers to give city comedy a try. Why did the theatres decide to take a chance on *A Mad World, My Masters* twice during the eighteenth century, when most of the Middleton canon lay forgotten? Why did the city comedies of Jonson and Fletcher seem to hold the stage longer than the rest of their works? What was there about Sir Giles Overreach that Garrick and his successors could not leave alone?

Recall the three bases of city comedy appeal discussed in chapter 2. The topical references to Renaissance London neighborhoods and character types contributed to the original theatrical popularity of city comedy, a popularity that led to both its conventionalization and its preservation, hence its availability for subsequent revival. While essential for this preservation, however, topicality does not go very far toward explaining the eighteenth-century enthusiasm for the genre. London had changed vastly since the Elizabethan age, and the plays' particular allusions and satire were too outdated even for nostalgia. Nor does the archetypal appeal of the trickster suffice to account for why this genre was favored over the other Renaissance plays that also expressed enduring human interests and dilemmas exceedingly well. Any type of appeal that is categorized as "universal," such as the attractions of antistructure embodied in a trickster, is by definition invariant. While the powerful literary expression of generally acknowledged truths about the human condition has much to do with a work's ability to enter and remain in the canon, and with the decision of someone like Dodsley to publish a play for reading, it does not account for significant shifts in popular interest.

The solution to the puzzle lies in the social import of city comedy, especially the way in which city comedy presented and formally resolved the tension between rampant economic mobility and the social stability entailed in the preservation of the existing social hierarchy. This theme of economic mobility within a stable social order continued to appeal to the tastes of the eighteenth-century audience long after other Renaissance themes had lost their savor because it addressed a concern salient to them. Moreover, it suggested a resolution that both court and Town could applaud, though for rather different reasons.

Eighteenth-century London was an arena of commerce and consumption, and its producers and consumers were organized in a gradually sloping social structure.[64] The city was a center of aggressive commercial capitalism, small-scale entrepreneurial and manufacturing activities, and an increasing number of intermediaries between producer and consumer. Indeed, London itself was such an intermediary, a clearinghouse for colonial products bound for European markets. It was also a financial center of increasing complexity. An essayist in 1749 commented on the growth of "Agents, Factors, Brokers, Insurers, Bankers, Negotiators, Discounters, Subscribers, Contractors, Remitters, Ticket-Mongers, Stock-Jobbers, and of a great Variety of other Dealers in Money, the Names of whose Employments were wholly unknown to our Forefathers."[65] In addition to this expansion of the commercial and financial sectors, Augustan England experienced an unprecedented growth in the number, size, wealth, and social status of the professions.[66] Lawyers, physicians and surgeons, apothecaries, clergy, civil servants, army and naval officers, schoolmasters—all constituted a social group that was expanding more rapidly than any other in the late seventeenth century and the first half of the eighteenth. Moreover, entrance into this professional sector was easier than ever before, for a shift from the requirement of a university education to various forms of professional apprenticeships made the necessary years of training for the would-be professional man less expensive.

For most eighteenth-century Londoners of the middle and upper middle classes, who constituted the bulk of the theatregoers, opportunities seemed plentiful and the social system porous, a "gradual and easy transition from rank to rank."[67] No Industrial Revolution had yet made apparent a gap between the owners of the means of production and those forced to sell their labor. It was not until the end of the eighteenth century that this division would begin to seem obvious to many, and even then not as starkly in London as in the northern industrial centers, for London grew relatively less, not more, industrial during the eighteenth century.[68]

City comedy could appeal to these men and women of the Town, who were not at all embarrassed by plots involving the headlong pursuit of money and a desirable way of life, for they were pursuing these things themselves. The typical audience member was probably not born in London; two-thirds or more adult Londoners had come from distant parts seeking a career and the pleasures money could buy.[69] He may well have been a younger son; primogeniture was still forcing these young men into commercial life, though the elite disapproval of engaging in "traffic" had largely disappeared, probably because the practice was so common and so rewarding. He was concerned with fashion and display. Even if he was not one of the young fops excoriated by the soberer members of the audience, a London theatregoer could not help but be caught up in the ethos of conspicuous consumption so typical of the eighteenth century. Above all, he was interested in improving himself financially and socially.

A finely graded system of stratification along with the availability of consumer goods meant that visible social distinctions were all but erased. Witnesses frequently commented on not being able to "know the mistress from the maid by their dress."[70] Defoe reported that he once, when greeting a company of ladies, "kis'd the chamber jade into the bargain for she was as well dress'd as the rest."[71] Maids were not the only imitators of fashion; "the Tradesman vies with my Lord," and "the different stations of Life so run into and mix with each other, that it is hard to say, where the one ends, and the other begins."[72] Fashionable goods were available for anyone with money, and more and more people had money.

Members of the middle class wanted not to overturn the elite but to join it. They believed elite circles were open to them, and this belief persisted in spite of any evidence to the contrary.[73] Acquiring land was the desideratum; failing that, imitation of high society fashion was one way to proclaim membership in circles above your own. Such anticipatory socialization may not have fooled snobbish aristocrats (as *The British Magazine* sniffed in 1763, "The present rage of imitating the manners of high life hath spread itself so far among the gentlefolks of lower life, that in a few years we shall probably have no common folk at all"), but it fueled the fashion revolutions of the day and lent support to the impression of a fluid social structure.[74] Large social leaps were difficult to achieve, but moving up a peg or two seemed easier, for there were plenty of pegs and no one was too sure about their order. There was money to be made and the material wherewithal with which to flaunt one's success. The immediate satisfactions of money, consumer products, and individual social mobility contented most representatives of the Town for most of the century, despite the fact that they lacked political power commensurate with their economic importance. They were occupied with other concerns, chiefly, as one representative put it, "the getting of Money, and whatever some divines would teach to the contrary, this is true that it is the main business of the life of man."[75]

Activism, striving, and conflict in the England of Elizabeth and James had taken place along three dimensions: political, religious, and economic. In contrast, Georgian England saw relative tranquility in the first two of these three potential arenas of contest. Following the political turbulence of William III and Anne's reigns, the Hanovers and their Whig managers brought an era of unprecedented political stability during the century following 1714. An oligarchy of landed gentry and their retainers adroitly managed government affairs, bought power with the patronage plums of an expanding government, and engineered legislation to quell dissent. Georgian England may not have been the Eden of patronizing squires and their grateful beneficiaries that is sometimes envisioned—riots, crime, and public violence of all sorts, including the violence that periodically closed the theatres, bore witness to the social tensions and dislocations of the age—but revolution, or even a widespread movement for political change, never materialized.[76] Episodes of social protest were specific and issue-oriented, not directed toward broad social change. Commercial and professional groups never united for greater political power, but instead sought economic benefits for their own particular groups or patronage prizes for themselves as individuals; they received enough to stand content. Political life remained in the hands of the landed few. Running for office was expensive, elections were infrequent and manipulated, and complaints did not arouse concentrated political action.

This same pattern of general tranquility punctuated by occasional outbursts of enthusiasm or bigotry marked the religious life of the eighteenth century. The Anglican church was prosperous from tithes. Among its other agreeable features, it provided a good source of livings for younger sons. The old Puritan gentry and commercial groups shifted their allegiance to Anglicanism, causing the total number of Dissenters to drop by some forty percent during the period 1700–1740; it was said that "the Dissenter's second horse carried him to Church."[77] The common people drifted from Anglicanism to one of the Dissenting sects or, more often, to religious apathy. From mid-century on, Methodism fanned religious enthusiasm among certain groups of laborers, especially miners, but its qualified populism did not create new coalitions or mobilize secular political conflicts as Puritanism had done in the preceding century. Religious passions were like political passions in the eighteenth century: they burned brightly in individual breasts, occasionally flared up in some episode like the anti-Catholic Gordon riots of 1780, but never came close to igniting a general conflagration.

Only in the arena of economic advancement, and the consequent or anticipatory display of social status, was there a sustained struggle obvious to all observers. The passionate pursuit of interest, which now had come to be defined in economic terms alone, was taken for granted as a given fact of life.[78] Adam Smith could construct an entire social philosophy on this bedrock of individual acquisitiveness. What the medieval mind had deplored, the Georgian mind assumed.

City comedies, as we have seen, constituted a collective representation of such economic acquisition. Censorship and audience composition had filtered out much of the Renaissance political and religious controversies from city comedy; what remained was getting and spending, and social climbing on the rungs of a firm social ladder. This partial representation of Elizabethan and Jacobean social concerns expressed the manifest collective concerns of the middle and upper middle classes of Georgian London. Indeed, insofar as religious, political, and economic struggles preoccupied Renaissance Londoners but the Town of the eighteenth century concentrated primarily on the economic sphere, city comedy might be said to have "fit" the eighteenth century better than it fit its original era.

At the same time, city comedy reassured the aristocratic members of the

eighteenth-century audience, for it offered the accommodating myth that enterprise could be rewarded within a stable social order. The court and the
landed gentry visiting the theatres during a trip to the city undoubtedly ap-
preciated the point about the stable social order more, while the numerous
representatives of the Town were more attentive to the economic gains of
clever individuals who saw and seized the main chance. All enjoyed the celebration of London as a city great in opportunity. There were multitudes of
people who knew otherwise, whose experience of the metropolis was one of
disease, poverty, and an absence of opportunity, but these less fortunate Londoners did not constitute an influential part of the theatre audience. City
comedy's fit with the economic optimism and social conservatism of its eighteenth-century audience gave the genre some protection from the institutional factors working against the revival of Renaissance plays. Throughout
the century, a city comedy remained a candidate for consideration in shaping
the theatrical repertory, and thus constituted an exception to the general rule
keeping non-Shakespearean Renaissance drama off the London stage.

Plate 1: Kirkman's 1672 print of the Red Bull theatre is believed to be the only representation of the interior of an Elizabethan-Jacobean theatre dating from the period. The heads on the sides and bottom of the picture show how intimate the actor-audience relationship was in this platform stage theatre. (Harvard Theatre Collection)

INSIDE OF THE DUKES THEATRE
in Lincoln's Inn Fields,
as it appeared in the reign of King Charles II.

Plate 2: The Restoration theatre at Dorset Garden showing the ornamented proscenium that dwarfed the actors. During this period most of the acting still took place in front of the prosenium arch. (Harvard Theatre Collection).

For the Benefit of

Mr. DU-BELLAMY, and Mrs. PITT.

Theatre Royal in Covent Garden,

This prefent TUESDAY, being the 5th of MAY, 1767,

Every MAN in his HUMOUR.

Kitely by Mr. S M I T H,
Old Knowel by Mr. G I B S O N,
Young Knowel by Mr. D Y E R,
Wellbred by Mr. M A T T O C K S,
Capt. Bobadil by Mr. W O O D W A R D,
Mafter Stephen by Mr. S H U T E R,
Juftice Clement by Mr. W I G N E L L,
Mafter Matthew by Mr. C U S H I N G,
Brainworm by Mr. D U N S T A L L,
Cafh by Mr. PERRY,   Formal by Mr. MURDEN,
Downright by Mr. W A L K E R,
Bridget by Mrs. B A K E R,
Dame Kitely by Mifs W I L F O R D.

End of Act I. At TOTTERDOWN HILL, a favourite Song,
End of Act IV. the Cantata of CYMON and IPHIGENIA, (By Particular Defire)
will be fung, By Mr. DU-BELLAMY.
End of the Play, a grand Pantomime Ballet, called The WAPPING LANDLADY,
Jack in Diftrefs by Mr. FISHAR,   The Landlady by Mr. MILES,
The Milk-woman by Signiora M A N E S I E R E.
With a Double Hornpipe by Mr. FISHAR and Signiora MANESIERE.
To which will be added (Not performed thefe four Years) a Burlefque Opera, call'd

The DRAGON of WANTLEY.

The MUSIC compofed by Mr. JOHN FREDERIC LAMPE.
Moor of Moor-Hall by Mr. DU-BELLAMY,
Gaffer Gubbins by Mr. S H U T E R,
The Dragon by the G I A N T,
Mauxalinda by Mifs P O I T I E R,
Margery by Mrs. P I N T O.
Tickets delivered for THEODOSIUS, will be taken.

To-morrow, (acted but once thefe 25 Years,)
DOUBLE FALSHOOD; Or, The DISTREST LOVERS,
With MIDAS. For the Benefit of Mr. HULL.
On Thurfday, CATO. For the Benefit of Mr. DAVIS and Mr. DIBDIN.

Plate 3: A typical playbill from the eighteenth century. In addition to the mainpiece, the entertainment included a burlesque opera afterpeice, a song, a cantata, and a pantomime ballet. (Harvard Theatre Collection)

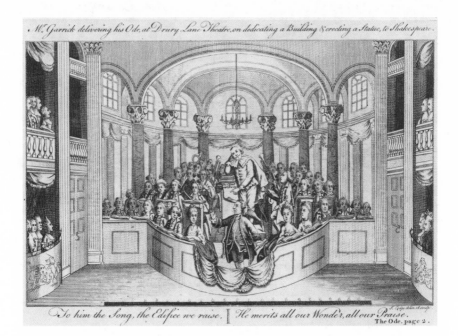

Mr Garrick delivering his Ode, at Drury Lane Theatre, on dedicating a Building & erecting a Statue, to Shakespeare.

To him the Song, the Edifice we raise. | *He merits all our Wonder, all our Praise.*

The Ode. page 2.

Plate 4: Garrick's tireless promotion of Shakespeare firmly established the playwright's unique position in the dramatic canon. Here Garrick presents his ode to, and statue of, Shakespeare to the Drury Lane audience, many of whom may have attended the earlier Shakespeare festival af Stratford. (Harvard Theatre Collection)

Plate 5: Merging the pugnacious characteristics of Kastril with the simplicity of Abel Drugger, Garrick created a star vehicle. The role of Drugger offered a challenge to comic actors that helped maintain *The Alchemist,* and the shortened version called *The Tobacconist,* on the London stage well into the nineteenth century. (University of Chicago Library)

Plate 6: Drury Lane in the eighteenth century was by no means small, for it accommodated roughly 2,000 people, but it still allowed some degree of intimacy between the actors and the audience. (Harvard Theatre Collection)

Plate 7: By the nineteenth century Drury Lane had become, as Sarah Siddons complained, a "vast wilderness," where it was difficult for the audience to hear the lines of a legitimate drama. (Harvard Theatre Collection)

Plate 8: The "little theatre" in the Haymarket was more suited to the performance of spoken drama than were the two larger legitimate playhouses, Covent Garden and Drury Lane. But the Haymarket performances were restricted to the summer months, when many fashionable people left London for Bath or the seaside. (University of Chicago Library)

Publish'd Jan.ʳ 25, 1804 by LAURIE & WHITTLE, 53, Fleet Street, London.

C A R L O,
THE ROSCIUS OF DRURY-LANE THEATRE.

No actor great in histrionic name,
Than Carlo, boasts a prouder, nobler fame:
E'en Garrick, nature's fav'rite child, must yield;
Nature *herself* with Carlo takes the field.
The buskin'd hero, or the mottled fool,
Must *sink*, before great Carlo, in the *pool*.
E'en mighty Rolla *ducks*, a bridge he crost,
And to his mother gave the babe she'd lost.
No bridge, no boat, no friendly log at hand,
Carlo the sinking urchin brings to land:
With dauntless heart, the stormy waves he dares,
And from the dreadful deep the infant bears:
Safe to his mother's arms restores the boy,
Shakes his rough coat, and wags his tail for joy.—
Approving shouts reward the gen'rous deed,
And greet the actor of Newfoundland breed:
Each lounging *puppy* joins his friendly *paws*;
The lobby quits, and aids his brother's cause.

Curst is the *cur* who growls when Carlo plays,
Mongrel the *hound* that can withhold his praise.
Was ever part so naturally play'd?
E'en *snarling* critics his eulogiums made;
Both sock and buskin mummers, all agree,
They cannot " play the Dog " so well as he.
Was Carlo e'er reprov'd (like many a clown)
For *speaking* more than was for him set down?
Ne'er was he found imperfect in his part,
His character was always GOT BY HEART.
When he perform'd, an *overflowing* house
Ne'er fail'd to witness gallant Carlo's souse.
Be it recorded in historic page,
A mime more perfect never swam the Stage:
Nor can his envious *brethren* e'er destroy
The fame of Carlo, and the *drowning boy*.
" Let Hercules himself say what he may,
" The cat will mew, the DOG WILL HAVE HIS DAY."

Plate 9: Spectacles and melodramas that appealed more to the eye than to the ear became the staple of the nineteenth-century stage. Sensations like Carlo the hero dog or Master Betty the infant prodigy disgusted many educated audience members but allowed the legitimate theatres to maintain solvency. (Harvard Theatre Collection)

Plate 10: After the theatrical monopoly ended in 1843, minor theatres could stage legitimate drama, including Renaissance revivals. This scene is from an 1848 Olympic Theatre production of *A New Way to Pay Old Debts*. A mélange of historical costuming is evident: Sir Giles seems to have stepped straight out of the Renaissance, Lady Allworth is pure Victorian, and Wellborn combines a seventeenth-century costume with a nineteenth-century hairstyle. (University of Chicago Library)

Plate 11: Mid-nineteenth-century playbills continued to advertise an evening of various entertainments; this was soon to give way to performance of a single play as the dinner hour of the middle class grew later. The star vehicle of Sir Giles Overreach, established for almost a century, kept Massinger's city comedy on the London stage when other Renaissance revivals were rare. (Harvard Theatre Collection)

Plate 12: *Titus Andronicus* shares the awkward sensationalism of other Kydian revenge tragedies, but the exceptional status of the Shakespeare canon plus the star vehicle offered by Aaron, arch-villain and tender father, have caused it to be revived more frequently than other examples of the genre. This scene of Aaron defending his baby (having just slain its nurse) is from the 1957 production at the Old Vic. (Harvard Theatre Collection)

Plate 13: Looming thrones, overhanging crowns, and similar symbols of authority, which appear often in modern revenge tragedy sets, emphasize the contrast between individual human passions and established human institutions. This scene of Bosola's revenge is from the 1960 Aldwych production of *The Duchess of Malfi*. (Harvard Theatre Collection)

RENAISSANCE REVIVALS FROM CARLO THE HERO DOG TO THE ELIZABETHAN STAGE SOCIETY

Undoubtedly the most familiar depiction of nineteenth-century English theatre comes from Charles Dickens's classic account of Vincent Crummles and his touring company.[1] This fictional impresario offers a none-too-exaggerated picture of how a contemporary manager conceived of his repertory when Nicholas Nickleby informs Crummles that he must leave the company, and the manager immediately plans the actor's final appearance:

> 'Then I am to make three last appearances, am I?' inquired Nicholas, smiling.
>
> 'Yes,' rejoined the manager, scratching his head with an air of some vexation; 'three is not enough, and it's very bungling and irregular not to have more, but if we can't help it we can't so there's no use in talking. A novelty would be very desirable. You couldn't sing a comic song on the pony's back, could you?'
>
> 'No,' replied Nicholas, 'I couldn't indeed.'
>
> 'It has drawn money before now,' said Mr. Crummles, with a look of disappointment. 'What do you think of a brilliant display of fireworks?'
>
> 'That it would be rather expensive,' replied Nicholas, drily.
>
> 'Eighteenpence would do it,' said Mr. Crummles. 'You on the top of a pair of steps with the phenomenon in an attitude; "Farewell" on a transparency behind; and nine people at the wings with a squib in each hand—all the dozen and a half going off at once—it would be very grand—awful from the front, quite awful.'
>
> As Nicholas appeared by no means impressed with the solemnity of the proposed effect, but, on the contrary, received the proposition in a most irreverent manner and laughed at it very heartily, Mr. Crummles abandoned the project in its birth, and gloomily observed that they must

> make up the best bill they could with combats and horn-
> pipes, and so stick to the legitimate drama.

A theatre open to caricature for having such a conception of legitimate drama
was not apt to be hospitable to Renaissance plays.

While the previous chapter attempted to explain the presence of certain
Renaissance revivals on the eighteenth-century London stage, the present
chapter must explain their nineteenth-century absence. As figure 4 illustrates,
neither city comedy nor revenge tragedy found much favor during most of
the nineteenth century. Nor did important new genres, comparable to the
comedy of manners, emerge. The London stage produced few dramatists or
plays of any lasting value, at least until the late Victorian era. Spectacle and
melodrama dominated. The ponies and fireworks favored by Crummles and
his real-life counterparts overwhelmed and altered the legitimate stage.

What is surprising about Renaissance revivals in the nineteenth-century
theatre is not that there were very few, but that there were any at all. For a
number of attempts were made to revive a city comedy or revenge tragedy,
and some productions generated great interest. Edmund Kean transfixed his
audiences with his portrayal of Sir Giles Overreach. A determined mid-century revival of the less familiar part of the Shakespeare canon introduced an
audience to *Titus Andronicus* and a sanitized version of *The Maid's Tragedy*.
William Poel presented unfamiliar Elizabethan and Jacobean drama to theatregoers at the turn of the century. Notable productions of revenge tragedy
and city comedy were thus seen occasionally on the nineteenth-century stage,
but they did not generate further productions. They did not start a trend,
such as the one we saw in the eighteenth-century vogue for city comedy.
What needs to be explained, therefore, is not only why theatre managers were
usually disinclined to take a chance on a Renaissance revival in the nineteenth
century, but why those revivals that were mounted failed to catch on.

Nineteenth-Century London Theatre

Institutional factors, above all else, prevented Renaissance drama from gaining a firm foothold on the nineteenth-century stage, despite the success of
any individual production. The most prominent of these factors, and the one
most deplored by the educated commentators of the age, was the change in
the social composition and theatrical expectations of the theatre audience.
The history of the London theatre from the late eighteenth to the late nineteenth century is the history of the middle-class audience's rapid desertion
and slow return.[2] Too strong a statement perhaps, for the middle class never
entirely abandoned the London theatres, this observation was nevertheless
shared by both the respectable and the intellectual groups who mourned the
theatre's decline.

In *New Grub Street,* George Gissing's naturalistic novel published in 1891, a writer named Reardon contends that intelligent men no longer need to live in London, one of his arguments being: "And as for recreation, why, now that no English theatre exists, what is there in London that you can't enjoy in almost any part of England?"[3] Reardon's statement was less true in the 1890s than a few decades before, for the serious attempts that had been made to reform the theatres were beginning to pay off, but melodrama was still the staple fare. It would be another several years before Shaw and the little theatre movement might be able to convince a man like Reardon, or Gissing, that the English theatre still existed. While in the eighteenth century an upwardly mobile young man used the theatre as arena for a display of his wit before the trendsetters and the prosperous of the Town, by the mid-nineteenth century a similar young man would seldom have attended the theatres, and, if he did, might avoid mentioning it in the company of those whom he wished to impress.

The middle-class abandonment of the theatre to the working class coincided with a low point in dramatic writing and a theatre of spectacles, dancing horses, farce, and melodrama, a theatre in which legitimate drama was at a distinct disadvantage. This raises the question of cause and effect. Many commentators at the time felt that the gentler classes had left the theatre because of the low quality of the productions therein. As has been shown before, however, managers of commercial theatres are usually more concerned with responding to the tastes of their audiences than with changing or violating them, and the nature of their audience largely determines the nature of what goes on their stages. The nineteenth-century theatre was indeed a popular one, and its urban working-class audiences wanted such entertainment as "Lions! Tigers! Panthers! And Other Wild Animals in a State of Native Ferocity!"[4] Like that of the courtly Restoration audiences of two centuries earlier, this audience's taste may have been deplorable according to middle-class standards, but it got what it wanted.

Analysis must not substitute one simple determinism for another, however, for the problems of the nineteenth century theatre involved all points on the cultural diamond. Why did talented writers avoid drama and hacks dominate it? Why did spectacles flourish in this theatre? What brought the working class into the theatres at the beginning of the century and drove them out at its close? How did changes in the social world, from the demographic change in London to the political ascendancy of the middle class, influence the theatre? And what were the consequences of this combination of factors for the English drama as it was written and as it was revived?

To address these questions, it is useful to break down the theatrical changes of the nineteenth century into three periods. The first followed the age of Garrick in the previous century. From the 1780s until about 1815 theatres grew larger, their audiences rowdier, and their expenses greater.

During the second period, which lasted from 1815 to the 1850s, the theatrical monopoly was dismantled, all theatres were in the financial doldrums, and members of the educated class were conspicuous by their absence. Then from the 1850s to the end of the century, concentrated efforts succeeded in bringing back the middle-class audience. To the disgust of the Reardons of the world, however, the boisterous working-class audience was replaced by a dull Philistine one equally incapable of appreciating innovative or unfamiliar drama. The following sections examine these three periods, so harshly characterized by their contemporaries as well as by twentieth-century accounts, in greater detail.

The Decline of Fashion

The reasons for the change in audience composition from the age of Garrick to the age of Kean are manifold. One contributing factor was that high society became enamored of the Italian opera in the late eighteenth century. Opera was by no means a novelty to English audiences. The Queen's (later King's) Theatre in the Haymarket had performed opera since Queen Anne's reign; ballad opera, most notably John Gay's *The Beggar's Opera,* had enjoyed remarkable popularity in the mid-eighteenth century; Handel's operas and oratorios won enthusiastic acclaim. By the end of the century, going to an opera was more fashionable than going to a play. A century earlier, *The Gentleman's Magazine* had reported that "operas abroad are plays where every word is sung; this is not rellished in England."[5] By the opening of the nineteenth century, opera was relished above all else. Its dominance was proclaimed unmistakably in 1847 when Covent Garden, the venerable house of legitimate drama, was converted once and for all into the Royal Italian Opera House.

A second factor contributing to the withdrawal of the more affluent members of the theatre audience was the change in the dinner hour of upper-class people and their emulators. While most people dined at 4:00, people of quality ate later, and took longer, thus finding it impossible to make an early evening curtain time. Class and curtain times coincided; in 1832 the Italian opera (King's Theatre, Haymarket) began its performance at 8:00 each evening, the patent houses at 7:00, several minor theatres at 6:30 or 6:45, and the notorious Coburg, home of the most sensational variety of melodrama, at 6:15. Such matters of convenience might not have deterred a committed theatre audience, but they contributed to preventing a new generation from forming the habit of regular attendance.

Most important in terms of its effect on audiences, the patent theatres simply got too big. Theatres lie at the intersection of the horizontal and vertical axes of the cultural diamond, mediating between social world and cultural product, as well as between artist and audience. In the present case, demographic change combined with legal constraints to produce theatres of expanded seating capacity, which in turn brought about changes in the nature of the works performed in these theatres.

The increasing size of the legitimate playhouses was the consequence of the system of theatrical monopoly (see plates 6–8). In the late eighteenth century, London was expanding in population, reaching about 900,000 by the turn of the century. Such growth increased the size of the potential theatre audiences, but there still could be only two legitimate theatres, plus the Haymarket for the summer season.

Theatrical entrepreneurs responded to this situation in two ways. First, the owners and managers of the patent houses kept increasing the seating capacities of their theatres. After its reconstruction in 1782, Covent Garden seated about 2,500 people; it was enlarged again in 1792 to hold over 3,000. Two years later, Drury Lane was rebuilt, going from a seating capacity of 2,300 to over 3,600.[6] Sarah Siddons referred to the Drury Lane as "a wilderness of a place." The size of such theatres made it impossible for many to hear, especially in the galleries where the cheaper seats were located. Increasing noisiness and rowdy behavior resulted. Size and difficulties in hearing made staging drama dependent on the spoken word more and more problematic. Of course, size alone does not preclude audience decorum or drama dependent on language, as the size of the second Globe attests. But during the eighteenth century, theatre forestages had become smaller, with much of the action moving behind the proscenium arch; this development was in sharp contrast to the raised open platform of the Elizabethan theatres, which had created intimacy between actors and audience. (See figure 2 in chapter 2.) Without such close physical proximity, the problem of size and unamplified voices became critical. Haymarket, with only 1,500 seats crowded together, was somewhat better; one playgoer recalled that "however the audience in this little theatre might be cramped for room and accommodation, they certainly could hear and see the performances upon its stage better than upon those two covered Salisbury Plains which now characterize the two grand winter houses."[7] Even Haymarket was hardly intimate by today's standards.

The second entrepreneurial response to a larger population that demanded more entertainment than the patent houses could supply was a proliferation of new theatres built at the end of the eighteenth and the first two decades of the nineteenth century. These were the minor theatres, whose right to exist was predicated upon their offering something other than straight "legitimate" drama. They circumvented the legal monopoly by presenting a variety of drama-music mixtures under the label of "burletta," a term that originally designated a popular version of opera with all lines sung.[8] Soon burlettas were staged that consisted of spoken dialogue interspersed with a number of songs, and eventually the term merged with and gave way to melodrama, in which the musical accompaniment might be reduced to a few pregnant chords.

The patent houses had a monopoly only on spoken, five-act, legitimate drama, so the minor theatres could operate legally as long as they confined their activities to burlettas, performing animals, one-man shows, and various forms of entertainment other than full-length nonmusical plays. The mushrooming minor theatres included Sadler's Wells (1765), the Lyceum (1765), the Royalty (1787), the Sans Souci (1796), Astley's Circus (1780; rebuilt as Astley's Amphitheatre in 1803), the Royal Circus (1782; rebuilt in 1804 and becoming the Surrey, without the circus ring, several years later), the Sans Pareil (1806; reopened as the Adelphi in 1819), and the Olympic (1806).[9] These theatres found an enthusiastic audience in the suburbs, the working-class areas of eastern London, and south of the Thames.

The minor theatres became so popular that, by the opening of the nineteenth century, managers of the two enlarged patent houses concluded that they had a monopoly on the wrong commodity. To meet their mounting expenses and attract an audience now accustomed to the delights of burletta and performing animals, they too began to offer fare that appealed to the taste for spectacle, novelty, and light entertainment. In 1803 Drury Lane managed to achieve a profit only by offering Frederick Reynolds's melodrama *The Caravan,* whose chief attraction was the scene where a dog named Carlo jumped into the water to save a drowning child (plate 9).[10] Several years later Covent Garden introduced Astley's performing horses on the legitimate stage. Lions were to follow. So were child prodigies; the "Master Betty" sensation, in which the thirteen-year-old "Infant Roscius" drew huge audiences to see the phenomenon at Covent Garden during the 1804–5 season, further demonstrated the depths to which the patent theatres were willing to sink in order to fill their houses. Of more lasting significance than animal spectacles and nine-day wonders was the increasing emphasis Drury Lane and Covent Garden were giving to burletta and melodrama, which appeared first as afterpieces and then mainpieces.

The decision to offer such entertainment was an economically sound one, for legitimate drama was no longer profitable—Covent Garden lost money on regular drama from 1809 to 1821, making profits only on the Christmas pantomimes and the spectacle productions[11]—but it had disastrous consequences. As the patent theatres tried to compete with the minors by producing burletta and spectacle, they further alienated the middle class and intellectual members of the audience even as they attracted the working class. Since the working-class patrons chose the least expensive seats, the management had to draw ever more of them. The changes snowballed. Larger working-class audiences meant more disruptions, more incidents of bottle throwing and other offenses to middle-class sensibilities. Middle-class men began to

express their fears of bringing their wives and families into such sordid sur-
roundings. These complaints sound a little contrived when we recall the tu-
mult and occasional violence among the well-bred patrons of the eighteenth-
century theatre, but the early nineteenth century was a time in which the
middle class was aggressively defining itself and marking its boundaries from
the working class; the theatres became one of many sites on which the battles
of class demarcation were fought.

The victory of the working-class audience was signaled by the Old Price
riots of 1809. When John Philip Kemble rebuilt Covent Garden, which had
burned to the ground the previous year, he reopened with higher ticket prices
and increased seating in the boxes at the expense of the gallery, thereby exhib-
iting a remarkable insensitivity to the changing nature of his audience. This
audience rebelled, calling for old prices, and for sixty-seven nights rioting
disrupted every performance. Finally Kemble capitulated to the demands of
the rioters and order was restored. The worst fears of the middle class had
been confirmed, however: the mob had won. From then on, middle-class
families found other forms of entertainment, while intellectuals and lovers of
literature contented themselves with reading drama rather than seeing it
performed.[12]

Of course there were exceptions. A star like Edmund Kean could bring an
audience from all classes back into the theatre. Nor did spectacle fail to appeal
to the more refined tastes of the elite. High society flocked to Drury Lane in
1838 to see Van Amburgh's trained lions; the queen herself went half a
dozen times, and it became fashionable to visit the theatre at feeding time. It
would therefore be a mistake to assume that the decline in the quality of
legitimate drama being performed or written was due solely to the peculiar
tastes of the working classes, for the Victorian fondness for sensation tran-
scended class divisions. On the whole, however, working-class patrons and
preferences dominated the theatre audiences of the first half of the nineteenth
century, just as the upper middle class had dominated the theatres a century
earlier. In 1826 an appalled German visitor summed up the prevailing atmosphere: "The most striking thing to a foreigner in English theatres is the
unheard-of coarseness and brutality of the audiences. The consequence of this
is that the higher and more civilized classes go only to the Italian opera, and
very rarely visit their national theatre. English freedom here degenerates into
the rudest license. . . ."[13]

Doldrums and the End of the Monopoly

There is no direct relationship between the social status of the theatre audience and the quality of the drama written for it, as the comparison of
Elizabethan with Restoration drama illustrates. The feeble condition of nineteenth-century drama was not simply a product of the debased tastes of the

working class, for their counterparts had applauded Marlowe and Shake-speare. Turning to the left point of the cultural diamond, therefore, one must ask why no Marlowe appeared in the first three-quarters of the nineteenth century.

One basic reason why few men or women of literary talent wrote for the theatre was that other forms of writing paid better, something not true for professional writers of the Elizabethan and Jacobean era. Nineteenth-century playwrights were vastly underpaid in comparison with their nondramatic peers, particularly the novelists. In a theatre of stars and visual spectacles, actors, designers technicians, even animal trainers drained a theatre manage-ment's resources, leaving little for the playwrights. The most famous play of the first half of the century, Dion Boucicault's *London Assurance,* earned only three hundred pounds for its author, while a writer who made fifty pounds on a melodrama was considered to be well recompensed.[14] Low pay encour-aged quantity over quality (James Robinson Planché turned out 152 plays between 1818 and 1849) and discouraged serious writers.[15]

If the prose writers had better things to do with their talent, the poets may have lacked the temperament for the craft of dramaturgy. Allardyce Nicoll has suggested that self-absorption on the part of the lyric poets, plus a certain snobbishness, rendered them incapable of transcending their own person-alities and seeing beyond themselves: "Both tragedy and comedy depend upon the ability of the author to forget for a moment his own petty loves and woes, or so to transform these that they become universal. This the romantic poets, because they were always thinking of themselves, failed to do."[16] Nic-oll's conception of the lyric poets as spoiled children may be a bit harsh, but it seems plausible that writers who see their output in terms of overflowing fountains of emotion, as did Wordsworth, will be little attracted to the struc-tural problems of dramaturgy. Those poets who did make some attempt to write drama tended to follow obsolete models and create characters of ex-quisite sensibility given to long monologues and little action. The gallery gods were not impressed.

While neither audience demand nor authorial capacities promoted dramat-ic quality, the organizational state of the London theatres perpetuated the general malaise. The patent theatres' economic troubles, caused by a com-bination of loss of an affluent audience, mismanagement, and inflation fol-lowing the Napoleonic Wars, continued. The financial debilitation of the legitimate houses, the competition from the minors, and the widespread per-ception of a decline in the drama being written and produced combined to exert pressure for reform.

Many looked to the end of the monopoly as the cure for the theatres' disease. In keeping with the laissez-faire spirit of the day, they argued that open competition among theatres would promote quality drama as well as economic efficiency. Furthermore, they pointed out, the constraints of the monopoly system were rapidly giving way in spite of the law. The patrons of the legitimate theatres demanded the same type of entertainment as that featured in the minors, and their demands were being met. At the same time, the minor theatres were openly challenging the majors even in the area of legitimate drama; by the 1840s, a few chords of music played during an otherwise nonmusical play qualified it for performance at one of the minors.[17] The border between burletta and drama was indistinct and crossed from both sides; Covent Garden labeled the music-free comedy *Tom Thumb* a burletta, while the Surrey offered a *Macbeth* with music.[18] Pieces from the repertory of the legitimate theatres began to be performed on the minor stages, often with the same actors on temporary leave from their regular homes. The distinction between the legitimate and illegitimate houses no longer obtained. An attempt to break the theatrical monopoly in 1832 narrowly failed. Finally, the Theatre Regulation Act of 1843 ended Drury Lane's and Covent Garden's century-old position of privilege.

The end of the monopoly, contrary to the expectations of the reformers, did not bring about an immediate revitalization of either the finances of the larger theatres or the quality of drama written and produced. From the 1820s to the 1860s neither the major nor minor theatres were able to sustain profitability from season to season. After 1843, the old patent houses and the minors engaged in a free-for-all competition for the same working-class audience. Convent Garden and Drury Lane now offered much the same spectacles and melodramas as their less illustrious counterparts, with the former finally giving up drama altogether in favor of opera. Theatre building ground to a halt under the laissez-faire system; while fourteen new theatres had been built during the 1830s through 1841, only one was built from the end of the monopoly until 1864.[19] Admission prices, which had been declining throughout the century, dropped still further. In 1839 a box seat at Drury Lane could be had for five shillings, a seat in the pit for two shillings sixpence; by 1852 the box seat went for four shillings, the pit seat for two.[20]

Playwrights still received little compensation from the major theatres and even less from the minors.[21] Writers with talent continued to direct their efforts to more rewarding fields, increasingly fiction. Authors of nondramatic literature, from Bryon to Dickens, did occasionally attempt to write a play, but since they lacked practical experience in the theatre, the results were usually dismal. Professional dramatists continued to be hacks, writing in volume with more speed than craft, borrowing freely from French drama, old plays, and the newspapers for their plots. The drama produced under such conditions did not immediately encourage the middle classes or the intellectuals to rediscover the national theatre.

Romantic criticism's veneration for Shakespeare and esteem for his contemporaries had the paradoxical effect of exacerbating the divorce between literature and the stage. Lamb's well-known view was that the very excellence of Shakespeare's plays made them less suited for performance than inferior works because stage enactment obscured the complexities of a character's mind and motivations; performances distracted the audience with irrelevant appeals to eye and ear through scenery, costuming, and the oratorical devices of "intellectual prize-fighters"; by giving material embodiment to dreams and abstractions, the stage either reduced them to a simple stimulus/response provoked by "the standard of flesh and blood" or, in the case of witches or fairies, shattered their hold over the imagination altogether. Worst of all, the stage eliminated distinctions between greater and lesser dramatic poets. Lamb's opinions went well beyond Shakespeare; while his *Dramatic Specimens* and essays introduced readers to the qualities of the less familiar Renaissance dramatists, he consistently represented their appreciation and criticism as responses of the reader, not the playgoer. For example, in a note describing his reaction to the episode in *The Revenger's Tragedy* where Vindici and his brother tempt their mother into urging their sister to become a courtesan, Lamb reports that "the reality and life of this Dialogue passes any scenical illusion I have even felt. I never read it but my ears tingle, and I feel a hot blush spread my cheeks, as if I were presently about to "proclaim" some such "malefactions" of myself. . . ."[22] Lamb's views were extreme, but even a practicing theatre critic like William Hazlitt was known to express a preference for reading plays over watching them. The coincidence of a highpoint of drama criticism in the early nineteenth century (the chief representatives being Coleridge, Leigh Hunt, Hazlitt, and Lamb) with a lowpoint in dramatic writing perhaps made such an attitude inevitable, for what was on the stage was indeed less rewarding than what was on the page, but this separation of literature from theatre did little to encourage either better writing or more revivals.

A comparison of the dramatic repertory of the Garrick years with that of the first half of the nineteenth century offers a striking illustration of the change undergone by the English theatre in less than a century. During the eighteenth century, a performance at one of the patent theatres usually included both a mainpiece (five acts) and an afterpiece (three or fewer acts). Thus the shorter afterpieces, which included farces, pantomimes, musicals, short comedies, and a variety of miscellaneous forms, did not compete with the mainpieces, which were predominantly comedies and tragedies; the long and short plays appeared together, complementing one another and producing a full evening's entertainment. Looking only at Drury Lane's repertory (Covent Garden followed the same pattern), one finds that there were actually a few more mainpieces than afterpieces during the Garrick era, both in terms of number of individual plays and in terms of performances.[23] This was because occasionally a long mainpiece precluded an afterpiece. As a rule however, long and short, "legitimate" drama and light entertainment, coexisted on the same bill.

In the early nineteenth century, on the other hand, legitimate and illegitimate dramatic forms were competing, as the minor theatres struggled with the patent houses for audiences. The result was a shift in the overall repertory of the theatres away from legitimate five-act, nonmusical drama and toward a wide variety of other types of entertainment. Table 6 tells the story of the vast differentiation that occurred.[24] The "miscellaneous" designation includes operettas, comic dramas, entertainments, ballad operas, domestic dramas, romantic dramas (Nicoll says these latter two should be considered as melodrama), one "eccentric drama," one "patriotic effusion," and some forty other designations.

If all works listed as "drama," "comedy," and "tragedy" are considered legitimate drama, the total accounts for less than a third of the dramatic output of the period (and even this estimate is generous, for many of the "comedies" were not full-length plays). In comparison with the Garrick era, there

TABLE 6   Early Nineteenth-Century Dramatic Repertory

Designation	Number	Percentage of repertory
Drama	180	21%
Melodrama	143	16%
Burletta	102	12%
Farce	96	11%
Comedy	56	6%
Tragedy	35	4%
Spectacle	29	3%
Pantomime	28	3%
Burlesque	22	3%
Comic opera	21	2%
Ballet	21	2%
Operatic farce	19	2%
Opera	16	2%
Comedietta	11	1%
Interlude	11	1%
Extravaganza	10	1%
Miscellaneous	67	8%
Total	867	98%

was a significant decline in the proportion of dramatic productions that were legitimate drama. The dominance of the hastily written and quickly forgotten short works featuring music, spectacle, pathos, and happy endings makes Vincent Crummles's ideas of novelty, and Reardon's disgust, perfectly understandable.

The Return of Respectability

Theatre managers, desperate for revenues during the mid-century, were willing to try anything. Some tried waterfalls, some tried displays of fireworks, some tried troops of elephants, and some even tried serious drama. Although its effect was slow in being felt, the end of the theatrical monopoly made possible the experimentation that was eventually to give new life to English drama.

Royal support gave critical impetus to the movement to restore the English stage. Queen Victoria, acceding the throne in 1837, gave prominent encouragement to theatrical revitalization. A lover of drama since childhood, she appealed to English patriotism for the restoration of the English theatre to its former stature. Setting a conspicuous example for her countrymen, she had Charles Kean produce entertainments for the royal family at Windsor Castle from 1848 until Albert's death in 1861. During the same period, she attended the public theatres, including the previously disreputable houses such as the Adelphi, the home of a particularly sensational form of gothic melodrama known as "Adelphi screamers." The hesitant middle classes could not help but be impressed.

Encouraged by such royal patronage and liberated from the monopoly, a number of managers tried, with a characteristic Victorian earnestness, to elevate their offerings and their audiences. Samuel Phelps at Sadler's Wells in the 1850s, Marie and Squire Bancroft at the Prince of Wales in the 1860s and '70s, and Henry Irving at the Lyceum in the 1880s and '90s made determined efforts to win back a middle-class audience and incorporate classical and serious modern works into their repertories. Perhaps the most important of these innovators was Charles Kean. During his management of the Princess Theatre from 1850 to 1859, he produced all but four of Shakespeare's plays. Using a combination of Shakespeare and "gentlemenly melodrama," Kean transformed his previously undistinguished theatre into a most respectable institution.

Samuel Phelps produced the greatest number of Renaissance revivals.[25] An eminent tragedian, Phelps took over the management of Sadler's Wells in 1844. Sadler's Wells was an old playhouse in Islington, far from the West End center of London theatre life. During the early nineteenth century it catered to a rough, suburban audience, offering them the usual fare of melodrama, acrobatics, and performing horses. It was especially renowned for its nautical melodramas, facilitated by two huge tanks of water above and under the stage. Neither the theatre nor the audience seemed promising for the reestablishment of legitimate drama, but Phelps opened his tenure with a handbill proclaiming his intentions: to make Sadler's Wells into "what a Theatre ought to be; a place for justly representing the works of our great dramatic poets" and "a resort of the respectable inhabitants of the neighborhood."[26] Phelps encouraged a certain middle-class standard of behavior in the old Sadler's Wells audience, for example by forbidding patrons to bring babies under three years old into the theatre. More important, he attracted a new audience through such appeals to refined sensibilities as increasing the number of high-priced box seats and providing the boxes with separate entrances so the genteel playgoers did not have to rub shoulders with the hoi polloi in the lobby.

Beyond such theatrical innovations, Phelps made a dramatic one: he offered legitimate English drama, which had become virtually unheard of in the West End. Phelps's devotion to Shakespeare is demonstrated by the fact that of the 3,472 performing nights of his eighteen-year tenure, 1,632 included a Shakespeare play.[27] He did not limit himself to the most popular plays of the canon, but performed thirty-one plays attributed to Shakespeare, neglecting only *Troilus and Cressida, Henry VI, Richard II,* and *Titus Andronicus.* Going even beyond the less familiar works of Shakespeare, he produced *The Duchess of Malfi* and Rowley's *The New Wonder—A Woman Never Vext* for a single season apiece. He also staged four plays of the Beaumont and Fletcher canon, including an adaptation of *The Maid's Tragedy,* and three of Massinger's plays, including *A New Way to Pay Old Debts,* in which Phelps himself played Sir Giles. Sheridan Knowles's 1837 adaptation of *The Maid's Tragedy,* named *The Bridal,* had converted it into a star vehicle for the actor playing the noble Melantius, devoted to honor and friendship; it also catered to nineteenth-century delicacy by obscuring the nature of the relationship between Evadne and the king and by deleting the coarser lines. Phelps starred in the Sadler's Wells productions of the play, which was performed during eight seasons.

Although Albert's death ended her own attendance, Victoria retained an interest in encouraging the middle classes to return to the theatres. Her knighting of Henry Irving in 1895, the first actor to be so honored, capped the effort to bring respectability, and the respectable, back to the London theatres. By the last two decades of the nineteenth century, attending the theatre had once again become proper and even fashionable.

As the middle class returned to the late nineteenth-century theatre, the working class began to abandon it in favor of the music halls. Descendants of the old minor theatres, the music halls offered an appealing combination of farce and variety acts, plus a convenient tavern in an adjoining room. By the turn of the century, the entertainment demands of the working class were being met by the music halls and, increasingly, the cinema. In a complete reversal, the audience for the legitimate stage had become not heterogeneous, but solidly middle class.

In addition to the end of the theatrical monopoly and the desertion and return of the middle class, the nineteenth-century theatre is remembered for its advances in technology. Improvements in the means for moving flats and backdrops, elaborate traps that allowed characters to make their entrances and exits through walls and floors, devices for sending angels and demons flying above the stage, the introduction of gaslights—all such developments facilitated catering to the pleasures of the eye. The sense of illusion was heightened by the final disappearance of the jutting apron. The acting now was entirely behind the proscenium arch, which was painted and ornamented like the picture frame it suggested.

Within this frame, the settings contained greater detail and authenticity than had previously been known. Charles Kean's antiquarianism led him to produce Shakespeare not in anything like an actual Elizabethan stage setting, but in the setting of a Danish court or Roman forum as suggested by the play. Madame Vestris expended the same attention to detail on interior settings such as drawing rooms, a trend that eventually culminated in the complete box set. The actor-audience intimacy of the eighteenth-century theatre, an intimacy that had emphasized the artificiality of the production, was transformed into the late nineteenth-century theatre of illusion. Now the audience was an unacknowledged observer looking through a picture frame or a fourth wall. Such was the style of presentation inherited by the twentieth century.

RENAISSANCE REVIVALS IN THE NINETEENTH CENTURY

The nineteenth-century theatre seldom produced any old plays. Shakespeare, who now occupied an orbit completely different from that of his contemporaries, was the only Renaissance dramatist who maintained a continuing presence on the English stage.

City comedies lost the privileged position they had occupied in the eighteenth century. Jonson all but disappeared from the stage after the first quarter of the century, although *Every Man in His Humor* was occasionally revived, the role of Captain Bobadil having become something of a star vehicle. Other city comedies were absent, the single exception being *A New Way to Pay Old Debts*. Edmund Kean created a sensation with his portrayal of Sir Giles Overreach in 1816. During his first performance, the audience cheered and screamed; one of the actresses fainted from the intensity of Kean's performance; Lord Byron rushed backstage to pump Kean's hand and exclaim, "Great! Great! By Jove, that was acting."[28] Thereafter, the challenge of

Kean's Sir Giles, which itself followed the success of Cooke and Kemble, attracted both established stars and aspiring actors, and the pleasure of comparing different performances of this role appears to have overcome the Victorian audience's general distaste for Renaissance comedy (see plates 10 and 11).

The absence of revenge tragedies continued. Every now and then a revival was attempted. Kean produced *The Jew of Malta* in 1818, taking the role of Barabas himself. In the 1850s, the American Negro actor Ira Aldridge brought *Titus Andronicus* to London twice. Phelps made *The Bridal* (*The Maid's Tragedy*) and *The Duchess of Malfi* briefly popular in mid-century. But such individual attempts were regarded as novelties, did not remain long in the repertories as a rule, and spawned no successors. Spectacular and bloody as revenge tragedies were, they were no match for lions and tigers in their state of native ferocity.

At the close of the century, a small audience, under the tutelage of William Poel, began to take a renewed interest in the performance of classic English drama. Influenced, if not always captivated, by the wave of realistic drama coming from the Continent, some theatregoers had finally begun to weary of the spectacles, melodramas, and farces that had been the staples of the Victorian theatre. Through prodigious efforts to turn the attention of the intellectual and affluent members of the audience toward serious national drama, Poel almost single-handedly constructed and promoted a turn-of-the-century Elizabethan revival.[29] Poel himself came from a privileged background. His father was a distinguished civil engineer and musician, a professor of engineering at University College, London, a vice-president of the Royal Society as well as vice-president of the Royal College of Organists; his mother came from a family of eminent clergymen and musicians. He did not follow his elder brothers to Oxford and Cambridge because of his supposedly frail constitution (he lived to be eighty-two). Instead, after a rather aimless youth spent working for a building firm and keeping a journal of theatre criticism, Poel was moved to join a provincial touring company as the first step toward a stage career. He got his practical training from working in several theatre companies in the 1870s, and in 1879 he had organized a small touring company, "The Elizabethans," dedicated to bringing Shakespeare to the provinces. By the 1880s he was producing and directing a variety of plays, including Shakespeare, and advocating his Elizabethan reform ideas in lectures and publications.

Poel emphasized both authenticity and rediscovery.[30] He wanted to perform Shakespeare in conditions that approximated those of the Elizabethan theatre, without the elaboration of scenery and special effects that had been increasing ever since the Restoration. Having attracted some interest and financial backing, Poel formed the Elizabethan Stage Society in 1894. Its productions, which generally ran for only one or two performances, featured Elizabethan costumes, a minimum of scenery, and a determined effort to eschew Victorian conventions in favor of what was understood to be the stagecraft of Shakespeare's day.

The Elizabethan Stage Society dusted off some of the non-Shakespearean canon of the Renaissance period as well. Poel had produced *The Duchess of Malfi* for the Independent Theatre Society in 1892. The third production of his Elizabethan Stage Society, performed in 1895, was the long-neglected *Doctor Faustus,* and by the turn of the century he had produced *Arden of Feversham,* Beaumont and Fletcher's *The Coxcomb,* Middleton and Rowley's *The Spanish Gipsy,* Ford's *The Broken Heart,* and *The Alchemist.* Poel's revival activity exhibited no particular intention beyond his desire to stage neglected masterpieces in something approaching their original production conditions. Plays were aired for the sake of the airing, and were usually given only one or two performances.

His revivals were not random, however, and their pattern reveals Poel's view of Shakespearean comedy as the key to building an audience for Renaissance drama. Five of the seven productions of the Society's first three years (1895–98) were Shakespearean comedy; the other two were Renaissance tragedies.[31] During the next three years, the Society branched out, producing unfamiliar Renaissance comedies (*The Spanish Gipsy*), plays by foreign playwrights, and Shakespeare's rarely performed *Richard II,* with only one Shakespeare comedy staged during this middle period. Poel later returned to the comedies (although not so exclusively as before) in what may have been an attempt to build up the Society's sagging fortunes. Clearly Poel believed that Shakespeare's comedies would prepare the way for less familiar and more somber revivals.

Poel's Renaissance revivals did not catch on or make the jump to the commercial theatre. They made no profits, with the happy exception of the 1901 production of *Everyman.* But the critics strongly supported Poel's objectives. They approved of the restoration of the original texts of Shakespeare and other Renaissance dramatists, the use of Elizabethan costumes rather than those of Rome or Denmark, and the paring away of the scenic elaboration that had accumulated throughout the previous two centuries. They were somewhat harsher toward the actual productions, for many of the actors were amateurs and Poel himself was untalented as a player. Overall, theatre critics applauded Poel's aims while recognizing his limits. One typical reviewer said of the 1904 production of *Doctor Faustus:*

> Like all the Society's work, the performance of *Faustus* keeps you, at any rate while it lasts, in that state of grave and childlike absorption and of freedom from our modern affliction of knowingness. . . . Everybody's mind was for the

> moment simplified—not, indeed, to the point of sharing
> Elizabethan joy in such a play, but to the point of genuine
> interest in that joy and partial comprehension of it.[32]

Admired though he was, Poel's achievements were an exception to the rule. During most of the Victorian period and beyond, institutional constraints prevented commercial theatre managers from taking chances on Renaissance revivals, for their theatres simply could not afford the experimentation of an Elizabethan Stage Society. The size of the theatres and behavior of the audiences discouraged drama dependent on hearing the spoken word. The social composition of the audience during most of the century discouraged drama that required much education or the motivation to cope with unfamiliar material. The competition among the varieties of available entertainment discouraged legitimate drama in general.

Moreover, the nineteenth-century theatrical public understood a specific set of dramatic conventions, those associated with melodrama.[33] The problem that melodrama posed for Renaissance revivals was not simply that melodrama was a formulaic genre that somehow stupefied its audiences. Popular culture is always formulaic; Kydian revenge tragedy and Middletonian city comedy were clearly so. The problem was that the presuppositions cultivated by melodrama were antithetical to the conventions of city comedy and revenge tragedy. Melodrama is characterized by moral certitude. The good characters are unfalteringly good, the bad characters bad from beginning to end, and deserts are always just. Such a "moral fantasy" is diametrically opposed to the ambiguities of revenge tragedy and city comedy, where revengers are good but also evil, where gallants are immoral but also heroes.[34] An audience schooled in melodrama was ill-equipped to appreciate the ironies offered by the Renaissance masters.

So while a Renaissance play was occasionally revived throughout the century, when a city comedy or revenge tragedy was staged because of its star role, the will of the manager, or some other reason, it did not catch on and start a trend, for its audience was unprepared to receive it. It was unprepared not only because of its training in the conventions of spectacle and melodrama, but because the social sources of appeal of these plays were not especially salient for it. The revenge tragedy tension between order and freedom, the central government versus the rights of the individual, was a pressing concern for a John Stuart Mill but not for the working-class members of the mid-century theatre audiences. This same audience neither anticipated much social mobility nor had reason to favor the existing social hierarchy, so the city comedy theme of economic opportunity within a rigid system of social stratification had no special appeal. Such themes might have been of greater interest to the middle-class audiences who had returned to the theatres by the end of the century, but they too had been trained by the prevailing theatrical conventions. Their tastes were conservative; they liked "gentlemanly" melo-drama, but melodrama nonetheless. The ambiguities and ironies of revenge tragedy and city comedy were neither attractive nor especially relevant to the dominant groups within the nineteenth-century audience. Kean, Phelps, and Poel might experiment with non-Shakespearean Renaissance revivals, but these remained experiments and not harbingers.

RENAISSANCE REVIVALS FROM
THE EDWARDIANS TO
THE ARTS COUNCIL

During the twentieth century, Renaissance revivals changed from being an endangered species to one that was stable and self-reproducing. Modern theatregoers have enjoyed more opportunities to see Renaissance drama than have any of their counterparts since the early Restoration. Shakespeare's warhorses have been trotted across the stage as always, but they have been joined by a herd of less familiar beasts: morality plays, pastorals, mystery cycles, masques, and our genres of particular interest, city comedies and revenge tragedies.

The first task of this chapter is to examine the institutional changes that allowed and encouraged the rediscovery and reconstruction of old plays. Next comes an analysis of the patterns of revivals of various types of Renaissance drama. Here, taking advantage of the detailed data available for this period, I shall distinguish among various categories of drama: popular and infrequently performed Shakespeare; Renaissance comedies, tragedies, and miscellaneous categories; and then city comedy and revenge tragedy. Finally I shall attempt to account for the particular success of revenge tragedy since the mid-1950s.

TWENTIETH-CENTURY LONDON THEATRE

The modern London theatre emerged from institutional changes established around the turn of the century. During the Edwardian era most of the major influences on the twentieth-century theatre were in place, including the persistence of an affluent and highly educated audience, the continued absence of the working class, the split between commercial ("West End") and art theatres, and the competition between the theatre and the electronic media. The one major development still to come was the public subsidization of the theatre following the Second World War. These factors have set the possibilities and limits for modern Renaissance revivals.

Turn-of-the-Century Transition

By the closing decades of the nineteenth century, the theatres of London had
become eminently respectable.[1] Evening dress was the rule for those sitting
in the stalls (orchestra) or dress circle (first balcony). Performances began at
8:00, allowing for the later dining hour of people above the working class. As
a consequence, the evening's bill had been reduced to a single play, with
perhaps some modest opening entertainment. Theatres were luxuriously fur-
nished and appointed. The ratio of reserved to unreserved seats increased.
Matinees, available only to persons of leisure, were popular. Birthdays and
other middle-class celebrations took the form of theatre parties.

The basis of the London audience grew broader geographically and nar-
rower socially. Theatregoers were not limited to the elite coterie of a Blackfriars or a Dorset Gardens; less privileged people could well afford gallery
seats, though they were required to adhere to middle-class standards of behavior. Most members of the working class, however, sought the livelier atmosphere of the music halls and, after the turn of the century, the cinema. At
the same time improvements in public transportation enabled middle-class
residents of the outskirts and suburbs of London to attend the theatre regularly and easily. Drawing patrons from the periphery into the cultural center
of the West End, the London theatre increased its potential audience of the
relatively well-to-do.

One consequence of this increase was to encourage theatre managers to
offer longer and longer runs of popular productions. In the 1850s there had
been only fifteen productions running over one hundred nights.[2] During the
period 1900 to 1914, forty-nine productions ran over 350 performances.[3]
Such hits, far more profitable than the varied offerings of a repertory system,
became the goal of the West End managers.

Like their audiences, the actors, managers, and dramatists rose in reputation and affluence. Salaries of actors increased markedly, and actors moved
freely from theatre to theatre with each new production. Their training was
no longer a matter of what they picked up while touring the provinces; the
Royal Academy of Dramatic Art opened in 1904, the Central School of
Speech and Drama two years later. Dramatists' revenues and their rights to
their literary property, following the modernization of copyright laws, took a
turn for the better. The traditional actor-manager, whose lineage went back
to Shakespeare and Garrick, finally began to give way; Henry Irving, who
died in 1905, was one of the last. Commercial theatre managers became businessmen who ran their theatres like any other company.

Most significant for the future of Renaissance revivals was the split that
took place between commercial and noncommercial theatres, a split that to
some extent occurred within the theatre audience as well. This was the split
between "serious," "progressive," or "modern" drama on the one hand and

"entertainment" on the other. It was the split between "little" or "art" theatres and the West End, the split between intellectuals like Gissing's Reardon,
who claimed there was no theatre in England, and the well-dressed members
of polite society who filled the playhouses.

Many intellectuals complained that the theatre had become like its audience: prosperous, conservative, and dull. They compared the English musical comedies and melodramas with the revolutionary drama on the continent,
the realism of Ibsen, the theatrical experiments of André Antoine's Théâtre
Libre. They saw Ibsen reviled as "wretched, deplorable, loathsome" by Clement Scott, the period's most influential and reactionary critic.[4] They saw that
the innovations of Chekhov, Hauptmann, Strindberg, and other continental
playwrights were virtually unknown in England. They saw only one of
Shaw's plays performed in public theatre before 1900. They saw Oscar
Wilde imprisoned for violating English standards of decency. They saw a
theatre more concerned with catering to and perpetuating such standards
than with offending its audiences with naturalism, social criticism, or too
much intellectual challenge.

The intellectuals responded to the conservatism of the West End with an
outburst of "little" or "independent" theatre societies.[5] The movement in
England began in 1891 when J. T. Grein, a Dutch immigrant influenced by
Antoine's example, founded the Independent Theatre to produce plays having artistic rather than commercial value. He opened with *Ghosts,* to the outrage of Scott and other conservative critics as well as the general public.
Thérèse Raquin, Grein's second production, similarly offended with its harsh
naturalism. The next year the Independent Theatre presented *Widowers'
Houses,* Shaw's first play and one that contributed to the theatre's reputation
for controversy. Grein produced contemporary European plays for five more
years, though his theatre's audience remained small and its finances dismal.

A direct and more enduring successor to the Independent Theatre was the
Stage Society, founded in 1899 to "promote and encourage Dramatic Art;
to serve as an Experimental Theatre."[6] The Stage Society performed on
Sunday afternoons with professional actors, minimal scenery, and low production costs. Subscribers paid annual dues of one pound, plus an additional
entrance fee for each performance; by the outbreak of World War I, there
were 1,500 members. Since technically it was not a theatre, the Society was
able to avoid the censorship, the long runs, and the star system of the commercial West End. Best remembered for its productions of Shaw, the Stage
Society performed Yeats, Somerset Maugham, Arnold Bennett, Granville
Barker, Ibsen, Chekhov, Tolstoy, Hauptmann, and all of the important contemporary dramatists of both England and the continent. Lasting until the
beginning of World War II, it produced some two hundred plays, never for
more than one or two performances each.

Wanting to maintain its devotion to modern drama, the Stage Society generated an offshoot in 1919 named the Phoenix Society, which was dedicated to the revival of English classics. Many other theatre societies and experimental theatres appeared during the first quarter of the century: the Pioneer (1905), the Play Actors Society (1907), the English Drama Society, which revived the Chester mystery plays during the 1906–7 season, the Fellowship of Players (1922), which was dedicated to Shakespeare, Poel's Elizabethan Stage Circle (1927), and the Renaissance Theatre (1925). One important variation on the private theatre society theme was the Lyric, Hammersmith, whose first producer, Nigel Playfair (1918–32), emphasized the amateur qualities of his theatre, dedicated to "amusement" only; at the same time he employed professional actors, staged an important series of eighteenth-century revivals and modern experimental works, and managed to create that rarity, a theatre that was at once prosperous, fashionable, and dramatically challenging. The Gate Theatre (1925–41) similarly straddled the line between art and commercial theatres; it was a private club catering to intellectuals, but its innovative offerings, many continental or American, ran for several weeks and drew considerably more attention than those of the "Sunday societies."

The repertory theatre movement, in which an ensemble of actors offered a rotating variety of plays in the manner of the eighteenth-century theatre, was another innovation that grew up with the theatre societies and was similarly opposed to the long-run commercial system. The Lyceum (1899), the Court (1904, later the Royal Court), the Duke of York (1910), and the Old Vic, where Lilian Bayles produced every play in Shakespeare's First Folio between 1914 and 1923, were repertory theatres outstanding in ambition and achievement. Offering a far wider variety of classic and modern drama than could be found in the West End, the repertory theatres fueled the old dream of a national theatre (a dream not to be fulfilled until 1976). Like the theatre societies, they made possible revivals that the West End would never attempt.

The World Wars and Between

The Great War disrupted every aspect of English life, and the theatre was no exception. Young actors left the stage, many never to return. Theatres were forced to close early, and reductions in public transportation made them harder to reach. Paper for advertising posters was scarce. The more frail of the art and repertory theatres closed for good. What audience there was flocked to see light, escapist entertainment; the oriental musical extravaganza *Chu Chin Chow* (Norton and Asche, 1916) achieved the longest run the London stage had ever seen (2,238 consecutive performances), while patriotic hearts were stirred by such fare as *For England, Home, and Beauty* (Andrew Emm, 1915).

Perhaps the war's most lasting theatrical legacy was economic. Production costs quadrupled, and would increase still further after Versailles. Investors, often businessmen who had profited during the war, bought up groups of theatres, then subleased them. By the end of the war the actor-manager had given way almost entirely to the prudent businessman. High costs, a management unencumbered by literary or dramaturgical aspirations, and the increasing competition from Hollywood films and later radio encouraged a conservative theatrical strategy. Managers aimed at long runs, and they favored musicals, spectacles that might attract patrons of the cinema, and inexpensive plays having small casts and single sets. Such strategy worked at first, with the theatre enjoying an economic boom during the early 1920s, but prosperity did not last. By 1930 three-quarters of the nonmusical plays produced in London lost money.[7] Reviews, musical comedies, star vehicles for matinee idols, mysteries, farces, and occasionally serious plays were all mounted in the endless search for a hit.

The impetus for "the other theatre," an intellectual alternative to the West End, thus continued, and new art theatres replaced those lost during the war.[8] Most significant for the present study was the aforementioned Phoenix Society. Founded by Allen Wade in 1919, this company revived twenty-six Renaissance and Restoration plays, many for the first time, in the six years of its existence. Its productions never ran for more than one or two performances, nor did they attract a mass audience, but following Poel's precedent, they generated intense interest in revivals of the less familiar classics of English drama.[9] For several years the Phoenix was blessed with an aristocratic clientele, Lady Cunard being a prominent supporter. Its performances "drew a more distinguished audience than any ordinary first night," until the film societies seduced the attention of the fashionably fickle.[10] Though only in existence for a half-dozen years, the Phoenix Society is generally credited with having firmly reestablished non-Shakespearean Renaissance drama on the English stage through the quality of its performances and the prestige of its audience.

Other noncommercial theatres revived English classics during the interwar years. The Renaissance Theatre, a Sunday society similar to the Phoenix, produced several Renaissance and Restoration plays during its short life in 1925. The Old Vic continued to present Shakespeare and other old plays, and its company attracted the finest actors emerging in the interwar period, including Tyrone Guthrie, John Gielgud, Alec Guinness, Ralph Richardson, and Laurence Olivier, who was to become its manager following the Second World War. Audiences for the noncommercial theatres included intellectuals and serious students of drama, as well as some members of the middle-class audience of the West End.

The gap between the commercial and art theatres troubled a number of observers. In 1924 Frank Vernon described "two theatres," that of serious drama and of the musical comedy and reviews.[11] "The ear beats the eye in the theatre proper; in the other theatre (which shall not be called improper), in the theatre of light entertainment, the eye beats the ear" (p. 17). Vernon speculated that the serious theatre was improving in quality "in sheer self-defense" against pressure from the more popular theatre. More likely, the fortunes of "proper" theatre were enhanced by a narrowing base of intellectual and educated middle-class theatregoers. Both theatre audiences were becoming more "serious," for the mass audience was in the cinema, and the theatre, as always, was responding to its audience's tastes.

World War II permanently altered the physical face and economic life-blood of the English theatre. The bombing of London demolished many theatres, partially destroying the Old Vic, Drury Lane, the Queen's and Sadler's Wells, while obliterating the Shaftesbury; only the Windmill ("We never closed") remained operating throughout the Battle of Britain. Air raids, the blackout, wartime restrictions, and the evacuation of London caused the struggling city theatres to close and reopen on an irregular basis. The general evacuation encouraged the development of touring companies and regional theatres to meet the entertainment needs of a nation at war, and, for the first time, the government itself took on the responsibility for meeting those needs.

The Council for the Encouragement of Music and the Arts, formed in 1939 from a combination of state (Board of Education) and private (Pilgrim Trust and Carnegie United Kingdom Trust) resources, bolstered English morale by bringing cultural programs to the dislocated urban population while providing artists with employment. CEMA, which became entirely state-funded after 1942, sponsored touring companies that played in army camps, hospitals, air-raid shelters, factories, evacuation centers throughout the provinces, and wherever the war had thrown people together. The Old Vic company, which could no longer play in its damaged playhouse, was active as a CEMA touring company, as was the Sadler's Wells opera and ballet. At one time there were sixteen different touring companies playing throughout the nation, and they brought classic works of English culture, especially Shakespeare, to new audiences. The creation of a taste for serious drama among a substantial portion of this captive audience had three postwar legacies: continued government support of serious theatre, the growth of repertory theatre outside of London, and the renewed demand for a national theatre.

The theatrical consequences of the First and Second World Wars were thus remarkably different. The earlier war had halted the movement toward more challenging drama. Patriotic jingoism and lightweight escapism dominated the stage; serious modern drama all but disappeared, and the classics held out only at the Old Vic. The London theatre participated in the odd wartime bifurcation of English life, as Tommies on leave from the trenches took their girls to see *Chu Chin Chow*. The theatres were taken over by businessmen and combines attracted to the sure profits of the wartime theatre; these groups had no incentive to experiment, and the West End became even more safe, predictable, and dull.

In contrast, the Second World War gave a boost to serious drama, especially classics, through its government-supported attempts to bring the best of English culture to the dispersed population. The BBC contributed to this effort, for its radio drama likewise reached a captive audience and cultivated the dramatic tastes of some of its listeners. Thus, by the end of this war, the potential audience for more substantial theatrical fare had been broadened geographically, and the precedent for state provision of cultural welfare had been firmly established.

Postwar Theatre

Public support of the arts, the one aspect of the welfare state that was virtually unchallenged, changed the face of the postwar English theatre by allowing far greater innovation than was possible in the commercial theatres.[12] CEMA, reformed as the Arts Council of Great Britain in 1946, expanded its role

> to develop a greater knowledge, understanding, and practice of the fine arts exclusively, and in particular to increase the accessibility of the fine arts to the public . . . and to improve the standard of execution of the fine arts and cooperate with our Government Departments, local authorities and other bodies on any matters concerned directly or indirectly with those objects.[13]

The Arts Council makes direct grants to noncommercial (non-profit-distributing) theatre companies in London and the provinces, and it assists in the revivals of neglected older plays, as well as approved new ones, by direct guarantees against financial loss. It also sponsors training programs for theatre managers and designers and gives some support to new playwrights. Arts Council grants constitute roughly half of the revenue of the major noncommercial theatres.[14]

The National Theatre, opened amid much fanfare in 1976, symbolized the government's commitment to the proposition that the English theatre should not be totally dependent on the market. In addition to the National, the major subsidized London theatres during the postwar era have been the Royal Shakespeare Company, the Mermaid, the Royal Court, and the Old Vic. As appendix B indicates, these are the theatres in which Renaissance revivals have flourished.

The existence of government-supported, noncommercial theatres created a new phenomenon: large-scale, even lavish, productions of serious drama, old and new. Noncommercial theatres have also been experimental in design, with flexible staging arrangements used to reestablish the actor-audience closeness lost during the preceding century. They have not been successful at being a truly popular theatre, however. The nation as a whole may pay for these theatres, but it is still the upper and middle classes, the intellectuals, and the tourists who attend them.

For despite government support and the attempts of the theatres to draw a popular following, the London theatre audience has remained obdurately educated and affluent. The entertainments that have successfully competed with the theatres in winning a mass audience have changed almost entirely during the course of the century. The music halls started to decline following the licensing acts beginning in 1902, which prohibited them from offering alcoholic refreshment along with the entertainment, but the cinema and later television took their place in capturing the working-class audiences, who never returned to the theatres. Nowadays, the upper circle is likely to be filled with students and tourists, a far more passive group than the gallery gods of previous centuries.

A 1965 survey of the audiences of British performing arts, which included ballet, symphony, and opera as well as theatre, revealed that while 60.5% of the total male population was engaged in blue-collar occupations, only 4.5% of the performing arts' audience came from this class.[15] Audience members were wealthier than their nonattending contemporaries, with median incomes of £1,676, as opposed to the national average of £990, and they were far better educated. Almost half of the males (48.5%) and 42.3% of the females had been in school until the age of twenty or older; for the population at large, only 3.7% of the males and 2.7% of the females had stayed in school that long. Although these percentages are from a combination of audiences, the conclusions of the survey go on to say that

> the British theatre seems to draw its audience from a partic-
> ularly exclusive group. In our sample the members of the-
> atre audiences have higher educational levels and higher
> incomes and are more frequently in the professional classifi-
> cation then the members of other audiences. The theatre
> also has the highest frequency of attendance. . . .[16]

London theatres depend upon this educated, affluent, and faithful audience, plus a large number of overseas tourists, to fill their houses.[17]

The twentieth-century repertory of both commercial and noncommercial London theatres has been shaped by the tastes of this privileged group. Their influence is especially direct in the case of the major commercial theatres collectively known as the West End, in which box-office ticket sales are the sole measure of success. As discussed above, sharply increased production costs during and following World War I made these theatres dependent on long-running comedies, melodramas, and musicals, popular forms with proven ability to draw large audiences. Today the situation remains the same. Musicals, mysteries, American imports, and shows specifically aimed at the tourist trade such as *No Sex, Please—We're British* predominate in the West End.

After World War II, the noncommercial or "other" theatre movement followed two channels. The larger theatres like the Old Vic, now relatively secure thanks to Arts Council support, produced classics and contemporary drama that the West End would not risk. At the same time a number of smaller alternative theatres, also known as the fringe theatres because of their location outside of the West End, emerged. Both types of non–West End theatre have had two basic objectives. One goal has been to allow innovative dramatists, iconoclastic directors, and (especially in the case of the fringe theatres) inexperienced actors to get a showing. This goal was resoundingly achieved by the success of the English Stage Company at the Royal Court theatre, notably with John Osborne's *Look Back in Anger* in 1956. Fringe theatres, typically small, experimental, politically engaged, and economically shaky, have continued to provide an alternative to the more commercially oriented fare of the West End. Many have been short-lived; some alternative theatres like the Royal Court have been rather domesticated by their success; all have provided training grounds for actors and dramatists.

The second objective, that of luring the mass public back into the theatre, has not been achieved. Perhaps the boldest attempt to bring back the working class was Joan Littlewood's Theatre Royal, Stratford East, founded in the run-down East End of London in 1953. Littlewood wanted to form a proletarian theatre audience by setting a "fun palace" in the center of a working-class neighborhood. Plays were selected for their topicality and social message. To her distress, the Stratford East productions were a great success with the intellectuals and liberal-to-radical segments of the upper middle class, but the working class stayed home with the telly. Audiences for fringe threatres have continued to be a young, intellectual, left-wing subset of the upper-middle-class general theatre audience, while the larger noncommercial theatres attract both groups.

RENAISSANCE REVIVALS IN THE TWENTIETH CENTURY

As an institutional context for repertory decisions, the twentieth-century London theatre has favored a wide variety of Renaissance revivals. Since the documentation of productions is richer than that of the previous century, and since the beginning and end of any individual revival is more clearly defined than in the case of the eighteenth-century repertory system, revival trends during the modern period can be analyzed in considerable detail, as indicated by the tables for this chapter.

Table 7 shows the number of new productions in the London theatre during five-year periods following World War I, and the proportion of these productions that were revivals.[18] (All tables and figures for the chapter are collected at its end.) General patterns of theatrical activity emerge, as illustrated in figure 5. The early 1930s had the greatest number of new productions, with the late twenties and late thirties also ranking high on this measure of theatrical activity. Following the decline of activity during World War II (though it is amazing how active the London theatre was during the war), the theatre recovered quickly and rose to equal the immediate prewar level of new productions.

A sharp decrease in the number of new productions occurred in the mid-fifties, from which the London theatre has never recovered. From an average of over 250 individual productions per year for more than three decades except during wartime, the average dropped to about 180 per year during the twenty-five years after 1955. The reason for this abrupt drop is not hard to find: in 1955 Independent Television began its commercial broadcasting. The response to ITV, representing the demand for light entertainment which the BBC had left unfulfilled, was enormous: in 1955, forty percent of the population had a television, by 1960, the figure was over ninety percent.[19] Theatre-going declined correspondingly. For many middle-class Britons, going to the theatre changed from a habit to an event.

Over the course of the century, about one-quarter of all new productions have been revivals. There was an unusually high revival rate in the early 1920s, when the theatre was still recovering from the war and a generation of new dramatists had been decimated. In the period of high theatrical activity beginning in the mid-twenties, the revival rate had dropped to less than a quarter of all productions, declining further in the late 1930s. During World War II, it rose to well over one-third of all productions; both the wartime restrictions on theatrical activity and the preferences of what remained of the London audience favored the familiar. After the war, the percentage of revivals declined gradually through the 1950s. During the early 1960s there was a significant jump in the revival rate, and revivals have continued to account for about one-quarter of all productions in the London theatre.

What does this pattern of productions and revivals mean? To begin with, one must not draw hasty conclusions regarding the "health" of the London theatre from the figures in table 7. A large number of new productions might mean either a lively, growing theatre scene or one having an abnormally high number of failures, the early thirties being a case in point. As chapter 4 showed, the robust theatre of Garrick had relatively few new productions. Similarly, a high rate of revivals may indicate a theatre whose managers want to avoid risk by choosing plays of known audience appeal. On the other hand, some revivals are extremely risky; *Blithe Spirit* may be a certain crowd-pleaser, but *Women Beware Women* is a different proposition altogether.

Without making any assumptions about the general meaning of the number of new productions or the proportion of revivals, one may nevertheless make a few observations about the patterns observable in figure 5. First, there seems to be no simple relationship between theatrical activity and the general state of the economy. New productions were frequent during the Depression and during the prosperous early 1950s; they rose with the economy in the twenties, yet also rose in the seventies when the economy was increasingly troubled. Aside from the fact that a massive shift in resources during wartime curtails theatrical activity, one can find no direct indication of the prosperity of the nation by looking at the production activity of the theatre.

Revival activity usually corresponds with the general level of theatrical activity as measured by new productions. The two rates rise and fall together; relatively flat periods in terms of new productions, as in the sixties, are flat for revivals as well. Some modest changes in the proportion of revivals are suggestive. A rise in overall theatrical activity is apt to be associated with a decline in the proportion of that activity accounted for by revivals. Of the six periods of rising theatrical activity, three reveal a significant decrease in revivals, one reveals an increase, and in two there is no significant change. (See appendix C for relevant statistics.) The period from the late fifties to the early sixties is an oddity, in that an increase in overall theatrical activity is associated with an increase in the percentage of that activity accounted for by revivals. The late fifties were an unusual period, having the lowest revival rate of the century, perhaps because theatres were all looking for another John Osborne.

If increases in new productions are often associated with a decreasing proportion of revivals, the reverse does not seem to be the case. Of the four periods showing decreasing productions, three showed no significant change in the proportion of revivals; only the World War II decline saw revivals accounting for a disproportionate share of the diminished theatrical activity. The period from the late sixties to the early seventies was unusual, for while overall theatrical activity was declining, the absolute number and the percentage of revivals went up, though the change was not statistically significant.

Now we may examine where Renaissance drama fits into this general picture. Tables 8 through 12 give the number of productions of frequently performed and infrequently performed Shakespeare plays, non-Shakespearean Renaissance plays, and revenge tragedies and city comedies. In these tables, each separate production of an individual play is counted as one revival. (This is in contrast to the number of plays revived as shown in figure 4 and listed in appendix B, which consider only whether or not a particular play was revived during a given decade and do not reflect the number of productions.) Since ample data exist on the stage histories of the specific plays listed, I have been able to trace revivals back to the beginning of the century for these tables.

The comparison of the general pattern of theatrical activity with the revivals of classics of the English drama begins with a look at the patterns of the most frequently performed plays of the Shakespeare canon, as indicated in table 8 and figure 6. I have taken roughly the top third of Shakespeare's comedies (five of seventeen) and tragedies (three of ten) in terms of frequency of performance and compared them.[20] Plays of Shakespeare are unusual in that they are performed in both the commercial and noncommercial theatres, and frequently revived Shakespearean plays straddle the line between popular theatre and theatre for the intellectual elite.

Overall, the performances of popular Shakespearean plays are evenly distributed over the century, with no trend toward increasing or decreasing numbers of performances. Unusually large numbers of productions occurred in the decade before World War I, the result of Poel's and the theatre societies' activities, and again in the 1930s. The multiplicity of productions during the Depression, high even for this period of many new productions, was perhaps due to the precarious financial state of the theatre during those years; many managers sought to produce a sure thing. There is also a high point in the early 1960s that can be credited to the Royal Shakespeare Company, which took over the Aldwych Theatre in 1961 and for several years produced much of the best-known portion of the Shakespeare canon for London audiences. Unlike the overall revival rate, which continued to increase during the late 1960s, the number of frequently performed Shakespeare plays dropped in the second half of the decade, but picked up again during the 1970s.

Two points seem clear: first, frequently performed Shakespeare plays fluctuate with the general changes in theatrical activity as measured by new productions, and second, comedies and tragedies fluctuate together as a rule. The exceptions to these general patterns are instructive. Frequently produced Shakespeare was at a low point in the late forties, a buoyant period for theatre in general. An overexposure of the classic plays during the war in relation to other plays, plus the competition from new drama that the war held back, may account for this. Frequently produced Shakespeare also took an unexpected dip in the late sixties, against the trend of theatre in general, making a strong recovery in the seventies. The late sixties was a time of cultural iconoclasm and creative innovation, which probably worked to the disadvantage of the standard canonical works. As for the relationship between comedies and tragedies, the popular tragedies seem to have been disproportionately selected in the late twenties and the late seventies, while comedies were favored during the early sixties. There was only one period during which comedies and tragedies were moving in opposite directions, the early to the late fifties, when frequently produced comedies were gaining ground while tragedies were slipping.

An examination of the infrequently produced plays of the Shakespeare canon, represented in table 9 and figure 7, produces a different picture.[21] High points for these less popular Shakespeare plays included the early seventies, when overall theatrical activity was low, and the late sixties and early twenties, when overall theatrical activity was only moderate. Much of the activity in the twenties is accounted for by the fact that Lillian Baylis was finishing up her series of productions of the entire First Folio at the Old Vic; by the early twenties, she had produced most of the better-known plays and was working on the more obscure ones. Much of the post–World War II boom, particularly that of the 1950s, may be attributed to the new government support of the theatres, which permitted managers to depart from the better known portions of the canon. Subsidized theatres also help account for the continued robust revival rate of all Shakespeare plays since 1955, a period during which new productions as a whole declined.

Tragedies and comedies generally rise and fall together, but there seems to be a tendency for less familiar Shakespeare comedies to lead the comparable tragedies. A high point for comedy in the twenties was followed by a high point for tragedy in the thirties, and comedy's strength in the sixties preceded tragedy's strength in the seventies. This is the pattern observed before in the case of Poel's Elizabethan Stage Society productions: comedy seems to prepare an audience for more serious fare. It also appears that, prior to World War II, high points of frequent Shakespeare productions preceded high points of infrequent Shakespeare. For example, the more popular plays of the canon were at an all-time peak during the early thirties, while the less popular plays reached a high point during the late thirties; this pattern seems to hold for the sixties as well. From this I conclude that the more familiar plays pave the way for the less familiar ones by developing new cohorts of audiences for Shakespeare; playgoers who have seen *Twelfth Night* will take a chance on *Two Gentlemen of Verona*. Similarly, unfamiliar comedy prepares the audience for unfamiliar tragedy; *Two Gentlemen* is apt to come before *Timon of Athens*.

Twentieth-century productions of other Renaissance plays, those neither written by Shakespeare nor falling into the categories of city comedy or revenge tragedy, have had careers similar to those of infrequently produced Shakespeare plays. Table 10 and figure 8 show the patterns of the "other" Renaissance revivals. (A play-by-play breakdown is given in appendix D.) These plays received an unusually large number of productions in the 1920s, largely through the Phoenix and Renaissance theatre societies. They had another period of considerable production in the early seventies. They underwent a surprising number of productions during the Second World War (four plays, as opposed to only one of the infrequently produced Shakespeare plays). During the twenties the comedies-leading-tragedies pattern appears for these "other" Renaissance plays, but later disappears.

One rather surprising observation is that government subsidies have apparently had little influence on the sheer number of productions of these lesser-known plays. There were thirty-three productions during the quarter-century before 1940, and seventeen productions during the quarter century after 1944. The productions were on an entirely different scale, however. The early Sunday-society productions ran for only one or two performances in front of very small audiences, while some of the later productions were far more elaborate and had substantial runs.

Finally come our plays of particular interest: city comedies are recorded in table 11 and revenge tragedies in table 12, and both are represented in figure 9. (Again, note that these figures represent independent productions; there may be more than one production of the same play counted in a single decade or even in a single year.) City comedies were often produced during the early fifties and early sixties; in fact, forty percent of the twentieth-century productions occurred during the fifteen-year period from 1950 to 1964. Both city comedies and revenge tragedies were produced relatively frequently during the early twenties, under the auspices of the Phoenix Society and Renaissance Theatre. City comedies also did fairly well immediately after the Second World War, and during the late seventies. Of the eleven city comedies receiving twentieth-century performances, only two have had over three productions; half seem to have been just occasionally trotted out, receiving only one or two productions. Three of our city comedy population have never been performed in the present century, namely *Ram Alley, Wit without Money,* and *A Mad World, My Masters.* (There was a play by Barrie Keefe produced in 1977 that had the same title and spirit as Jonson's comedy, but its plot was entirely different.)

Revenge tragedies as a category were more popular during the twentieth century than city comedies, receiving a third more total productions. While the average city comedy was produced three times during the century if it was produced at all, the average revenge tragedy, if revived at all, received 4.4

productions. Seven revenge tragedies, including (surprisingly) *The Spanish Tragedy,* were ignored, but if produced at all, they were apt to be produced often.[22] Revenge tragedies sometimes fluctuated with city comedies and infrequently produced Shakespeare, with revenge tragedies being popular in the twenties and late seventies, as were the two latter groups. Like city comedies, revenge tragedies reached a high point in the early sixties, and they declined less markedly during the later half of that decade. In one respect revenge tragedies differed sharply from city comedies, frequently or infrequently produced Shakespeare, and theatrical activity in general: revenge tragedies showed strength during the late fifties, a low point for most other categories. During the period after World War II, the pattern of comedies preceding tragedies reappears: city comedies had surge immediately after the war, and peaked in the early fifties, a decade earlier than revenge tragedies.

In table 13 and figure 10, all of the preceding categories of Renaissance drama have been translated into production coefficients to facilitate comparison among them. A category's production coefficient for a given half-decade is simply the number of productions of that category of play during the period divided by the total number of plays in that category revived during the century. For example, there have been ten city comedies revived in this century. Since there was only one production of a city comedy during the period 1900–1904, the city comedy production coefficient for that period is .10; for the period from 1920 to 1924 when there were four city comedy productions, the coefficient is .40. The translation allows for simultaneous longitudinal comparison within categories and cross-sectional comparison among categories.

Figure 10 reveals two different systems, that of the most popular Shakespeare plays and that of all other Renaissance plays, including the less familiar works of Shakespeare. The less popular Shakespeare plays are nevertheless almost twice as frequently produced as the categories of non-Shakespearean Renaissance drama. Peaks in frequently produced Shakespeare tend to precede peaks in infrequently produced Shakespeare by about a decade. Generally, all categories of plays rise or fall during the same period, though at different rates; a notable exception is the period from the early to the late fifties, when revenge tragedies and frequently produced Shakespeare comedies rose while all other categories fell. There were two odd periods: the post–World War II period, when the frequently produced Shakespeare plays dipped while all other categories rose, and the early sixties, when both revenge tragedies and to a lesser extent city comedies were doing better than infrequently produced Shakespeare. In the postwar period we see city comedy and infrequently produced Shakespeare peaking in the early fifties, with revenge tragedies peaking a decade later.

For the system of less frequently performed Renaissance plays, the mid-fifties seems to be a dividing point, after which revenge tragedies enjoyed a disproportionate revival. Before this time, revivals of infrequently produced Shakespeare, city comedies, and revenge tragedies rise and fall together; afterwards they have markedly different careers. Revenge tragedies are the only category of play for which over half of the twentieth-century productions occur after 1955. Revenge tragedies are significantly overrepresented in the post-1955 period when compared with all new productions, revivals only, or popular Shakespearean plays; they also appear overrepresented when compared with infrequently produced Shakespeare, other Renaissance drama, and city comedies, although these differences are smaller (see appendix C). Every revenge tragedy that has received a twentieth-century revival has been produced during the period 1955–79, which is true of no other category of Renaissance play aside from the Shakespeare favorites.

REVENGE TRAGEDY EXCEPTIONALISM

Except for the wave of revenge tragedies starting in the late fifties, institutional factors account for the abundant Renaissance revivals in the twentieth century. An intellectual subsection of an affluent and well-educated theatre audience supported experimental theatrical endeavors of various sorts, from Ibsen to Webster. Coming together in small, clearly demarcated groups, such as the theatre societies of the century's early decades, these intellectuals were able to exhibit a fine disdain for the commercial theatre and give free rein to their aesthetic inclinations. They could afford to do so, for both the producers and their subscribers were from privileged backgrounds.

After the Second World War the situation changed, but not entirely. No longer did the wealthy and the intellectuals have to provide full support for theatrical endeavors of the noncommercial sort, though they were in a position to see that such support went to what they regarded as quality drama. Since the theatre audience in the age of television was more unrepresentative than ever, what the intellectual elite wished to see in the theatre and what the producers were interested in producing and what the funders felt was worth supporting all tended to coincide. Each level of theatrical involvement drew from this elite within an elite, all of whom shared similar conceptions of what was worthwhile theatre. The postwar theatre outside the West End has enjoyed a golden age for a golden few.

This situation has favored Renaissance revivals. As the conventions of language change, a drama heavily dependent on language requires increasingly more effort on the part of its audience in order to understand and enjoy it, as Dryden noted three centuries ago. Such effort is not simply a matter of will; it must be based on sufficient education to provide both the linguistic tools and the historical context for appreciation, an aesthetic training to allow recognition and emotional response to the dramatic embodiment of ideas, and the motivation to invest energy to wrestle with difficult cultural materials, thereby demonstrating one's refinement and taste to others and to oneself. Any elite group will celebrate and invest in those cultural institutions that seem to legitimate its superiority; this was particularly easy for the educated upper middle class in twentieth-century Britain, inasmuch as the lower-class groups were not contesting the control of the theatres. In contrast to the nineteenth century, when the theatre had been an arena of symbolic class conflict, the less educated of the present century were happy to relinquish any remaining interest they might have had in the theatre; movies and later commercial television were better able to satisfy their entertainment needs.[23] Without any need to appeal to an audience lacking the education or status motivation to comprehend Elizabethan language and conventions, the revivers of Renaissance drama could proceed free from concerns about broad commercial appeal, a freedom unknown to the Renaissance playwrights themselves.

Great Britain's declining power and prestige during the post–World War II era may have given additional thrust to the interest in reviving classic drama. As we have seen, productions of Shakespeare and other classics were surprisingly plentiful during the war, for they offered the displaced and the frightened a heartening reminder of English culture, their particular version of "the best that has been thought and known." After the war this cultural pride waxed as evidence of economic and international power waned; English theatrical classics have provided national self-satisfaction from the Battle of Britain to the Battle of the Falklands. Far more important, however, have been the institutional factors—a highly educated audience and some kind of patronage (in the form of either elite backing of the theatre societies or government subsidy, which have relieved certain theatres from box-office pressure)—that have made possible the production of a vast number of Renaissance plays during the twentieth century.

What remains to be accounted for is the particular appeal revenge tragedy has had during the period from the mid-fifties through the seventies. This genre, which has seldom been revived since the Restoration and enjoyed only average success during the early twentieth century, occupied a dominant position among the Renaissance revivals on the post-1955 London stage. From the mid-fifties on, the production coefficients of revenge tragedies stayed higher than those of city comedies, higher than those of other Renaissance plays, and during the early sixties even higher than the infrequently performed plays of Shakespeare. Previously neglected revenge tragedies received multiple productions: three productions of *Titus Andronicus* in 1957 (see plate 12), seven Webster productions from the late fifties through the seventies, and long-ignored masterpieces like *The Revenger's Tragedy* and

Women Beware Women back on the stage. Nor was it the case that less familiar plays were taking the place of better-known ones; plays like *The Maid's Tragedy, 'Tis Pity She's a Whore,* and *The Changeling,* staged earlier in the century, were revived again during the post-1955 period. *The Changeling* received two productions during the early fifties, two in the sixties, and two more in the seventies, an astonishing exhibit of strength for a play that had not been produced in its original form since the 1660s.

So the question is, Why was the postwar theatre, which was kind to Renaissance revivals in general, so especially kind to revenge tragedy after the mid-fifties? Institutional factors do not allow us to discriminate among Renaissance genres in terms of their likelihood of revival; a theatre institutionally hospitable to *A Woman Killed with Kindness* can also be expected to welcome *'Tis Pity She's a Whore,* but it will not favor the one over the other. Nor is it simply the case that the postwar era was a gloomy one for Britons and therefore tragedies were unusually consonant with the national mood, for, as we have seen, neither the popular nor the less popular works of Shakespeare reveal any lasting bias toward tragedy during this period. It seems that there was something about revenge tragedy itself that led to its disproportionate selection during the late fifties and afterward.

The social meaning of revenge tragedy had a particular salience for the educated elite that selected and supported the drama produced at the subsidized theatres during this period. Archetypal themes cannot themselves explain the difference in response between any two time periods, such as before and after 1955; the meaning of life in face of the certainty of death is always a problem for thinking people, and the horrible always fascinates. Nor can topical themes account for the strength and endurance of the revenge tragedy revival—drama urging a Protestant nationalism centered on the monarchy would have limited appeal during the twentieth century, and the pleasures of decoding ideological messages would be unlikely to provide enduring audience support for any genre.

Revenge tragedy's social meaning, I have previously suggested, lies in its depiction of the dilemma between order and justice as focused on the institutions of governmental authority. The central authority, or those human beings who embody it, are not always adequate to the tasks they take upon themselves. In one specific historical instance, the Elizabethan and Jacobean court could not always ensure the provision of justice. At the same time, the alternative to the central monopoly of justice, a reversion to feudal decentralization and localized warfare, was unthinkable. So revenge tragedy, with all its blood and cynicism, nonetheless represented the dogged optimism of its era, wherein governors might be corrupt but high hopes were held for their institutional successors. Even a late and somewhat atypical Revenge Tragedy like *The Changeling* perpetuated this pattern. The governor Vermandero, left issueless by the death of his corrupt daughter, is assured in the final lines by his son-in-law of twenty-four hours that "you have yet a son's duty living, please you accept it." The court of Alicant, no House of Usher, will stand in spite of the corruption of the main line of descent. Such institutional optimism marked the key break from the Senecan prototype.

The preoccupation with revenge followed the Tudor monopoly of justice and punishment, and the revenge tragedy conventions displayed the revenge theme so as to maintain the compatibility of justice and order. What resonance did such a display have, one must ask, for twentieth-century British intellectuals? I shall suggest a contemporary interpretation of the justice-and-order dilemma, then offer evidence that such an interpretation did obtain for those people, both managers and audience members, institutionally capable of influencing the selection and perpetuation of Renaissance revivals.

Revenge tragedy is of particular interest when there is widespread concern over the ability of the government to accomplish what is expected of it. It offers a reconciliation despite—indeed, because of—the fact that it avoids actually answering the question of the king's or state's capacities. Revenge involves taking what has been declared to be a public function into private hands. In revenge tragedy, the authorities cannot or will not provide justice. The revenger acts, and since the object of his wrath is usually evil, justice is served. But unlike the city comedy rascal, the revenger does not get away with it. In the plays that established the conventions of the genre, the revenger undergoes a moral change in the course of his revenge, becomes corrupt, and is destroyed. It cannot be otherwise. If the authority of the central government is to be preserved, people cannot run around carrying out their personal systems of justice. Justice is accomplished, corruption purged, but revenge tragedies end with a ritual restoration of the central authority. The revenger is never a revolutionary; his revenge and his destruction are individual. Thus in revenge tragedy one can have it both ways: just deserts on an individual level plus the maintenance of the existing structure of authority.

This highly artificial balance of justice and order has no special appeal when little is expected of the government, or during revolutionary times, or during times of complacency about the strength of the center, but it is exceedingly attractive during times when there is concern about state capacities coupled with a fear that the center may in fact not hold. Such was the situation during the late Elizabethan and Jacobean period, and such has been the situation in England since the mid-1950s.

Following World War II, England enjoyed a decade or so of confidence that the national government could create a just, humane society for all its members through the welfare state.[24] The "age of austerity" following the war gave way to "the age of affluence." Politicians of both major parties had accepted the thrust, if not always the recommendations, of the 1942 Beveridge Report: the state had a responsibility for providing protection against the five "giants" of want, disease, ignorance, squalor, and idleness. There was bipartisan support for such legislative pillars of the welfare state as the National Insurance Act (1946) and the National Health Service (inaugurated 1948). On the international front, politicians made a virtue of necessity in the case of Indian independence, congratulating themselves that Britain was setting a constructive example in how to grant independence to former colonies.[25] The lifting of rationing and the economic prosperity of the early fifties seemed to justify the British optimism, their confidence that they were a people exceptionally endowed with the capacity to provide both social justice and order, internally and internationally.

By the late 1950s, and accelerating in the sixties and seventies, however, confidence in both the welfare state and Britain's international role was undermined, perhaps permanently. One may trace the growing sense of malaise in two ways: by looking at objective events and the English response, and by looking at some key expressions of doubt by the intellectual sector. First the events. Optimistic plans for economic recovery were dealt a series of jarring blows in the late 1940s: the slow pace of industrial recovery, the run on the pound during the convertibility crisis of 1947, the devaluation of the pound in 1949 to check inflation, the continued rigors of the age of austerity. Labour's fall from power in 1951 seemed to signal national dissatisfaction, but it was not a strong signal; the election of 1950, when Labour managed to hold on, and that of the following year, when it didn't, were both very close. Furthermore, the two parties were in considerable agreement on welfare state objectives (though not on the means to achieve them, notably nationalization) and foreign policy.

The early 1950s saw a spectacular economic improvement and a national mood of buoyancy. Confidence was boosted by the change from a deficit of 700 million pounds in 1951 to a surplus of 300 million the following year. The end of food rationing made daily life less frustrating for the average Briton. The stock market boomed, with prices doubling between 1952 and 1955. Production and wages rose as well. Huge housing programs under Harold Macmillian got underway. Britain's explosion of a nuclear bomb in 1952 and Anthony Eden's diplomatic coup in crafting the Paris Agreements of 1954 seemed to justify Britains's self-image as a world-class power, one of the "Big Three," and enjoying a "special relationship" with the United States. In the Festival of Britain and Elizabeth II's coronation, the Britain of the early fifties gave ritual expression to its optimism.[26] The age of affluence was welcomed.

Subsequent events have proved just how unwarranted this optimism was, for neither internal economic trends nor international relations justified Britain's mood of self-confidence. It took a series of blows to shake and finally shatter public complacency. The most dramatic was the Suez Crisis of 1956, which revealed that Britain had become a second-class power, unable to muster effective military action or to count on American support for such action, "special relationship" notwithstanding. The humiliation was deeply felt. More gradual, yet more significant in the long run, was a continuing series of economic crises. Economic problems including unfavorable trade balances, the weakness of the pound, low productivity compared with European competitors, and an increasing inflation were proving far more stubborn than had been anticipated. The "Super-Mac" of the 1959 elections proved a disappointment. By 1963 the Profumo affair and scandal, which unleashed months of media innuendo, suggested widespread government corruption. Meanwhile, many people were taking their political views into the streets: the Campaign for Nuclear Disarmament of the fifties was followed by the Vietnam War protests of the sixties. The relative industrial cooperation of the postwar years began to give way to the strike-torn period of the later sixties and seventies. Law and order became an issue in the elections of 1966 and 1970.

The mid-fifties constituted an intellectual watershed as well, for the fifties produced hints and the sixties facts regarding the failure of postwar Britain in general, and the welfare state in particular, to achieve all that had been expected. There were some early warnings as to the limited capacities of the welfare state; a charge was imposed for eyeglasses in 1951, for prescriptions and dental service in 1952. Perhaps more unnerving for the educated groups were influential articles appearing in highbrow magazines suggesting that class distinctions were flourishing. Nancy Mitford's notorious article in the September 1955 issue of *Encounter* made "U" and "non-U" a part of the common parlance and reminded readers of the social distinctions such usage represented.[27] The following year C. P. Snow's analysis of the "two cultures" generated fierce debates about the coherence of the intellectual sector.[28] Drama and fiction became "angry." Richard Hoggart's widely read study *The Uses of Literacy* suggested a cultural impoverishment of the working class that was being exacerbated, not offset, by their increased purchasing power.[29]

The sixties brought an acceleration of anxiety. Social scientists pointed out the widespread persistence of poverty and inequality.[30] These findings produced some results (the Child Poverty Action Group pushed through increases in family allowances in the late sixties and seventies) but also a new cynicism. At the same time, educated men and women were deeply troubled by the debates over colored immigration and the nationalist movements in Scotland and Wales, for such issues revealed fundamental divisions in British society at odds with the welfare state ideal of justice and plenty for all.

"The decade of disillusion" has been the label given to the sixties, a period that saw a fall from the heightened expectations following World War II regarding the state's ability to satisfy the economic and social needs of its citizens.[31] The welfare state began to be seen as, if not exactly a failure, at least as not working as had been hoped. People's expectations and demands on the system of social services were outstripping its capacities. As one writer put it,

> Behind the sniping was the feeling that the welfare state represented an alarmingly open-ended commitment . . . Lord Beveridge's assumption that national assistance would be a tide-over phenomenon till his social security scheme got off the ground, and Aneurin Bevan's confident pronouncement about the levelling out and probable decline in costs of the health service had become sick jokes.[32]

Another observer stressed the results of the discrepancy between popular expectations and the state's ability to deliver:

> For the British economy, the sixties were years of bitter disappointment. The real failure of Governments lay not so much in their economic policies as in their extravagant claims of omnipotence. A credulous public was led to expect El Dorado, found only plenty, and became understandably dissatisfied. Some of the economic problems were found to be intractable. Others could be disposed of, like the heads of the hydra, only at the cost of creating more numerous and more horrifying new ones. Each of the problems became more serious as the decade wore on. The traditional instruments to deal with them seemed less and less effective. The battery of new devices rarely improved upon the old.[33]

The left's disappointment with the welfare state was matched by the right's denunciation of the "permissive society," the sixties' noisy revolution in popular morality.[34] The wine of affluence had soured into the vinegar of disillusion, and intellectuals were first to notice the bad taste.

As early as the mid-fifties, the increasing disappointment felt by the educated groups was finding artistic and literary expression. The most powerful response to the increasing sense of malaise was that made by the Angry Young Men. *Lucky Jim,* Kingsley Amis's best-selling novel and the first work of the Angry Young Men to reach a wide audience, appeared in 1954. In 1956 *Look Back in Anger* rocked London. Jimmy Porter's bitter diatribes against life in contemporary England resonated with the hitherto unacknowledged discontent of the intellectuals, and Osborne's masterpiece of disillusion saved the Royal Court Theatre from bankruptcy. A series of plays by "angry" dramatists like John Arden, Shelagh Delaney, and Arnold Wesker followed Osborne's success.[35] Though Jimmy Porter quickly grew dated, this was in large degree because of the play's ability to express the frustrations of the intellectual left at a particular moment. Even today few would disagree with the assessment made in the mid-sixties that "everything now in modern British drama dates before or after May 1956, and that is John Osborne's achievement."[36]

Such a period was ripe for the rediscovery of revenge tragedy for, as we have seen, the genre structurally resolves the dilemma of government incapacity versus social anarchy. The encouraging message of revenge tragedy is, even if the government cannot provide, it will endure; even if the state is impotent, justice will be accomplished somehow. Individual claims are satisfied, but nothing is really changed. From the mid-fifties on, this quasi-resolution of the dilemma, the notion that the temple could be cleansed without being torn down, was increasingly attractive to London's disillusioned audiences.

On the level of individual characters, revenge tragedies have considerable congruence with the plays of the Angry Young Men. Compare Vindici to Osborne's Jimmy Porter. Both young men are near, but not part of, the centers of social power: Vindici is from the declining landed aristocracy hanging around the court, while Jimmy Porter, though from a working-class background, is a cultural snob married to an upper-middle-class woman. Both become unspeakably cruel, as their energy and the initial justice of their causes turns rotten within them. Both achieve an ambiguous victory over their adversaries: Vindici kills his enemies but throws his own life away in a moment of bravado, while Jimmy Porter, having destroyed his unborn child, only recovers his wife in an infantile retreat from reality. The festering court of *The Revenger's Tragedy* and the "Brave New Nothing-very-much-thank-you" of *Look Back in Anger* were both suitable arenas for the representation of a profound disillusionment with existing institutions coupled with a final, dramatically awkward optimism.[37]

To summarize, I have suggested that the disproportionate interest in revenge tragedies after the middle of the 1950s may have been due to the growing awareness among many educated men and women that the capacities of the British government to provide peace, happiness, and social justice were less than they had hoped. Structurally, their dilemma was the same as that felt by late Elizabethan and Jacobean observers of contemporary affairs: on the one hand the central government seemed increasingly unable to guarantee justice, while on the other hand to relieve government of its ultimate responsibility in this regard was to court chaos. In such circumstances a formal, artificial display of justice plus order emerging from corruption took on, and takes on, renewed salience.

Such an explanation is plausible, but one must seek evidence to support it. There are three groups of decision makers who influence the repertory of the contemporary London theatre: the artistic personnel, including directors, producers, and sometimes important actors; the reviewers; and the affluent, educated audience.[38] While the noncommercial theatre can be somewhat more independent of the audience than the West End, ticket sales nevertheless account for at least half of these theatres' revenues. Theatres may try to shape their audiences' tastes, but they cannot defy them for long. Box-office popularity is an imperfect measure of success in the noncommercial theatre, because most plays are set for limited runs regardless of their reception. Since the audience is articulate only through its purchase of tickets, however, one must assume that when a type of play is produced steadily over some time, it has won audience approval. From the mid-fifties on, English audiences have approved of revenge tragedy.

More individually articulate are the directors. When asked about their reasons for reviving a certain play, directors almost invariably mention the work's contemporary relevance, why it is a "play for our time," as they often put it. This may mean several things: that the play addresses current concerns, that it lends itself to a mode of presentation currently fashionable, that it displays universal themes currently being rediscovered or represented artistically, or some mixture of these.

Sometimes directors have a very particular connection in mind. Peter Barnes directed *Antonio,* formed from Marston's comedy *Antonio and Mellida* followed by his revenge tragedy *Antonio's Revenge,* at the Nottingham Playhouse in 1979. He told me that he is interested in reviving only those plays that "say something for today."[39] In *Antonio,* that something had to do with heads of state in the modern world who exhibit a form of comic tyranny, doing wicked deeds while remaining essentially ludicrous; the "buffoonery of evil," he called it, Idi Amin and Richard Nixon being two of his examples. Tyranny need not be awesome; it could be, as in the case of Piero, essentially ridiculous without losing its capacity for destructiveness. In *Antonio,* Barnes explored his vision of the cruel comedy at the center of authority, while an enormous crown hung menacingly over the set of the production. (The same visual point was made by the throne looming over the dead and dying in the production of *The Duchess of Malfi,* as shown in plate 13). One reviewer who praised Barnes's achievement as "the most notable rep production in ages" saw *Antonio* as presenting its viewers with "insatiability for its own sake . . . a good bad-dream play."[40] He went on to remark on effective portrayal of the "rottenness of court life," implying contemporary comparisons.

Robert Brustein, an American director interested in applying revenge tragedy to current concerns, revived *The Revenger's Tragedy* at the Yale Repertory Theatre. He wanted to portray the corrupting capacity of violence, even violence in a good cause—"Vindici as a Weatherman."[41] As his program notes put it:

> Like so many of today's radical avengers, Vindici begins
> with an authentic grievance against his violent society and

an honest determination to purify it. To do this, however, he must 'put on the knave for once,' and use the tactics of the world he abhors. . . . Having lost his initial purpose somewhere along the way, he inadvertently becomes identified with the objects of his vengeance. . . . The revenger's tragedy is that he cannot escape the cursed circle he has sworn to break.

Brustein, like most contemporary directors, sees his productions as indirect, metaphoric comments on current events; his *Julius Caesar* followed the political assassinations of the sixties, while *'Tis Pity She's a Whore* was staged as a vision produced by hallucinogenic drugs.

When Tony Richards revived *The Changeling* at the Royal Court in 1961, he argued similarly that "there is no point in producing a classical play at all unless it had an aliveness and a relevance to the times we are living in."[42] Specifying the nature of this relevance, he gave three lines of connection between the play and the contemporary audience:

> There is, first, the extraordinary existentialism of the theme of *The Changeling,* the idea that you are solely and wholly responsible for your own actions. . . . Secondly, Middleton shows an understanding of a certain kind of sexual violence, an almost Strindbergian love-hatred relationship. . . . And thirdly, there is a curious and ironic mixture of styles within the play, of abrupt switches from farce to thriller, from thriller to tragedy which to me is very much in tone with contemporary attitudes to writing and in the other arts—a sort of super Hitchcock if you like.

Notice here that the second connection is the universal appeal of blood-plus-sex. The third connection, the stylistic mixture concocted to satisfy a particular heterogeneous audience, now appeals to afficionados of high culture. Richard's first point about existential individualism refers to only half of what I have designated as the social level of meaning: the individual may ultimately be responsible for moral outcomes, but the combined acts of moral individuals will wreck social institutions. Richardson's insight must be combined with Brustein's, for each director concentrates on a different horn of the dilemma.

Reviewers and critics might or might not catch the directors' intentions, but they, too, have often sought contemporary applications. This is a twentieth-century phenomenon; eighteenth- and nineteenth-century theatre (as opposed to drama-as-literature) critics confined their comments to the quality of the acting and the reception of the audience, seldom mentioning the substance, let alone the relevance, of the play in question. Their modern counterparts similarly discuss production values and audience response, in the case of revenge tragedy often mentioning the degree of stylization and whether or not the audience laughed at the gory extravagances. For example, a reviewer of *The White Devil* at the Old Vic, making little mention of the actual content of the play, made the familiar complaint that the production "dazzles the eye [but] starves the ear"; in his view the play's art-deco hotel lobby set suffered from "an acute attack of trendiness."[43] This type of review reminds us of the elite nature of theatre audiences in the London noncommercial theatre; a reviewer may assume that his readers know what the Webster play is about and will form their own interpretation.

Most reviewers go ahead and interpret anyway. One reviewer of *The Revenger's Tragedy* found its contemporary application in the conflict between "the permissive society" and those who would impose their individual moral visions on it:

> While these Jacobean horror plays . . . do visibly revel in sadistic sex fantasies and horrors, they are also very much of their time in that clearly they are also pointing an accusing finger at a permissive society, that they are in fact an expression of a deep puritanical disgust with sex, the flesh and mortality itself. The insight which *The Revenger's Tragedy* in this brilliant production gives is thus an insight into the conflict of our own time, the battle between the permissive society and the Mrs. Whitehouses of this world; and what it shows is that in fact both are two sides of the *same* coin. The castigators of filth and immorality on our screens who spend their lives ferreting out ever more horrid examples of pornography are in exactly the same position as Vendice [*sic*], Tourneur's hero, who, to clean up the horribly corrupt . . . enters its service as a self-confessed bawd and purveyor of human flesh.[44]

An earlier review of the same production while it was still at Statford-upon-Avon commented on the institutional setting of Vindici's paradoxical position: "In a corrupt tyranny where law has no meaning, the individual must seek his own redress. . . . Vendice is fighting a corporate evil rather than isolated individuals."[45]

Perhaps the reviewer who comes closest to articulating our social level of meaning is Hugh Leonard, who, in his review of *The Jew of Malta*, warns his readers not to be taken in by the producer's joke of pretending the play is four hundred years old: Marlowe is clearly a dramatist of the mid-sixties and his play "shrieks of the contemporary."[46] Leonard goes on to suppose that Marlowe must be a disciple of John Osborne's, the Jew being clearly an Angry Old Man. Marlowe uses the wildest black farce to mount an attack upon both the Establishment and religion in general, and cunningly pretends to be writing about Malta in the sixteenth century. Barabas, unlike his model, Jimmy Porter, is a man devoid of self-pity. His fearful crimes have an aura of wholesomeness in contrast to the hypocrisies of the Church and the mealy-mouthed tyrannies of the State.

Leonard suggests that, given the state of contemporary society, young Christopher Marlowe ("is that a pseudonym?") is a promising writer whose work should be watched.

What do all of these interpretations and analogies—Vindici as a Weatherman or as Mrs. Whitehouse—add up to? Producers, reviewers, and, it must be assumed, audiences, drew connections between revenge tragedy and a permissive society that seemed increasingly out of control, saw the genre as representing the individual versus social institutions, watched the corruption of its moral individualists, and compared the tyrannies of the state to the terrors of anarchy. These concerns, salient in post-1955 England for the intellectual elite, well reflected the era of disillusion, a disillusion with the state of England in its national and international context. They lend support to the contention that revenge tragedy offered a formal, indirect rendering of post-1950s concerns about justice versus order, state capacity versus individual morality, social control versus social anarchy.

Revenge tragedy spoke in a slightly different voice to the two overlapping segments of the noncommercial theatre audience, the intellectuals and the affluent. For the generally left-of-center, the students, the highly educated, and those audience members professionally connected to academic or artistic institutions, revenge tragedy's contemporary meaning involved the corruption of authority, the injustice of the very institutions of justice. For the middle class, the civil servants and professionals unconnected with either radical politics or intellectual discourse, revenge tragedy's meaning had more to do with permissiveness, showing what happens when freely acting zealots run amok. Both interpretations are justified, and perhaps both were sensed by the majority of the audience, for such is the nature of multivocal drama. More significant, both segments belonged to a narrow social stratum, the relatively educated and relatively well-off, and this stratum shared a common question, if not a common solution, about state capacities for justice and order. Modern English directors, audiences, and reviewers from this intellectual elite peered into the mirror of revenge tragedy and saw their own worried faces.

TABLE 7 New Productions and Revivals, 1921–79

July,	1921–24	1925–29	1930–34	1935–39	1940–44	1945–49	1950–54	1955–59	1960–64	1965–69	1970–74	1975–79	Totals
New productions (including revivals)	683	1400	1629	1397	655	1282	1393	849	894	900	808	1094	12,984
Yearly average	195	280	326	279	131	256	279	170	179	180	162	219	
Revivals	206	338	393	295	250	320	309	152	224	230	247	270	3,234
Yearly average	59	68	79	59	50	64	62	30	45	46	49	54	
Revivals as percentage of new productions	30%	24%	24%	21%	38%	25%	22%	18%	25%	26%	31%	25%	25%

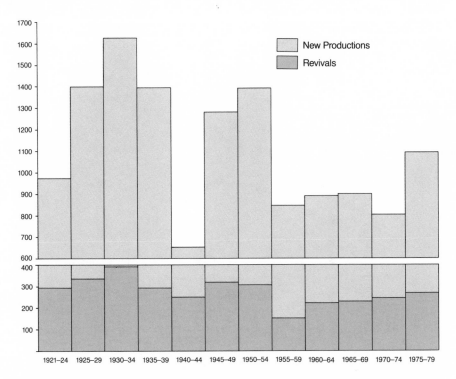

FIG. 5 New Productions and Revivals, 1921–79

TABLE 8   Shakespeare: Frequently Produced Plays

Play Period:	1900–1904	1905–9	1910–14	1915–19	1920–24	1925–29	1930–34	1935–39	1940–44	1945–49	1950–54	1955–59	1960–64	1965–69	1970–74	1975–79	Total revivals of plays
Comedies (5)																	
Twelfth Night	4	5	5	2	2	2	9	7	4	2	3	3	7	1	6	5	67
Midsummer Night's Dream	2	1	2	1	3	3	3	9	4	1	1	1	6	3	4	4	48
Merchant of Venice	2	4	6	2		5	5	1	3		4	1	3	2	2	4	44
As You Like It	3	4	2		3	1	4	3			1	4	1	4	1	4	35
The Tempest	3	2			1	2	5	3	2		1	3	2	1	3	3	31
Total comedies	14	16	15	5	9	13	26	23	13	3	10	12	19	11	16	20	225
Tragedies (3)																	
Hamlet	1	4	2	3	3	8	12	8	3	2	3	2	3	2	5	6	67
Romeo and Juliet	1	6	3	1	2	4	3	2	2	1		1	2		3	6	37
Macbeth		2	1		2	3	4	3	2	2	3	2	2	3	2	5	36
Total tragedies	2	12	6	4	7	15	19	13	7	5	6	5	7	5	10	17	140
Total revivals for each period	16	28	21	9	16	28	45	36	20	8	16	17	26	16	26	37	365

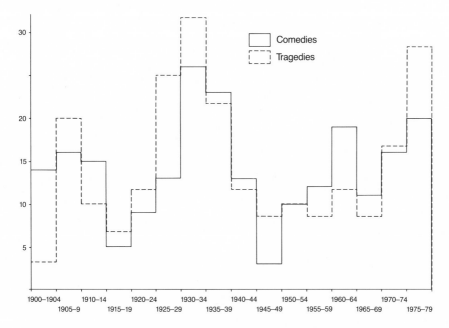

FIG. 6 Shakespeare: Frequently Produced Plays

TABLE 9 Shakespeare: Infrequently Produced Plays

Play / Period:	1900–1904	1905–9	1910–14	1915–19	1920–24	1925–29	1930–34	1935–39	1940–44	1945–49	1950–54	1955–59	1960–64	1965–69	1970–74	1975–79	Total revivals of plays
Comedies (5)																	
All's Well That Ends Well					1			1	1		1	1					5
Pericles					1						1	1		1	2		6
Cymbeline					1		1	1		1	1				1		6
Troilus and Cressida					1			1		1	1	1	1	2		1	9
Two Gentle-men of Verona					1	2				1	1			2	2	1	10
Total comedies	0	0	0	0	5	2	1	3	1	3	5	3	1	5	5	2	36
Tragedies (3)																	
Timon of Athens	1							1			1						3
Coriolanus					1		1	1		1	1	1	1				7
Antony and Cleopatra		1				1	1	1		1	2	1		1	3	3	15
Total tragedies	1	1	0	0	1	1	2	3	0	2	4	2	1	1	3	3	25
Total revivals for each period	1	1	0	0	6	3	3	6	1	5	9	5	2	6	8	5	61

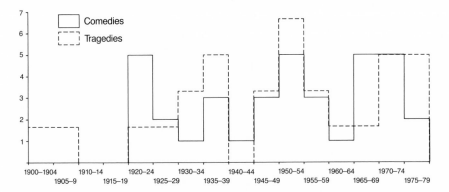

FIG. 7 Shakespeare: Infrequently Produced Plays

TABLE 10 Other Renaissance Plays

Type Period:	1900–1904	1905–9	1910–14	1915–19	1920–24	1925–29	1930–34	1935–39	1940–44	1945–49	1950–54	1955–59	1960–64	1965–69	1970–74	1975–79	Total revivals of plays
Comedies	1	0	0	2	6	3	2	3	3	1	1	1	1	2	2	2	30
Tragedies	2	0	0	0	3	5	0	1	1	1	2	1	4	1	5	1	27
Other, including medieval	3	2	3	1	1	2	2	2	0	0	0	0	1	1	3	0	21
Total revivals for each period	6	2	3	3	10	10	4	6	4	2	3	2	6	4	10	3	78

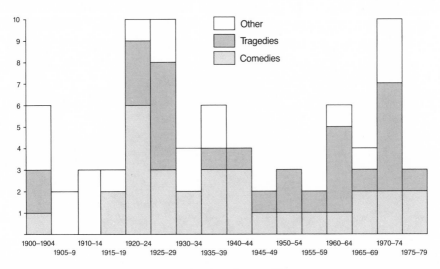

FIG. 8 Other Renaissance Plays

TABLE 11   City Comedies

Play (10)* Period:	1900–1904	1905–9	1910–14	1915–19	1920–24	1925–29	1930–34	1935–39	1940–44	1945–49	1950–54	1955–59	1960–64	1965–69	1970–74	1975–79	Total revivals of plays
The Alchemist	1				1			1		2			1		1	1	8
Bartholomew Fair					1						1			2		2	6
The Dutch Courtesan											1	1	1				3
A New Way to Pay Old Debts					1						1		1				3
Eastward Ho!											2						2
Epicoene					1						1						2
Every Man in His Humour										1			1				2
A Chaste Maid in Cheapside		1												1			2
A Trick to Catch the Old One													1				1
The Devil Is an Ass																1	1
Total revivals for each period	1	1	0	0	4	0	0	1	0	3	6	1	5	3	1	4	30

*Only the city comedies actually performed during the period 1900–1979 are listed here.

TABLE 12　Revenge Tragedies

Play (9)* Period:	1900– 1904	1905– 9	1910– 14	1915– 19	1920– 24	1925– 29	1930– 34	1935– 39	1940– 44	1945– 49	1950– 54	1955– 59	1960– 64	1965– 69	1970– 74	1975– 79	Total revivals of plays
The Duchess of Malfi				1				2		1		1	1		2		8
The White Devil		1						1		1			1	1		1	6
The Changeling						1							1		2	2	6
Titus Andronicus					1						2	3					6
The Maid's Tragedy	1				1	1							1	1			5
'Tis Pity She's a Whore					1		1		1				1			1	5
The Jew of Malta					1								1				2
Women Beware Women													1				1
The Revenger's Tragedy														1			1
Total revivals for each period	1	1	0	1	4	2	1	3	1	2	2	4	7	3	4	4	40

*Only the revenge tragedies actually performed during the period 1900–1979 are listed here.

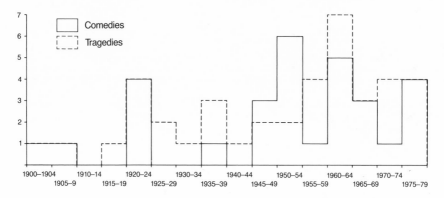

FIG. 9 City Comedies and Revenge Tragedies

TABLE 13 Production Coefficients

Type of play / Period	1900–1904	1905–9	1910–14	1915–19	1920–24	1925–29	1930–34	1935–39	1940–44	1945–49	1950–54	1955–59	1960–64	1965–69	1970–74	1975–79	Total production coefficient for type of play in twentieth century
Shakespeare: frequently performed																	
Comedies	2.80	3.20	3.00	1.00	1.80	2.60	5.20	4.60	2.60	.60	2.00	2.40	3.80	2.20	3.20	4.00	45.00
Tragedies	.67	4.00	2.00	1.33	2.33	5.00	6.33	4.33	2.33	1.67	2.00	1.67	2.33	1.67	3.33	5.67	46.67
Total	2.00	3.50	2.63	1.13	2.00	3.50	5.63	4.50	2.50	1.00	2.00	2.13	3.25	2.00	3.25	4.63	45.63
Shakespeare: infrequently performed																	
Comedies	0	0	0	0	1.00	.40	.20	.60	.20	.60	1.00	.60	.20	1.00	1.00	.40	7.20
Tragedies	1.33	.33	0	0	.33	.33	.66	1.00	0	.66	1.33	.66	.33	.33	1.00	1.00	8.33
Total	.13	.13	0	0	.75	.38	.38	.75	.13	.63	1.13	.63	.25	.75	1.00	.63	7.63
Other Renaissance																	
Comedies	.09	0	0	.18	.55	.27	.18	.27	.27	.09	.09	.09	.09	.18	.18	.18	2.73
Tragedies	.18	0	.25	0	.27	.45	0	.09	.09	.09	.18	.09	.36	.09	.45	.09	2.45
Other	.25	.27	.09	.08	.08	.17	.17	.17	0	0	0	0	.08	.08	.25	0	1.75
Total	.18	.06	0	.09	.29	.29	.12	.18	.12	.06	.09	.06	.18	.12	.29	.09	2.29
City comedies	.10	.10	0	0	.40	0	0	.10	0	.30	.60	.10	.50	.30	.10	.40	3.00
Revenge tragedies	.11	.11	0	.11	.44	.22	.11	.33	.11	.22	.22	.44	.78	.33	.44	.44	4.44

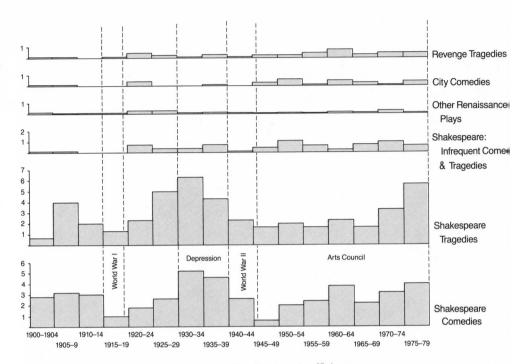

FIG. 10 Production Coefficients

REVIVALS AND THE REAL THING

"Renaissance revivals" is a redundancy, but one that nevertheless expresses a fundamental property of cultural objects: no cultural object is ever created wholly anew. Instead, a cultural object is an artifact constructed from previously used cultural elements, current conventions, contemporary aesthetic and social interests, the individual vision and expertise of the artist, the demands of the audience mediated through an existing institutional structure, and sometimes a dollop of unpredictability which heirs to Romanticism label genius. The birth of a cultural object is always, in part, a renaissance. Conversely, since cultural objects live only insofar as they are experienced by human beings, every human interaction with such an object is a revival.

In this study, as in common usage, Renaissance and revival have more particular meanings. I have tried to understand why drama written during a few decades of the English Renaissance was rediscovered and reproduced—revived—at some times more than others. I have maintained that the creation, production, reception, preservation, and revival of plays are all social actions in the Weberian sense, for they all involve people, with an eye on other people, making meanings. I have attempted to interpret and explain these social actions, with a special emphasis on the action of dramatic revival.

At the beginning of this study, I suggested that one may conceive of revivals in terms of "fit," in that there are some times when a certain type of play fits a theatre, in its current institutional and social context, better than at other times. Now it is time to sum up and account for the variations in fit that have been discovered with respect to Renaissance plays and London theatre. After reviewing the findings, I shall formulate some general propositions regarding Renaissance revivals, following the points indicated by the cultural diamond. Finally, drawing on what has been learned about revivals, I shall suggest the following theory of cultural meaning: when an accessible cultural object interacts with topical, archetypal, or social interests of relevant human beings to generate an elegant metaphor of their experience, cultural meaning is produced.

An Explanatory Model of Renaissance Revivals

As I suggested in the opening chapter, revivals entail both archive and activity; any revival of an English play is the result of someone who goes through the English cultural archive, rediscovers something of interest therein, and brings it out for contemporary inspection. A cultural archive is like an attic, filled with trunks of old clothes, discarded furniture, odd remnants of our historical experience, any of which may be brought out and put to new uses. Just as a family is vaguely aware of its store of possessions in the attic, so we know we have a cultural archive—it is "ours," just as *The Faerie Queene* is part of "our culture"—but we rarely go through its contents. (There is one exception to this: children are ritually, institutionally exposed to the contents of the attic in an educational procedure that ensures that most of them will value the cultural objects in storage, however incomprehensible they may be.) From time to time, however, the attic is opened and items are taken out for airing, inspection, reinterpretation, use.

To analyze revivals, rediscoveries in the attic, one must first understand what is there in the first place. Why were the old clothes, old furniture, or old plays made the way they were? Second, one must inquire why they, and not other cultural objects, were preserved. (We save old wedding dresses, but not old pajamas—will our descendants conclude we wore wedding dresses more often than pajamas?) Third, we must try to determine when and why an old cultural object is pulled out and put to new use.

The preceding investigation has yielded two sets of empirical results regarding Renaissance revivals. First, the general findings are as follows:

1. Renaissance drama dominated the early Restoration stage, but was quickly displaced.
2. Renaissance revivals declined from the late seventeenth century until the late nineteenth. Certain playwrights such as Jonson and Beaumont and Fletcher maintained a stage presence longer than their contemporaries. Shakespeare's preeminence was established during the eighteenth century, but only some of his plays were performed regularly.
3. Renaissance drama, except for some Shakespeare plays, was rarely performed during the nineteenth century, and no one type was dominant.
4. During the twentieth century, and particularly during the decades following World War II, Renaissance revivals have flourished. Non-Shakespearean plays and the less familiar plays of the Shakespeare canon have exhibited especially strong revival patterns in the postwar period.
5. Revivals of the less familiar Shakespeare plays prepared the way for revivals of non-Shakespeare Renaissance plays in the twentieth century.
6. Revivals of unfamiliar Renaissance comedies prepared the way for revivals of unfamiliar Renaissance tragedies in the twentieth century.

Second, the following observations can be made concerning the two Renaissance genres of city comedy and revenge tragedy:

1. In comparison with other non-Shakespearean Renaissance drama, city comedies were overrepresented during the eighteenth century. They declined during the nineteenth century.
2. During both the eighteenth and nineteenth centuries, revenge tragedies were seldom revived and did not enjoy much success when they were.
3. City comedies have continued to reflect the general fortunes of Renaissance revivals during the twentieth century.
4. Revenge tragedies have been overrepresented from the mid-1950s until at least the end of the 1970s.

To account for these patterns, it has been necessary to specify what has happened to the cultural diamond as it has moved over time. The theatre has changed, both as an organizational system and as a set of constraining and facilitating influences. Audiences have changed in their social and demographic composition. Artists, including managers, producers, and directors as well as actors and contemporary playwrights, have been subject to changing pressures and considerations. The cultural objects have been seen in relation to changing standards and conventions of dramatic writing as well as changing competition from other media. And the concerns, interests, and common sense of all the human agents involved in the theatrical world have changed.

These changes and their effect on Renaissance revivals are represented by the causal pattern pattern, derived from the general cultural diamond heuristic, shown in figure 11. At any point in time, the theatre audience has a specifiable socioeconomic and demographic composition. Any segment of the audience that is influential in terms of numbers or social prestige shares some social concerns, attitudes, values, and knowledge. The theatre audience, characterized by both its composition and its interests, exerts pressure on theatrical decision makers, especially the managers, to provide certain types of entertainment. (For the sake of consistency I shall continue to use the term manager, although the functions of manager are usually divided between the artistic director and the producer in the modern theatre.) Audience pressure is not the only thing a manager must take into account—he must consider the demands and capabilities of his actors, his own professional aspirations, the technical capacities of his theatre, and whether his theatre receives enough patronage from sources other than the box office to be somewhat more independent of audience tastes than a wholly commercial theatre—but it is the principal one. Subject to these institutional and exogenous influences, managers make their repertory decisions, including decisions about whether or not to revive a Renaissance play. Not all Renaissance drama is available to them; they must select from plays that have been preserved, and they are most

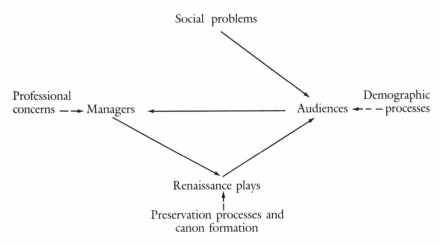

FIG. 11 A Model of the Renaissance Revival Process

apt to consider plays that have achieved some prominence in the literary canon. If they do select a Renaissance play for performance, that production influences the theatre audience, and its reception of the play in turn influences subsequent repertory decisions. A favorable audience response will encourage managers to revive comparable, perhaps even less familiar Renaissance plays of the same genre; an audience that stays away, on the other hand, will discourage managers from mounting similar productions. This is the essential causal mechanism that accounts for general patterns of Renaissance revivals.

REVIVALS AND THE THEATRE MANAGER

To follow the revival process represented by figure 11, the analysis will move from the individual to the societal level. I shall first review the microclimate in which a theatre manager makes repertory decisions, and then discuss the various types of audience influence on the encouragement of Renaissance revivals. Finally I shall take up the relationship, mediated by the audience and the theatre as institution, between drama and topical, archetypal, and social concerns, a set of relationships that accounts for specific patterns of the revival of particular Renaissance genres.

Nonecomonic motivations influence theatre managers' repertory decisions, and these should not be lost sight of, despite the obvious weight of financial considerations, for they are the most immediate factors behind any choices a manager makes. A manager's simple, possibly idiosyncratic, desire to produce a certain play is probably the single most important reason a revival takes place. Men and women whose life and livelihood is the theatre, individuals familiar with all forms of English drama, like to share their enthusiasms; their constantly proclaimed desire to please the audience notwithstanding, they will admit that revivals are often mounted first of all to please themselves. These labors of love may be successful, as with Garrick's *The Alchemist,* but often they are not: even Kean could not make a nineteenth-century audience like *The Jew of Malta,* despite his brilliant performance. Nevertheless, within the limits of financial and company constraints, what remains necessary for a revival to occur is that some manager or director "really wants to do it."

There are a number of reasons for wanting to produce a Renaissance play, with the high prestige of Elizabethan and Jacobean drama being only the most obvious. In the cases of Kean and Garrick, the manager's desire for novelty coincided with the actor's desire to play a certain role. In the twentieth century, the functions of manager (artistic director) and leading actor are usually separate, but the desire of important actors to play a certain role carries considerable weight with contemporary managers, for they depend on their actors' being professionally satisfied. Another reason for a Renaissance revival is the manager's sense of responsibility to the canon. This can range from the wish to give a play an airing just for the sake of doing so—*Titus Andronicus* was revived in 1923 during Lilian Baylis's forced march through the first folio—to a more specific aesthetic or theatrical commitment to the qualities of a work the manager regards as unjustly neglected. Peter Barnes described his hopes for one day reviving *The Roaring Girl* just because "it's such a marvelous play."

The manager also must consider issues of repertory balance and keep an eye on the competition. Repertory theatres seem to have general, though often unacknowledged, ratios operating at any given time, as in the case of the mid-eighteenth century's three-to-one comedy-to-tragedy ratio. The Royal Shakespeare Company currently tries for about an even balance between light and serious drama, with the problem plays such as *Measure for Measure* casting a swing vote.[1] During the nineteenth century, the critics called for novelty, but novelty in the form of new plays or revivals carried risks and, especially during the monopoly period, was conspicuous by its very absence. In the twentieth century, on the other hand, the competition has encouraged dramatic innovation. Since film and television are better able to produce realistic fourth-wall effects, theatre managers (as well as contemporary playwrights) often rely on stylized productions, actor/audience contact, and distinctly artificial "theatrical" conventions, for it is in such self-aware theatricality that the stage holds an advantage over its rivals.

Contemporary plays and competing forms of entertainment influence a play as it is first written and performed, and these "other plays"—potential competitors or fellow travelers—also influence revival decisions. Revivals sometimes seem to coincide with the drama being written at the time. Revenge tragedies, with their black humor and grotesque horrors, have been heavily revived in the era of Harold Pinter, Peter Shaeffer, and the Angry Young Men; they were not revived when contemporary drama was heroic and classical, or melodramatic and sentimental. Sometimes old plays are adapted to suit contemporary tastes, and in the process they come to resemble contemporary drama. Sheridan Knowles cleaned up *The Maid's Tragedy* for Victorian audiences, and the notorious sentimentalized versions of *King Lear* by Nahum Tate and George Colman made the play considerably more congruent with eighteenth-century drama than the original had been.

Revivals often directly stimulate similar revivals, for a manager learns from observing what has worked. Sometimes a company carves out a fixed audience, as William Poel or the Phoenix Society did, and as the regional theatres try to do. Sometimes the success of one play opens the door for another by the same author. For example, in 1818 advertisements for *The Duke of Milan* emphasized that it was by Massinger, who was known for the popular *A New Way to Pay Old Debts*. Such piggy-backing does not assure the success of the revival, *The Duke of Milan* being a case in point, but it does seem to influence whether or not a revival will even be attempted. Of the city comedies and revenge tragedies that have never been revived, most are by playwrights such as Chettle and Barry whose other works are unknown or unrevived. Managers know that a drama prepares an audience for comparable drama. This preparation may amount to an ossification, as when a set of conventions becomes so prevalent that an audience rejects deviation from it, but it does not necessarily work in such a conservative direction. The Stage Society, discussed in chapter 6, prepared its audience to accept controversial and intellectually demanding plays that had little else in common; works by Shaw paved the way for Hauptmann and Pirandello. Patrons of the Court Theatre under George Devine's direction (1956–65) expected a certain type of dramatic experience, one that challenged the complacent assumptions of the age of affluence, but not a specific dramatic formula. Shakespeare creates the audience for more Shakespeare.

Moreover, as has been shown, experienced managers sense the distinct patterns by which drama facilitates drama. Productions of works by well-known playwrights make the rediscovery of a lesser-known contemporary possible, as happened with Massinger in the eighteenth century. Comedies prepare the way for tragedies. Lesser-known works of Shakespeare precede other Elizabethan plays. Black comedy prepares the way for ironic tragedy.

The relationship between revenge tragedy and the plays of the Angry Young Men, which burst on the theatrical scene with John Osborne's *Look*

Back in Anger in 1956, demonstrates how schools of contemporary dramatic writing can enhance the likelihood that a manager will attempt certain types of revivals. Osborne's Jimmy Porter has a great deal in common with Renaissance revengers: he feels that he has been unjustly dealt with by a corrupt society; he strikes out at those in authority; although his grievances are justified, he becomes a monster as he obsessively nurses his wounds; and, like most revenge tragedies, the ending of *Look Back in Anger* is more form than substance, the achievement of peace without an actual resolution of the underlying dilemma between the individual and the established order. Jimmy Porter and his fellow malcontents represented the social strains of postwar Britain, but they also enabled their audience to comprehend the brooding malcontents who make their bloody ways through revenge tragedies. The post-1956 audience was well prepared to see Barabas as an "Angry Old Man."

The publication of the plays for reading can also spur revivals. Dodsley's publications did not begin the mid-eighteenth-century Elizabethan revival, but they helped it to gain momentum, and the publication of Massinger's plays prompted Colman's appeal to Garrick for some performances of them. In the twentieth century, when drama is less commonly read except in schools, the reverse seems to take place as well: revivals are followed by publication activity. In the case of *The Revenger's Tragedy,* a half-dozen editions of this long-neglected play came out in the early 1970s following the RSC revival. Similarly, the multiple productions of *The Changeling* preceded, and undoubtedly influenced, its addition to A-level lists of required texts in the late 1970s.[2]

While all of these proximate factors impinge on individual revival decisions, economic considerations usually set the manager's boundaries of possibility in repertory decisions. As a rule, Renaissance plays are more expensive to produce than are works from later periods. They have very large casts, and they are usually conceived as requiring some forms of historical costume and perhaps music. It is difficult to imagine an inexpensive production of *Bartholomew Fair,* for example, with its animals, puppet shows, and over thirty speaking roles.[3]

Their large casts present particular obstacles to a manager attempting a Renaissance revival. Actors' salaries and production costs constitute somewhere around 40% of most theatre companys' expenses. The Royal Shakespeare Company devoted 27.5% of its expenditures to actors' salaries in the 1978–79 season and an additional 11.5% to production.[4] For the same season, the National Theatre's figures were 16.7% and 21.9%, respectively.[5] Production costs can be reduced to some extent, but often the very obscurity of a Renaissance revival makes it dangerous to attempt the type of modern-dress, austere productions that occasionally succeed with the better-known plays of Shakespeare. One need only compare any Renaissance play with a twentieth-century counterpart, in which four or five roles is normal and two not unusual, to see that the differences in production costs between the two would be considerable. A theatre in a precarious financial state will generally avoid Renaissance productions, with the possible exception of Shakespeare.

A related consideration for the manager is the degree to which productions must achieve box-office success. No manager can afford to be totally indifferent to the box office, but theatres subsidized by private patrons or public grants can take more risks with the repertory than can theatres that are entirely commercial. Revivals in the post–World War II theatre reflect this: although there were many Renaissance revivals, almost all took place in publicly subsidized theatres and had fixed or limited runs. (It is difficult to gauge the "success" of such a production, especially in comparison with plays in the West End like *The Mousetrap* that have extraordinarily long runs and large profits.) Clearly, theatres like the Royal Shakespeare, with forty percent of its income coming from public grants, or the National Theatre, with a government subsidy of over fifty percent, could afford to take risks with box-office appeal that would be bad business for commercial theatres of this or any previous era.

Public subsidies can have unanticipated effects on Renaissance revival decisions. From its inception, the Arts Council has been concerned with community-based theatre, and its funding policies have favored the development of regional repertory companies at the expense of London-based touring companies. The results have been dramatic: regional theatres increased from about 20 in the mid-1950s to over 100 in the early 1970s, while during the same period touring companies decreased from 120 to 30.[6] Touring companies from the commercial theatres bring the most popular London plays to the provinces. Regional companies operating through public grants, on the other hand, can be far more experimental and innovative. Thus, we have seen the Glasgow Citizen's Theatre revive Kyd's *The Spanish Tragedy* in 1978, while in 1979 Peter Barnes revived *Antonio,* a production that combined *Antonio and Mellida* and *Antonio's Revenge,* in Nottingham. Clearly this system of subsidized regional theatre permits revivals of obscure plays; neither *The Spanish Tragedy* nor *Antonio's Revenge* had been revived in London since the seventeenth century. Whether such revivals achieve the objectives of community-oriented theatre is another question. *Antonio* was a success with the London critics, but did not enthrall the local audience. Subsidized regional theatres promote innovative, challenging productions, raise the level of the theatrical sophistication of those who attend them, give actors and directors an arena for experimentation, and are favorable for Renaissance revivals. They do not necessarily cater to the local tastes, however, because they don't have to.

Given these economic constraints, a third factor influencing a manager's repertory decisions is the physical nature of the theatre itself. Because Renaissance plays are so dependent on language, if a theatre is too large or has unsatisfactory acoustics, no amount of competence in the production can make up for the audience's missing the lines. In the late eighteenth and nineteenth centuries, as the patent theatre got bigger and the actors retreated behind the proscenium, even long-surviving dramatists like Jonson and Beaumont and Fletcher began to disappear from the stage.

The twentieth-century trend toward more intimate theatres, especially predominant in those noncommercial theatres where Renaissance productions are staged, grew out of the recognition of the physical requirements of live theatre. The Olivier, largest of the three performance halls at the National Theatre and with a seating capacity of 1,160, was designed for "concentrated intimacy." Its sharply banked seating, open thrust stage, and fan shape create something like the Elizabethan actor/audience relationship. The designer, Denys Lasdun, tried to facilitate a sense of intimacy between the players and the audience both because plays dependent on language required it and because this was one area in which live theatre could successfully compete with television and films. As he expressed it: "The personal relationship, flesh and flesh, is unique to theatre. Make it too big and you've lost it."[7]

The question of a theatre's physical capacities has a reverse side as well: since Renaissance plays were originally given on bare stages with minimal sets, they do not require elaborate stage technologies, and thus they allow set designers and technicians relatively limited opportunity to show off their skills. Nineteenth-century dramas often included a waterfall scene, a fire scene, a succession of elaborate settings, which made good use of the new stage technologies their managers had available; the two water tanks at Sadler's Wells both responded to and perpetuated the vogue for nautical melodrama, for example. Such scenic innovations further whetted the audience's taste for spectacle. A Renaissance play, which might be set in a single courtyard, was less attractive to nineteenth-century managers because it capitalized on neither their theatres' facilities nor their audiences' appetite for spectacular visual effects.

Professional aspirations, economic factors, and the physical capacities of the theatre all impinge on the individual manager's repertory decisions, and the appropriate configuration of these elements brings the revival of a Renaissance play into the realm of possibility. This microlevel of decision making is not entirely determined by institutional exingencies, of course. While usually operating within the perceived realm of the feasible, a manager will occasionally take a chance on a production that seems to defy the contemporary theatrical wisdom regarding what is possible. When he does, either a hitherto unrecognized audience or other source of patronage emerges to support this effort and encourage similar productions, or it does not. Too many idiosyncratic decisions, and the manager is out of business.

This brings us to the critical role played by audience feedback in the causal mechanism. The audience does more than ratify or reject a manager's repertory decisions; it exerts specific pressures for specific types of plays. To put this in terms of Renaissance revivals, while the cumulation of proximate institutional elements such as those we have been considering goes a long way toward explaining why any period's theatrical system will produce few or many Renaissance plays, such factors do not account for the favoring of any particular thematic cluster or genre. To understand the variations within the overall pattern of Renaissance revivals, one must take a closer look at audiences and their influence.

REVIVALS AND AUDIENCES

The theatre is social in its very essence, and the actual or potential audience provides the fundamental context for all theatrical activities. The composition of his audience is critically important to the manager whose theatre is market-dependent to any significant degree, as the London theatre always has been, so the changing characteristics of London audiences must be a central concern in the study of repertory choices in London theatres. As the previous chapters have shown, shifts in English audience composition have never been complete; a middle-class merchant and his wife would not have felt out of place in most London theatres from Burbage's day to the present. Nevertheless, different groups have been dominant in defining audience tastes, and it is their preferences that theatre managers have had to satisfy. "Citizens" may have been present in a Restoration audience, for example, but Killigrew and Davenant had little incentive to cater to their tastes, for the tastes of the court and the courtly were what mattered.

The basic demographic and social composition of contemporary playgoers is the principal audience factor affecting repertory choice. A manager must know his theatre's actual and potential audience, and must try to attract the latter without alienating the former. While age, geographic background, and gender may exert important influence in fostering some types of drama, social class and education have been the most significant audience variables influencing Renaissance revivals. These audience variables interact with organizational ones. The more segmented a theatre audience is, the more certain theatres can specialize in serving a middle-to-upper-class, highly educated audience, and then theatres will be especially hospitable to Renaissance revivals.

One characteristic of much Renaissance drama, including city comedy and revenge tragedy, is its tonal variety, its indecorous mixing of comic and serious, low and genteel, and such variety appeals to some audiences more than others. As we have seen, these mixed forms of drama were fashioned by play-wrights who wanted to appeal to mixed audiences, like those of the Elizabethan and Jacobean theatres, in which a wide variety of tastes had to be simultaneously satisfied. At the same time, city comedy and revenge tragedy do not appeal to every palate. The blunt language, violent action, and sensationalism of these genres (and indeed, of most public Renaissance drama except for Beaumont and Fletcher) make them unattractive to either courtly or sentimental tastes. Their mixtures of tone, ideas, and emotions makes them unappealing to those looking for classical decorum. On the other hand, the complexity of their imagery and the ambiguity of their moral messages make them unappealing to an audience that seeks only to be entertained or uplifted.

Therefore, other things being equal, one might expect these two Renaissance genres to be revived in periods of heterogeneous audience values and tastes, such as the period in which they originated, and to lose favor in periods when audiences overwhelmingly favored polite wit, sentimentality, or simple forms of entertainment. Such has been the case. Taking into account only audience preferences, one would not expect city comedies or revenge tragedies (or most other Renaissance drama) to be popular with the court-dominated audiences of the Restoration, the working-class audiences of the nineteenth century, or the middle-class and tourist audiences of the twentieth-century West End theatre, for such relatively homogeneous audiences can be better satisfied by drama that concentrates on their relatively homogeneous demands.

The importance of a mixed audience to the enjoyment of mixed dramatic forms decreases over time, however, for any literary object grows increasingly inaccessible to a popular audience as its conventions and language become ever more removed from the common understanding. Even old popular genres such as cony-catching pamphlets are received and studied as "high culture" after several centuries, for they demand more effort at comprehension than consumers of popular entertainment are usually willing to expend. Therefore, while it is true that one part of a twentieth-century audiences may especially enjoy the dirty jokes in *A Chaste Maid in Cheapside,* while another group is slightly embarrassed by the smut but amused by the representation of a new middle class struggling to ape the manners of the aristocracy, both parts of this audience tend to belong to a cultural elite, highly educated and motivated enough to work at comprehending and enjoying unfamiliar language and situations.

A second characteristic shared by city comedy and revenge tragedy is multivocality, a specific type of two-pronged thrust that appealed to a specific type of audience, one composed of the elite and the rising. As we have seen, each genre apparently said two rather contradictory things: city comedy promised economic change without social dislocation, while revenge tragedy suggested that both justice and order were possible under the centralized state despite its manifest tendencies toward corruption or ineffectualness. Underneath their apparently modern stories about highly individualistic actors who act outside social institutions to achieve their ends, both genres were fundamentally alike in their reiteration of existing social or political structures. Thus they would appeal to audience segments having some stake in the preservation of the status quo, while paradoxically they would also appeal to those hungry for change. An audience having prominent representation of both positions, such as the middle class and the aristocracy of the eighteenth century or the intellectuals and the affluent of the twentieth, might be especially responsive to a genre with a dual message, for such an audience could agree about the importance of certain problems while disagreeing about their solutions. Either side of the house could interpret a multivocal genre to its own satisfaction.

Beyond mixed tone and multivocality, a variety of other factors influenced the degree to which revenge tragedies and city comedies fit the tastes of London playgoers. Audiences are sometimes swept by fads, which may help or hinder revivals. During the eighteenth century, the shapely limbs of Peg Woffington playing Sir Harry Wildair in *The Constant Couple* set off a vogue of "breeches parts," in which actresses played the roles of young men.[8] Roles that called for handsome young lovers who were played by women were found in romantic comedies, not in city comedies; the device would have made no sense in male-acted Renaissance plays. The fad worked against the revival of Renaissance drama, since it contained no such roles. In a contrasting case, the popular English vogue for the black American actor Ira Aldridge, called the "African Roscius" and applauded as a novelty (another specimen of the exotica craved by nineteenth-century audiences), facilitated the Victorian revival of *Titus Andronicus*.

In the eyes of theatre managers, an audience consists not only of those who actually attend the theatre, but of those who might attend, and the hypothetical preferences of this latent audience carry considerable weight. For example, the RSC at Stratford depends on a large tourist audience and must be responsive to the projected tastes of tourists, including how these tastes are estimated by the townspeople. The residents of Stratford-upon-Avon put pressure on the RSC to produce the more familiar plays of the Shakespearean canon: they fear the more obscure works by other Elizabethans, or even by Shakespeare himself, will attract smaller audiences and hence a smaller contribution to the regional economy.[9] And they are quite right, according to the RSC's own study. During the early winter season at the Aldwych, twenty-six percent of the audience for two popular Shakespeare plays were overseas visitors, while only twelve percent of the audience for the three non-Shakespeare plays being offered at the same time were from overseas.[10] This local pressure to attract a potential audience works against the RSC producing non-Shakespearean Renaissance drama, and hence discourages revivals of most city comedies and revenge tragedies.

Potential audiences can, however, be cultivated. The Prospect Company of the Old Vic pays close attention to which plays have been selected for study in the schools, for such reading prepares an audience for touring productions of the same plays.[11] Productions in other media help form a potential theatre audience. Especially important for Renaissance revivals has been the role of the BBC in introducing forgotten drama. Radio productions of serious classical and contemporary plays are far more frequent in Great Britain than in the United States. The dramatist Peter Barnes, who has recently revived a number of Jacobean plays, says that he likes to do a radio production preceding a stage presentation, for it educates and awakens interest in a potential theatre audience.

During times when drama is read by large portions of literate people, new publications of old plays help create a potential new audience. Robert Dodsley's 1744 publication of a *Select Collection of Old Plays* is a case in point. Dodsley was encouraged by the Shakespearean revival to see if other forgotten Renaissance writers might be marketable. His popular collection paved the way for some attempts at producing Renaissance revivals, including some city comedies. Similarly, during the Commonwealth period, play publication nurtured the literate portion of the latent theatre audience.

The relationship between the size of the potential audience and the number of revivals is not a simple one. Some observers assume a supply-and-demand relationship: when the audience demand exceeds the capacity of the creators to create, the difference will be made up with revivals. Robert Brustein, commenting on the American theatre's recent proliferation of remakes and nostalgic revivals, which he refers to as "the retread culture," speculates that

> apparently, America's appetite for entertainment is becoming simply insatiable, and as a result, is far outstripping the industry's capacity to generate new products. With all that television time to be filled, all those movie theatres to be occupied, all those records to be sold, remakes not only have become essential to popular media like TV, films, musicals, recordings, fashions and advertising, but are also becoming an important element of scholarship, serious literature, drama, and painting.[12]

Yet one should be cautious here. We have seen that the heightened dramatic activity in London during the 1930s did not coincide with a greater percentage of revivals; even with over 300 new productions being staged per year, less than one-quarter of these were revivals. Cultural creators like potential playwrights respond to market demand rather swiftly; in fact, they often anticipate it. Even if the overall proportion of revivals does not increase in response to audience demand, however, the absolute number probably does. The early 1930s saw an average of seventy-nine revivals per year, although revivals constituted a fairly small proportion of all new productions. By contrast, revivals approached one-third of all new productions in the early 1980s, but only an average of forty-nine per year were staged. So if the unit of analysis is an individual play or set of plays, by and large the chances for a revival are apt to be improved in periods of high audience demand and many new productions.

The theatrical and audience factors that influence Renaissance revivals may be summarized in the following series of propositions. All else being equal, Renaissance revivals will increase:

1. When a competitive market creates a demand for many new productions.
2. When the theatrical system is segmented so that individual theatres may specialize by catering to particular types of audiences.
3. When the theatre audience (or a significant segment of it) is highly educated.
4. When the theatre audience (or a significant segment of it) is composed of members of the middle and upper classes.
5. When a theatre is free from total reliance on the box office for its revenues through government or private patronage.
6. When a theatre is financially sound enough to be able to mount productions having large casts.
7. When an intellectual subsection of producers, directors, and actors is dissatisfied with mainstream contemporary drama.
8. When a theatre building has a spatial organization allowing for intimacy between actors and audience.

The likelihood of any particular Renaissance play's being revived will increase:

1. When the play has been successfully revived in the recent past.
2. When another play by the same author has been successfully revived in the recent past.
3. When plays of the same genre have recently enjoyed successful runs.
4. When the play contains a role that actors regard as a professional challenge.
5. When the play has recently had a new edition published.
6. When the play has been presented on radio, television, or in other media.
7. When a producer, director, or manager has a personal interest in the play.

These propositions define what might be termed a period's "structural susceptibility" to Renaissance revivals, and can account for the revival of a particular play, but they still cannot explain why a specific set of themes resonates with a specific audience, or, in other words, why a genre like revenge tragedy or city comedy occasionally gets revived more than its Renaissance counterparts. We know that any particular Renaissance genre, or individual play, stands an improved chance of being revived when other types of Renaissance drama are being revived, but this does not explain what appear to be thematic distinctions whereby a certain type of play dealing with certain issues finds exceptional favor. Since the two genres under consideration share attributes of multivocality, mixed tone, canonical prestige, unfamiliar language and conventions, and expensive production characteristics, we now need to ask why some periods disproportionately favor revenge tragedy revivals and other times favor city comedy. What makes a play from a specific dramatic genre appeal to a certain audience at a certain time so as to generate positive audience feedback, which in turn encourages managers to attempt similar revivals? The answer to this question involves thinking about the relationship between lived experience and literary expression.

REPRESENTATION AND THE REAL THING

To understand revivals, one must first understand how cultural objects actually work. Consider the process whereby a powerful cultural object possesses the symbolic capacity to enable a significant portion of a population to "communicate, perpetuate, and develop their knowledge about and attitudes toward life."[13] One may conceive of the operation of such a cultural object in terms of metaphor and elegance. Metaphor establishes the relationship between a cultural object and human experience, while elegance denotes the object's efficient resolution of literary and representational problems. Let us examine each of these.

The Interaction of Metaphor

A metaphor equates one thing with something else, something that it literally is not: "Juliet is the sun." Patently untrue at a literal level, the metaphoric statement draws the receiver's attention to the possibility that Juliet, the tenor of the metaphor, and the sun, the vehicle, have some common characteristics.[14] In such a metaphoric equation, the tenor and vehicle interact; the sun prompts us to think of Juliet's brightness and warmth, while Juliet reminds us of the sun's love-inspiring and life-giving properties. "Juliet is the sun" changes the way we see Juliet and the way we see the sun. A metaphor organizes the recipient's understanding of both vehicle and tenor by having characteristics of the one suggest similar characteristics of the other.

In the same way social experience and cultural objects interact and thereby organize the participant's understanding of each. A cultural object, analogous to the vehicle of a metaphor, displays aspects of the social world, emphasizing certain features and suggesting an attitude toward them. Sir Giles Overreach clarified the Jacobean audience's understanding of newly wealthy men hungry for social prestige; at the same time, it was the socially based interest in these new men that gave the character his meaning. Similarly, revenge tragedy offers a vehicle through which the troubling problem of the capacity of the state to provide justice was explored; the Elizabethan social tenor, which had provided new conceptions (e.g., optimism about the stability of the central government), combined with old dramatic conventions (e.g., Senecan horrors) to shape the revenge genre. The revenge tragedy vehicle was then able to display, organize, and formally resolve tensions within the social context precisely because, as a cultural object, it was removed from that context.

This last point bears closer examination. In their metaphoric interaction with society, cultural objects organize and illuminate social concerns by presenting the structure of the particular concerns in an arena removed from everyday life. The separateness, the "other-than-real-life" quality of a cultural work enables human beings to examine the dilemmas represented and assess the solution offered, in terms of attitude or behavior, without being distracted by the complexities and randomness of the real world.

Russian formalist literary critics aptly termed this separation as a "making strange," by which they meant setting a datum of experience apart from the welter of everyday life, freeing and freezing it so it becomes available for contemplation.[15] By being brought to the foreground of the field of vision, being made palpable, the datum may be affirmed or criticized, compared and contrasted with other data, accepted or rejected as part of the reader's cognitive and ethical systems. City comedy, for example, makes strange the acquisitory activities of entrepreneurs, criminals, social climbers, gallants, and the various buyers and sellers of Renaissance London. These activities are expressed not just *in* a play, but in play form.[16] Like all play, the activities in "a play" are distinct from everyday life; viewing them is voluntary, marked off as a special occasion; assessments of them are made irrespective of market value. Separate from the economic struggles of daily life in Elizabethan London, the economic activities of the gallants and rogues became available for an intensified gaze and consideration by those who voluntarily invested money and energy to see them.

Strangeness requires complicity, however. It is produced by an interaction between a work and a human receiver. If a paragraph from a newspaper is typeset in poetic stanzas, does it become a poem? No, if the reader sees an error, a trick, or a technical failure whereby prose is masquerading as something else. Yes, if the reader receives it as a poem, weighing the words and rhythms, assessing its literary qualities. Strangeness requires recognition by, and interaction with, human receivers, whose horizons of expectations are evoked by the knowledge that they are experiencing a cultural object.

This otherness of cultural works, taken to its extreme, amounts to the removal of art or literature from time or historical contingency. Culture becomes Keats's "still unravished bride of quietness," or Yeats's golden bird in a timeless Byzantium. Any sociologist, and most post-Romantic humanists, will reject such an extreme vision of art's otherness, for it denies connections between culture and social context, but cultural works do possess the capacity to suppress temporarily the world of daily experience. One consequence of this capacity is the ability of the work to remove the sting from contradictions without resolving them, although the relief afforded is easily confused with resolution. In the realm of culture, conflict seems to be suspended. Such a suspension is exceedingly attractive to participants in real-world conflicts; it seems to take away their fears by offering a myth of accommodation. In culture, the lion lies down with the lamb beyond accusations of false representation, for they are after all in the arena of play. Just as metaphor has the power to organize characteristics of its tenor because it is patently false at the literal level, cultural objects can organize our attitudes toward real life because they are so clearly set apart from it.

Cultural metaphors exist only in the minds of human beings, who must be attracted to the cultural object in the first place. Attraction begins with the recognition of aesthetic and expressive conventions; a work attracts insofar as it suggests and fulfills expectations skillfully and perhaps surprisingly. The recipients who know what to expect are satisfied by the tension and ultimate release created by such a work.[17] If a cultural object defies all expectations, all of the cognitive and perceptive skills that normally enable people to "understand" sculpture or comedy or what have you, the object is mystifying and without lasting attraction. If the object sets up expectations and then violates too many of them too brutally, it offends its recipients (except, of course, those whose expectation is that they will witness a violation of the expected); on the other hand, if it satisfies all expectations in an easily anticipated way, it is formulaic and lacks aesthetic tension. The creator, the artist, has a limited range within which to work; he seeks to innovate or demonstrate skill beyond prediction within a context of comprehensibility for his known audience. The gallant was a successful innovation, for example, because he was the familiar antistructure trickster given a timely and dramatically effective twist.

A cultural object like a play may be said to work, therefore, insofar as it establishes, in the minds of its audience, a metaphoric connection between itself and some of their shared interests and concerns. But there is a difference between working and working well. This difference may be understood as consisting in varying degrees of elegance, and it is to the question of elegance that we must now turn.

Elegance

> True Wit is Nature to Advantage drest,
> What oft was Thought, but n'er so well Exprest,
> Something, whose Truth convinc'd at Sight we find,
> That gives us back the image of our Mind.[18]

Alexander Pope's familiar definition of wit expresses the desideratum of cultural elegance: the efficient, recognizably accurate, and handsome representation of otherwise inchoate thoughts and experiences. Elegance, which has its etymological roots in words denoting choice or selection, is the embrace of amplitude by simplicity. In reference to style, as in literary composition or attire, elegance means a luxuriousness controlled by taste and refinement. When referring to scientific processes, it means neat ingenious, simple, and effective; an elegant experiment is one that produces the most significant results through the simplest procedures (a high ratio of output to input), and an elegant mathematical proof is one that reaches its conclusion with a minimum of steps. When a number of problems may be solved with a single solution, that solution is elegant, and the more problems solved, the more elegant it is.

Cultural objects are elegant in the degree to which they efficiently solve a number of problems, tie up a number of loose ends, or convey a number of meanings. One type of elegance is that which is internal to the cultural work. An elegant plot device, for example, is one that economically solves several dramaturgical problems. When a Renaissance playwright was writing the final scene of a revenge tragedy, he needed to assemble his male and female characters and give them some believable, ostensibly peaceful reason for interacting with one another, underneath which they could carry out their deadly designs. He wanted to incorporate some trickery, some disguises, perhaps some music and dance—all crowd-pleasing stage devices—and he may have wanted to bring in some allegory as well. He also liked to allow his slaughtered characters time to utter their last sententious lines, so he needed a means of death that took a while to work. A battle scene would solve his problem of assembling the males and, straining credibility, the playwright could give the slain fighters elaborate dying words. A banquet scene was far more elegant, however, because it solved more problems. Its eating and drinking allowed poisoning as well as swordplay; its entertainments facilitated trickery and spectacle as well as allegory; it constituted a perfectly plausible reason for court members of both sexes to get together. The banquet was an elegant solution that became a convention.

Beyond the strictly internal level, elegance refers to the cultural object's striking yet efficient rendering of ideas, conceptions, and concerns, whether they be topical, archetypal, or social. As previously suggested, the topical appeal of Renaissance drama lay in those aspects of the plays that had immediate relevance to the economic, political, and social understandings and issues of the day. The frequent references to aristocrats forced to sell their lands is one example of this topical level. In *The Revenger's Tragedy,* Vindici, himself a member of the dispossessed landed gentry, says:

> I have seen patrimonies washed apieces,
> Fruit fields turned into bastards,
> And in a world of acres
> Not so much dust due to the heir 'twas left to
> As would well gravel a petition.
>
> (1.3.50–54)

His audience had seen the same, and the image of lands reduced to less than the sand required to blot the signature on an entreaty gave elegant expression to the specific complex of contemporary social dislocations that lay at the root of some of the audience's worst fears. The humorous references to London neighborhoods in city comedies were similarly elegant metaphors for extensive practical knowledge. Ram Alley was not only a notorious London neighborhood, but one with which Barry knew his audience was very familiar, for it lay right behind the Whitefriars playhouse where the play was to be produced, and it had the additional advantage of double-entendre. Plays that express particular knowledge and topical concerns in an elegant manner are apt to be popular, for they gratify the human desire to be in the know, to "get" a joke or allusion, to solve an implied riddle.

Elegance at the archetypal level of metaphor, in contrast, refers to the simple, striking, efficient depiction of broad human concerns and contradictions which are, if not actually universal, at least recurrent in Western thought. Archetypes may be represented formally in sets of analogies and oppositions—the relations between the strong and the weak, men and women, parents and children, vanity themes that explore the value of life in the face of the inevitability of death, and the horrible mingling of sex and death—and their elegant representation makes Renaissance plays comprehensible to other societies or eras. An example is Vindici pondering the vanity of pursuing love in a life where only death is certain, as he holds the skull of his mistress and asks,

> Does the silkworm expend her yellow labours
> For thee? For thee does she undo herself?

> Are lordships sold to maintain ladyships
> For the poor benefit of a bewitching minute?
> Why does yon fellow falsify highways,
> And put his life between the judge's lips
> To refine such a thing, keeps horse and men
> To beat their valors for her?
> Surely we're all mad people, and they
> Whom we think are, are not: we mistake those;
> 'Tis we are mad in sense, they but in clothes.
>   (*The Revenger's Tragedy* 3.5.71–81)

This vanity theme, formally expressed as the contradiction between the body's delights and its decay, is an archetypal question, and the senseless spinning of the silkworm is an elegant symbol connoting misdirected endeavor, appearance versus reality, and the worm that clothes the flesh versus the worm that eats the flesh.[19] Such memorable rendering of universal conundrums has ensured the preservation of the play as literature, as poetry, even when it was not performed as theatre.

The topical component of the metaphoric relationship between society and culture contributes to the original audience's understanding and enjoyment of a cultural object, hence to its popularity, but the potency of this level fades over time; Ram Alley means nothing to modern Londoners, for it is not found on their actual or cognitive maps. The elegant rendering of archetypes makes the meaning of some cultural objects transcend the time and place of their origins, but because it is based on a more or less constant human response to formal categories and their mediation, it cannot explain how cultural works can be revaluated. This question about the changes in the relationship between a society and its cultural objects over time is best approached through that metaphoric interaction by which culture represents issues of recurring social relevance. Here, elegance involves the infusion of multiple social meanings into simple cultural objects, and this is the key to cultural revivals.

Revivals and Social Meaning

Cultural objects may represent certain social concerns that, neither constant nor historically specific to one time and place, reemerge at different historical moments. When these concerns recur, cultural works that are related to an earlier manifestation of analogous concerns will be reimbued with social significance. Their meaning will be somewhat different, for the societal tenor of the metaphor is different, but meaning there will be. The revenge theme is a metaphor on this level, its tenor being the dilemma of the state's apparent inability to carry out public expectations versus the need for centralized control. Similarly, city comedy rascals stand in a metaphoric relationship to the dilemma posed by the visible conflict between a rising economic group and an established social elite.

The social concern component of the dramatic metaphor explains the loss and reapproporiation of meaning in the following way. When a play is written, its social themes are drawn from contemporary experience. During the late Elizabethan and Jacobean periods, for example, revenge themes were expressions of the growing concern about the ability of the state to hold together, monopolize violence, provide justice, and satisfy the demands of both newly powerful commercial groups and an insecure aristocracy. Revenge tragedies constituted an elegant, artificial resolution to a number of concerns; they presented the image that the state would hold, despite its incapacities, but at the same time justice would be served on an individual level. Similarly, the city comedy rascals embodied the artifice whereby extensive economic mobility would bring no social disruption, younger sons would reassume their inherent social status, and projectors and protocapitalists would achieve their economic ends without displacing the social elite. Both of these quasi-resolutions were conservative in their original context, representing individual freedom of action contained within a stable system of social power, and both genres were elegant in their ability to represent and resolve problems pressing on different segments of their audiences.

During the Restoration, different problems prevailed and different questions were being raised by those elements of English society in a position to influence the drama that was written or revived, The former social questions had lost their interest, and their cultural vehicles, the revenge tragedies and city comedies, therefore lost much of their meaningfulness. These plays did not fit Restoration social concerns very well; the metaphor between them and society was moribund.

As social issues and theatre audiences continue to change, cultural objects may become reinvested with meaning when issues resembling those surrounding the object's origin become salient to the contemporary audience. Such was the case, I have suggested, with concerns about social mobility and the disproportionate revival of city comedies in the eighteenth century, and with concerns about state capacity and the rediscovery of revenge tragedies in the mid-twentieth. Fits and misfits between a society and cultural works are not permanent. A work loses and gains meaning; a metaphor loses and gains elegance, as attention shifts away from and back to the social tensions that the work addresses. An artificial solution to a social problem can only be seen to be elegant, or inelegant, when there is the shared recognition that the problem exists; in other words, the problem must oft be thought in order for the audience to admire how well it is expressed.

Cultural objects are, among other things, arenas for the display of collective preoccupations. Their separation from daily life makes them safe vehicles for the exploration of that which is deeply disturbing. Following such exploration, they can suggest strategies for coping with the problem at hand, a set of attitudes and even practices.[20] At the very least, they can display and thus legitimize issues and dilemmas of intense interest to a portion of their audience.[21]

If social anxieties constitute questions for which cultural objects suggest answers, or at least affirm the importance of the questions, then, other things being equal, the questions and the cultural objects that treat them will vary together. The actual selection of cultural forms—books to publish, plays to revive, artists to exhibit, as well as the acts of initial cultural creation themselves—is done on an individual level, but the recurring patterns stem from a social impetus. When artistic directors or drama critics say, "This is a play for our time," as they do repeatedly, they mean that the work fits the contemporary concerns of their audiences by establishing a powerful social metaphor.[22]

The social metaphor of city comedy is the genre's representation of the collective concern with economic change, social mobility, and social stability. For revenge tragedy, the social metaphor expresses the collective worry regarding the central government's ability to provide both order and justice. When these concerns recur among those with the capacity to influence revival decisions, managers and audiences, the genre representing them takes on a renewed salience, and its chances for revival increase.

The metaphoric relationship between social concern and cultural objects, I have contended, allows cultural works to lose and recover meaningfulness. Now, in light of the previous suggestion that the revival of cultural meaning is the activity of going into the archive, some final questions about the archival nature of cultural works must be addressed. What is it about a cultural object that allows it to retain latent significance, and makes it available for revival perhaps centuries after its initial appearance?

The creation and re-creation of meaning is possible because of the formal properties of cultural objects. An artist formally organizes individual and social experience, embodying it in a symbolic medium that will enable it to be communicated to others. Such formal embodiment gives cultural works a fixed quality, a permanence, that does not exist in real-life experience. A cultural work seems as unchanging as Keats's Grecian urn, a still and forever unravished bride of quietness, while "real life" just seems to go on.

Georg Simmel gave a suggestive account of what he called this "ominous independence" of culture, which he regarded as removed from subjective experience from the very moment of its creation:

> Although these forms arise out of the life process, because
> of their unique constellation they do not share the restless
> rhythm of life, its ascent and descent, its constant renewal,
> its incessant division and reunifications. [Cultural forms] ac-

quire fixed identities, a logic and lawfulness of their own;
this new rigidity inevitably places them at a distance from
the spiritual dynamic which creates them. . . .[23]

Simmel regarded this separation of form and social context as radical and
permanent. Forms devoid of content persist, as in Simmel's example of so-
ciability, but such forms become subjectively and increasingly meaningless.
This, for Simmel, was the inevitable "tragedy" of culture.

Simmel was too dismayed by this tragedy to pursue the question of how a
cultural work can recover meaning, but his own logic suggests that if real life
is in a constant state of flux, social experiences analogous to those at the
moment of the cultural work's creation will recur. Just as the union between
experience and culture is impermanent, so is the cleavage. Looking at a cultural object's career over time, as in a study of revivals, reveals the union,
separation, and reunion that may take place between a society and one of its
cultural objects.

Cultural objects can be reimbued with meaning, but only under certain
circumstances: (1) when the object has been preserved; (2) when it is accessible; and (3) when a new social context arises similar enough to the original
one that the object, if applied to it, can organize it in a metaphoric relationship. New concern over rising social groups or the capacities of the state
can therefore reinvest city comedies and revenge tragedies with meaning if
the conditions of preservation and accessibility have first been satisfied.

Although preservation of Renaissance plays was partly a matter of historical accident, theatrical and dramatic merit played an important part. A Renaissance play that was not popular on the stage was not likely to have ever
been published and hence preserved. Plays that have been preserved are
biased in the direction of popularity on the Renaissance stage; they were
"good theatre" in their own day. Part of theatrical success has to do with the
dramatist's skill, of course, but part is due to the elegant exploration of contemporary concerns, in other words, topicality.

Plays that are read, that appear in new editions, that are taught in schools,
and that are thus preserved and given some prominence in the cultural archive, are plays considered to possess literary merit. Literary quality depends
in large part on the elegant articulation of archetypes, as when Vindici uses
the silkworm to express the vanity of human life. Such striking and multivocal images helped ensure the preservation of certain Renaissance plays in
the literary canon, after their topicality helped them to be popular and get
published in the first place.

Accessibility comes from those institutional and audience factors that
bring the production of Renaissance plays within the realm of possibility.
Non-Shakespearean Renaissance drama was accessible to the English theatre
from the Restoration through most of the eighteenth century. It became

accessible again in the 1890s, and even more so in the post–World War II period. It was during these periods that social concerns could be represented by the theatrical forms of revenge tragedies and city comedies.

While I have maintained that society poses questions that culture addresses, the cultural archive is not ransacked for the best possible answer to some current question. Instead, preservation and then accessibility arrange the cultural archive in such a way that certain cultural works will be encountered more readily than others. This stacking of the deck is what characterizes a canon. It is as if cultural decision makers, first managers and ultimately audiences, when perplexed by social dilemmas, go to the cultural archive for representations of these dilemmas. Their search is neither random nor exhaustive, but is ordered by the nature of the canon and by factors of accessibility that come from the current institutional state of the theatre. The search stops when something that looks satisfactory is found. The work is produced as a "play for our time," and its new meaning is created when people see it as forming a metaphor with some of their concerns.

To recapitulate, plays are preserved because of their theatrical and then literary power. If preserved, they become accessible for theatrical revival in certain institutional contexts. They are revived disproportionately if they address some currently salient social concern shared by members of the audience.

Now a final question: Why is it that cultural objects address the dilemmas and concerns of human experiences in such a satisfying way? Again, the answer lies in the formal characteristics of culture. Cultural objects formally resolve dilemmas by creating a tension and then providing a release from that tension. Aesthetic enjoyment depends on knowing that the release is coming; knowledgeable audience members are aware of roughly what shape it will take. It is this formal aspect of cultural narratives that distinguishes them from our daily experience. In what we call "real life," one thing just seems to lead to another; experiences appear to be random, continuous, inexplicable, and morally unsatisfying. Cultural objects, in contrast, seem purposeful, have clearly delineated beginnings and outcomes, satisfy expectations, and hence are immensely pleasing. All dramatic narratives have this formal resolution, and specific genres like revenge tragedy and city comedy have more specific resolutions. An audience familiar with these types of play knows just what to expect. They play will not come to just any ending; the revenger will be satisfied yet destroyed, or the rascal unmasked yet forgiven. If they are reproduced often enough, genres become conventionalized, and much audience enjoyment comes from recognizing the convention at hand, knowing how it works, and having the satisfaction of seeing it work.

Such release and resolution, enjoyable though they are, are after all only formal. Cultural objects display ambiguities incapable of resolution, and these may be present along any of the three metaphoric dimensions. In literature, including drama, aesthetic enjoyment of this content comes from these artificial resolutions, these elegant renderings of "What oft was Though, but ne'er so well Exprest." Vindici depicts the plight of the dispossessed landed aristocracy by saying they do not have enough land left to provide the sand to blot a petition. This is an appealing metaphor, but it did nothing to resolve the actual problems of those who had lost their lands, any more than the image of the futile labors of the silkworm resolves the problem of death. These are some of the ambiguities and dilemmas of lived human experience, and culture cannot solve them.

In presenting topical, archetypal, or social materials in elegant language and images, what a cultural object *can* do is satisfy its audience by giving memorable, legitimating expression to certain issues, ideas, and problems. In and of itself, culture cannot remove the sting from class conflicts, state incapacities, or the inevitability of death, but in displaying such collective concerns, a cultural object affirms their significance. It suggests attitudes that may lead to action. And more, it offers a satisfying testament to humans as social beings. The audience sees that the concerns set forth on the cultural stage are commonly felt, and members of the audience feel less alone after witnessing their private concerns publicly displayed and acknowledged.

Those cultural objects possessing a combination of satisfying formal qualities and elegant metaphoric content have the capacity to be enjoyed, preserved, and revived. This study has demonstrated the continuing interaction between English society and such cultural objects. Like the timbers from the Theatre that were used to construct the Globe, the cultural resources of revenge tragedy and city comedy have been used to structure the social experience of succeeding generations of London playgoers.

Henry James had one of his characters explain his love of the theatre by saying, "I'm fond of representation—the representation of life: I like it better, I think, than the real thing."[24] James's theatre afficionado, like Simmel, overestimated the estrangement between culture and the real thing. It is because the cleavage is not necessarily permanent that revivals are correctly named. A revival, I have stressed, is neither an exhumation nor a resurrection. It is a moment in which a collection of human beings witness a conjunction between a cultural object and a set of social experiences. In such a moment, representation and the real thing become one.

ENGLISH DRAMA, 1571–1642: TOTAL PLAYS, LOST PLAYS, AND GENRES

Table 14 shows the numbers of the known English plays first performed during the years from 1571 to 1642. The counts, which I have grouped in three-year intervals, have been taken from the plays listed in Alfred Harbage's *Annals of English Drama;* Harbage lists each play under the probable year of its first performance. I have used his classifications of the dramatic genre of each play, but I have been conservative in counting as a comedy or tragedy only those plays he listed as such without modification; thus I have considered such categories as "Latin Comedy," "Classical Legend (Comedy)," and "Romantic Comedy" as "Other," not as comedy. In the case of lost plays, Harbage sometimes labels a play as "Comedy (?)" or "Tragedy (?)" when the title seems clearly to indicate a specific genre, and I have included these in my counts of comedies and tragedies. Harbage usually hazards a guess as to the genre of a lost play based on its title, so the proportion of "Others" that are "Unknowns" is very low. The way to read table 14 is: we know of thirty-four plays that were first performed during the period 1586–88, of which thirteen have been lost and twenty-one survive. Of the thirty-four plays, three were comedies, four were tragedies, and the remaining twenty-seven were of some other genre or their genre is unknown.

One must remember that the figures for "Total plays" by no means represent all the dramatic activity of the time, only that minority of plays that we happen to know about. As pointed out in chapter 2, Bernard Beckerman's work has indicated that perhaps seventy percent of the plays introduced during the years not documented by Henslowe are completely unknown to us. "Lost plays" therefore are members of that privileged group of works that have left some trace, even if only a title.

Using the Henslowe performance records for the years from 1592 to 1597 as assembled by John Leeds Barroll in *The Revels History of Drama in English,* vol. 3, I have made some rough comparisons of the performances of lost versus surviving plays, and of the performances of comedy, tragedy, and other genres. Table 15 suggests that plays that have survived were significantly more popular, in terms of the number of known performances, than their lost contemporaries. Of the 884 known performances during this six-year period, 642 were of 92 lost plays and 242 were of 22 surviving plays. Thus each lost play averaged 7 performances, while each surviving play averaged 11 performances.

Table 16 breaks down the known performances by genre. It appears that comedy occupied the Elizabethan stage considerably more often than did tragedy. On the

other hand, these performances were of 26 different comedies and 9 different tragedies. Therefore each tragedy received an average of 14.9 performances that we know
of, while each comedy averaged 7.7 performances. During the 1590s several very
popular tragedies by Marlowe and Kyd were performed, while the heyday of comic
writers such as Jonson, Middleton, and other city comedy writers came a decade later.
So it seems unwise to draw conclusions from these data regarding the relative popularity of comedy and tragedy; if the average tragedy had indeed been twice as popular
as the average comedy, more tragedies would have been written. Table 17 lists the
dozen plays having the most known performances during the period 1592–97; I have
taken this count from Barroll's listing.

TABLE 14   English Drama, 1571–1642

Period	Comedies	Tragedies	Other or unknown	Total plays	Lost plays
1571–73	0	1 (5%)	19 (95%)	20	16 (80%)
1574–76	1 (3%)	1 (3%)	30 (94%)	32	23 (72%)
1577–79	5 (11%)	1 (2%)	39 (87%)	45	37 (82%)
1580–82	3 (9%)	2 (6%)	29 (85%)	34	21 (62%)
1583–85	2 (9%)	1 (4%)	20 (87%)	23	14 (61%)
1586–88	3 (9%)	4 (12%)	27 (79%)	34	13 (38%)
1589–91	5 (12%)	4 (9%)	34 (79%)	43	5 (12%)
1592–94	13 (23%)	9 (16%)	35 (61%)	57	23 (40%)
1595–97	20 (26%)	7 (9%)	49 (64%)	76	49 (64%)
1598–1600	36 (29%)	19 (15%)	71 (56%)	126	82 (65%)
1601–3	34 (30%)	15 (13%)	66 (57%)	115	71 (62%)
1604–6	29 (33%)	13 (15%)	46 (52%)	88	18 (20%)
1607–9	15 (24%)	15 (24%)	33 (52%)	63	8 (13%)
1610–12	14 (24%)	10 (17%)	34 (59%)	58	12 (21%)
1613–15	18 (24%)	9 (12%)	47 (64%)	74	25 (34%)
1616–18	6 (11%)	8 (14%)	43 (75%)	57	13 (23%)
1619–21	16 (23%)	11 (15%)	44 (62%)	71	27 (38%)
1622–24	29 (30%)	14 (15%)	53 (55%)	96	52 (54%)
1625–27	17 (30%)	8 (14%)	31 (55%)	56	11 (20%)
1628–30	13 (33%)	6 (15%)	21 (53%)	40	10 (25%)
1631–33	29 (42%)	7 (10%)	33 (48%)	69	12 (17%)
1634–36	22 (27%)	4 (5%)	57 (69%)	83	16 (19%)
1637–39	24 (30%)	12 (15%)	43 (54%)	79	15 (19%)
1640–42	20 (33%)	9 (15%)	31 (52%)	60	15 (25%)
1599[a]	7 (17%)	1 (2%)	33 (80%)	41	41 (100%)
1571–1642	381 (25%)	191 (12%)	968 (63%)	1540	629 (41%)

[a]Addenda from Harbage: plays revived during 1590s, original dates unknown.

TABLE 15   Performances of Surviving and Lost Plays, 1592–97

Year	Performances of 22 surviving plays	Performances of 92 lost plays	Total known performances
1592	53	55	108
1593	15	16	31
1594	65	143	208
1595	31	183	214
1596	40	132	172
1597	38	113	151
Total	242 (27%)	642 (73%)	884
Performance per play	11	6.98	7.75

TABLE 16   Genres of Known Performances, 1592–97

Year	Comedy	Tragedy	Other genres	Total known performances
1592	18	24	66	108
1593	10	5	16	31
1594	33	53	122	208
1595	58	19	137	214
1596	41	18	113	172
1597	40	15	96	151
Total	200 (23%)	134 (15%)	550 (62%)	884

TABLE 17   The Twelve Most Frequently Performed Plays 1592–97

Play	Genre	Survived or lost	Known performances
The Jew of Malta	T	S	36
The Wiseman of Westchester	O[a]	L	32
The Spanish Tragedy	T	S	29
Doctor Faustus	T	S	25
Belin Dun	O[b]	L	25
The Blind Beggar of Alexandria	C	S	22
Seven Days of the Week	O[c]	L	21
A Knack to Know an Honest Man	O[d]	S	21
The French Comedy	C (?)	L	17
Henry VI	O[b]	S	17
Crack Me This Nut	C (?)	L	16
Long Meg of Westminster	C (?)	L	16

a. Pseudo-history
b. History
c. Morality (?)
d. Tragicomedy

CITY COMEDY AND REVENGE
TRAGEDY LONDON REVIVALS

Table 18 lists all of the known London revivals of the city comedies and revenge tragedies included in this study. I have considered a revival to be one or more London performances of a play during the decade; therefore, regardless of the number of independent productions or individual performances of the play, the play can have no more than one revival in any single decade. I have used this definition of a revival because, during the seventeenth and eighteenth centuries, a play might remain in a company's repertory and be performed regularly over a number of years, so it is difficult to speak of a production in the modern sense of the term. A revival, as I have defined it, is a somewhat crude measure, for it equates a popular play having several productions during a single decade with a one-performance flop. It does, however, indicate the primary dependent variable of this study: the fact that a theatre company (or manager) decided that a certain play might appeal to its audience and committed resources to implementing this decision. Figure 4 in chapter 4 is a graph of the trends of these city comedy and revenge tragedy revivals from 1660 to 1979.

The data on revivals have come from several sources. *The London Stage 1660–1800* provides as full an account as is available of the Restoration and eighteenth-century productions. The twentieth-century London theatre was traced through the playbills listed in the seventeen editions of *Who's Who in the Theatre*. The nineteenth century presented the greatest challenge, for there were many theatres and a compilation such as *The London Stage* has yet to be done. I have gone through collections of playbills in the British Library and Victoria and Albert Theatre Museum, as well as looking for mention of revivals in secondary sources. John Genest's *Some Account of the English Stage, from the Restoration in 1660 to 1830* was useful for the century's first three decades, while J. P. Wearing's *The London Stage, 1890–1899*, covered the final decade.

The "Sunday societies" produced a number of Renaissance plays during the early twentieth century, and I have indicated the two most active in terms of city comedy and revenge tragedy revivals. PS denotes a Phoenix Society production; RT indicates the Renaissance Theatre Society.

TABLE 18   City Comedy and Revenge Tragedy Revivals

Decade	Plays	Theatres and dates
1660–69	**8 city comedies, 7 revenge tragedies**	
	The Alchemist	Vere Street (1660–62); Bridges (1664, 1669); Lincoln's Inn Fields (1668)
	Wit without Money	Red Bull (1660, 1663); Cockpit (1660); Vere Street (1663); At Court (1666)
	Bartholomew Fair	Vere Street (1661); Bridges (1664, 1667–68); At Court-King's Co. (1669)
	Epicoene	Red Bull (1660); Vere Street (1660–61); Cockpit (1661–62); Bridges (1664, 1667–69); At Court-King's Co. (1666)
	The Devil Is an Ass	Unknown (1663); Bridges (1669)
	A New Way to Pay Old Debts	Red Bull (1662)
	A Mad World, My Masters	Red Bull (1661)
	A Trick to Catch the Old One	Lincoln's Inn Fields (1662–25)
	The Maid's Tragedy	Vere Street (1660–62); Red Bull (1660); Bridges (1667–69)
	Valentinian	Bridges (1669)
	'Tis Pity She's a Whore	Salisbury (1661)
	The Spanish Tragedy	The Nursery (1668)
	The Changeling	Lincoln's Inn Fields (1661); Salisbury (1661); At Court (1668)
	The Duchess of Malfi	Salisbury (1660); Lincoln's Inn Fields (1662, 1668)
	The White Devil	Vere Street (1661); unknown (1664); Drury Lane (1665)
1670–79	**5 city comedies, 4 revenge tragedies**	
	Wit without Money	Lincoln's Inn Fields (1672)
	The Alchemist	Drury Lane (1674–75)
	Bartholomew Fair	Drury Lane (1674)
	Epicoene	Unknown (1673)
	Every Man in His Humour	Bridges (1670)
	Valentinian	Unknown (1975)
	Titus Andronicus	Drury Lane (1678)
	The Duchess of Malfi	Dorset Garden (1672–76)
	The White Devil	Bridges (1671)
1680–89	**4 city comedies, 4 revenge tragedies**	
	Eastward Ho! (an adaptation by Tate entitled *Cuckold's Haven*)	Dorset Garden (1685)

(*continued*)

TABLE 18   (*Continued*)

Decade	Plays	Theatres and dates
	Bartholomew Fair	Drury Lane (1682)
	Epicoene	Dorset Garden or Drury Lane (1685)
	The Dutch Courtesan (an adaptation by Behn entitled *The Revenge*)	Dorset Garden (1680)
	The Maid's Tragedy	Unknown (1685); Drury Lane (1687)
	Valentinian	Unknown (1684, 1687–89); At Court (1685, 1688); Drury Lane (1687)
	Titus Andronicus	Drury Lane (1685, 1687)
	The Duchess of Malfi	At Court (United Co.) (1686)
1690–99	**0 city comedies, 3 revenge tragedies**	
	The Maid's Tragedy	Unknown (1691); Lincoln's Inn Fields (1698)
	Valentinian	Unknown (1691, 1693)
	Titus Andronicus	Unknown (1698 [?])
1700–1710	**5 city comedies, 4 revenge tragedies**	
	The Alchemist	Lincoln's Inn Fields (1702; Drury Lane (1700–1702, 1709)
	Bartholomew Fair	Drury Lane (1702–10), performed almost every season from 1702 to 1722; Queen's (1707)
	Epicoene	Drury Lane (1700–1710), performed almost every season from 1700 to 1742; Queen's (1707)
	A New Way to Pay Old Debts (an adaptation entitled *The Debaucher*)	Drury Lane (1708)
	Wit without Money	Queen's (1707, 1709)
	The Maid's Tragedy	Drury Lane (1704, 1708); Queen's (1706–7)
	Valentinian	Lincoln's Inn Fields (1704); Drury Lane (1706)
	Titus Andronicus	Drury Lane (1704)
	The Duchess of Malfi	Lincoln's Inn Fields (1705); Queen's (1707)
1710–19	**5 city comedies, 3 revenge tragedies**	
	The Alchemist	Drury Lane (1711–13); Queen's (1710)
	Bartholomew Fair	Drury Lane (regularly); Queen's (1710)
	Epicoene	Drury Lane (regularly); Queen's (1710)
	Wit without Money	Drury Lane (regularly), performed almost every season from 1711 to 1735
	A Mad World, My Masters (adapted as short farce)	Lincoln's Inn Fields (1715)
	A Maid's Tragedy	Drury Lane (1710, 1715–19); Queen's (1710)

(*continued*)

TABLE 18 (*Continued*)

Decade	Plays	Theatres and dates
	Valentinian	Drury Lane (1710–11); Lincoln's Inn Fields (1715)
	Titus Andronicus	Drury Lane (1717–19)
1720–29	**5 city comedies, 2 revenge tragedies**	
	The Alchemist	Drury Lane (1721–30), performed almost every season from 1721 to 1787; adapted into a farce entitled *The Tobacconist* in 1770
	Bartholomew Fair	Drury Lane (regularly)
	Epicoene	Drury Lane (regularly)
	Ram Alley	Drury Lane (1723 or 1724; Genest's report)
	Wit without Money	Drury Lane (regularly)
	The Maid's Tragedy	Drury Lane (1720–21, 1723–25, 1728); Lincoln's Inn Fields (1729)
	Titus Andronicus	Lincoln's Inn Fields (1720–24); Drury Lane (1721)
1730–39	**4 city comedies, 1 revenge tragedy**	
	The Alchemist	Drury Lane (regularly); Haymarket (1733)
	Bartholomew Fair	Drury Lane (1731); Lincoln's Inn Fields (1735)
	Epicoene	Drury Lane (regularly)
	Wit without Money	Drury Lane (1730–35); Covent Garden (1736–39)
	The Maid's Tragedy	Lincoln's Inn Fields (1730, 1732); Covent Garden (1735)
1740–49	**4 city comedies, 1 revenge tragedy**	
	The Alchemist	Drury Lane (regularly); Covent Garden (1740–41)
	Wit without Money	Covent Garden (1740, 1748)
	Epicoene	Drury Lane (regularly); Covent Garden (1745–46, 1748)
	A New Way to Pay Old Debts	Drury Lane (1748–49)
	The Maid's Tragedy	Covent Garden (1744–45)
1750–59	**6 city comedies, 0 revenge tragedies**	
	Eastward Ho!	Drury Lane (1751)
	Epicoene	Drury Lane (1752)
	The Alchemist	Drury Lane (regularly)
	Every Man in His Humour	Drury Lane (regularly), performed almost every season from 1751 to 1788
	Wit without Money	Covent Gardent (1753, 1757–59)
	A New Way to Pay Old Debts	Drury Lane (1759)

(*continued*)

TABLE 18 (*Continued*)

Decade	Plays	Theatres and dates
1760–69	**5 city comedies, 0 revenge tragedies**	
	Wit without Money	Covent Garden (1760–61, 1764)
	Eastward Ho!	Drury Lane (1763)
	The Alchemist	Drury Lane (regularly)
	Every Man in His Humour	Drury Lane (regularly); Covent Garden (1762–69)
	A New Way to Pay Old Debts	Drury Lane (1760, 1769)
1770–79	**4 city comedies, 1 revenge tragedy**	
	Eastward Ho! (an adaptation entitled *Old City Manners*)	Drury Lane (1775–77)
	The Alchemist	Drury Lane (regularly); Haymarket (1770)
	The Tobacconist (farce by Francis Gentleman; not counted separately from *The Alchemist*)	Haymarket (1770, 1771, 1773, 1775); Drury Lane (1772, 1773)
	Epicoene	Drury Lane (1776)
	Every Man in His Humour	Drury Lane (regularly); Covent Garden (1770–74, 1777, 1779)
	The Duke of Milan (an adaptation by Cumberland)	Covent Garden (1779)
1780–89	**6 city comedies, 3 revenge tragedies**	
	The Alchemist	Drury Lane (regularly to 1787); Haymarket (1784)
	The Tobacconist	Haymarket (1782, 1784)
	Wit without Money	Haymarket (1782)
	Epicoene	Covent Garden (1784)
	Every Man in His Humour	Drury Lane (regularly)
	A New Way to Pay Old Debts	Drury Lane (1783–88); Covent Garden (1781–85)
	A Mad World, My Masters (an adaptation by MacNally entitled *The April Fool*)	Covent Garden (1786)
	The Maid's Tragedy	Drury Lane (1785)
	The Duke of Milan (an adaptation by Cumberland)	Covent Garden (1780)
	The Changeling (an ad-	Covent Gardent (1789)

(*continued*)

TABLE 18   (*Continued*)

Decade	Plays	Theatres and dates
	aptation entitled *Marcella*)	
1790–99	**3 city comedies, 0 revenge tragedies**	
	Every Man in His Humour	Drury Lane and King's (1791); Covent Garden (1798)
	The Tobacconist	Covent Garden (1798–99)
	A New Way to Pay Old Debts	Covent Garden (1796)
1800–1809	**3 city comedies, 0 revenge tragedies**	
	Every Man in His Humour	Covent Garden (1800–1802, 1806–9); Drury Lane (1802)
	A New Way to Pay Old Debts	Covent Garden (1801–2, 1804, 1807–9)
	The Tobacconist	Haymarket (1800)
1810–19	**3 city comedies, 2 revenge tragedies**	
	Every Man in His Humour	Covent Garden (1810–11); Drury Lane (1816)
	The Tobacconist	Drury Lane (1815)
	A New Way to Pay Old Debts	Covent Garden (1810–12, 1814, 1816–17); Drury Lane (1816–19)
	The Jew of Malta	Drury Lane (1818)
	The Duke of Milan	Drury Lane (1816)
1820–29	**2 city comedies, 0 revenge tragedies**	
	Every Man in His Humour	Covent Garden (1825)
	A New Way to Pay Old Debts	Drury Lane (1820, 1822, 1824–25); Covent Garden (1820, 1827–28)
1830–39	**2 city comedies, 1 revenge tragedy**	
	Every Man in His Humour	Drury Lane (1832)
	A New Way to Pay Old Debts	Drury Lane (1832, 1834, 1838); Covent Garden (1836); Haymarket (1831–33); New City (1831)
	The Maid's Tragedy (an adaptation by Sheridan Knowles entitled *The Bridal*)	Haymarket (1837)
1840–49	**2 city comedies, 0 revenge tragedies**	
	Every Man in His Humour	Haymarket (1848)

(*continued*)

TABLE 18 (*Continued*)

Decade	Plays	Theatres and dates
	A New Way to Pay Old Debts	Haymarket (1840, 1842–43); Victoria (1844, 1848); Royal Olympic (1848); City of London (1847); Sadler's Wells (1844); Marylebone (1848)
1850–59	**1 city comedy, 2 revenge tragedies**	
	A New Way to Pay Old Debts	Drury Lane (1850, 1854, 1857); City of London (1853); Royal Grecian Saloon (1854); Marylebone (1852)
	Titus Andronicus	Britannia Saloon (1852, 1857)
	The Duchess of Malfi	Sadler's Wells (1850); Standard (1855, 1859)
1860–69	**1 city comedy, 1 revenge tragedy**	
	A New Way to Pay Old Debts	Haymarket (1861)
	The Duchess of Malfi	Sadler's Wells (1864)
1870–79	**1 city comedy, 1 revenge tragedy**	
	A New Way to Pay Old Debts	Gaiety (1871); St. James (1877)
	The Duchess of Malfi	Standard (1870)
1880–89	**0 city comedies, 0 revenge tragedies**	
1890–99	**1 city comedy, 1 revenge tragedy**	
	The Alchemist	Apothecaries Hall (1899)
	The Duchess of Malfi	Opera Comique (1892)
1900–1910	**2 city comedies, 1 revenge tragedy**	
	The Alchemist	Imperial (1902)
	Epicoene	Great Queen St. (1905)
	The Maid's Tragedy	Royalty (1904); Court (1908)
1910–19	**0 city comedies, 1 revenge tragedy**	
	The Duchess of Malfi	Lyric, Hammersmith (1919–PS)
1920–29	**4 city comedies, 5 revenge tragedies**	
	Bartholomew Fair	New Oxford (1921–PS)
	A New Way to Pay Old Debts	Old Vic (1922)
	The Alchemist	Regent (1923–PS)
	Epicoene	Regent (1924–PS)
	The Maid's Tragedy	Lyric, Hammersmith (1921–PS); Scala (1925–RT)
	The Jew of Malta	Daly's (1922–PS)
	'Tis Pity She's a Whore	Shaftesbury (1923–PS)
	Titus Andronicus	Old Vic (1923)

(*continued*)

TABLE 18   (*Continued*)

Decade	Plays	Theatres and dates
	The White Devil	Scala (1925–RT)
1930–39	**1 city comedy, 3 revenge tragedies**	
	The Alchemist	Embassy (1935); production later moved to Princess
	'Tis Pity She's a Whore	Arts (1934)
	The Duchess of Malfi	Embassy (1935); Tavistock (1937)
	The White Devil	St. Martins (1935)
1940–49	**2 city comedies, 3 revenge tragedies**	
	The Alchemist	King's, Hammersmith (1945); New Theatre (Old Vic Company–1947)
	Every Man in His Humour	Toynbee Hall Curtain Theatre (1949)
	'Tis Pity She's a Whore	Strand (1941)
	The Duchess of Malfi	Haymarket (1945)
	The White Devil	Duchess (1947)
1950–59	**5 city comedies, 3 revenge tragedies**	
	Bartholomew Fair	Old Vic (1950)
	A New Way to Pay Old Debts	Richmond (1950); King's, Hammersmith (1953)
	A Trick to Catch the Old One	Mermaid (1952)
	Eastward Ho!	Royal Exchange (1953)
	The Dutch Courtesan	Theatre Royal, Stratford E15 (1954, 1959)
	The Changeling	Interval Club (1950); Wyndham's (Pegasus Society–1954)
	Titus Andronicus	Old Vic (1957); Aldwych (1957); Stoll (1957)
	The Duchess of Malfi	Theatre Royale, Stratford, E15 (1957)
1960–69	**6 city comedies, 8 revenge tragedies**	
	Every Man in His Humour	Theatre Royale, Stratford E15 (1960)
	A Chaste Maid in Cheapside	Embassy, Swiss Cottage (1961), Royal Court (1966)
	Eastward Ho!	Mermaid (1962)
	The Alchemist	Old Vic (1962)
	The Dutch Courtesan	Old Vic (1964)
	Bartholomew Fair	Royal Court (1966); Aldwych (1969)
	The Duchess of Malfi	Aldwych (1960)
	'Tis Pity She's a Whore	Mermaid (1961)
	The Changeling	Royal Court (1961); Jeanetta Cochraine (1966)
	The White Devil	Old Vic (1961); National Theatre (at Old Vic–1969)
	Women Beware Women	New Arts (1962)

(*continued*)

TABLE 18   (*Continued*)

Decade	Plays	Theatres and dates
	The Jew of Malta	Aldwych (1964)
	The Maid's Tragedy	Mermaid (1964)
	The Revenger's Tagedy	Aldwych (1969)
1970–79	**3 city comedies, 5 revenge tragedies**	
	The Alchemist	Old Vic (1970); Aldwych (1977)
	The Devil Is an Ass	Lyttelton (1977)
	Bartholomew Fair	Young Vic (1978); Roundhouse (1978)
	The Duchess of Malfi	Young Vic (1970); Royal Court (1971)
	Titus Andronicus	Roundhouse (1971); Aldwych (1973)
	The White Devil	Old Vic (1976)
	'Tis Pity She's a Whore	Warehouse (1978)
	The Changeling	Riverside (1978); Aldwych (1978)

STATISTICAL COMPARISONS

Following are some statistical comparisons referred to in chapter 6.

TWENTIETH-CENTURY NEW PRODUCTIONS AND REVIVALS

If the period from 1921 to 1979 is taken in five-year units, as shown in table 7, the number of new productions rose six times (excluding the tiny rise in the 1960s). Two of these increases, from the late 1920s to the early 1930s and from the late 1940s to the early 1950s, show no significant changes in the proportion of new productions that were revivals. The other four periods show three significant (below the .01 level) decreases and one increase in the revival rates, as indicated in table 19 below. For the period from the late 1960s to the early 1970s, which saw a decrease in overall theatrical activity as measured by new productions, coupled with an increase in revivals, the change during the two periods was not statistically significant; $\chi^2 = 5.317$; $P(\chi^2) = .021$.

MODERN RENAISSANCE REVIVALS BEFORE AND AFTER 1955

Following the mid-fifties, revenge tragedies received relatively more revivals than did other categories of Renaissance drama. Table 20 shows some comparisons of revenge tragedy with other types of Renaissance plays.

TABLE 19   Revivals When New Productions Were Increasing

Type	July 1921–24	1925–29	Total productions
Revivals	206 (30%)	338 (24%)	544
New plays	477 (70%)	1,062 (76%)	1,539
Total	683	1,400	2,083

$\chi^2 = 8.617; P(\chi^2) = .003$

Type	1940–44	1945–49	Total productions
Revivals	250 (38%)	320 (25%)	570
New plays	405 (62%)	962 (75%)	1,367
Total	655	1,282	1,937

$\chi^2 = 36.410; P(\chi^2) < .001$

Type	1955–59	1960–64	Total productions
Revivals	152 (18%)	224 (25%)	376
New plays	697 (82%)	670 (75%)	1,367
Total	849	894	1,743

$\chi^2 = 13.168; P(\chi^2) < .001$

Type	1970–74	1975–79	Total productions
Revivals	247 (31%)	270 (25%)	517
New plays	561 (69%)	824 (75%)	1,385
Total	808	1,094	1,902

$\chi^2 = 8.144; P(\chi^2) = .004$

TABLE 20 Revenge Tragedy Revivals and Other Plays

Type	1900–54	1955–79	Total productions
New productions	8,421	4,523	12,944
Revenge tragedies	18	22	40
Total	8,439	4,545	12,984
$\chi = 7.051$; $P(\chi^2) = .008$			
Revivals only	2,093	1,101	3,194
Revenge tragedies	18	22	40
Total	2,111	1,123	3,234
$\chi = 7.345$; $P(\chi^2) = .007$			
Shakespeare: Frequent	243	122	365
Revenge tragedies	18	22	40
Total	261	144	405
$\chi = 7.324$; $P(\chi^2) = .007$			

For the following comparisons, although the percentages go in the anticipated direction (i.e., suggesting a disproportionate increase in revenge tragedy revivals relative to other Renaissance plays in the period following 1955), the differences are not significant at the .01 level. Percentages of twentieth-century productions for each type before and after 1955 are indicated.

Type	1900–1954	1955–79	Total productions
Shakespeare: Infrequent			
Comedies	20 (56%)	16 (44%)	36
Tragedies	15 (60%)	10 (40%)	25
Total	35 (57%)	26 (43%)	56
Other Renaissance plays			
Comedies	22 (73%)	8 (27%)	30
Tragedies	15 (56%)	12 (44%)	27
Other	16 (76%)	5 (24%)	21
Total	53 (68%)	25 (32%)	78
City comedies	16 (53%)	14 (47%)	30
Revenge tragedies	18 (45%)	22 (55%)	40

MODERN REVIVALS OF OTHER RENAISSANCE PLAYS

The following tables offer a closer look at the modern revivals of "other" Renaissance plays, that is, plays that are neither revenge tragedies, nor city comedies, nor by Shakespeare. Table 21 lists the revivals of eleven Renaissance comedies during the twentieth century, and table 22 lists the revivals of eleven tragedies. Table 23 lists revivals of Renaissance (and medieval) plays that are outside the preceding two genres. These tables include all of the modern London revivals of "other" Renaissance plays that I have been able to find. The figures from these three tables have been cumulated in table 10 in chapter 6.

TABLE 21 Other Renaissance Plays: Comedies

Play (11) Period:	1900–1904	1905–9	1910–14	1915–19	1920–24	1925–29	1930–34	1935–39	1940–44	1945–49	1950–54	1955–59	1960–64	1965–69	1970–74	1975–79	Total revivals of plays
Volpone					2		1	1	2	1	1	1		2		1	12
The Shoemaker's Holiday						1		1	1				1		2		6
The Knight of the Burning Pestle	1				1		1										3
Ralph Roister Doister					1	1											2
The Poetaster				1													1
The Return from Parnassus				1													1
The Fair Maid of the West					1												1
The Chances					1												1
Rule a Wife and Have a Wife						1											1
Gammer Gurton's Needle								1									1
A Fair Quarrel																1	1
Total revivals for each period	1	0	0	2	6	3	2	3	3	1	1	1	1	2	2	2	30

TABLE 22 Other Renaissance Plays: Tragedies

Play (11) Period:	1900–1904	1905–9	1910–14	1915–19	1920–24	1925–29	1930–34	1935–39	1940–44	1945–49	1950–54	1955–59	1960–64	1965–69	1970–74	1975–79	Total revivals of plays
Doctor Faustus	1					1			1	1			1		2		7
Arden of Faversham						1					1		1		2		5
Edward II					1						1		1	1			4
The Witch of Edmonton					1			1				1					3
Tamburlaine the Great													1			1	2
The Broken Heart	1																1
Fratricide Punished					1												1
Bonduca						1											1
Charles, Duke of Byron						1											1
Sejanus						1											1
A Woman Killed with Kindness															1		1
Total revivals for each period	2	0	0	0	3	5	0	1	1	1	2	1	4	1	5	1	27

TABLE 23 Other Renaissance Plays: Other

Play (12) Period:	1900–1904	1905–9	1910–14	1915–19	1920–24	1925–29	1930–34	1935–39	1940–44	1945–49	1950–54	1955–59	1960–64	1965–69	1970–74	1975–79	Total revivals of plays
Everyman (morality)	1	2		1				1									5
Wakefield mystery plays (mystery cycle)													1	1	1		3
Comus (masque)	1						1										2
The Faithful Shepherdess (pastoral)					1	1											2
The Raigne of King Edward, II (history; episode entitled *The King and the Countess*)	1					1											2
The Masque of Beauty (masque)			1														1
Jacob and Esau (biblical interlude)			1														1
When You See Me, You Know Me (history)			1														1
David and Bethsabe (biblical history)							1										1
Fulgens and Lucrece (romantic interlude)															1		1
Genesis mediaeval mystery play								1									1
Magnyficence (morality)															1		1
Total revivals for each period	3	2	3	1	1	2	2	2	0	0	0	0	1	1	3	0	21

NOTES

CHAPTER 1: TIMBERS

1. Stephen Orgel sketches the "intimacy and danger," the tensions of attraction, legitimation, and dependency, that existed between the theatre and the courts of both Elizabeth and James I, in "Making Greatness Familiar," *The Power of Forms in the English Renaissance,* ed. Stephen Greenblatt (Norman, Oklahoma: Pilgrim Books, 1982), 41–47. Edmund Tilney, master of the revels from 1579 to 1609, was responsible for licensing all plays before their first performance. An order of the Privy Council (1581) commissioned him to "order and reforme, auctorise and put downe [plays, players, and playmakers], as shalbe thought meete or unmeete unto himselfe or his said Deputie in that behalfe." Seven years later the Council elaborated on what was meant by "meete": Tilney was called "to stryke oute or reforme suche partes and matters as they shall fynd unfytt and undecent to be handled in playes, both for Divinitie and State . . ." (E. K. Chambers, *Notes on the History of the Revels Office Under the Tudors* [London: A. H. Bullen, 1906], 72, 77).

2. The despondency felt by post-Renaissance men of letters in England is discussed by W. Jackson Bate in *The Burden of the Past and the English Poet* (1970; rpt. New York: Norton, 1972).

3. Ben Jonson's notes on literature, notes that themselves included collections of classical maxims and comments thereon, were published posthumously in 1640. Their title, most appropriately, was *Timber, or Discoveries: Made upon Men and Matter as They Have Flowed Out of His Daily Readings or Had Their Reflux to His Peculiar Notion of the Times.*

4. *Economy and Society: An Outline of Interpretive Sociology,* ed. Guenther Roth and Claus Wittich (Berkeley: University of California Press, 1978), 4.

5. The example comes from Thomas Middleton's city comedy, *A Trick to Catch the Old One.*

6. The meaning of a book, play, or other cultural object is not even fixed for the individual, for it changes as he or she changes; as Edmund Wilson put it, "there is really no way of considering a book independently of one's special sensations in reading it on a particular occasion. In this as in everything else one must allow for a certain relativity. In a sense, one can never read the book that the author originally wrote, and one can never read the same book twice" (*The Triple Thinkers,* revised ed. [New York: Oxford University Press, 1948] ix).

7. Primary groups and subcultures participate in larger cultural arenas, of course, but they also create a set of their own cultural objects, rich in connotation for members of the group. Gary Allen Fine has explored the capacity small groups have for culture creation; see "Small Groups and Culture Creation," *American Sociological Review* 44, no. 5 (October 1979): 733–45. For an exploration of how subcultures develop their styles (including, in my terminology, cultural objects) in opposition to other cultural systems, see Dick Hebdige, *Subculture: The Meaning of Style* (New York: Methuen, 1979).

8. Anthropologist Victor Turner described a Ndembu circumcision ritual he observed in which the participants forgot to construct one of the central symbols, an archway. No one seemed to mind or even notice the omission until after the circumcision was over; cultural participants can always, unconsciously, fill in the pattern. See "Mukanda" in *The Forest of Symbols: Aspects of Ndembu Ritual* (Ithaca, N.Y.: Cornell University Press, 1967), 151–279.

9. For a discussion of the problem of distinguishing between culture and social structure while avoiding reductionism, see Robert Wuthnow, James Davison Hunter, Albert Bergeson, and Edith Kurzweil, *Cultural Analysis* (London: Routledge and Kegan Paul, 1984). Wuthnow et al. suggest that culture and social structure be considered as "mutually influencing aspects of behavior," the former oriented toward the expressive, the latter toward differentially distributed resources.

10. This archive image is prominent in those schools of literary criticism that accept as unproblematic a canon or, in F. R. Leavis's now somewhat notorious phrase, a "great tradition." Spokesmen for the archive position were and are unembarrassed in their claims regarding cultural value. From the mid-nineteenth to the mid-twentieth century, many prominent thinkers from the world of arts and letters associated culture with an ideal of human perfection. This recalls the root word *cultivation*, as in agriculture, and implies the cultivation of the human spirit. Matthew Arnold maintained that culture has "its origin in the love of perfection; it is a study of perfection. . . . [It seeks] to make the best that has been thought and known in the world current everywhere" ("Culture and Anarchy," *The Portable Matthew Arnold*, ed. Lionel Trilling [New York: Viking, 1949], 473, 499). Culture overrides class distinctions by making the perfection of beauty and intelligence, sweetness and light, available to all. T. S. Eliot, who similarly maintained a traditional belletristic position, disagreed with Arnold's emphasis on individual perfection, arguing that culture was better thought of as an attribute of an entire society, but, like Arnold, Eliot had no doubt that some cultures were better than others and that there was some ideal against which any particular culture might be measured. Cultures might be more or less "developed," which may just be the twentieth-century version of being more or less "perfect," and the degree of cultural development a society possesses determines the overall value of that society.

> Culture may even be described simply as that which makes life worth living. And it is what justifies other peoples and other generations in saying, when they contemplate the remains and the influence of an extinct civilisation, that it was *worth while* for that civilisation to have existed. [Emphasis is Eliot's.] ["Notes towards the Definition of Culture," in *Christianity and Culture* (New York: Harcourt, Brace, & Co., 1940, 1949), 100]

During the past quarter century, when the conception and construction of "the canon" has come under devastating attack by feminist and Marxian critics among others, considerations of value, at least in the domain of literature, have been eclipsed by what has been said to be more "objective" scholarship. For an illuminating discussion of the history and costs of this "exile of evaluation," see Barbara Herrnstein Smith, "Contingencies of Value," in *Critical Inquiry* 10 (1983): 1–35.

11. The social science view of culture, its lineage going back to Romanticism and particularly Herder's advocacy of cultural relativism, is that culture has to do with a particular society's overall way of life. The anthropologist A. L. Kroeber offered a general functionalist definition:

> The essential characteristic things about a culture are its forms and patterns, the interrelations of these into an organization, and the way these parts, and the whole, work or function as a group of human beings lives under them. A culture is a way of habitual acting, feeling, and thinking channeled by a society out of an infinite number and variety of potential ways of living. The particular channeling adopted is heavily preconditioned by antecedent ways and organizations or systems of culture; though it is not predetermined thereby except within certain limits. ["Values as a Subject of Natural Science Inquiry," read before the National Academy of Sciences, 25 April 1949; published in *Proceedings* 35 (1949); rpt. in A. L. Kroeber, *The Nature of Culture* (Chicago: University of Chicago Press, 1952), 136–38]

Kroeber believed that the cultural order, like the social and physical orders, was a part of the natural world, hence subject to empirical investigation but not to evaluation (except perhaps in terms of how well cultural traits are integrated with the rest of the social system). Evaluation according to any external standard, let alone an ideal of human perfection, has been strenuously avoided by almost all social scientists; "the scientific rhetoric, tight-lipped and non-normative, brooks no invidious distinctions" (Gertrude Jaeger and Philip Selznick, "A Normative Theory of Culture," *American Sociological Review* 39, no. 5 [October 1964]: 654.) Except for this general reluctance to evaluate, social scientists have varied widely in their use of the concept of culture. In a survey of the definitions of culture used in modern anthropology, sociology, and psychology, Kroeber and Clyde Kluckhohn identified 164 distinct meanings, including among others those based on the concepts of tradition, habit, learning, ideas, symbols, and artifacts (A. L. Kroeber and Clyde Kluckhohn, *Culture: A Critical Review of Concepts and Definitions,* Papers of the Peabody Museum of American Archeology and Ethnology, Harvard University, 47, 1 [Cambridge, 1952]). Richard A. Peterson has recently tried to restore some order by a fourfold grouping of definitions: "In contemporary parlance, culture consists of four sorts of elements: norms, values, beliefs, and expressive symbols" ("Revitalizing the Culture Concept," *Annual Review of Sociology* 5 (1979)) 137–66). Such a compact statement is both all-encompassing and typically noncommital regarding any association between culture and some ideal of perfection in the formulation of human experience.

12. For a useful account of the present state of "new literary history," see Herbert Lindenberger, "Toward a New History in Literary Study," *Profession 84* (Modern Language Association, 1984), 16–23; see also Smith, "Contingencies of Value."

Renaissance studies have been particularly influenced by the new literary history; the work of Steven Orgel, Steven Greenblatt, Louis A. Montrose, Jonathan Goldberg, and Frank Whigham, cited in the following two chapters, exemplifies this approach.

13. Howard S. Becker, *Art Worlds,* (Berkeley: University of California Press, 1982), 35.

14. The "production-of-culture" approach, with its plumbing-inspired emphasis on organizational channels and filters through which cultural objects flow or are blocked, is described by one of its leading practitioners, Richard Peterson, in "Revitalizing the Culture Concept"; see also Paul M. Hirsch, "Processing Fads and Fashions," *American Journal of Sociology* 77 (1972): 639–59.

15. For a discussion of some varieties of reflection theory, see Milton Albrecht, "The Relationship of Literature and Society," *American Sociological Review* 59 (1954): 425–31; for a critique of the reflection model, see Peter Laslett, "The Wrong Way through the Telescope," *British Journal of Sociology* 27 (1976): 319–42.

16. "The Triumph of Mass Idols," *Literature, Popular Culture, and Society* (Palo Alto, Calif.: Pacific, 1968), 109–36.

17. See, respectively, R. Howard Bloch, *Medieval French Literature and Law* (Berkeley: University of California Press, 1977); Will Wright, *Sixguns and Society: A Structural Study of the Western* (Berkeley: University of California Press, 1975); Dorothy Hobson, "Housewives and the Mass Media," in *Culture, Media, Language,* ed. Stuart Hall et al. (London: Hutchinson, 1980); César Graña, *Bohemian versus Bourgeois* (New York: Basic, 1964); and Michael Baxandall, *Painting and Experience in Fifteenth-Century Italy* (New York: Oxford University Press, 1972).

18. Hans Robert Jauss, "Literary History as a Challenge to Literary Theory," in *Toward an Aesthetic of Reception,* trans. Timothy Bahti (Minneapolis: University of Minnesota Press, 1982), 3–45.

19. *Sociology of Literature,* trans. Ernest Pick, 2d ed. (London: Frank Cass, 1971), 75–86.

20. George H. Ford, *Dickens and His Readers: Aspects of Novel Criticism Since 1836* (1955; rpt. New York: Norton, 1965).

21. Paul DiMaggio and Kristen Stenberg, "Conformity and Diversity in the American Resident Theatre," in *Art, Ideology and Politics,* ed. Judith Balfe and Margaret J. Wyszomirski (New York: Praeger, 1985); Rosanne Martorella, *The Sociology of Opera* (New York: Praeger, 1982).

22. Adena Rosmarin, " 'Misreading' *Emma:* The Powers and Perfidies of Interpretive History," *English Literary History* 51 (1984): 315–42, and "Hermeneutics versus Erotics: Shakespeare's *Sonnets* and Interpretive History," *PMLA* 100 (1985): 20–37; Jerome J. McGann, "The Text, the Poem, and the Problem of Historical Method," *New Literary History* 12 (1981): 269–88.

23. George Steiner, *Antigones* (New York: Oxford University Press, 1984). All of the studies cited look at reception over time; for an exemplary microscopic, synchronic study of literary reception, see Janice A. Radway, *Reading the Romance: Women, Patriarchy, and Popular Literature* (Chapel Hill: University of North Carolina Press, 1984).

24. John H. Mueller, *The American Symphony Orchestra: A Social History of Musical Taste* (Bloomington: Indiana University Press, 1951). The original data and an update to 1970 is provided in Kate Hevner Mueller, *Twenty-seven Major American Sym-*

phony Orchestras: A History of Their Repertoires 1842–3 through 1969–70 (Bloomington: Indiana University Press, 1973).

25. John Mueller, *American Symphony Orchestra,* 239, 208–10.

26. Becker, in *Art Worlds,* 365–68, also uses the conception of art as either "lasting" or dying.

27. In an exception to the implicit assumption that art either lasts or doesn't, Francis Haskell has studied the wide variety of circumstances that produced a general rediscovery of early Italian, eighteenth-century French, Spanish, and certain Dutch (Vermeer) painters in the nineteenth century; see *Rediscoveries in Art: Some Aspects of Taste, Fashion, and Collecting in England and France* (Ithaca, New York: Cornell University Press, 1976).

28. See Gaye Tuchman and Nina E. Fortin, "Fame and Misfortune: Edging Women Out of the Great Literary Tradition," *American Journal of Sociology* 90 (1984): 72–96, and Wendy Griswold, "American Character and the American Novel," *American Journal of Sociology* 86 (1981): 740–65; for a study of the editorial decisionmaking process in nonfiction books, see Lewis Coser et al., *Books: The Culture and Commerce of Publishing* (New York: Basic, 1982).

CHAPTER 2: CITY COMEDIES

1. The first full study devoted to treatment of the city comedy as a distinct genre was Brian Gibbons, *Jacobean City Comedy: A Study of Satiric Plays by Jonson, Marston, and Middleton,* 2d ed. (London: Methuen, 1980). See also M. C. Bradbrook, *The Growth and Structure of Elizabethan Comedy,* new ed. (London: Chatto & Windus, 1973), chap. 9, and *Four Jacobean City Comedies,* edited and introduction by Gāmini Salgādo (Harmondsworth: Penguin, 1975). In *Citizen Comedy in the Age of Shakespeare* (Toronto: University of Toronto Press, 1973), Alexander Legatt has delineated a broader category encompassing all plays of the period set in a middle-class social milieu, thus including the sanguine accounts of London life by dramatists such as Thomas Dekker and Thomas Heywood. I am following Gibbons and Salgādo in labeling as city comedies only those plays having a darker, more satirical view of urban mores.

2. Although *Every Man in His Humour* was set in Italy when performed in 1598, Jonson later gave it a London setting, using sites such as Moorfields, the Windmill Tavern, and the Old Jewry, all rich with connotation for a London audience. This change may have been made as early as the 1605 revival of the play, perhaps was not made until 1612, but in any case had been established by the 1616 folio and has been perpetuated.

3. Any selection criteria introduce some arbitrariness, of course. For example, while Gibbons (*Jacobean City Comedy*) includes both Jonson's *Volpone* and Middleton's *Michaelmas Term,* I exclude the former because it is set in Venice and the latter because it has never been revived. On the other hand, I do include *Ram Alley,* although its revival status is questionable; see appendix B.

4. Dates and companies are from Alfred Harbage, *Annals of English Drama 975–1700,* 2d ed. rev. by S. Schoenbaum (Philadelphia: University of Pennsylvania Press, 1964). I have used Harbage's estimated date of first performance to order the plays, and I have indicated his limits of possible dates in parentheses.

5. See especially Gāmini Salgādo's introduction to *Four Jacobean City Comedies,* 9–27, and Gibbons, *Jacobean City Comedy.*

6. Even the two plays not actually set in London, *A Mad World, My Masters* and *A New Way to Pay Old Debts,* share the London orientation. In the former, for example, the nonexistent but emblematic Lord Owemuch is said to have "great acquaintance i' th' city," and a courtesan, feigning gentility, asks to be remembered "to all my good cousins in Clerkenwell and St. Johns," such illustrations implying that country diseases come from London germs. Other casual references are made to London hospitals, fairs, and prisons. Similarly, though *A New Way to Pay Old Debts* is set in Nottinghamshire, Welborn has lived on Bankside, Margaret is to be presented in London, Sir Giles sends debtors to the Counter and may himself be sent to Bedlam, and Marrall has learned his table manners in Ram-Alley. Both plays are included as city comedies by Gibbons, Leggatt, and Salgādo, although Salgādo expresses some reservations.

7. In Elizabethan usage, the term "rogue" was associated with someone operating outside society, specifically a vagrant. Originally a rogue was a con artist bearing false papers, but by the Elizabethan era, a rogue might be the term for any idle rascal, and was occasionally a term of endearment. See C. T. Onions, *A Shakespeare Glossary,* 2d ed. (Oxford: Oxford University Press, 1978).

8. Some of the most familiar city comedy rogues are the trio of Subtle, Face, and Doll Common of *The Alchemist,* Meercraft of *The Devil Is an Ass,* and Ursula of *Bartholomew Fair.*

9. The term "elite" refers to peers, lesser titled nobility such as knights and baronets (after 1611), and untitled gentry in this study. See Peter Laslett, *The World We Have Lost,* 2d ed. (London: Methuen, 1971), chap. 2, for a discussion of the "one-class society." Laslett so labels early modern England because only the peers and lesser nobility, all of whom fall into the category of gentry, hold effective social power.

10. The term "grandsire" referred to any old man in Elizabethan usage.

11. In these cases one sometimes finds a split between the gallant as lover and the trickster who assists the gallant. For example, Sir Penetent Brothel's desire for Mistress Harebrain (*A Mad World, My Masters*) is consummated only through the machinations of the Courtesan, who seeks to profit by aiding the lovers. Similarly, Allwit's secret marriage to Sir Giles's daughter (*A New Way to Pay Old Debts*) is facilitated through the good offices of Lord Lovell. Lovell is an atypical trickster, in that he is of a high and secure social position; he is motivated by his desire to reward the worthy, stymie the vicious Sir Giles, and preserve traditional social distinctions. In this play Allwit and Welborn share the gallant's characteristics of being reduced by poverty, but they split other characteristics: Welborn has the tricks, Allwit is the young lover, and both achieve their rightful social position at the end of the play.

12. The sentimental and even romantic view of middle-class life in London portrayed by Dekker and Heywood, in contrast with the far more critical portraits by Middleton, Jonson, and Marston, is discussed by Ashley Thorndike in *English Comedy* (New York: Macmillan, 1929). See also Leggatt, *Citizen Comedy.*

13. See George F. Watson's introduction to the New Mermaids edition of *A Trick to Catch the Old One* (London: Benn, 1968).

14. Thus L. C. Knights discriminates among city comedy dramatists according to the firmness with which they represent an "anti-acquisitive attitude"; Jonson is the paramount exemplar of a playwright who shows a "healthy" popular distaste for greed and accumulation, while Middleton falls short because he lacks a steady moral position. See *Drama and Society in the Age of Jonson* (London: Chatto & Windus, 1937).

15. See Richard Hosley, "The Playhouses," in *The Revels History of Drama in English* (London: Methuen, 1975), 3:119–236.

16. See Alfred Harbage, *Shakespeare's Audience* (New York: Columbia University Press, 1941), and *Shakespeare and the Rival Traditions* (1952; rpt. Bloomington: Indiana University Press, 1970).

17. Harbage, *Shakespeare's Audience,* 59.

18. See Hosley, "Playhouses," 143 and his figures 36 and 52.

19. The masques presented at court involved far more elaborate scenic design. Inigo Jones's sets included painted backdrops in perspective, a front curtain, and a proscenium arch.

20. Theatres were "restrained" during sixteen of the thirty years from 1580 to 1610, for example, and restraints often lasted for months. See E. K. Chambers, *The Elizabethan Stage,* vol. 4 (Oxford: Clarendon Press, 1923), appendix E, 345–51 for a chronological list of plague restraints.

21. H. S. Bennett, "Shakespeare's Audience," *Studies in Shakespeare: British Academy Lectures,* ed. Peter Alexander (London: Oxford University Press, 1964), 68.

22. J. Leeds Barroll, "The Social and Literary Context," in *Revels History of Drama in English,* 3:48.

23. *Shakespeare's Audience,* 90.

24. *The Privileged Playgoers of Shakespeare's London 1576–1642* (Princeton, N.J.: Princeton University Press, 1981).

25. She claims the "privileged" to be "the nobility, the gentry, the wealthier merchants, and the professionals (advocates, clerics, military officers, and an occasional physician), together with their wives and children" (p. 16), the "aristocrats" (p. 80), and "soldiers, courtiers, and men up from the country" (p. 125).

26. Cook estimates that 15% of Londoners in 1603 were "privileged," as opposed to 4–6.6% of the English population as a whole (p. 94). Harbage estimates that "gentry, professional men, and officials" constituted about 10% of the city's population, with perhaps another 20% being "dealers and retailers"; craftsmen, laborers, and servants made up the majority by far (*Shakespeare's Audience,* 54–55).

27. Chambers, *The Elizabethan Stage,* 3:130.

28. The contrasting interests of professional and amateur writers are discussed in Edwin H. Miller, *The Professional Writer in Elizabethan England: A Study of Non-Dramatic Literature* (Cambridge, Mass.: Harvard University Press, 1959), and Gerald Eades Bentley, *The Profession of Dramatist in Shakespeare's Time, 1590–1642* (Princeton, N.J.: Princeton University Press, 1971).

29. Bentley, *The Profession of Dramatist,* chap. 2.

30. The decline of the patronage system for writers and consequent discontent among them is described in Phoebe Sheavyn, *The Literary Profession in the Elizabethan Age,* 2d ed. rev. by J. W. Saunders (1909; revised Manchester: Manchester University Press, 1967). There is some disagreement as to how financially pressed the professional dramatists actually were. Sheavyn regards the dramatists as poor, but better off than nondramatic writers; Bentley (*Profession of Dramatist*) goes even further, contending that dramatists' incomes compared favorably with those of other men of comparable education, including schoolteachers and curates. Miller (*Professional Writer*) argues, on the other hand, that with the exception of Shakespeare and Spenser, "the lives of Elizabethan authors comprise case histories of poverty" (p. 12), pointing out that even the relatively successful Ben Jonson, who was unusual in his ability to attract patrons, died in poverty. All agree that dramatists were prone to the discontents shared by intellectuals of the period, the result of their financial and social positions not being in keeping with their educational backgrounds or professional activities. For a discussion of this frustration, especially as experienced by those trained for the clergy who were unable to obtain a living, see Mark Curtis, "The Alienated Intellectuals of Early Stuart England," *Past and Present* 23 (1962): 25–41; see also Knights, *Drama and Society,* appendix B, "Seventeenth-Century Melancholy."

31. See Bentley, *The Profession of Dramatist,* chap. 6.

32. See Sheavyn, *Literary Profession,* chap. 3, and Bentley, *Profession of Dramatist,* chap. 10.

33. The first quotation is from the title page of the first edition, the 1608 quarto, of *A Mad World, My Masters,* and the second is from the first edition, 1611, of *The Atheist's Tragedy.*

34. Bernard Beckerman, *Shakespeare at the Globe 1599–1609* (New York: Macmillan, 1964), appendix A, 217.

35. Data are taken from J. Leeds Barroll, "Table 2: a calendar of plays 1576–1613," in *Revels History of Drama in English,* 3:53–94.

36. David Riesman discussed the "inside dopester" in his classic *The Lonely Crowd* (1950; New Haven, Conn.: Yale University Press, 1969). Riesman's inside dopster was one who wanted to enter elite political circles, or at least know what was going on inside them. He was "other directed," as was true of the coteries of gallants attending the public theatres; like them, the inside dopester was both cosmopolitan and a conformist at heart.

37. The first two illustrations come from *Every Man in His Humour,* while the last is from *A Mad World, My Masters.*

38. There is some debate over how constraining Elizabethan official censorship actually was. Bentley (*The Profession of Dramatist*) emphasizes the power of the master of the revels, who was supposed to approve and license all plays before performance. Sheavyn (*Literary Profession*) also stresses the paralyzing role of the censorship apparatus, particularly the corporation of the City of London, which made vigorous efforts to suppress theatres as hang-outs for the idle. Miller (*Professional Writer*), in contrast, argues that the heavy hand of Elizabethan censorship has been exaggerated, and points out that objectionable works frequently achieved publication or performance.

39. See Gwendolen Murphy, *A Bibliography of English Character-Books 1608–1700* (Oxford: The Bibliographic Society, 1925) for a list of titles. For more examples of English characters, a tradition that has been perpetuated into the present century, see Chester Noyes Greenough, *Theophrastan Characters in English,* prepared for publication by J. Milton French (Cambridge, Mass.: Harvard University Press, 1947).

40. In *The Antitheatrical Prejudice* (Berkeley: University of California, 1981), Jonas Barish points out that Jonson defied the custom whereby printed plays were claimed to be identical reproductions of the acted version. Jonson implied that the printed version of *Every Man Out of His Humour* would be different from the acted version, presumably better, and he included the Theophrastan characters as a lure for readers, since these sketches would have added nothing to the play's performance. See 136–37.

41. George Macaulay Trevelyn, *England Under the Stuarts,* 10th ed. (New York: Putnams, 1922), 59.

42. *Timber of Discoveries,* ed. Ralph S. Walker (1640; Syracuse, N.Y.: Syracuse University Press, 1953), 33; see also Knights, *Drama and Society.*

43. David Garrick missed the point so completely that he cast the role of Epicoene with a woman in his 1776 production of George Coleman's alteration. When Epicoene threw off her female attire to reveal herself to Morose and the audience as a boy, the entire trick fell flat. The prompter noted that the play "does not seem to hit the present taste—A little hissing at the End." Henry Bate's review in the *Morning Post and Daily Advertiser* was more direct: "The character of *Epicoene* should be played by a *male*, if the denoument is to be brought about by any natural means, or produce the least effect—the coolness with which the audience received the discovery is a proof of the propriety of this remark." After three performances Garrick substituted a male actor for Mrs. Siddons, but the change came too late to save the production. Eight years later the play was again revived, this time at Covent Garden, and again a woman played Epicoene. The play lasted but a single performance. Robert Gale Noyes, *Ben Jonson on the English Stage, 1660–1776* (Cambridge, Mass.: Harvard University Press, 1935), 204–19.

44. Throughout this study I am using the term archetype in its most general literary sense: "in poetry, an archetype may be any idea, character, action, object, institution, event, or setting containing essential characteristics which are primitive, general, and universal rather than sophisticated, unique, and particular" (*Princeton Encyclopedia of Poetry and Poetics,* 48). I do not intend the term to imply the Jungian-based approach of Northrop Frye and other "archetypal critics."

45. See Stith Thompson, *The Folktale* (New York: Holt, Rinehart & Winston, 1946), 319–28 for an overview of trickster tales.

46. Stith Thompson, *Motif-Index of Folk Literature,* rev. ed. (Bloomington: Indiana University Press, 1958), 4:101.

47. Karl Kerenyi, "The Trickster in Relation to Greek Mythology," trans. R. F. C. Hull, in Paul Radin, *The Trickster: A Study in American Indian Mythology* (London: Routledge & Kegan Paul, 1956), 185. For a discussion of the liminal aspects of the trickster, including his ambiguity, his defiance of authority, and his energy, see Victor W. Turner, "Myth and Symbol," in *International Encyclopedia of the Social Sciences* (New York: Macmillan and Free Press, 1968), 10:576–82.

48. Joel Chandler Harris, *Uncle Remus: His Songs and Sayings* (1880; New York: Appleton, 1926), 18.

49. Jonson's Brainworm and Face are exceptions. See Madelein Doran, *Endeavors of Art: A Study of Form in Elizabethan Drama* (Madison: University of Wisconsin Press, 1954), chap. 7 for a discussion of this point and of the Elizabethans' uses and transformations of the Roman models.

50. The quotation from Plautus is taken from *Five Roman Comedies,* edited by, and *Mostellaria,* translated by, Palmer Bovie (New York: E. P. Dutton, 1979), 111.

51. The comic relief in the mystery plays was provided by human characters, such as

Herod, presented as a braggart, and Noah's wife, who didn't want to get into the ark when it started raining because she was busy gossiping.

52. See L. W. Cushman, *The Devil and the Vice in English Dramatic Literature before Shakespeare* (Halle A.S.: Max Niemeyer, 1900); E. K. Chambers, *The Medieval Stage* (London: Oxford University Press, 1903); Keith Thomas, *Religion and the Decline of Magic* (New York: Scribner's, 1971).

53. There has been considerable discussion of the Vice's origins. Cushman (*The Devil and the Vice*) argued that the Vice and devil were independent in origin, the devil being a theological figure derived from saints' legends and biblical tales, the Vice being an ethical figure developed from the seven deadly sins. T. E. Allison modified Cushman by arguing that the Vices derived from not major sins but minor vices, which had always had some comic characteristics ("The Paternoster Play and the Origin of the Vices," *PLMA* 39 [1924]: 789–804). Recent scholarship has emphasized in influence of the folk traditions of the fool and Lord of Misrule; see Francis Hugh Mares, "The Origin of the Figure called 'The Vice' in Tudor Drama," *Huntington Library Quarterly* 22 (1958): 11–29, and Frank Percy Wilson and G. K. Hunter, *The English Drama, 1485–1585* (Oxford: Clarendon Press, 1969).

54. David M. Bevington, *From Mankind to Marlowe* (Cambridge, Mass.: Harvard University Press, 1962).

55. See Robert Carl Johnson, "Audience Involvement in the Tudor Interlude," *Theatre Notebook* 24 (1970): 101–11, and Robert C. Jones, "Dangerous Sport: The Audience's Engagement with Vice in the Moral Interludes," *Renaissance Drama*, n.s., 6 (1973): 45–64.

56. See L. C. Knights (*Drama and Society*).

57. See Gāmini Salgādo ed., *Cony-Catchers and Bawdy Baskets* (Harmondsworth: Penguin, 1972), and Gibbons, *Jacobean City Comedy*, appendix A, "A Minor Genre: The Coney-Catching Pamphlet," 161–67.

58. Gilbert Walker, "A Manifest Detection of Dice-play," in Salgādo, *Cony-Catchers and Bawdy Baskets*, 27–58.

59. Walker, in Salgādo (*Cony-Catchers and Bawdy Baskets*), 38–39.

60. See Wendy Griswold, "The Devil's Techniques: Cultural Legitimation and Social Change," *American Sociological Review* 48 (1983): 668–80.

61. Salgādo (*Cony-Catchers and Bawdy Baskets*), 99.

62. Ibid., 101.

63. Ibid., 343.

64. Ibid., 356–57.

65. Ibid., 346.

66. The Elizabethan theatre's creative intermixing of humanist and popular cultural elements is analyzed by Robert Weimann in *Shakespeare and the Popular Tradition in the Theatre* (Baltimore: Johns Hopkins, 1978); see esp. chap. 5. A comparable account of a cultural moment of mixture and innovation is Mikhail Bakhtin's classic, *Rabelais and His World*, trans. Helene Iswolsley (Bloomington: Indiana University Press, 1984).

67. The following discussion draws on Lawrence Stone's study, "Social Mobility in England, 1500–1700," *Past and Present* 33 (1966): 16–55 (the quotation is from p. 15); Stone, *The Crisis of the Aristocracy 1558–1641*, (Oxford: Clarendon Press, 1965), and Valerie Pearl, *London and the Outbreak of the Puritan Revolution* (London: Oxford University Press, 1961).

68. Roger Finlay, *Population and Metropolis: The Demography of London 1580–1650* (Cambridge: Cambridge University Press, 1981). Finlay points out that the urban death rate exceeded its birth rate; thus the increase was due entirely to immigration.

69. William Harrison, *The Description of England* (1587), ed. George S. Edelen (Ithaca, N.Y.: Cornell University Press, 1958), 94.

70. Joan Thirsk, "The European Debate on Customs of Inheritance," in *Family and Inheritance: Rural Society in Western Europe, 1200–1800*, ed. Jack Goody, Joan Thirsk, and E. P. Thompson (Cambridge: Cambridge University Press, 1976), 177–91.

71. The increase in the numbers of lesser gentry was due to the greater availability of land following the dissolution of the monasteries, the prosperity that a century of inflation had brought to many land-owning yeoman and merchants, and a higher fertility rate among the elite in general. Grants of arms to the newly prosperous were at an all-time high during the 1570s, and almost as high during the 1580s. See Anthony Richard Wagner, *English Genealogy* (Oxford: Clarendon Press, 1960); T. H. Hollingsworth, "A Demographic Study of British Ducal Families," *Population Studies* 11 (1957): 4–26.

72. Sir Thomas Wilson, "The State of England (1606)," ed. F. J. Fisher; *Camden Miscellany* 16; Camden 3d ser. 52 (1936):24.

73. See Finlay, *Population and Metropolis,* and Hollingsworth, "A Demographic Study."

74. The perception that commercial or industrial wealth was readily converted into elite status through the acquisition of land may have been stronger than the reality during most of post-Tudor English history; Lawrence and Jeanne C. Fawtier Stone have recently argued that the "open elite" was largely a myth, though a long-lasting and potent one. See *An Open Elite? England 1540–1880* (Oxford: Clarendon Press, 1984).

75. See Stone, *Crisis of the Aristocracy.*

76. *Description of England,* pp. 115–16.

77. Louis B. Wright, *Middle-Class Culture in Elizabethan England* (1935; rpt. Chapel Hill: University of North Carolina Press, 1958); F. J. Fisher, "The Development of London as a Centre of Conspicuous Consumption," *Transactions of the Royal Historical Society,* 4th ser., 30 (1948): 37–50.

78. In "Social Mobility in England," Stone discusses two subsections of "citizens and burgesses" that were greatly increasing during the period: lawyers and government administrators. Both callings tended to draw younger sons of the gentry, for both carried slightly more social prestige than the other alternatives, commerce or the clergy. Both also recruited from the more ambitious and upwardly mobile sons of the citizens.

79. For a compact discussion of the problem engendered by London's rapid growth, and the ineffectual attempts by court and city to stem the tide, see Thomas Fiddian Reddaway, "London and the Court in Elizabethan England," *Shakespeare Survey* 17 (1964): 3–12.

80. This prejudice against going into "traffic" was harmful to the landed gentry as a class, not just the helpless younger sons, because it encouraged the further selling off of lands by the heirs to provide for their sons and brothers. Lu Emily Pearson discusses this predicament in *Elizabethans at Home* (Stanford: Stanford University Press, 1957).

81. John Earle, *Microcosmography* (1628), ed. Harold Osborne (London: University Tutorial Press, 1933), 23.

82. Knights attributes the widespread expression of melancholy in the late Elizabethan and Jacobean periods to the large numbers of educated men whose social and financial expectations were not fulfilled. Literary men were especially sensitive to this problem, because of their own constant indebtedness. "Seventeenth-Century Melancholy," appendix B in *Drama and Society in the Age of Jonson*. See also Curtis, "The Alienated Intellectuals."

83. See Frank Whigham, *Ambition and Privilege: The Social Tropes of Elizabethan Courtesy Theory* (Berkeley and Los Angeles: University of California Press, 1984).

84. E. M. W. Tillyard thus expressed what he saw as the general mentality, which now is regarded as one "world picture" among several:

> If Elizabethans believed in an ideal order animating earthly order, they were terrified lest it should be upset, and appalled by the visible tokens of disorder that suggested it upsetting. They were obsessed by the fear of chaos and the fact of mutability, and the obsession was powerful in proportion as their faith in the cosmic order was strong. To us *chaos* means hardly more than confusion on a large scale; to an Elizabethan it meant the cosmic anarchy before creation and the wholesale dissolution that would result if the pressure of Providence relaxed and allowed the law of nature to cease functioning. (*Elizabethan World Picture* [1943; rpt. Harmondsworth: Penguin, 1976], 23–24.)

85. Hardin Craig remarks that "the cruel snobbery with which Malvolio is treated in *Twelfth Night* is perhaps a commonplace reflection of the general attitude toward the man who aspired to rise above his station." *The Enchanted Glass* (New York: Oxford University Press, 1936), 192.

86. Fanciful as they sound, Meercraft's land-improvement and manufacturing projects were based on actual enterprises during this period of speculation and money-making schemes. See J. W. Gough, *The Rise of the Entrepreneur* (London: Batsford, 1969).

87. Nowhere is the depiction of economic change and social stability more paradoxically expressed than in *A New Way to Pay Old Debts*. See Michael Neill, "Massinger's Patriarchy," in *Renaissance Drama*, n.s., 10 (1979): 185–213.

CHAPTER 3: REVENGE TRAGEDIES

1. *A Warning for Fair Women*, ed. Charles Dale Cannon (The Hague: Mouton, 1975), Induction, ll. 50–61.

2. The classic discussions of the genre include John Addington Symonds, *Shakespeare's Predecessors in the English Drama*, new ed. (London: Smith, Elder, 1900); Ashley H. Thorndike, "The Relations of *Hamlet* to Contemporary Revenge Plays," *PMLA* 17 (1902): 125–220; Lily B. Campbell, "Theories of Revenge in Renaissance England," *Modern Philology* 28 (1931):257–96; Percy Simpson, "The Theme of Revenge in Elizabethan Tragedy," *Proceedings of the British Academy* (1935), 101–36; Fredson Bowers, *Elizabethan Revenge Tragedy 1587–1642* (Princeton, N.J.: Princeton University Press, 1940). More recent studies include Robert Ornstein, *The Moral Vision of Jacobean Tragedy* (Madison and Milwaukee: University of Wisconsin Press, 1960); Irving Ribner, *Jacobean Tragedy: The Quest for Moral Order* (London: Methuen, 1962); J. W. Lever, *Tragedy of State* (London: Methuen, 1971); and Charles A. Hallett and Elaine S. Hallet, *The Revenger's Madness* (Lincoln: University of Nebraska, 1980).

3. In *A Study of Elizabethan and Jacobean Tragedy* (Cambridge: Cambridge University Press, 1964), T. B. Tomlinson claims that no literary form, including metaphysical poetry, Augustan moral epistles, and nineteenth-century family romances, ever equaled the unity and dominance of the revenge plot. In his view only Restoration heroic tragedy or the modern detective story come close, but their literary products are minor. Tomlinson includes the later plays by Ford, Middleton, and Webster in his definition.

4. Sociologically, the returned revenger shares in the objectivity, freedom, and existential homelessness of Georg Simmel's "stranger" or Robert Park's "marginal man." This freedom is comparable to that of the city comedy gallant as well.

5. Poisoned corpes occur in *The Duke of Milan* and *The Revenger's Tragedy*. The poisoned Bible is from *The Duchess of Malfi*. The Jew of Malta is boiled in oil; *Hoffman's* father and his victims are crowned with a burning crown; Hieronimo's son is hung up in an arbor in *The Spanish Tragedy*. Human flesh is served for dinner in *Titus Andronicus* and *Antonio's Revenge*. Death's-heads are carried in *The Revenger's Tragedy* and *Titus Andronicus,* hands in *The Duchess of Malfi* and *Titus Andronicus,* a finger is waved about in *The Changeling,* a leg (by report) in *The Duchess of Malfi,* a heart in *'Tis Pity She's a Whore.*

6. Necrophilia occurs in *The Revenger's Tragedy, The Atheist's Tragedy,* and *The Duke of Milan.*

7. For a discussion of the evidence for various dates of composition, see Philip Edwards's introduction to the Revels edition of *The Spanish Tragedy* (Manchester: Manchester University Press, 1977). Edwards favors a date a few years later than the widely accepted date of the mid-eighties. The upper limit is fixed, for Henslowe recorded performances of the play by Lord Strange's Men at the Rose in early 1592.

8. Thomas Lodge, *Wit's Miseries.*

9. See Thorndike, "Relations of *Hamlet* to Contemporary Revenge Plays," 135.

10. Philip Massinger did follow up his success with *A New Way to Pay Old Debts* by writing *The City Madam* a decade later; it first appeared in 1632, long after the vogue for city comedy had faded. Like *The Cardinal,* it was more an echo than the end of a trend.

11. Hamlet asks why the city tragedians were free to travel, and Rosencrantz explains it is because they have lost their following "the late innovation" of boy companies:

> ROSENCRANTZ: But there is, sir, an aery of children, little eyases, that cry out on the top of question, and are most tyrannically clapped for't. These are now the fashion. . . .
> HAMLET: What, are they children? Who maintains them? . . . Will they pursue the quality no longer than they can sing?
> (2.2.339–47)

Hamlet goes on to express dismay at this turn of events and its threat to the acting profession. All this was in reference to the "War of the Theatres," which was raging in the opening years of the seventeenth century.

12. In *The Multiple Plot in English Renaissance Drama* (Chicago: University of Chicago Press, 1971), Richard Levin argues that tragedy demands a clear and, in retrospect, inevitable line of causation and a concentration of emotional effect, both of which are apt to be blurred by too great a reliance on multiple plotting. Comedy, on the other hand, thrives on intersecting causation and the cumulation of comic actions. Thus although multiple plots are found in tragedy, especially the direct contrast type of *The Changeling,* Levin contends that the tragic equivalent to *Bartholomew Fair* or *A Chaste Maid in Cheapside* is inconceivable.

13. See John N. King, *English Reformation Literature: The Tudor Origins of the Protestant Tradition* (Princeton, N.J.: Princeton University Press, 1982); see King's figures 2 and 3 for the title pages of the Coverdale Bible and the Great Bible.

14. William Haller, *Foxe's Book of Martyrs and the Elect Nation* (London: Jonathan Cape, 1963).

15. Malcolm Smuts compares Elizabeth's effective use of cultural symbolism for political ends with "The Political Failure of Stuart Cultural Patronage" in *Patronage in the Renaissance,* ed. Guy Fitch Lytle and Stephen Orgel (Princeton, N.J.: Princeton University Press, 1981), 165–87.

16. The standard discussion of the history of the English conception of royal perogative culminating in the Stuart adherence to divine right is John Neville Figgis, *The Divine Right of Kings,* 2d ed. (Cambridge: Cambridge University Press, 1922).

17. Ernst H. Kantorowicz, *The King's Two Bodies: A Study in Medieval Political Theology* (Princeton, N.J.: Princeton University Press, 1957).

18. See Marie Axton, *The Queen's Two Bodies: Drama and the Elizabethan Succession* (London: Royal Historical Society, 1977) for a discussion of how plays performed during the Christmas revels at the Inns of Court dramatized the political controversies over the dual nature of the monarch.

19. Stephen Greenblatt, *Renaissance Self-Fashioning: From More to Shakespeare* (Chicago: University of Chicago Press, 1980).

20. Robin Clifton, "The Popular Fear of Catholics in England," *Past and Present* 52(1971):23–55.

21. John Leon Lievsay, *The Elizabethan Image of Italy* (Ithaca, N.Y.: Cornell University Press, 1964).

22. *The Unfortunate Traveller and Other Works,* ed. J. B. Steane (Harmondsworth: Penguin, 1971), 342. The English imagined some international competition in revenge; an Iberian in *'Tis Pity She's a Whore* says, "I rejoice that a Spaniard outwent an Italian in revenge" (5.6). Bowers (*Elizabethan Revenge Tragedy*) notes that the English considered the Spanish fully equal to the Italians in villainy and vengefulness, while the French were seen as more inclined to threaten revenge than actually carry it out. Germans, Danes, and Turks were also regarded as singularly prone to revenge. In fact, England appeared to be a remarkable exception in a world bent on vengeance.

23. Felix Raab, *The English Face of Machiavelli: A Changing Interpretation 1500–1700* (London: Routledge & Kegan Paul, 1964).

24. Ibid., 59.

25. Francis A. Yates has traced the history of this association to the ideal of political-religious unity in the Holy Roman Empire; see *Astraea: The Imperial Theme in the Sixteenth Century* (London: Routledge and Kegan Paul, 1975).

26. Lawrence Stone, *The Causes of the English Revolution 1529–1642* (London: Routledge & Kegan Paul, 1964), 86, and *Crisis of the Aristocracy*, 97–119, 494–99.

27. For a comparison of the ideological styles of James and Elizabeth, and a discussion of how the *arcana imperii* were used by James in service of his conception of divine right, see Jonathan Goldberg, *James I and the Politics of Literature* (Baltimore: Johns Hopkins University Press, 1983); for a study of how Elizabeth managed to turn the liability of her gender to political advantage, see Louis Adrian Montrose, "The Elizabethan Subject and the Spenserian Text" in *Literary Theory and Renaissance Texts*, ed. Patricia Parker and David Quint, (Baltimore: Johns Hopkins University Press, forthcoming).

28. See Philip Edwards, *Threshold of a Nation: A Study in English and Irish Drama* (Cambridge: Cambridge University Press, 1979).

29. Robert Dodsley, *A Select Collection of Old Plays*, 3d ed., 12 vols., ed. Isaac Reed, Octavius Gilchrist, and "The Editor" [J. Payne Collier] (London: Septimus Prowett, 1825–27). Dodsley's first edition was published in 1744; Isaac Reed published a second edition in 1780. Collier brought out a supplementary volume, the thirteenth, in 1828, adding five more plays. The fourth edition, enlarged from sixty to eighty-four plays, was published by W. C. Hazlitt, 1874–76.

30. Charles Lamb, *Specimens of English Dramatic Poets, Who Lived about the Time of Shakespeare, with Notes* (London: Longman, 1808). A second edition appeared in 1813, another in 1854, and another in 1893.

31. Thomas Kyd, *The Spanish Tragedy*, ed. Philip Edwards, in the Revels Plays series (Manchester: Manchester University Press, 1959), editions listed on pp. lxix–lxx.

32. Allardyce Nicoll ed., *The Works of Cyril Tourneur* (1930); Mermaid Dramabook edition (J. A. Symonds introduction), *John Webster and Cyril Tourneur (Four Plays)* (1956); Irving Ribner ed., *The Atheist's Tragedy* (1964); Brian Morris and Roma Gill eds., *The Atheist's Tragedy* (1976); George Parfitt ed., *The Plays of Cyril Tourneur* (London: Cambridge University Press, 1978).

33. As always, "universal" must be qualified; I use the term not in an absolute sense, but rather to designate a relatively wide range of time and space within the Western, Judeo-Christian tradition. Tragedy as a dramatic form appears to be confined to the Western world.

34. G. K. Hunter has pointed out that the nineteenth-century critical term "tragedy of blood" was something of a redundancy; see *Dramatic Identities and Cultural Tradition* (New York: Harper & Row, 1978), 175.

35. The following draws on Mary Douglas's classic monograph, *Purity and Danger: An Analysis of Concepts of Pollution and Taboo* (London: Routledge and Kegan Paul, 1966).

36. Even under the Christian image of life after death, there remains the appeal of "that church were the blind don't see and the lame don't walk and what's dead stays that way." Flannery O'Connor, *Wise Blood* (1949), in *Three by Flannery O'Connor* (New York: New American Library, 1983), 54.

37. Victor Turner, "Betwixt and Between," *The Forest of Symbols*, 93–111.

38. One widely perceived horror that is not prominent in revenge tragedy is homosexuality, which was considered an abomination and and offense against the social order, punishable by death following a 1533 statute. Homosexuality was not unknown to the Renaissance stage (e.g., Marlowe's *Edward II*), but was not used by revenge tragedy writers; perhaps their interest in Senecan models made other forms of horror occur more readily to the earlier dramatists, while the later ones writing during the reign of James I were inclined toward discretion on the subject. See Derrick Sherwin Bailey, *Homosexuality and the Western Christian Tradition* (London: Longmans, Green & Co., 1955) for a review of English laws on homosexuality, and Caroline Bingham, "Seventeenth-Century Attitudes toward Deviant Sex," *Journal of Interdisciplinary History* 1 (Spring 1971):447–67, for an account of the 1631 trial and execution of the earl of Castelhaven for sodomy.

39. During the Renaissance, Seneca was believed to have been the author of ten plays: *Hercules Furens, Troades, Medea, Hippolytus, Oedipus, Agamemnon, Thyestes, Hercules Oetaeus, Octavia,* and the fragment *Phoenissae. Octavia* is now generally believed to have been written by an imitator of Seneca, and the authorship of *Hercules Oetaeus* is in doubt.

40. The debate over the degree of Senecan influence on Elizabethan drama has lasted for close to a century. John W. Cunliffe put forward vast claims in *The Influence of Seneca on Elizabethan Tragedy* (London: Macmillan, 1893); three decades later F. L. Lucas, while believing Cunliffe had overstated his case by seeing "influence" wherever there was coincidence, agreed that melodramatic excess, a rhetoric of gorgeous oratory, the frequent use of line-by-line repartee (stichomythia) and epigrams, a fascination with the horrible, and some stock characters like the tyrant and the ghost were the Elizabethans' Senecan legacies (*Seneca and Elizabethan Tragedy* [1921; rpt. New York: Haskell House, 1966]). More recent scholarship has severely qualified Seneca's direct influence, stressing the importance of folk traditions as well as other classical writers; see Willard Farnman, *The Medieval Heritage of Elizabethan Tragedy* (Berkeley: University of California Press, 1936) and T. W. Baldwin, *Shakespeare's Five-Act Structure* (Urbana: University of Illinois Press, 1947). G. K. Hunter argues that many of the so-called Senecan elements in Renaissance drama are more Gothic than classical; see *Dramatic Identities and Cultural Tradition,* chap. 6. In a review of the debate, Anna Lydia Motto and John L. Clark conclude that while teasing out of a traces of Senecan influence was something of an intellectual fad around the turn of the century, it would be foolish to submit to the opposing fad of seeing only medieval and popular infuences; see "Senecan Tragedy: A Critique of Scholarly Trends," *Renaissance Drama* n.s. 6 (1973):219–35. Recently in *Renaissance Tragedy and the Senecan Tradition: Anger's Privilege,* (New Haven: Yale University Press, 1985), Gordon Braden has argued for the rhetorical affinity between Senecan and Elizabethan drama, seeing both as sharing a hyperbolic rhetoric of self-summoning unlike either Greek or medieval drama, through which autonomous individuals muster and direct their fury.

41. The next classical dramatist to have all of his plays available in English, Sophocles, was not fully translated until 1759 (Lucas, *Seneca and Elizabethan Tragedy,* 17–18).

42. Quotations from *Thyestes* are from *Four Tragedies and Octavia,* trans. E. G. Watling (Harmondsworth: Penguin, 1966); this quotation is from 1.46–48.

43. Because any count of this sort involves some arbitrary decisions over what to include, I am listing the data behind my counts so the reader may see my procedures. A. *Seneca's plays (total of 9 plays, including all of the traditional Senecan canon except for the fragment Phoenissae); there are 3 murders and 3.33 violent deaths per play. Murder of kin—17:* Clytemnestra kills husband (*Ag.*); Medea kills her 2 children (*Med.*); Hercules kills his wife and 3 sons (*Her.f.*); Theseus kills his son (*Hip.*); Oedipus kills his father (*Oed.*); Deianira kills her husband (*Her. oet.*) (last two are both unwitting); Agrippina kills Nero, Nero kills mother, stepbrother, wife (*Oct.*); Atreus kills 3 nephews (*Thy.*). Kin murders account for 57% of the 30 total deaths, or 63% of the 27 murders. *Murder of nonkin—10:* Aegisthus kills Agamemnon, Clytemnestra kills Cassandra (*Ag.*); Medea kills Creon and Creusa (*Med.*); Hercules kills Lichas (*Her. oet.*); Nero kills Plautus and Sulla (*Oct.*); Hercules kills Lycus (*Her. f.*); Greeks kill Polyxena and Astyanax (*Tr.*). *Suicides—3:* Deianira (*Her. oet.*); Phaedra (*Hip.*); Jocasta (*Oed.*). B. *Revenge tragedies (total of 16 plays); there are 6 murders and 7 violent deaths per play. Murder of kin—28:* Barabas kills Abigail (*JM*); Titus kills Mutius and Lavinia (*TA*); Ferdinand and Cardinal kill Duchess, Antonio, 2 children (*DM*); Ambitioso and Supervacuo kill Junior, Ambitioso kills Supervacuo, Spurio kills Ambitioso (*RT*); Eudoxa kills Maximus (*Val*); Livia kills Isabella, Isabella kills Livia, Bianca kills Duke, Livia kills Hippolito (*WBW*); Duke kills wife, Francisco kills Duke, Duke orders Francisco's execution (*Duke of M*); D'Amville kills Montferrers (*Atheist'sT*); Brachiano kills Isabella, Flamineo kills Camillo and Marcello (*WD*); Giovani kills Annabella, Florio (inadvertantly), and Soranzo, Soranzo (via bandetti) kills Giovanni (*TPSW*); Mathias kills Lodowick, Jerome kills Prussia (*Hoff*). Kin murders (28) account for 25% of the 112 total deaths, or 29% of the 96 total murders. *Murder of nonkin—68:* Balthazar and Lorenzo kill Horatio, Hieronimo kills Lorenzo and Castile, Bel-Imperia kills Balthazar, Pedrigano kills Serberine, Lorenzo kills (allows to be executed) Pedrigano (*ST*); King kills Guise, Clermont kills Montsurry in duel (*RBD'A*); Barabas kills 2 friars, convent of nuns (I am counting this as one slaying), Ithamore, Bellamira, Pilia-Borsa, and Turkish solders (counted as one killing), Mathias and Lodowick kill each other, Ferenze kills Barabas (*JM*); Tamora and sons kill Bassianus and Titus's 2 sons, Aaron kills nurse and midwife, Titus kills Tamora, Saturninus kills Titus, Lucius kills Saturninus (*TA*); Duke killed Vindici's mistress, Vindici and Hippolito kill Duke, Vindici and others kill Lussurioso and 3 lords, Lussurioso kills gentleman, fourth lord kills Spurio, Antonio kills Vindici and Hippolito (*RT*); Maximus kills Aecuis, Valentinian, Chilax and Balbus, women kill 2 bawds, troops kill general (*Val*); Hippolito kills Leanto (*WBW*); Beatrice and Deflores kill Alonzo and Diaphanta, Deflores kills Beatrice (*Ch.*); Charlemont kills Borachio, Sebastian and Belforest kill each other (*Atheist'sT*); Lodovico (in conspiracy with Francisco, Duke of Florence, who is Brachiano's brother-in-law) kills Brachiano, Victoria Corombona, Flamineo, and Zanche, ambassdors kill Lodovico (*WD*); Grimaldi kills Bergetto, Vasques kills Hippolita (*TPSW*); Piero kills Feliche, Andrugio, and Strozo, Antonio kills Julio, Antonio, Pandulpho and others kill Piero (Ant'sR); Hoffman kills Otho, Austria, and Lorrique, Saxony, Duchess, Mathias and Lucibella kill Hoffman (*Hoff*); Evadne kills King, Amintor kills Aspatia (*Maid'sT*). Nonkin murders (68) account for 61% of the 112 total deaths, or 71% of the 96 murders. *Suicides—16:* Isabella, Bel-Imperia, Hieronimo (*ST*); Clermont (*RBD'A*); Antonio's wife (*RT*); Pontius and Lucina (*Val*); Bianca, Guardino (accident)(*WBW*); Deflores kills self (*Ch.*); Levidulcia, D'Amville (accident) (*Atheist'sT*); Jerome kills self(accident) (*Hoff.*); Evadne, Amintor kill selves, Melantius vows to do so (*Maid'sT*). Suicides (intentional or accidental) account for 14% of the 112 deaths.

44. Seneca's notorious sensationalism compared with his Greek models is illustrated by the different treatments Euripides and Seneca give to the scene where the mad Hercules kills his sons and his wife, a scene that is bloody and pathetic by its very nature. Euripides describes the killing of the second son thus:

> The boy leaped first, fell at his father's knees
> and held his hand up to his father's chin.
> "Dearest Father," he cried, "do not murder me.
> I am your own son, yours, not Eurystheus'!"
> But he stared from stony gorgon eyes,
> found his son too close to draw the bow,
> and brought his club down on that golden head,
> and smashed the skull, as though a blacksmith
> smiting steel.

Full of pathos and horror to be sure, but considerable more restrained than Seneca's account of the same scene:

> See, how he stretches out coaxing hands to his fathers knees, and
> with piteous voice begs—oh, impious crime, grim and horrid sight!
> With his right hand he has caught the pleading child, and, madly
> whirling him again and yet again, has hurled him; his head crashed
> loudly against the stones; the room is drenched with scattered brains.

Similarly, Euripides concludes the slaugher with "one arrow brought down son and wife," while Seneca elaborates how "the child died ere he felt the blow; fear snatched his life away. Against his wife now he poises his heavy club—her bones are crushed, her head is gone from her mangled body, gone utterly." (The Euripides quotations are from *Heracles*, trans. William Arrowsmith, in *Euripides II*, ed. David Grene and Richard Lattimore [1952; rpt. Chicago: University of Chicago Press, 1962], ll. 986–94, 1000; the Seneca quotations are from *Hercules Furens*, trans. Frank Justus Miller, in *Seneca VIII* [Cambridge, Mass.: Harvard University Press (Loeb Classical Library), 1979], 89, 91.)

45. *Dramatic Identities and Cultural Tradition*, chap. 6.

46. The Spanish honor plays used for this comparison, all in English translation, are: Pedro Calderón de la Barca (Calderón), *The Mayor of Zalema* and *The Secret Vengeance for Secret Insult*, trans. Edwin Honig, in *Calderon de la Barca: Four Plays* (New York: Hill & Wang, 1961), *The Painter of His Own Dishonour* and *Three Judgments at a Blow*, "freely translated" by Edward Fitzgerald, in *Eight Dramas of Calderon* (London: Macmillan, 1921), and *The Surgeon of His Honour*, trans. Roy Campbell (Madison: University of Wisconsin Press, 1960); Lope Felix de Vega Carpio (Lope de Vega), *Peribanez, Justice without Revenge, and Fuenteovejuna*, trans. Jill Booty, in *Lope de Vega: Five Plays* (New York: Hill & Wang, 1961). Lope de Vega lived from 1562 to 1635, Calderón from 1600 to 1681. For a comparison of Spanish and English Renaissance drama that argues some of their similarities derive from the absolutist politi-

cal contexts in which their theatres were situated, see Walter Cohen, *Drama of a Nation: Public Theater in Renaissance England and Spain* (Ithaca: Cornell University Press, 1985).

47. William Painter, *The Palace of Pleasure* (1566, 1567, 1575), ed. Hamish Miles, ed., 4 vols. (New York: AMS Press, 1967). Most of the 101 tales are from Boccaccio, Bandello, or Margaret of Navarre: the classical tales are mainly from Aulus Gellius and Livy.

48. Tales involving revenge are numbers 4, 5, 17, 39, 41–43, 49, 51, 54, 57–59, 69, 89, 90, 93, and 97.

49. *Murder of kin—9:* Virginius kills daughter (5); Tancredi kills daughter unwittingly (39); Violenta kills husband (42); husband kills wife by locking her in room with lover's rotting corpse (43); husband poisons wife (58); brothers of Duchess of Malfi kill their sister and her three children (89).

Murder of nonkin—7: Tancredi kills daughter's lover (39); husband kills wife's lover (43); brother kills duke who is trying to seduce his sister (54); husband kills lover (57); Timoclia kills knight who had raped her (69); brothers kill Duchess's maid (89); Countess of Celant kills ex-lover (90).

50. Charles Lamb, *Specimens of English Dramatic Poets,* ed. William Macdonald (London: Dent, 1903), 2:34.

51. My count appears below. Based on this count, there are 24 revenge dyads, in which someone declares he or she will be revenged on someone else, in the 9 complete Senecan plays, 2.67 per play; there are 111 revenge dyads in the 16 Revenge Tragedies, almost 7 per play.

Senecan Revenge Dyads:

Rulers on nonrulers—7: Atreus on Thyestes (*Thy.*); Theseus on Hippolytus (*Hip.*); Greeks on Trojans (as Hecuba and Andromache view it) (*Tro.*); Oedipus on Laius' murder (*Oed.*); Nero on enemies (counted as one) (*Oct.*); Nero on Octavia (*Oct.*); Nero on Romans (*Oct.*)

Gods on mortals—4: Juno on Hercules (*Herc. f.*); Juno on Hercules (*Herc. oet.*); Venus on Phaedra (*Hip.;* Venus' revenge on Hippolytus is emphasized in Euripides' version, but not in Seneca's); gods on family of Octavia (*Oct.*)

Ghosts on mortals—4: Tantalus on house of Pelops (*Thy.*); Thyestes on house of Atreus (*Ag.*); Achilles on ungrateful Greeks (*Tro.*); Agripina on Nero (*Oct.*)

Possessors of magic on nonpossessors—4: Medea on Jason, Creon, and Creusa (*Med.*); Nessus on Hercules (*Herc. oet.*)

Nonrulers on rulers—3: Aegisthus on Agamemnon (*Ag.*); Clytemnestra on Agamemnon (*Ag.*); Hercules on Lycus the usurper (*Her. f.*)

Nonrulers on nonrulers—2: Phaedra on Hippolytus (*Hip.*); Romans on Poppea (*Oct.*)

Revenge Tragedy Revenge Dyads:

Weaker on stronger—68: Hieronimo on Lorenzo and Balthazar, Bel-Imperia on Lorenzo and Balthazar (*ST*); Clermont, Charlotte, and Tamyra on Montsurry (*RBD'A*); Barabas on Ferneze and town, Ferneze on Barabas (after their positions are reversed), Ferneze on Turks, Mathias on Lodowick (*JM*); Titus on Demetruis, Chiron, Tamora, Saturninus, and Aaron, Aaron on Bassianus (*TA*); Bosola on Ferdinand and Cardinal (*DM*); Vindici and Hippolito on Duke and Lussurioso; Duchess on Duke; Spurio on Duke, 3 sons of Duchess and Lussurioso; Hippolito, Antonio, and other

Lords on Junior and Lussurioso; Ambitioso and Supervacuo on Lussurioso (*RT*); Maximus on Valentinian, Eudoxa on Max. (*Val.*); Francisco on Duke, Graccio on Francisco, Isabella and Mariana on Duchess, Eugenia on Duke (*Duke of M*); Deflores on everyone of higher status (*Ch.*); Vittoria Corombona on Monticelso, Lodovico on Brachiano and Vittoria Corombona (*WD*); Grimaldi, Richardetto, Hippolita, and Giovanni on Soranzo (*TPSW*); Antonio, Pandulpho, Maria, Alberto on Piero (*Ant'sR*); Hoffman on Duke of Lunenburg, his son, and 3 other Dukes; Jerome on Otho and his father; Lodovick on Duke of Prussia, Duchess of Lunenberg on Hoffman, Mathias and Lucibella on Hoffman (*Hoff.*); Melantius on King, Evadne on King, Amintor on King (*MT*). *Total (68) is 61% of 111 total revenges, or 65% of human revenges.*
Stronger on weaker—21: Balthazar and Lorenzo on Horatio (*ST*); Barabas on daughter, on friars, on 3 plotters; Lodowick on Mathias (*JM*); Saturninus on Titus and family (*TA*); Ferdinand and Cardinal on Duchess and Antonio (*DM*); Lussurioso on Piato (*RT*); Duke on Duchess (*Duke of M.*); Alsemero on Beatrice, Beatrice on Diaphanta (*Ch.*); Monticelso and Francisco on Vittoria Corombona (*WD*); Piero on Andrugio and family (*Ant'sR*); Soranzo on Giovanni (*TPSW*). *Total (21) is 19% of total revenges.*
Ghost on human—5: Andrea's on Balthazar (*ST*); Bussy's on Montsurry (*RBD'A*); Alonzo's on Beatrice and Deflores (*Ch.*); Andrugio's on Piero (*Ant'sR*). Ghost of Montferrer warns against revenge (*Ath's T.*). Total (5) is 5% of total revenges.
Equals—17: Alexandro on Villupo (*ST*); Livia on Hippolito and Isabella, Guardiano on Hippolito and Isabella; Hippolito and Isabella on Livia, Bianca on Cardinal (*WBW*); Tomaso on his brother's killer (*Ch.*); Charlemont (potentially) on D'Amville (*Ath's T.*); Montcelso and Francisco on Brachiano, Marcello on Flamineo (*WD*); Mathias on Greek, Austria on Saxony, Austria on Hoffman (*Hoff.*); Calianax on Melantius (relative positions ambiguous) (*MT*). *Total (17) is 15% of total revenges.*
52. Catherine Belsey has suggested that any Senecan vacillation is the result of fluctuating passions, not rational internal debate, in "Senecan Vacillation and Elizabethan Deliberation: Influence or Confluence?" *Renaissance Drama* n.3. 6 (1973): 65–88.
53. Douglas Cole, "The Comic Accomplice in Elizabethan Revenge Tragedy," *Renaissance Drama* 9 (1966): 125–39.
54. For a discussion of the theme of order, see Norman T. Pratt, *Seneca's Drama* (Chapel Hill: University of North Carolina Press, 1983). Pratt suggests a change from Greek tragedy, representing "disorder in nature," to Shakespeare, representing "nature in disorder"; in the latter, the forces of chaos are purged and moral order emerges at the end. He argues that this change had already occurred in Seneca, who held out the possibility of moral order through the rational faculty's control of the irrational, but this order was only on the individual and not the political level.
55. The triumph of order, embodied in the magnificence of the monarch and his court, was given frequent ritual enactment in the court masques; see Stephen Orgel, *The Jonsonian Masque* (1967; New York: Columbia University Press, 1980) and *The Illusion of Power* (Berkeley: University of California Press, 1975).
56. Some honor plays, it has been suggested, subvert the honor code by showing how it dehumanizes those who adhere to it; see, for example, Edwin Honig's discussion of *Secret Vengeance for Secret Insult* in chap. 4 of *Calderon and the Seizures of Honor* (Cambridge, Mass.: Harvard University Press, 1972).
57. The changing legal status of revenge is summarized in Bowers, *Elizabethan Re-*

venge Tragedy, chap. 1. The comparable French change, in which trial by ordeal organized by corporate kinship groups gave way to trial by inquest at the individual level, is described in Bloch, *Medieval French Literature and Law.*

58. The appeal was still theoretically available during the Tudor period, but its disadvantages seem to have precluded its actual use.

59. *The Commonwealth of England and Maner of Government Thereof,* 1st ed. (1589), quoted in Bowers, *Elizabethan Revenge Tragedy,* 7.

60. Other scriptural references invoked by the preachers included "To me belongeth vengeance, and recompence; their foot shall slide in due time" (Deut. 32:35) and "For we know him that hath said, vengeance belongeth unto me, I will recompence, saith the Lord. And again, The Lord shall judge his people" (Heb. 10:30). For a full account of the theological case against revenge, see Campbell, "Theories of Revenge"; Bowers, *Elizabethan Revenge Tragedy,* chap. 1; Eleanor Prosser, *Hamlet and Revenge,* 2d ed. *(Stanford, Calif.: Stanford University Press, 1971).*

61. Bowers, *Elizabethan Revenge Tragedy,* 40.

62. Prosser, *Hamlet and Revenge,* 34.

63. Susan Jacoby has recently written a thoughtful popular account of the contemporary revenge dilemma, *Wild Justice: The Evolution of Revenge* (New York: Harper & Row, 1983).

64. Francis Bacon, *A Selection of His Works,* ed. Sidney Warhaft (Indianapolis: Odyssey Press, 1965), 55–56.

65. Renaissance productions of Seneca's plays were revised to add a moral and political significance not found in the originals. For example, a production of *Oedipus* made it fit the "mirror for magistrates" convention; it made Oedipus personally responsible for Thebes' fate, a responsibility Seneca had specifically denied. Bruce R. Smith, "Toward the Rediscovery of Tragedy: Productions of Seneca's Plays on the English Renaissance Stage," *Renaissance Drama* n.s. 9 (1978): 3–37.

66. See Yates, *Astraea,* pt. 2.

67. In keeping with their Protestant nationalist ideology, revenge tragedy's message was neither Stoic nor Machiavellian, advocating neither submission to an inscrutable Providence nor manipulations to avoid the dictates of Providence; see Joseph S. M. J. Chang, "'Of Mighty Opposites': Stoicism and Machiavellianism," *Renaissance Drama* 9 (1966): 37–57.

68. Robert Bolton (1621); quoted in William Lamont, *Godly Rule: Politics and Religion 1603–1660* (London: Macmillan, 1969), 49.

69. For a discussion of these public resolutions, in which a judge of person of rank closes the play, see Bernard Beckerman, *Shakespeare at the Globe, 1599–1609* (New York: Macmillan, 1964), 36 and passim.

70. A very different reading of revenge tragedy, one that pays insufficient attention to the death-and-restoration endings in my view, sees the revenger as a folk-hero opposing a modern state that is tryannical by nature; see J. W. Lever, *The Tragedy of State* (London: Methuen, 1971) and Jonathan Dollimore, *Radical Tragedy: Religion, Ideology and Power in the Drama of Shakespeare and His Contemporaries* (Chicago: University of Chicago Press, 1984).

71. Hallett and Hallet (*The Revenger's Madness*) makes this argument for the Kydian revengers.

72. There may be a tension between the restoration endings, which neatly resolve the plot's dilemmas in the usual manner of formulaic endings, and the audience or reader's response to such artificial tidiness, a response of ambivalence and dissatisfaction with the implausibility of the ultimate political optimism expressed. For the argument that our experience of authentic works of art resists reduction to any central meaning, and therefore the generation of such an ambivalent experience demonstrates a play's power, see Norman Rabkin, *Shakespeare and the Problem of Meaning* (Chicago: University of Chicago Press, 1981); for the role of formulaic endings, see Cawelti, *Adventure, Mystery, and Romance.*

CHAPTER 4: RENAISSANCE REVIVALS FROM THE RESTORATION
THROUGH THE AGE OF GARRICK

1. Since these terms are somewhat loaded in contemporary criticism, I should perhaps make clear what I mean by them. I take "intention" to be what an author wants his work to mean, and "significance" to be the meaning that a playgoer, reader, or the author himself finds in the finished work. "Meaning" applies to both; indeed, it applies to every case where a subject "makes something" of an object. Recently there has been considerable debate over whether intention or significance should be the primary focus for critical attention. I am attempting to encompass both, and while my own primary interest is in significance, I contend that first some attempt must be made to reconstruct intention, at least so far as to begin to understand why certain conventions are present in a work in the first place. For representative statements of the intentionist position, see E. D. Hirsch, Jr., *Validity in Interpretation* (New Haven: Yale University Press, 1967) and Quentin Skinner, "On Performing and Explaining Linguistic Actions," *The Philosophical Quarterly* 21 (1971):1–21; for the significance argument, specifically one that places "literature in the reader," see Stanley Fish, *Is There a Text in This Class?: The Authority of Interpretive Communities* (Cambridge, Mass.: Harvard University Press, 1980).

2. The gatekeeper metaphor was used by Paul M. Hirsch ("Processing Fads and Fashions") in his discussion of how products of the mass culture industry are connected to a potential public by being either blocked or facilitated by media gatekeepers such as disk jockeys and film critics.

3. For a historical and philosophical account of the Puritan antipathy, see Jonas Barish, *The Antitheatrical Prejudice* (Berkeley and Los Angeles: University of California Press, 1981). In *Puritanism and Theatre* (Cambridge: Cambridge University Press, 1982), Margot Heinemann points out that the hostility between Puritans and men of the theatre was by no means unremitting. At times the political interests of the Puritans and (some) dramatists coincided; she regards Thomas Middleton as manifesting their shared opposition to the court.

4. Harbage, *Annals of English Drama 975–1700.*

5. For an account of dramatic activity under the Commonwealth, see Louis B. Wright, "The Reading of Plays during the Puritan Revolution," *Huntington Library Bulletin* 6 (1924): 72–108. Wright emphasizes how the plays, always written by royalists, provided solace for those gentlemen temporarily removed from political power.

6. Harbage, *Annals of English Drama.*

7. Wright, "Reading of Plays," p. 75; Wright was quoting Giovanni Sagredo, the

Venetian ambassador to London, who wrote this remark on 12 November 1655, as published in *Calendar of State Papers, Venetian 1655–1656,* 138.

8. See David Cressy, "Levels of Illiteracy in England 1530–1730," in *Literacy and Social Development in the West,* ed. Harvey J. Graff (Cambridge: Cambridge University Press, 1981), 105–24. Cressy's data are drawn for Norwich, which he believes resembles the pattern for London more closely than it does the rest of England. The data suggest that during the seventeenth century literacy was near universal for clergy, professional men, and the gentry. Somewhat over half of the tradesmen and craftsmen were literate to some extent, about two-thirds of the yeomen, but only some fifteen percent of common laborers (and even fewer women). Furthermore, the Civil War had a catastrophic effect on popular education, so the literacy of the lower classes actually declined during the period.

9. Samuel Pepys, *The Diary of Samuel Pepys,* Robert Latham and William Matthews (Berkeley and Los Angeles: University of California Press, 1970), 1:171. See also Helen McAfee, *Pepys on the Restoration Stage* (New Haven: Yale University Press, 1916).

10. As John Loftis puts it: "The two most important dramatists of the first decade, Dryden and Sir George Etherege, repaid royal friendship and patronage with comedies achieving a conversational brilliance to which the court aspired." "The Social and Literary Context," *The Revels History of Drama in English,* vol. 5, 1660–1750, ed. John Loftis, Richard Southern, Marion Jones, and A. H. Scouten (London: Methuen, 1976), 11.

11. Emmett L. Avery, "The Restoration Audience," *Philological Quarterly* 45 (1966): 54–61.

12. Pepys, *Diary* (1976), 9:398.

13. *Diary,* 1 January 1663; quoted with several other examples of Pepys's distaste for "the Çitizens," by Emmet L. Avery and Arthur H. Scouten, *The London Stage 1660–1700* (Carbondale: Southern Illinois University Press, 1968), clxv.

14. Avery ("Restoration Audiences") emphasizes the wide range of backgrounds of Restoration audiences. This wide range included only the higher strata of society, but it went well beyond the court and titled aristocracy.

15. See Laslett, "The Wrong Way through the Telescope," for a warning against the use of Restoration comedy as social evidence.

16. Pepys condemned Dryden's *Mock Astrologer* for being "smutty," while he lauded another play for being "without one word of ribaldry." Much as he admired his aristocratic neighbors in the audience of the Restoration theatres, Pepys's taste may have had something in common with that of the despised "citizens." See McAfee, *Pepys,* 17–33, for a discussion of Pepys as a dramatic historian and critic.

17. John Dennis, *A Large Account of the Taste in Poetry, and the Causes of the Degeneracy of It,* in *Critical Works* (1939), 1:294; quoted in *The Revels History of Drama in English,* vol. 5 (London: Methuen, 1976).

18. See Barish, *The Antitheatrical Prejudice,* chap. 8.

19. Jeremy Collier, *A Short View of the Immorality and Profaneness of the English Stage* (1698; rpt. New York: AMS Press, 1974).

20. Arthur Bedford, *The Evil and Danger of Stage Plays* (London, 1706), emphasis Bedford's; quoted in Barish, *The Antitheatrical Prejudice,* 232.

21. Lewis Theobald, *The Censor* 87 (11 May, 1717); quoted *The Revels History of Drama in English,* vol. 5, 1660–1750, 30.

22. Since taking over the management of the Little (Haymarket) Theatre, Samuel Foote had aspired to rival the patent houses. Drury Lane's interventions prevented him from encroaching on legitimate drama, however, and he was unable to get a royal patent in spite of the popularity of the chocolate-and-entertainments he offered. In 1766 an accident brought him his wish. Foote was visiting with some aristocratic friends, including the duke of York, who mounted him on an unruly horse as a joke; he was thrown and his broken leg had to be amputated. The conscience-strikenn peers prevailed upon King George III to grant Foote a patent in recompense. The patent was for summer performances only.

23. W. R. Chetwood, *A General History of the Stage* (London: W. Owen, 1749), 28, 40.

24. A famous exception was the "battle of the Romeos" in 1750, when Spranger Barry and Mrs. Cibber played the leads at Covent Garden and David Garrick and George Anne Bellamy opposed them at Drury Lane. Some members of the audience rushed from Drury Lane, where they saw Garrick in the earlier acts, to Covent Garden just in time to catch Barry for the tomb scene, in which he was considered superior.

25. British Library, *Drury Lane Clippings,* vol. 1; the newspaper is not identified.

26. For detailed analyses of the composition of eighteenth-century audiences, see Harry William Pedicord, *The Theatrical Public in the Time of Garrick* (New York: Kings Crown, 1954), and James J. Lynch, *Box, Pit, and Gallery* (Berkeley: University of California Press, 1953).

27. Pedicord compares the cost, in modern equivalent dollars, of theatre attendance. For the cheapest seat, the Elizabethan paid the equivalent of $0.62, and the eighteenth-century workman $4.56. (The 1950s cheap seat cost $1.95.) In contrast, the Elizabethan and the eighteenth-century worker paid about the same for a pot of beer or a cheap meal. Pedicord, *The Theatrical Public,* 27.

28. Reported in the London *Chronicle,* 26 October 1759, in British Library, *Drury Lane Clippings,* vol. 1.

29. Dame Farnsworth Smith remarks how the Town "felt a responsibility for making the established conception of wit and good taste prevail," in *The Critics in the Audience of the London Theatres from Buckingham to Sheridan* (Albuquerque, N.M.: University of New Mexico Press, 1953), 181.

30. Julian L. Ross discusses this antagonism, which often took the form of economically insecure dramatists heaping scorn on their audiences' lack of taste, in "Dramatist vs. Audience in the Early Eighteenth Century," *Philological Quarterly* 12 (1933): 78–81. The height of contempt for one's audience was expressed by Henry Fielding in his advice to dramatists: "If you must write, write nonsense. . . . Be profane, be scurrilous, be immodest; if you would receive applause, deserve to receive sentence at the Old Bailey; and if you would ride in a coach, deserve to ride in a cart" (*The Author's Farce* 1.5).

31. *An Apology for the Life of Colley Cibber* (1740), ed. B. R. S. Fone (Ann Arbor: The University of Michigan Press, 1968), 100.

32. British Library, *Drury Lane Clippings,* vol. 1.

33. Pedicord, *The Theatrical Public,* 138–48.

34. George Winchester Stone, Jr., "The Making of a Repertory," in *The London Theatre World, 1660–1800,* ed. Robert D. Hume. (Carbondale: Southern Illinois University Press, 1980), 181–209. Stone's figures include both mainpieces and afterpieces; the data are drawn from the computerized *Index* to *The London Stage,* comp. Ben Ross Schneider, Jr. (Carbondale: Southern Illinois University Press, 1979).

35. *The London Stage, Part 5, 1776–1800,* ed. Charles Beecher Hogan (Carbondale: Southern Illinois University Press, 1968), clxvii.

36. Lynch, *Box, Pit, and Gallery,* 23.

37. Emmett L. Avery and Arthur H. Scouten in "Critical Introduction," *The London Stage 1660–1800,* pt. 1, cxxviii, have compiled the figures here and following.

38. Although comedy of manners is the most distinctive and lasting form of Restoration drama in the modern view, the majority of new plays written during the period were in fact tragedies. Avery and Scouten, *The London Stage,* cxxix.

39. Lawrence Bergmann Wallis, *Fletcher, Beaumont and Company, Entertainers to the Jacobean Gentry* (New York: King's Crown, 1947), 26; see also Arthur Colby Sprague, *Beaumont and Fletcher on the Restoration Stage* (Cambridge, Mass.: Harvard University Press, 1926), for an account of the popularity of these playwrights.

40. Gerald Eades Bentley compared the allusion to Shakespeare and Jonson made by seventeenth-century writers in *Shakespeare and Jonson: Their Reputations in the Seventeenth Century Compared,* 2 vols. (Chicago: University of Chicago Press, 1945). He found 1,839 allusions to Jonson and 1,430 allusions to Shakespeare. Jonson led in every decade except the last, in which Shakespeare had a slight majority. Jonson was consistently more often alluded to as setting the standard for dramatic quality, and Jonson's plays were more often mentioned, but Shakespeare's characters were alluded to more than Jonson's.

41. John Dryden, "*Troilus and Cressida* Preface" (1679). In *Essays of John Dryden,* ed. W. P. Ker (Oxford: Clarendon Press, 1900), 2:203.

42. Arthur H. Scouten, in "The Increase in Popularity of Shakespeare's Plays in the Eighteenth Century," *Shakespeare Quarterly* 7 (Spring 1956): 189–203, has demonstrated that during the decade before Garrick's management of Drury Lane, twenty-three percent of all performances were of Shakespeare, which was exactly the same percentage as that during the three decades of Garrick's management.

43. *The London Stage,* pt. 4, 1: clxii–clxvi.

44. For an overview of eighteenth-century critics, see Herbert Spencer Robinson, *English Shakespearean Criticism in the Eighteenth Century* (New York: H. W. Wilson, 1932).

45. Letter to Reverend Charles Jenner, 30 April 1770; this letter is number 584 in *The Letters of David Garrick,* ed. David M. Little and George Kahrl, 3 vols (Cambridge, Mass.: Harvard University Press, 1963), 2:690.

46. R. G. Noyes, in his account *Ben Jonson on the English Stage 1660–1776* (Cambridge, Mass.: Harvard University Press, 1935), emphasizes the early eighteenth century's admiration for Jonson as being based on his classicism in dramatic construction: "critics more typical of the neo-classic love of chaste outline and the rules praised him as law-giver and model" (11).

47. Letter to Herbert Lawrence, 10 January 1774; letter number 817 in *Letters.*

48. I must disagree with Lynch's (*Box, Pit, and Gallery*) attribution of the failure of

Eastward Ho! to its attack on social climbers, which he suggests "proved too strong fare for an audience that included many of the *nouveau riche.*" That same audience was amused by the social climbers of *The Alchemist,* and in a few years was to support the far harsher judgment on "overreachers" in *A New Way to Pay Old Debts.*

49. See Noyes, *Ben Jonson on the English Stage,* chap. 3, for the history of *The Alchemist.*

50. Charles Gildon, *The Complete Art of Poetry;* quoted in Noyes, *Ben Jonson on the English Stage,* 114. See also Robinson, *English Shakespearean Criticism,* 23–28.

51. Noyes, *Ben Jonson on the English Stage,* 117.

52. My count and categorization are taken from Harbage, *Annals of English Drama.* I have excluded *The Faithful Shepherdess* (pastoral), *The Knight of the Burning Pestle* (burlesque romance), *Four Plays* (morality), and *The False One* (classical history). The only plays of the remaining fifty that were never revived were the comedy *The Woman Hater* and the tragedies *The Jeweller of Amsterdam* and *Sir John van Olden Barnavelt.*

53. Wallis, *Fletcher, Beaumont and Company.*

54. All quotations from Sprague, *Beaumont and Fletcher on the Restoration Stage,* xix–xx; the "witty obscenity" quotation was from Richard Flecknoe, *Love's Kingdom* (1664).

55. *The Memoirs of Robert Wilks,* written by an anonymous author in 1732; quoted by Sprague, 124. *The Scornful Lady* shares many city comedy characteristics and is discussed by Leggatt (*Citizen Comedy*). I did not include it in this study because it seems to go further than even *Wit without Money* in parodying the city comedy conventions, but it was a close call.

56. See Robert Ball, *The Amazing Career of Sir Giles Overreach* (Princeton: Princeton University Press, 1939).

57. *A Select Collection of Old Plays,* vol. 8 (London, 1744).

58. London, published posthumously by Dell, 1759.

59. "Critical Reflections on the Old English Dramatick Writers," prefix to second edition of *The Dramatic Works of Philip Massinger.*

60. Quoted in Ball, *The Amazing Career,* 37.

61. Ibid., 33.

62. From *Memoirs of Richard Cumberland;* quoted in Ball, *The Amazing Career,* p. 39.

63. Figures are from *Index to The London Stage.* See also appendix B.

64. See Roy Porter, *English Society in the Eighteenth Century* (Harmondsworth: Penguin, 1982), chap. 2, and M. Dorothy George, *London Life in the Eighteenth Century* (1925; New York: Harper & Row, 1965), chap. 4, for detailed discussion of the immense variety of social gradations during the eighteenth century.

65. Quoted in P. J. Corfield, *The Impact of English Towns 1700–1800* (Oxford: Oxford University Press, 1982), 72–73.

66. For a detailed account of this expansion, see Geoffrey Holmes, *Augustan England: Professions, State and Society, 1680–1730* (London: George Allen & Unwin, 1982).

67. Joseph Harris, *An Essay upon Money and Coins* (1757); quoted in Neil McKendrick, John Brewer, and J. H. Plumb, *The Birth of a Consumer Society: The Commercialization of Eighteenth-Century England* (London: Europa Publications, 1982), 20.

68. See George, *London Life,* chap. 1, for a comparison of the seventeenth- and eighteenth-century industrial milieux of the city.

69. Corfield, *Impact of English Towns;* a survey of the patients of the Westminster General Dispensary, 1776–81, that found only twenty-five percent of the adult patients were born in London (68).

70. *A Trip through the Town* (1735), quoted in McKendrick et al., *Birth of a Consumer Society,* 60; chap. 2 of this study contains dozens of similar remarks.

71. McKendrick et al., *Birth of a Consumer Society,* 59.

72. Ibid., 53.

73. See Stone and Stone, *An Open Elite?*

74. (1763); quoted in McKendrick et al., *Birth of a Consumer Society,* 25. For the role fashion, especially calicoes, played in obscuring social distinctions, see Chandra Mukerji, *From Graven Images* (New York: Columbia University Press, 1983).

75. Jedediah Strutt (1767), quoted in Porter, *English Society,* 96.

76. "The political fabric—much abused, pulled, torn, tattered, and patched—was never ripped up. . . . Piecemeal violence never turned into general insurrection." Porter, *English Society in the Eighteenth Century,* 119.

77. Ibid., 195.

78. For the development of the concept of interest, see Albert Hirschman, *The Passions and the Interests: Political Arguments for Capitalism before Its Triumph* (Princeton: Princeton University Press, 1977).

CHAPTER 5: RENAISSANCE REVIVALS FROM CARLO THE HERO DOG
TO THE ELIZABETHAN STAGE SOCIETY

1. *Nicholas Nickleby* (1839; Harmondsworth: Penguin, 1978); quotation from pp. 463–64.

2. Joseph Donohue provides a detailed account of the transformation the English theatre underwent in the late years of the eighteenth century and first decades of the nineteenth century in *Theatre in the Age of Kean* (Oxford: Basil Blackwell, 1975).

3. 1891; rpt. Harmondsworth: Penguin, 1978, 474.

4. Playbill for *The Lion King,* Lyceum Theatre, 5 September 1842. British Library, *Playbills,* vol. 147.

5. 1693; quoted in *The Oxford Companion to the Theatre,* 3d ed., 702.

6. Donahue, *Theatre in the Age of Kean,* 18; see also Charles Beecher Hogan, *The London Stage 1776–1800* (Carbondale: Southern Illinois University Press, 1968).

7. Richard Brinsley Peake, *Memoirs of the Colman Family* (London, 1841), 2:19–20, quoted in Hogan, *London Stage,* xliv.

8. George Rowell, in *The Victorian Theatre 1792–1914,* 2d ed. (Cambridge: Cambridge University Press, 1978), points out that burletta is not to be confused with burlesque. The latter refers to the whimsical or mocking treatment of some other dramatic form, while burletta refers to the central role of music in the production. In the nineteenth century, burlettas were often burlesque as well, culminating in Gilbert and Sullivan's operatic takeoffs of romantic comedies.

9. See Michael R. Booth, Richard Southern, Frederick Marker, Lise-Lone Marker, and Robertson Davies, *The Revels History of Drama in English: Volume VI 1750–1880* (London: Methuen, 1975), for compact accounts of the histories of the minor theatres.

10. Allardyce Nicoll, *A History of English Drama 1660–1900* (1930; 2d ed., Cambridge: Cambridge University Press, 1955), 4:25.

11. Donohue, *Theatre in the Age of Kean,* 56.

12. Thus the "Elizabethan revival" associated with Charles Lamb involved a renewed interest in the poetry and moral structure of Renaissance drama, not in its performance. See Enjer J. Jensen, "Lamb, Poel, and Our Postwar Theatre: Elizabethan Revivals," *Renaissance Drama,* n.s., 9 (1978): 211–34.

13. Prince Hermann von Puckler-Muskau, *Tour of a German Prince,* vol. 3 (London, 1832), quoted in Booth et al., *Revels History,* 4:23.

14. Nicoll, *History of English Drama,* 4:53.

15. Ibid., 376–83.

16. Ibid., 61; see also 58–78.

17. See Rowell, *The Victorian Theatre,* 1–29, for a discussion of the decreasing distinction between the minors and the patent houses.

18. See Watson Nicholson, *The Struggle for a Free Stage in London* (Boston: Houghton, Mifflin, 1906), chap. 9.

19. See "Table of the London Theatres from 1800 to 1870," opp. p. 59 in Ernest Bradlee Watson, *Sheridan to Robertson: A Study of the Nineteenth-Century London Stage* (1926; New York: Benjamin Blom, 1963).

20. Watson, *Sheridan to Roberston,* 146.

21. For a discussion of the dramatists' pay during the period, see Booth et al., *Revels History,* 4:43–57.

22. Charles Lamb, *Specimens of English Dramatic Poets;* from *The Complete Works of Charles and Mary Lamb,* ed. E. V. Lucas (London: Methuen, 1904), 4:160.

23. I am using the figures and categorizations from the introduction to *The London Stage, 1747–1776,* clxii–clxix. There were 5,353 performances of 212 different mainpieces from 1747 through 1776 at Drury Lane. Comedy accounted for half of the plays and slightly more than half of the performances, and the remaining mainpieces included tragedies, operas, histories, tragicomedies, and masques. During the same years there were 5,013 performances of 189 different afterpieces; 44% of the performances were of farces, with pantomime accounting for another 27%. See *The London Stage* for a further breakdown of these figures; on p. clxii the number of mainpiece performances is incorrectly given as 5,363.

24. These percentages are derived from taking a 10% sample of the plays listed in "Handlist of Plays 1800–1850" in Nicoll, *History of English Drama,* 4:245–558. I counted the plays listed on every tenth page, which totaled 867 plays. The designations used by Nicoll are those from the original playbills whenever possible. The handlist included published plays for which no performance is known; it is my impression that this may have inflated the figures for "Tragedy" a bit. It also includes plays performed outside of London. While the proliferation of theatres makes any count incomplete, Nicoll's list of the vast majority of plays from the major and minor theatres provides a good general portrait of the types of drama written and produced during the early nineteenth century.

25. Shirley S. Allen, *Samuel Phelps and Sadler's Wells Theatre* (Middletown, Conn.: Wesleyan University Press, 1971).

26. Ibid., 82–83.

27. Ibid., appendix 1.
28. See Ball, *The Amazing Career.*
29. See Robert Speaight, *William Poel and the Elizabethan Revival* (London: Heinemann, 1954).
30. See Enjer, "Lamb, Poel, and Our Postwar Theatre."
31. Poel's full-length Elizabethan Stage Society Productions, which I have drawn from Speight, *William Poel,* appendix 1, were as follows: 404–405

1895	*Twelfth Night; The Comedy of Errors*
1896	*Doctor Faustus; The Two Gentlemen of Verona*
1897	*Twelfth Night; Arden of Feversham; The Tempest*
1898	*The Coxcomb; The Spanish Gipsy; The Broken Heart; The Sad Shepherd; The Merchant of Venice*
1899	*The Alchemist; Locrine; Such Stuff as Dreams Are Made Of* [from Calderón]: *Sakuntála; Richard II; Don Juan*
1900	*Hamlet; Samson Agonistes; The Death of Wallenstein; Marmion*
1901	*Everyman* (+ *The Sacrifice of Isaac*); *King Henry V*
1902	*The Alchemist*
1903	*Twelfth Night; King Edward the Second*
1904	*Much Ado about Nothing; Doctor Faustus; The Comedy of Errors*
1905	*The First Franciscans; Romeo and Juliet*

32. C. E. Montague, *The Manchester Guardian,* quoted in Speaight, *William Poel and the Elizabethan Revival,* 119.
33. See Michael R. Booth, *English Melodrama* (London: Herbert Jenkins, 1965).
34. For a valuable discussion of the "moral fantasies" conveyed in formulaic literature, see John Cawelti, *Adventure, Mystery, and Romance: Formula Stories as Art and Popular Culture* (Chicago: University of Chicago Press, 1976).

CHAPTER 6: RENAISSANCE REVIVALS FROM THE EDWARDIANS TO THE ARTS COUNCIL

1. For a discussion of the sources of this new respectability, see Nicoll, *A History of English Drama 1660–1900,* 7–27.
2. Michael R. Booth, Richard Southern, Frederick Marker, Lise-Lone Marker, and Robertson Davies, *The Revels History of Drama in English;* vol. 6: 1750–1880 (London: Methuen, 1975), 19.
3. J. C. Trewin, *The Edwardian Theatre* (Totowa, N.J.: Rowman & Littlefield, 1976), 155–60.
4. Scott was the leader of the critical faction labeled "the Ancients," who were opposed by "the Moderns," led by William Archer. The Ancients' response to a new play was emotional, the Moderns' analytic; the former deplored naturalism, Ibsen, and innovation in general, all of which the Moderns vigorously championed. Scott's influence was magnified by the fact that he wrote for the widely circulating *Daily Telegraph.*
5. Anna Irene Miller, *The Independent Theatre in Europe: 1887 to the Present* (New York: Long & Smith, 1931).
6. Quoted in Miller, *The Independent Theatre,* 177.

7. Hugh Hunt, Kenneth Richards, and John Russell Taylor, *The Revels History of Drama in English;* vol. 7: 1880 to the Present Day (London: Methuen, 1978), 136.
8. For an account of the noncommercial theatre between the wars, see Norman Marshall, *The Other Theatre* (London: John Lehmann, 1947).
9. The following plays were produced by the Phoenix:

1919	*The Duchess of Malfi* (Webster)
1920	*Marriage A-La-Mode* (Dryden); *The Fair Maid of the West* (Heywood); *Venice Preserved* (Otway)
1921	*Volpone* (Jonson); *Love for Love* (Congreve); *The Witch of Edmonton* (Dekker, Ford, and Rowley); *Bartholomew Fair* (Jonson); *The Maid's Tragedy* (Beaumont and Fletcher)
1922	*The Chances* (Fletcher and the duke of Buckingham); *All for Love* (Dryden); *Amphitryon* (Dryden); *The Jew of Malta* (Marlowe)
1923	*'Tis Pity She's a Whore* (Ford); *The Alchemist* (Jonson); *The Faithful Shepherdess* (Fletcher); *Edward II* (Marlowe)
1924	*The Country Wife* (Wycherly); *King Lear* (Shakespeare); *The Old Batchelor* (Congreve); *Epicoene* (Jonson)
1925	*The Assignation* (Dryden); *The Orphan* (Otway); *The Rehersal* (duke of Buckingham); *Dr. Faustus* (Marlowe); *The Gentleman Dancing Master* (Wycherly)

10. Marshall, *The Other Theatre*, p. 76.
11. Frank Vernon, *Twentieth-Century Theatre* (London: Harrap, 1924).
12. Two useful accounts of the postwar theatre are Ronald Hayman, *The Set-Up: An Anatomy of English Theatre Today* (London: Eyre Methuen, 1973), and John Elsom, *Post-war British Theatre* (London: Routledge & Kegan Paul, 1976). For a discussion of the unique immunity from fundamental criticism that government arts patronization enjoys, see Peter Calvocoressi, *The British Experience 1945–75* (London: Bodley Head, 1978), 42–43. In the mid-1980s, the English noncommercial theatres have felt severely threatened by government cost cutting.
13. *The Charter of Incorporation Granted by His Majesty the King to the Arts Council of Great Britain Ninth Day of August, 1946,* 3; quoted in John S. Harris, *Government Patronage of the Arts in Great Britain* (Chicago: University of Chicago, 1970), 40–41. For a more recent discussion of the effect of the Arts Council and its various types of grants, see *The Revels History of Drama in English,* vol. 7: 1880 to the Present Day, ed. Hugh Hunt, Kenneth Richards, John Russell Taylor (London: Methuen, 1978), 145–58.
14. England's support of the arts, though high by American standards, is not high for Europe. According to a report in *The New York Times* (19 June 1980), p. C15,

> Overall, the British Government spends far less per capita on the arts than most Western European governments. According to one compilation, West Germany last year laid out $18 per head of population for live theatre, opera and ballet; Sweden $14; Switzerland $4.75; Italy $2.35; and Great Britain about $1.05. In the United States, according to figures of the National Endowment for the Arts, the Federal Government spends 10 cents a person for dance, opera and theatre through its arts program.

Thatcher-era austerities of the mid-eighties have threatened even this level of support; shortage of funds, and a desire to dramatize their plight, closed one of the three National Theatre stages (the Cottlesloe) for some weeks in 1985.

15. William J. Baumol and William G. Bowen, "The Audience," *Performing Arts: The Economic Dilemma* (Cambridge, Mass.: MIT Press, 1966), 71–97; see table on 90–91.

16. Ibid., 90.

17. A Royal Shakespeare Company survey of five performances at its London theatre (Aldwych) revealed that overseas visitors constituted 17.5% of the audience. And the survey was conducted during late November and early December; the tourist portion of summer and Christmas audiences would be higher. Sandra Bratchell, Howard Austin, Stanislaus Hempel, Christine Komarynsky, and Ruth Tinning, *Aldwych Theatre Audience Survey* (March 1978), 3.

18. These tallies come from counting the London Playbills section of *Who's Who in the Theatre,* which began recording major productions in the middle of 1921. While all West End and most fringe, club, and noncommercial productions were recorded, some very small-scale or amateur productions may be missing.

Labeling a production a revival is somewhat arbitrary. A revival is "renewed performance of or interest in the drama or literature: a new presentation or publication, as of a play or book" (*Webster's Third New International Dictionary,* s.v. "revival"), but there is the question of how much adaptation of an older work can be done before it is no longer a revival but a new work "based on" a previous one. *Who's Who* has not followed any hard-and fast rule on the question of adaptations; some are marked as revivals, some not. American plays being given their first London productions are not considered revivals, nor are productions of plays that have premiered in the provinces. (I am grateful to Ian Herbert [letter dated 21 August 1980] for clarification of *Who's Who in the Theatre's* practices on these points.)

19. A. H. Halsey, ed., *Trends in British Society since 1900* (London: Macmillan, 1972), table 16.11, p. 552.

20. I have standardized the figures for figure 6 to facilitate comparison. The number of tragedies revived during each period has been multiplied by five-thirds.

21. Again, the figures for tragedy have been standardized for figure 7. It should also be noted that the overall figures for infrequently produced Shakespeare tragedies are inflated by the absence of *Titus Andronicus,* which has been reserved for the category of revenge tragedy; with only six productions in the twentieth century, *Titus Andronicus* was seen considerably less often than *Antony and Cleopatra.*

22. *The Spanish Tragedy* was given its first major revival in three centuries by the Glasgow Citizens' Theatre in October 1978. It was revised in London at the National Theatre in 1982.

23. Watching commercial television (or at least admitting to it) seems to be strongly associated with social class in Britain. In 1968, 34% of upper-middle and middle-class respondents claimed to watch ITV regularly; the comparable percentages were 49% for the lower middle class, 65% for the skilled working class, and 66% for the working class and poor. Halsey, *Trends in British Society,* table 16.17, p. 557.

24. My discussion of postwar Britain draws heavily from C. H. Bartlett, *A History of Postwar Britain 1945–1974* (London: Longman, 1977); Alan Sked and Chris Cook,

Post-War Britain: A Political History (London: Sussex: Harvester 1979), which gives full accounts of each election; and a social history that complements Sked and Cook by virtually ignoring politics in favor of social and institutional changes, Arthur Marwick's *British Society since 1945* (London: Allen Lane, 1982). A thoughtful and elegantly expressed account, organized topically rather than chronologically, comes from Calvocoressi, *The British Experience 1945–75*.

25. See Marwick, *British Society,* 107.

26. For the classic sociological analysis of the coronation as ritual, see Edward A. Shils and Michael Young, "The Meaning of the Coronation," in Shils, *Center and Periphery: Essays in Macrosociology,* (Chicago: University of Chicago Press, 1975), 135–52.

27. Nancy Mitford, "The English Aristocracy," *Encounter* 5 (September 1955): 5–12.

28. C. P. Snow, "The Two Cultures," *New Statesman and Nation* (6 October 1956), 413–14.

29. Richard Hoggart, *The Uses of Literacy* (1957; New York: Oxford University Press, 1970).

30. The work of Richard M. Titmuss was particularly influential; see *Essays on the Welfare State* (London: Allen & Unwin, 1958); *Income Distribution and Social Change* (London: Allen & Unwin, 1962); *Commitment to Welfare* (London: Allen & Unwin, 1968). Two other social scientists who documented and publicized the persistence of poverty under the welfare state were Brian Abel-Smith and Peter Townsend; see for example their jointly authored *The Poor and the Poorest: A New Analysis of the Ministry of Labour's Family Expenditure Surveys of 1953–4 and 1960* (London: G. Bell, 1965).

31. *The Decade of Disillusion: British Politics in the Sixties,* ed. David McKie and Chris Cook (London: Macmillan, 1972).

32. Anne Lapping, "Social Welfare and Housing," in McKie and Cook, *Decade of Disillusion,* 150.

33. Peter Sinclair, "The Economy—a Study in Failure," in McKie and Cook, *Decade of Disillusion,* 94.

34. See for example, James McMillan, *The Roots of Corruption: The Erosion of Traditional Values in Britain from 1960 to the Present Day* (London: Stacey, 1972).

35. See John Russell Taylor, *The Angry Theatre: New British Drama* (New York: Hill and Wang, 1962).

36. J. C. Trewin, *Drama in Britain 1951–1964* (London: Longmans, Green & Co., 1965).

37. John Boni has compared revenge tragedy and the modern novels of Vonnegut, Heller, Pyncheon and other writers of black comedy, finding that both "express a lack of reliance on value systems." See "Analogous Form: Black Comedy and Some Jacobean Plays," *Western Humanities Review* 28 (1974): 201–15.

38. In the early twentieth century the British used the term "producer" to designate what Americans, and now the British as well, usually call the "director." I use the term director consistently to refer to the person chiefly responsible for making dramatic, aesthetic, and staging decisions, while reserving "producer" for the person responsible for financial management. The two functions may be carried out by a single person; Garrick and Poel did both. In contemporary companies, however, they are usually divided.

39. Personal interview with the author, 2 January 1980.

40. Robert Cushman, *The Observer,* 30 September 1979, p. 14.

41. Robert Brustein, personal interview with author, 27 May 1980.

42. Tony Richards, "Why We Revived *The Changeling,*" *Plays and Players* (April 1961), p. 5.

43. John Barker, *Daily Telegram,* 13 July 1976.

44. Martin Esslin, review of Aldwych production of *The Revenger's Tragedy, Plays and Players* 17 (January 1970): 46–47. (Mary Whitehouse led the "Clean-up TV" campaign of the mid-sixties.)

45. *London Times* 6 October 1966, 18.

46. Review of *The Jew of Malta, Plays and Players* 12 (December 1964): 32–33.

CHAPTER 7: REVIVALS AND THE REAL THING

1. This was explained to me by Genista McIntosh, planning controller of the Royal Shakespeare Company.

2. Heinemann, *Puritanism and Theatre,* 1, n. 1; she comments that including *The Changeling* among the A-level texts "would scarcely have been possible even twenty years ago."

3. In his 1978 production of *Bartholomew Fair,* Peter Barnes transformed the Roundhouse into a huge fair, complete with live pigs and horses.

4. *RSC, 103rd Report of the Council,* 1978/79, Royal Shakespeare Theatre, Stratford-upon-Avon.

5. The figures were provided by John Goodwin, head of publicity and publications, National Theatre. In the United States, the proportion of expenses devoted to performers' salaries tends to be higher. The American Repertory Company spent 41% of its total expenses on artistic salaries in 1979–80, with an additional 16% going to production costs ("Summary of A.R.T. Income and Expenses for the 1979–80 Season," graph prepared by American Repertory Theatre).

6. These figures are from John Elsom, *Post-War British Theatre* (London: Routledge & Kegan Paul, 1970), 132. I have relied on Elsom's helpful discussion of the effect of the Arts Council and its policies on Britain theatre.

7. Denys Lasdun, "Building Vistas/1," *The Complete Guide to Britain's National Theatre* (London: Heinemann, 1977), 31.

8. "Breeches parts" should not be confused with roles in which women assume male disguise temporarily, as in *As You Like It.*

9. The attitude of the Stratford-upon-Avon residents was explained to me by Genista McIntosh.

10. See Bratchell et al., *Aldwych Theatre Audience Survey,* 9.

11. Information regarding Prospect Company and the Old Vic was provided by Joanna Caven, company administrator of the Old Vic Company.

12. "Remakes: The Retread Culture," in *Critical Moments* (New York: Random House, 1980), 97. In this essay, written in 1975, Brustein discussed the nostalgia vogue in the theatre, which shows no sign of abating. See Frank Rich, "What Makes a Play Seem Dated," *The New York Times,* 6 July 1980, sec. D, p. 11, for a later account of the proliferation of revivals on Broadway. The revivals of the early 1980s were mostly of popular musical comedies of the 1940s and 1950s, far less risky than revivals of more completely forgotten works.

13. The quotation is from Clifford Geertz definition of culture, the whole of which is "an historically transmitted pattern of meanings embodied in symbols, a system of inherited conception expressed in symbolic forms by means of which men communicate, perpetuate, and develop their knowledge about and attitudes toward life." This strikes me as an excellent working definition of culture as archive influencing activity, but I would want to add some attention to the question, culture of whom? A cultural object is powerful only insofar as it can move (establish moods and motivations, in Geertz's terms) an identifiable group of people. This group may correspond with the whole society in question, which I gather is what Geertz means by "men," but it also may be a subgroup (educated Londoners) or group cross-cutting societies (intellectuals). See "Religion as a Cultural System," in *The Interpretation of Cultures* (New York: Basic Books, 1973); quotation from p. 89.

14. The terms tenor and vehicle were established by I. A. Richards in his indispensable study of metaphor, *The Philosophy of Rhetoric* (1936; rpt. London: Oxford University Press, 1976). Of particular importance is his recognition that a metaphor is not just the vehicle, but the interaction of tenor and vehicle. See also Paul Ricoeur, *The Rule of Metaphor,* trans. Robert Czerny (Toronto: University of Toronto Press, 1977).

15. The term is from the Russian formalist Victor Shklovsky, who emphasized art's capacity to defamiliarize what is habitual and thoughtless.

16. Johan Huizinga, *Homo Ludens: A Study of the Play Element in Culture* (1950; rpt. Boston: Beacon, 1955).

17. Leonard B. Meyer, *Emotion and Meaning in Music* (Chicago: University of Chicago Press, 1956).

18. "An Essay on Criticism," in *Pastoral Poetry and an Essay on Criticism,* ed. E. Audra and Aubrey Williams (London: Methuen, 1961), 273.

19. The silkworm also operated as a topical metaphor, in that the changes being wrought by the textile industry had much to do with the troubles of the landed classes.

20. See Ann Swidler, in "Culture in Action: Symbols and Strategies," *American Sociological Review* 51 (1986):273–86; and Kenneth Burke, "Literature as Equipment for Living," in *The Philosophy of Literary Form* (Berkeley: University of California Press, 1974).

21. For example, while institutional factors such as Garrick's promotion facilitated the eighteenth-century growth of interest in Shakespeare's plays, at the same time the audience was receptive to Garrick's championing of Shakespeare because the playwright treated some issues that were of increasing interest to them. Shakespeare's exploration of the personalities of his characters was unusual among Renaissance dramatists, who typically presented "characters" in the sense of known types like Jonson's representatives of the humors. Shakespeare's more complex delineation of individual character appealed to an audience fascinated with probing the individual personality. The novel and the Shakespearean star rose at the same time, for both treated their audiences to a painstaking portrayal of individual human character, a subject of great concern to the eighteenth-century middle class. See Ian Watt, *The Rise of the Novel* (Berkeley: University of California Press, 1957), for the classic account of individualism and the novel.

22. Misfits between a play and social concerns are themselves illuminating, as the case of *Johnny on a Spot* illustrates. Just after Pearl Harbor, Charles MacArthur's play, a political farce about election skullduggery, opened on Broadway. The comedy clashed with the patriotic mood of the day and flopped. A successful revival was staged by the BAM Theatre Company in February 1980. This time the audience was very receptive to a comic representation of ridiculous candidates for office and crooked campaigns, in that the play corresponded with its young, urban, educated audience's cynicism and despair over politicians in general and the upcoming presidential election in particular. (The history of *Johnny on a Spot*, not a play for its time but a play for our own, was told to me by Richard Nelson, literary manager of the BAM [Brooklyn Academy of Music] Theater Company.)

23. "The Conflict in Modern Culture," translation of *Der Konflikt der modernen Kultur*, 2d ed. (Munich: Duncker and Humbolt, 1921), in *George Simmel: The Conflict in Modern Culture and Other Essays*, trans. K. Peter Etzkorn (New York: Teachers College Press, 1968), 11.

24. *The Tragic Muse* (1890; rpt. Harmondsworth, Middlesex: Penguin, 1978), 58.

BIBLIOGRAPHY

DATA SOURCES

Barroll, John Leeds; Alexander Legatt; Richard Hosley; and Alvin Kernan. *The Revels History of Drama in English*. Vol. 3: 1076–1613. London: Methuen, 1975.

British Library. Collections of playbills and clippings for individual London theatres.

Genest, John. *Some Account of the English stage, from the Restoration to 1830*. Bath: Carrington, 1832.

Harbage, Alfred. *Annals of English Drama 975–1700*. 2d ed. Revised by S. Schoenbaum. Philadelphia: University of Pennsylvania Press, 1964.

The London Stage 1660–1800: A Calendar of Plays, Entertainment, and Afterpieces. Part 1: 1660–1700. Edited by William Van Lennep; critical introduction by Emmett L. Avery and Arthur H. Scouten. Carbondale: Southern Illinois University Press, 1965.

————. Part 2: 1700–1729. 2 vols. Edited and critical introduction by Emmett L. Avery. Carbondale: Southern Illinois University Press, 1960.

————. Part 3: 1729–1747. 2 vols. Edited and critical introduction by Arthur H. Scouten. Carbondale: Southern Illinois University Press, 1961.

————. Part 4: 1747–1776. 3 vols. Edited and critical introduction by George Winchester Stone, Jr. Carbondale: Southern Illinois University Press, 1962.

————. Part 5: 1776–1800. 3 vols. Edited and critical introduction by Charles Beecher Hogan. Carbondale: Southern Illinois University Press, 1968.

Index to the London Stage 1660–1800. Compiled and introduction by Ben Ross Schneider Jr. Carbondale: Southern Illinois University Press, 1979.

Victorian and Albert Museum. Theatre Collection.

Wearing, J. P. *The London Stage, 1890–1899*. Metuchen, N.J.: Scarecrow, 1976.

Who's Who in the Theatre. 17 editions. Originally compiled by John Parker. London: Pitmen, 1912–81.

CITATION SOURCES

Citations refer to the following editions. I have modernized spelling and punctuation.

Barry, Lording. *Ram-Alley or Merrie-Tricks: A Comedy by Lording Barry*. Edited by Claude E. Jones. Louvain, Belgium: Ch. Uystpruyst, 1952.

Beaumont, Francis, and John Fletcher. *The Dramatic Works in the Beaumont and Fletcher Canon*. Edited by Fredson Bowers. 5 vols. Cambridge: Cambridge University Press, 1966–82. [Not yet complete; citations for *The Maid's Tragedy* and *Valentinian*.]

Beaumont, Francis and John Fletcher. *The Works of Beaumont and Fletcher*. Edited by Alexander Dyce. 2 vols. Boston: Phillips, Sampson, 1854. [Citation for *Wit without Money*.]

Calderón de la Barca, Pedro (Calderón). *The Painter of His Own Dishonour* and *Three Judgments at a Blow*. In *Eight Dramas by Calderon*. Translated by Edward Fitzgerald. London: Macmillan, 1921.

———. *The Surgeon of His Honour*. Translated by Roy Campbell. Madison: University of Wisconsin Press, 1960.

———. *The Mayor of Zalema* and *Secret Vengeance for Secret Insult*. In *Calderón de la Barca: Four Plays*. Translated by Edwin Honig. New York: Hill & Wang, 1961.

Chapman, George. *The Plays and Poems of George Chapman*. Edited by Thomas Mare Parrott. London: George Routledge & Sons, 1910.

Chettle, Henry. *The Tragedy of Hoffman, 1631*. Prepared by Harold Jenkins and checked by Charles Sisson. London: Malone Society, 1951.

Euripides. *The Complete Greek Tragedies: Euripides II, Four Tragedies*. Edited by David Grene and Richmond Lattimore. Chicago: University of Chicago Press, 1962.

Ford, John. *The Works of John Ford*. Edited by William Gifford and revised by Alexander Dyce. 3 vols. 1895; reissued New York: Russell & Russell, 1965.

Jonson, Ben. *Ben Jonson*. Edited by C. H. Herford and Percy Simpson. 11 vols. Oxford: Clarendon Press, 1925–52.

Kyd, Thomas, *The Works of Thomas Kyd*. Edited by Frederick S. Boas. 1901; reprint. Oxford: Clarendon Press, 1955.

Lope Felix de Vega Carpio (Lope de Vega). *Peribanez, Justice without Revenge,* and *Fuenteovejuna*. In *Lope de Vega: Five Plays*. Translated by Jill Booty. New York: Hill & Wang, 1961.

Marlowe, Christopher. *The Complete Works of Christopher Marlowe*. Edited by Fredson Bowers. 2 vols. Cambridge: Cambridge University Press, 1973.

Marston, John. *The Plays of John Marston*. Edited by H. Harvey Wood. 3 vols. Edinburgh: Oliver and Boyd, 1934–39.

Massinger, Phillip. *The Plays and Poems of Phillip Massinger*. Edited by Philip Edwards and Colin Gibson. 5 vols. Oxford: Clarendon Press, 1976.

Middleton, Thomas. *The Works of Thomas Middleton*. Edited by A. H. Bullen. 8 vols. Boston: Hougton, Mifflin, 1885–86.

Painter, William. *The Palace of Pleasure*. 4 vols. Edited by Hamish Miles. New York: AMS Press, 1967.

Seneca, Lucius Annaeus. *Four Tragedies and Octavia*. Translated by E. F. Watling. Harmondsworth: Penguin, 1966.

———. *Hercules Furens*. In *Seneca VIII*. Translated by Frank Justus Miller. Cambridge, Mass.: Harvard University Press, 1979.

Shakespeare, William. *The Complete Works of Shakespeare*. 3d ed. Edited by David Bevington. Glenview, Ill.: Scott Foresman, 1980.

Tourneur, Cyril. *The Plays of Cyril Tourneur: The Revenger's Tragedy and The Atheist's Tragedy*. Edited by Goerge Parfitt. Cambridge: Cambridge University Press, 1978.

Webster, John. *The Complete Works of John Webster.* Edited by F. L. Lucas. 4 vols. London: Chatto & Windus, 1927.

OTHER SOURCES

Abel-Smith, Brian, and Peter Townsend. *The Poor and the Poorest: A New Analysis of the Ministry of Labour's Family Expenditure Surveys of 1953–4 and 1960.* London: G. Bell, 1965.

Albrecht, Milton. "The Relationship of Literature and Society." *American Sociological Review* 59 (1954):425–31.

Allison, T. E. "The Paternoster Play." *PLMA* 39 (1924):789–804.

Avery, Emmet L. "The Restoration Audience." *Philological Quarterly* 45 (1966):54–61.

Axton, Marie. *The Queen's Two Bodies: Drama and the Elizabethan Succession.* London: Royal Historical Society, 1977.

Bacon, Francis. *A Selection of His Works.* Edited by Sidney Warhaft. Indianapolis: Odyssey Press, 1965.

Bailey, Derrick Sherwin. *Homosexuality and the Western Christian Tradition.* London: Longmans, Green & Co., 1955.

Baldwin, T. W. *Shakespeare's Five-Act Structure.* Urbana: University of Illinois Press, 1947.

Ball, Robert. *The Amazing Career of Sir Giles Overreach.* Princeton: Princeton University Press, 1939.

Barish, Jonas. *The Antitheatrical Prejudice.* Berkeley and Los Angeles: University of California Press, 1982.

Bartlett, C. H. *A History of Postwar Britain 1945–1974.* London: Longman, 1977.

Baumol, William J., and William G. Bowen. *Performing Arts: The Economic Dilemma.* Cambridge, Mass.: MIT Press, 1966.

Baxandall, Michael. *Painting and Experience in Fifteenth-Century Italy.* New York: Oxford University Press, 1972.

Becker, Howard S. *Art Worlds.* Berkeley and Los Angeles: University of California Press, 1982.

Beckerman, Bernard. *Shakespeare at the Globe, 1599–1609.* New York: Macmillan, 1964.

Bedford, Arthur. *The Evil and Danger of Stage Plays.* London: 1706.

Belsey, Catherine. "Senecan Vacillation and Elizabethan Deliberation: Influence or Confluence?" *Renaissance Drama* n.s. 6 (1973):65–88.

Bennet, H. S. "Shakespeare's Audience." *Studies in Shakespeare: British Academy Lectures.* London: Oxford University Press, 1964.

Bentley, Gerald Eades. *The Jacobean and Caroline Stage.* Oxford: Clarendon Press, 1941–68.

———. *The Profession of Dramatist in Shakespeare's Time, 1590–1642.* Princeton: Princeton University Press, 1971.

———. *Shakespeare and Jonson: Their Reputations in the Seventeenth Century Compared.* Chicago: University of Chicago Press, 1945.

Bevington, David M. *From Mankind to Marlowe.* Cambridge: Harvard University Press, 1962.

Bingham, Caroline. "Seventeenth-Century Attitudes toward Deviant Sex." *The Journal of Interdisciplinary History* 1, no. 3 (Spring 1971):447–67.

Bloch, R. Howard. *Medieval French Literature and Law*. Berkeley and Los Angeles: University of California Press, 1977.

Boni, John. "Analogous Form: Black Comedy and Some Jacobean Plays." *Western Humanities Review* 28 (1974):201–15.

Booth, Michael R. *English Melodrama*. London: Herbert Jenkins, 1965.

Bowers, Fredson. *Elizabethan Revenge Tragedy 1587–1642*. Princeton: Princeton University Press, 1940.

Bradbrook, M. C. *The Growth and Structure of Elizabethan Comedy*. New ed. London: Chatto and Windus, 1973.

Braden, Gordon. *Renaissance Tragedy and the Senecan Tradition: Anger's Privilege*. New Haven: Yale University Press, 1985.

Bratchell, Sandra; Howard Austin; Stanislaus Hempel; Christine Komarynsky; and Ruth Tinning. *Aldwych Theatre Audience Survey*. Report prepared for the Royal Shakespeare Company, March 1978.

Burke, Kenneth. "Literature as Equipment for Living." In *The Philosophy of Literary Form*. Berkeley: University of California Press, 1974.

Brustein, Robert. *Critical Moments*. New York: Random House, 1980.

Calvocoressi, Peter. *The British Experience 1945–75*. London: Bodley Head, 1978.

Campbell, Lily B. "Theories of Revenge in Renaissance England." *Modern Philology* 28 (1931):257–96.

Cawelti, John. *Adventure, Mystery, and Romance: Formula Stories as Art and Popular Culture*. Chicago: University of Chicago Press, 1976.

Chambers, E. K. *The Elizabethan Stage*. 4 vols. Oxford: Clarendon Press, 1923.

———. *The Medieval Stage*. London: Oxford University Press, 1903.

———. *Notes on the History of the Revels Office under the Tudors*. London: A. H. Bullen, 1906.

Chang, Joseph S. "'Of Mighty Opposites': Stoicism and Maciavellianism." *Renaissance Drama* n.s. 9 (1966):37–57.

Chetwood, W. R. *A General History of the Stage*. London: W. Owen, 1749.

Clifton, Robin. "The Popular Fear of Catholics in England." *Past and Present* 52 (1971):23–55.

Cohen, Walter, *Drama of a Nation: Public Theater in Renaissance England and Spain*. Ithaca: Cornell University Press, 1985.

Cole, Douglas. "The Comic Accomplice in Elizabethan Revenge Tragedy." *Reniassance Drama* n.s. 9 (1966):125–39.

Collier, Jeremy. *A Short View of the Immorality and Profaneness of the English Stage*. 1698; rpt. New York: AMS Press, 1974.

Cook, Ann J. *The Privileged Playgoers of Shakespeare's London 1576–1642*. Princeton: Princeton University Press, 1981.

Corfield, P. J. *The Impact of English Towns 1700–1800*. Oxford: Oxford University Press, 1982.

Coser, Lewis; Charles Kadushin; and Walter W. Powell. *Books: The Culture and Commerce of Publishing*. New York: Basic, 1982.

Craig, Hardin. *The Enchanted Glass*. New York: Oxford University Press, 1936.

Cressy, David. "Levels of Illiteracy in England 1530–1730." In *Literacy and Social Development in the West.* Edited by Harvey J. Graff. Cambridge: Cambridge University Press, 1981.

Cunliffe, John W. *The Influence of Seneca on Elizabethan Tragedy.* London: Macmillan, 1893.

Curtis, Mark. "The Alienated Intellectuals of Early Stuart England." *Past and Present* 23 (1962):25–41.

Cushman, L. W. *The Devil and the Vice in English Dramatic Literature Before Shakespeare.* Halle A. S.: Max Niemeyer, 1900.

DiMaggio, Paul, and Kristen Stenberg. "Conformity and Diversity in the American Resident Theatre." In *Art, Ideology and Politics.* Edited by Judith Balfe and Margaret J. Wyszomirski. New York: Praeger, 1985.

Dodsley, Robert. *A Select Collection of Old Plays.* 3d ed. 12 vols. Edited by Isaac Reed, Octavius Gilchrist, and "The Editor" [J. Payne Collier]. London: Septimus Powett, 1825–27.

Dollimore, Jonathan. *Radical Tragedy: Religion, Ideology and Power in the Drama of Shakespeare and His Contemporaries.* Chicago: University of Chicago Press, 1984.

Donohue, Joseph. *Theatre in the Age of Kean.* Oxford: Basil Blackwell, 1975.

Doran, Madelein. *Endeavors of Art: A Study of Form in Elizabethan Drama.* Madison: University of Wisconsin Press, 1954.

Douglas, Mary. *Purity and Danger: An Analysis of Concepts of Pollution and Taboo.* London: Routledge and Kegan Paul, 1966.

Dryden, John. *Essays of John Dryden.* 2 vols. Edited by W. P. Ker. Oxford: Clarendon Press, 1900.

Edwards, Philip. *Threshold of a Nation: A Study in English and Irish Drama.* Cambridge: Cambridge University Press, 1979.

Elsom, John. *Post-War British Theatre.* London: Routledge & Kegan Paul, 1976.

Escarpit, Robert. *Sociology of Literature.* 2d ed. Translated by Ernest Pick. London: Frank Cass, 1971.

Farnham, Willard. *The Medieval Heritage of Elizabethan Tragedy.* Berkeley: University of California Press, 1936.

Figgis, John Neville. *The Divine Right of Kings.* 2d ed. Cambridge: Cambridge University Press, 1922.

Fine, Gary Allen. "Small Groups and Culture Creation." *American Sociological Review* 44 (1979):733–45.

Finlay, Roger. *Population and Metropolis: The Demography of London 1580–1650.* Cambridge: Cambridge University Press, 1981.

Fish, Stanley. *Is There a Text in This Class?: The Authority of Interpretive Communities.* Cambridge, Mass.: Harvard University Press, 1980.

Fisher, F. J. "The Development of London as a Centre of Conspicuous Consumption," *Transactions of the Royal Historical Society.* 4th series, 30 (1948):37–50.

Ford, George H. *Dickens and His Readers: Aspects of Novel-Criticism Since 1836.* 1955; New York: Norton, 1965.

Garrick, David. *The Letters of David Garrick.* Edited by David M. Little and George Kahrl. Cambridge, Mass.: Harvard University Press, 1935.

Geertz, Clifford. "Religion As a Cultural System." *The Interpretation of Cultures*. New York: Basic Books, 1973.

George, M. Dorothy. *London Life in the Eighteenth Century*. 1925; New York: Harper & Row, 1965.

Gibbons, Brian. *Jacobean City Comedy: A Study of Satiric Plays by Jonson, Morston, and Middleton*. 2d. ed. London: Methuen, 1980.

Goldberg, Jonathan. *James I and the Politics of Literature*. Baltimore: Johns Hopkins University Press, 1983.

Gough, J. W. *The Rise of the Entrepreneur*. London: Batsford, 1969.

Graña, César. *Bohemian versus Bourgeois: French Society and the French Man of Letters in the Nineteenth Century*. New York: Basic Books, 1964.

Gray, Charles Harold. *Theatrical Criticism in London to 1795*. New York: Columbia University Press, 1931.

Greenblatt, Stephen. *Renaissance Self-Fashioning: From More to Shakespeare*. Chicago: University of Chicago Press, 1980.

———. ed. *The Power of Forms in the English Renaissance*. Norman, Okla.: Pilgrim Books, 1982.

Greenough, Chester Noyes. *Theophrastan Characters in English*. Prepared for publication by J. Milton French. Cambridge: Harvard University Press, 1947.

Griswold, Wendy. "American Character and the American Novel." *American Journal of Sociology* 86 (1981):740–65.

———. "The Devil's Techniques: Cultural Legitimation and Social Change." *American Sociological Review* 48 (1983):668–80.

Haller, William. *Foxe's Book of Martyrs and the Elect Nation*. London: Jonathan Cape, 1963.

Hallett, Charles A., and Elaine S. Hallett. *The Revenger's Madness: A Study of Revenge Tragedy Motifs*. Lincoln: University of Nebraska, 1980.

Halsey, A. H., ed. *Trends in British Society Since 1900*. London: Macmillan, 1972.

Harbage, Alfred. *Shakespeare and the Rival Traditions*. 1952; rpt. Bloomington: Indiana University Press, 1970.

———. *Shakespeare's Audience*. New York: Columbia University Press, 1941.

Harris, John S. *Government Patronage of the Arts in Great Britain*. Chicago: University of Chicago, 1970.

Harrison, William. *The Description of England 1587*. Edited by George S. Edelen. Ithaca, N.Y.: Cornell University Press, 1958.

Haskell, Francis. *Rediscoveries in Art: Some Aspects of Taste, Fashion, and Collecting in England and France*. Ithaca, N.Y.: Cornell University Press, 1976.

Hayman, Ronald. *The Set-Up: An Anatomy of English Theatre Today*. London: Eyre Methuen, 1973.

Hebdige, Dick. *Subculture: The Meaning of Style*. New York: Methuen, 1979.

Heinemann, Margot. *Puritanism and Theatre*. Cambridge: Cambridge University Press, 1982.

Hirsch, E. D., Jr. *Validity in Interpretation*. New Haven: Yale University Press, 1967.

Hirsch, Paul M. "Processing Fads and Fashions." *American Journal of Sociology* 77 (1972):639–59.

Hobson, Dorothy. "Housewives and the Mass Media." In *Culture, Media, Language.* Edited by Stuart Hall, Dorothy Hobson, Andrew Lowe, and Paul Willis. London: Hutchinson, 1980.

Hoggart, Richard. *The Uses of Literacy.* New York: Oxford University Press, 1970.

Hollingsworth, T. H. "A Demographic Study of British Ducal Families." *Population Studies* 11 (1957):4–26.

Holmes, Geoffrey. *Augustan England: Professions, State, and Society, 1680–1730.* London: George Allen & Unwin, 1982.

Honig, Edwin. *Calderón and the Seizures of Honor.* Cambridge, Mass.: Harvard University Press, 1972.

Huizinga, Johan. *Homo Ludens: A Study of the Play Element in Culture.* 1950; rpt. Boston: Beacon, 1955.

Hunter, G. K. *Dramatic Identities and Cultural Tradition.* New York: Harper & Row, 1978.

Jacoby, Susan. *Wild Justice: The Evolution of Revenge.* New York: Harper & Row, 1983.

Jaeger, Gertrude, and Philip Selznick. "A Normative Theory of Culture." *American Sociological Review* 29 (1964):653–69.

Jauss, Hans Robert. *Toward an Aesthetic of Reception.* Translated by Timothy Bahti. Minneapolis: University of Minnesota Press, 1982.

Jensen, Enjer J. "Lamb, Poel, and Our Postwar Theater: Elizabethan Revivals." *Renaissance Drama* n.s. 9 (1978):211–34.

Johnson, Robert Carl. "Audience Involvement in the Tudor Interlude." *Theatre Notebook* 24 (1977):101–11.

Jones, Robert C. "Dangerous Sport: The Audience's Engagement with Vice in the Moral Interludes." *Renaissance Drama* n.s. 6 (1973):45–64.

Kantorowicz, Ernst. *The King's Two Bodies: A Study in Medieval Political Theology.* Princeton: Princeton University Press, 1957.

Kerenyi, Karl. "The Trickster in Relation to Greek Mythology." Translated by R. F. C. Hull. In Paul Radin, *The Trickster: A Study in American Indian Mythology.* London: Routledge & Kegan Paul, 1956.

King, John N. *English Reformation Literature: The Tudor Origins of the Protestant Tradition.* Princeton: Princeton University Press, 1982.

Knights, L. C. *Drama and Society in the Age of Jonson.* London: Chatto and Windus, 1937.

Kroeber, A. L. *The Nature of Culture.* Chicago: University of Chicago Press, 1952.

Kroeber, A. L., and Clyde Kluckhohn. *Culture: A Critical Review of Concepts and Definitions.* Harvard University: Papers of the Peabody Museum of American Archeology and Ethnology 47, 1952.

Lamb, Charles. *Specimens of English Dramatic Poets.* Vol. 2. Edited by William Macdonald. London: Dent, 1903.

Lamont, William. *Godly Rule: Politics and Religion 1603–1660.* London: Macmillan, 1969.

Lasdun, Denys. "Building Vistas/1." *The Complete Guide to Britain's National Theatre.* London: Heinemann, 1977.

Laslett, Peter. *The World We Have Lost.* 2d ed. London: Methuen, 1971.

————. "The Wrong Way Through the Telescope." *British Journal of Sociology* 27 (1976):319–42.

Legatt, Alexander. *Citizen Comedy in the Age of Shakespeare.* Toronto: University of Toronto Press, 1973.

Lever, J. W. *The Tragedy of State.* London: Methuen, 1971.

Levin, Richard. *The Multiple Plot in English Renaissance Drama.* Chicago: University of Chicago Press, 1971.

Lewis, David K. *Convention: A Philosophical Study.* Cambridge, Mass.: Harvard University Press, 1969.

Lievsay, John Leon. *The Elizabethan Image of Italy.* Ithaca, N.Y.: Cornell University Press, 1964.

Lindenberger, Herbert. "Toward a New History in Literary Study." *Profession 84.* Modern Language Association (1984):16–23.

Lowenthal, Leo. *Literature, Popular Culture, and Society.* Palo Alto, Calif.: Pacific, 1968.

Lucas, F. L. *Seneca and Elizabethan Tragedy.* 1921; rpt. New York: Haskell House, 1966.

Lynch, James L. *Box, Pit, and Gallery.* Berkeley: University of California Press, 1953.

McAfee, Helen. *Pepys on the Restoration Stage.* New Haven: Yale University Press, 1916.

McGann, Jerome J. "The Text, The Poem, and the Problem of Historical Method." *New Literary History* 12 (1981):269–88.

Machery, Pierre. *A Theory of Literary Production.* Translated by Geoffrey Wall. London: Routledge & Kegan Paul, 1978.

McKendrick, Neil; John Brewer; and J. H. Plumb. *The Birth of a Consumer Society: The Commercialization of Eighteenth-Century England.* London: Europa Publications, 1982.

McKie, David, and Chris Cook, eds. *The Decade of Disillusion: British Politics in the Sixties.* London: Macmillan, 1972.

McMillan, James. *The Roots of Corruption: The Erosion of Traditional Values in Britain from 1960 to the Present Day.* London: Stacey, 1972.

Mares, Francis Hugh. "The Origin of the Figure called 'The Vice' in Tudor Drama." *Huntington Library Quarterly* 22 (1958):11–29.

Marshall, Norman. *The Other Theatre.* London: John Lehman, 1947.

Martorella, Rosanne. *The Sociology of Opera.* New York: Praeger, 1982.

Marwick, Arthur. *British Society since 1945.* London: Allen Lane, 1982.

Meyer, Leonard B. *Emotion and Meaning in Music.* Chicago: University of Chicago Press, 1956.

Miller, Anna Irene. *The Independent Theatre in Europe: 1887 to the Present.* New York: Long & Smith, 1931.

Miller, Edwin H. *The Professional Writer in Elizabethan England: A Study of Non-Dramatic Literature.* Cambridge, Mass.: Harvard University Press, 1959.

Mitford, Nancy. "The English Aristocracy." *Encounter* 5 (1955):5–12.

Montrose, Louis Adrian. "The Elizabethan Subject and the Spenserian Test." In

Literary Theory and Renaissance Texts. Edited by Patricia Parker and David Quint. Baltimore: Johns Hopkins University Press, forthcoming.

———. "The Purpose of Playing: Reflections on a Shakespearean Anthropology." *Helios* n.s. 7 (1980):53–74.

Morley, Henry. *The Journal of a London Playgoer from 1851 to 1866.* London: George Routledge, 1891.

Motto, Anne Lydia, and John L. Clark. "Senecan Tragedy: A Critique of Scholarly Trends." *Renaissance Drama* n.s. 6 (1973):219–35.

Mueller, John H. *The American Symphony Orchestra: A Social History of Musical Taste.* Bloomington: Indiana University Press, 1951.

Mueller, Kate Hevner. *Twenty-seven Major American Symphony Orchestras: A History of Their Repetoires 1842–3 through 1969–70.* Bloomington: Indiana University Press, 1973.

Mukerji, Chandra. *From Graven Images: Patterns of Modern Materialism.* New York: Columbia University Press, 1983.

Murphy, Gwendolen. *A Bibliography of English Character-Books 1608–1700.* Oxford: The Bibliographic Society, 1925.

Neill, Michael. "Massinger's Patriarchy." *Renaissance Drama* n.s. 10 (1979):185–213.

Nicholson, Watson. *The Struggle for a Free Stage in London.* Boston: Houghton, Mifflin, 1906.

Nicoll, Allardyce. *A History of English Drama 1660–1900.* Cambridge: Cambridge University Press, 1955.

Noyes, Robert Gale. *Ben Jonson on the English Stage, 1660–1776.* Cambridge, Mass.: Harvard University Press, 1935.

O'Connor, Flannery. *Three by Flannery O'Connor.* New York: New American Library, 1983.

Orgel, Stephen. *The Illusion of Power.* Berkeley: University of California Press, 1975.

———. *The Jonsonian Masque.* 1967; New York: Columbia University Press, 1980.

Ornstein, Robert. *The Moral Vision of Jacobean Tragedy.* Madison and Milwaukee: University of Wisconsin Press, 1960.

Pearl, Valerie. *London and the Outbreak of the Puritan Revolution: City Government and National Politics 1625–43.* London: Oxford University Press, 1961.

Pearson, Lu Emily. *Elizabethans at Home.* Stanford: Stanford University Press, 1957.

Pedicord, William. *The Theatrical Public in the Time of Garrick.* New York: Kings Crown, 1954.

Pepys, Samuel. *The Diary of Samuel Papys.* 11 vols. Edited by Robert Latham and William Matthews. Berkeley and Los Angeles: University of California Press, 1970–83.

Peterson, Richard A. "Revitalizing the Culture Concept." *Annual Review of Sociology* 5 (1979):137–66.

Porter, Roy. *English Society in the Eighteenth Century.* Harmondsworth: Penguin, 1982.

Pratt, Norman T. *Seneca's Drama.* Chapel Hill: University of North Carolina Press, 1983.

Prosser, Eleanor. *Hamlet and Revenge*. 2d ed. Stanford: Stanford University Press, 1971.

Raab, Felix. *The English Face of Machiavelli: A Changing Interpretation 1500–1700*. London: Routledge & Kegan Paul, 1964.

Rabkin, Norman. *Shakespeare and the Problem of Meaning*. Chicago: University of Chicago Press, 1981.

Reddaway, Thomas Fiddian. "London and the Court in Elizabethan England." *Shakespeare Survey* 17 (1964):3–12.

Ribner, Irving. *Jacobean Tragedy: The Quest for Moral Order*. London: Methuen, 1962.

Richards, I. A. *The Philosophy of Rhetoric*. 1936; London: Oxford University Press, 1976.

Ricoeur, Paul. *The Rule of Metaphor*. Translated by Robert Czerny. Toronto: University of Toronto Press, 1977.

Robinson, Herbert Spencer. *English Shakespearean Criticism in the Eighteenth Century*. New York: H. W. Wilson, 1932.

Rosmarin, Adena. "Hermeneutics versus Erotics: Shakespeare's *Sonnets* and Interpretive History." *PMLA* 100 (1985):20–37.

———. "'Misreading' *Emma:* The Powers and Perfidies of Interpretive History." *English Literary History* 51 (1984): 315–42.

Ross, Julian L. "Dramatist vs. Audience in the Early Eighteenth Century." *Philological Quarterly* 12 (1933):78–81.

Rowell, George. *The Victorian Theatre 1792–1914*. 2d ed. Cambridge: Cambridge University Press, 1978.

Salgādo, Gāmini, ed. *Cony-Catchers and Bawdy Baskets*. Harmondsworth: Penguin, 1972.

———. *Four Jacobean City Comedies*. Harmondsworth: Penguin, 1975.

Scouten, Arthur H. "The Increase in Popularity of Shakespeare's Plays in the Eighteenth Century." *Shakespeare Quarterly* 7 (Spring 1956): 189–203.

Sheavyn, Phoebe. *The Literary Profession in the Elizabethan Age*. 2d ed. Revised by J. W. Saunders. Manchester: Manchester University Press, 1967.

Simmel, George. *The Conflict in Modern Culture and Other Essays*. Translated by K. Peter Etzkorn. New York: Teachers College Press, 1968.

Simpson, Percy. "The Theme of Revenge in Elizabethan Tragedy." *Proceedings of the British Academy* (1935):101–36.

Sked, Alan, and Chris Cook. *Post-War Britain: A Political History*. London: Harvester, 1979.

Skinner, Quentin. "On Preforming and Explaining Linguistic Actions." *The Philosophical Quarterly* 21 (1971):1–21.

Smith, Barbara Herrnstein. "Contingencies of Value." *Critical Inquiry 10 (1983):1–35.*

———. *Poetic Closure: A Study of How Poems End*. Chicago: University of Chicago Press, 1968.

Smith, Bruce R. "Toward the Rediscovery of Tragedy: Productions of Seneca's Plays on the English Renaissance Stage." *Renaissance Drama* n.s. 9 (1978):3–37.

Smith, Dame Farnsworth. *The Critics in the Audience of the London Theatres from Buckingham to Sheridan.* Albuquerque: University of New Mexico Press, 1953.

Smuts, Malcolm. "The Political Failure of Stuart Cultural Patronage." In *Patronage in the Renaissance.* Edited by Guy Fitch Lytle and Stephen Orgel. Princeton: Princeton University Press, 1981.

Snow, C. P. "The Two Cultures." *New Statesman and Nation* (October 1956):413–14.

Speaight, Robert. *William Poel and the Elizabethan Revival.* London: Heinemann, 1954.

Sprague, Arthur Colby. *Beaumont and Fletcher on the Restoration Stage.* Cambridge, Mass.: Harvard University Press, 1926.

Steiner, George. *Antigones.* New York: Oxford University Press, 1984.

Stone, George Winchester. "The Making of a Repertory." In *The London Theatre World, 1660–1800.* Edited by Robert D. Hume. Carbondale: Southern Illinois University Press, 1980.

Stone, Lawrence. *The Causes of the English Revolution 1529–1642.* London: Routledge & Kegan Paul, 1972.

———. *The Crisis of the Aristocracy 1558–1641.* Oxford: Clarendon Press, 1965.

———. "Social Mobility in England, 1500–1700." *Past and Present* 33 (1966):16–55.

Stone, Lawrence, and Jeanne C. Fawtier. *An Open Elite? England 1540–1880.* Oxford: Clarendon Press, 1984.

Swidler, Ann. "Culture in Action: Symbols and Strategies." *American Sociological Review* 51 (1986):273–86.

Symonds, John Addington. *Shakespeare's Predecessors in the English Drama.* New ed. London: Smith, Elder, 1900.

Taylor, John Russell. *The Angry Theatre: New British Drama.* New York: Hill and Wang, 1962.

Thirsk, Joan. "The European Debate on Customs of Inheritance." In *Family and Inheritance: Rural Society in Western Europe, 1200–1800.* Edited by Jack Goody, Joan Thirsk, and E. P. Thompson. Cambridge: Cambridge University Press, 1976.

Thomas, Keith. *Religion and the Decline of Magic.* New York: Scribner's, 1971.

Thompson, Stith. *The Folktale.* New York: Holt, Rinehart & Winston, 1946.

———. *Motif-Index of Folk Literature.* Revised ed. Bloomington: Indiana University Press, 1958.

Thorndike, Ashley. *English Comedy.* New York: Macmillan, 1929.

———. "The Relations of *Hamlet* to Contemporary Revenge Plays." *PMLA* 27 (1902):125–220.

Tillyard, E. M. W. *Elizabethan World Picture.* 1943; rpt. Harmondsworth: Penguin, 1976.

Titmuss, Richard M. *Commitment to Welfare.* London: Allen and Unwin, 1968.

———. *Essays on the Welfare State.* London: Allen and Unwin, 1958.

———. *Income Distribution and Social Change.* London: Allen and Unwin, 1962.

Tomlinson, T. B. *A Study of Elizabethan and Jacobean Tragedy.* Cambridge: Cambridge University Press, 1964.

Trevelyn, George Macaulay. *England Under the Stuarts.* 10th ed. New York: Putnams, 1922.

Trewin, J. C. *Drama in Britain 1951–1964.* London: Longmans, Green & Co., 1965.

————. *The Edwardian Theatre.* Totowa: Rowman & Littlefield, 1976.

Tuchman, Gay, and Nina E. Fortin. "Fame and Misfortune: Edging Women out of the Great Literary Tradition." *American Journal of Sociology* 90 (1984):72–96.

Turner, Victor. *The Forest of Symbols: Aspects of Ndembu Ritual.* Ithaca, N.Y.: Cornell University Press, 1967.

————. "Myth and Symbol." *International Encyclopedia of the Social Sciences,* vol. 10. New York: Macmillan and Free Press, 1968.

Vernon, Frank. *Twentieth-Century Theatre.* London: Harrap, 1924.

Wagner, Anthony Richard. *English Genealogy.* Oxford: Clarendon Press, 1960.

Wallis, Lawrence Bergmann. *Fletcher, Beaumont and Company, Entertainers to the Jacobean Gentry.* New York: King's Crown, 1947.

Watson, Ernest Bradlee. *Sheridan to Robertson: A Study of the Nineteenth-Century London Stage.* New York: Benjamin Blom, 1963.

Watt, Ian. *The Rise of the Novel.* Berkeley: University of California Press, 1957.

Weber, Max. *Economy and Society: An Outline of Interpretive Sociology.* Edited by Guenther Roth and Claus Wittich. Berkeley and Los Angeles: University of California Press.

Weimann, Robert. *Shakespeare and the Popular Tradition in the Theatre.* Baltimore: Johns Hopkins, 1978.

Whigham, Frank. *Ambition and Privilege: The Social Tropes of Elizabethan Courtesy Theory.* Berkeley and Los Angeles: University of California Press, 1984.

Wilson, Frank Percy, and G. K. Hunter. *The English Drama, 1485–1585.* Oxford: Clarendon Press, 1969.

Wilson, Sir Thomas. "The State of England (1606)." Edited by F. J. Fisher. *Camden Miscellany* 16, Camden 3d ser. 52 (1936):24.

Wright, Louis B. *Middle-Class Culture in Elizabethan England.* 1935; rpt. Chapel Hill: University of North Carolina Press, 1958.

————. "The Reading of Plays During the Puritan Revolution." *Huntington Library Bulletin* 6 (1924):72–108.

Wright, Will. *Sixguns and Society: A Structural Study of the Western.* Berkeley and Los Angeles: University of California Press, 1975.

Wuthnow, Robert; James Davison Hunter; Albert Bergeson; and Edith Kurzweil. *Cultural Analysis: The Work of Peter L. Berger, Mary Douglas, Michel Foucault and Jürgen Habermas.* London: Routledge & Kegan Paul, 1984.

Yates, Francis A. *Astraea: The Imperial Theme in the Sixteenth Century.* London: Routledge and Kegan Paul, 1975.

INDEX